1.95

REVIEW TEXT IN
ENGLISH LANGUAGE ARTS

(Preliminary)

By JOSEPH BELLAFIORE

Principal,
Lafayette High School,
New York City

Dedicated to Serving Our Nation's Youth

AMSCO SCHOOL PUBLICATIONS, Inc.

315 Hudson Street   New York, N.Y.

Mailing Address: Box 315, Canal Street Station, New York, N.Y. 10013

TO

MARY ANN

FOR THE TEACHER

THE ENGLISH LANGUAGE ARTS

In *The English Language Arts,* a report prepared by the Commission on the English Curriculum of the National Council of Teachers of English, the major goals are set forth. Stated briefly they are these ten concepts:

1. Wholesome personal development—stability of mind and feeling
2. A heightened moral perception and a personal sense of values—dynamic and worthwhile allegiances
3. Growing intellectual curiosity and capacity for critical thinking
4. Effective use of language in the daily affairs of life—group planning, discussion, conducting meetings, actual situations
5. Habitual and intelligent use of the mass media of communication —radio, television, newspapers—and awareness of propaganda
6. Growing personal interests and increasingly mature standards of enjoyment
7. Effective habits of work-study skills, committee work, sharing responsibilities
8. Competent use of language and reading for vocational purposes—courteous speech, letter-writing, interviews, careers
9. Social sensitivity and effective participation in group life, human relations, world understanding
10. Faith in and allegiance to the basic values of a democratic society

This statement serves to keep before us the vision of our professional ideals. However, our task in the daily work of the classroom is to translate these into terms applicable to our boys and girls. The immediate goals for most pupils are competence in reading and writing and speaking. Thus, the present textbook aims to provide the teacher with the kind of materials, drills, tests, reviews, etc., that will help plan for mastery of fundamentals. Training pupils in effective habits of work is what parents, businessmen, and others expect of us as teachers. Meanwhile, we can also aim for those ultimate values referred to as the intangibles, which will be the outcome of our personal influence and guidance.

This book also provides a complete review in preparation for any standard examination in Preliminary English. Based on the New York State Syllabus, the topics cover the field of English and are organized to build skills as well as to assist youngsters in succeeding in the examination.

—J. B.

PURPOSES OF THE LANGUAGE ARTS

SCOPE

Your study of the language arts covers the entire field of English. It begins with the spoken word or oral communication, the give and take between people in everyday living. On a different level, it deals with the written word in social notes, business letters, and compositions. Here the mechanics of good usage come into play for decent acceptable expression. Then there is the technique of getting the meaning from the printed word when reading for comprehension. On a higher plane, you combine understanding with enjoyment in adventures in literature. Further enrichment comes from other channels of communication: television, radio, movies, newspapers, and magazines.

In other words, the scope of the language arts includes every means by which people can reach each other. Spoken and written words connect mind with mind and heart with heart, the present age with the past. Thus, every man can share in the history and traditions of our race, and, in his own way, contribute to the world of today.

That is why the English language arts are taught to all boys and girls in every school in our country. You should be proud and eager to master the language arts!

AIMS

You probably came to school today with a friend. You talked about things on your way. Perhaps, you met others and compared notes on the day's work, or planned to have lunch together, or agreed to play ball after school. This exchange of ideas is natural and desirable because all people have the urge to mix socially. The gift of language makes communication possible so all of us can share experiences. The "language arts" refer to the ways in which we do this; namely, by *speaking, listening, reading,* and *writing.*

But words are more than just labels for things. They serve as tools for learning, for thinking, for expressing our feelings, and for interpreting our experience. Language gives power. It builds knowledge. It gives skill in human relations. It develops appreciation. Language helps you grow up mentally, just as food and exercise help your body grow up physically. Besides personal growth, it increases your usefulness to serve others. And, finally, it aids you in discovering your own ability so that you may someday get the job you are best fitted for.

The language arts, therefore, are the human arts of communication between individuals. Just as the practical arts and the mechanic arts may build homes, provide food, comfort, and convenience in the world *around* us, the language arts enrich the world *within* us so we can live as social beings. It is a wonderful ability; learn to make the most of it.

—J. B.

CONTENTS

Good speech can become part of your personality...provided you care enough to make a determined effort to speak better.

I DEVELOPING ORAL COMMUNICATION SKILLS

WHY IS SPEECH IMPORTANT?

This is an age of direct person-to-person contact. Talking, interviewing, selling, broadcasting, discussing—all are done by personal communication, by word of mouth. In fact, about 95% of everything you express to others you do by *spoken* English.

Since you are not born with any particular language, your own speech is an imitation of what you hear at home, in school, in the neighborhood, and on the street. Often, it is an unconscious attempt to belong to the group, to sound like the rest of the boys and girls on the block.

HOW CAN YOU IMPROVE YOUR SPEECH?

As you grow older, you start making a more conscious effort to model your speech along the lines of clear voice and crisp diction by imitating the best speakers on television, radio, the movies, and elsewhere:

John Cameron Swayze, news commentator on television
Bishop Fulton J. Sheen, personality on *Life Is Worth Living*
Irene Dunne, movie actress
Red Barber, sports announcer
Basil Rathbone, actor of *Sherlock Holmes* stories
Maurice Evans, actor in stage plays
Julie Andrews, star of musical comedy

Listen to tape recordings and phonograph records of good speakers. Try making a tape recording of your own voice and have your teacher analyze it. Keep a notebook for new words and look up their pronunciation in the dictionary.

Practice speaking before your classmates or other groups in order to gain poise. Keep a scrapbook of pictures you clip from newspapers and magazines showing speakers who use dramatic gestures, good posture, and effective delivery. If you hesitate in talking, try singing to develop voice and breath control. If you are not sure of the correct position of your lips, teeth, and tongue in making certain sounds like *s* and *th,* practice in front of a small hand mirror.

1

SELF-RATING CHART FOR ORAL ENGLISH

Check yourself by means of this 100% scale to discover your strengths and weaknesses, if any. Have your teacher look over your score to compare the accuracy of your speech-analysis. Be *better* next time!

	Yes	No
1. Was my posture easily erect and natural?	☐	☐
2. Was my voice clear and loud enough to be easily heard by everyone in the room?	☐	☐
3. Was my manner friendly, relaxed, outgoing?	☐	☐
4. Was my pronunciation correct? (Any errors?)	☐	☐
5. Was my use of English marked by complete and smoothly connected sentences? (Any errors in usage?)	☐	☐
6. Was my choice of topic interesting to the listeners as well as to myself?	☐	☐
7. Was my opening sentence able to catch and hold the attention of the class?	☐	☐
8. Was the organization so clear that everybody could follow the ideas and happenings in good order?	☐	☐
9. Was my ending strong enough to close without leaving any loose ends?	☐	☐
10. Was the audience reaction a good sign that I had really reached them?	☐	☐

What's *your* score? (Give yourself 10 points for each **YES** answer.)

A TELEPHONE CONVERSATION

The nerve center of a modern business, factory, office, or home is the telephone. Try to imagine life without it. When the lines go down during a storm and service is interrupted, even for a few hours, we feel cut off from the world. We have grown so used to calling the stores, the doctor, the service companies, our relatives and friends, that the telephone has become almost a human appendage—a kind of extension of ourselves. It saves time and money. It brings us into immediate contact with others, whether locally or at a long distance. We shop by phone. We visit by phone. Some pupils even do their homework by phone. Let us value this great service as a convenience and a blessing!

SAMPLE TELEPHONE CONVERSATION

INVITATION TO A PARTY

Crude

Diane. Hi! Who's calling?
Marge. I'm nobody. Who are you?

Diane. You sound like Marge. Am I right?
Marge. Yep! Keep your lid on while I tell you some hot news. We're going to have a jam session at our place Saturday, and you're the first hepcat I'm asking. Coming over?

Diane. Try and make me. Just give me three good reasons!
Marge. Well, it's free, it's fun, and everybody'll be there. We'll have to keep those hungry boys eating while we cut a rug with the latest platters. Got any ideas?

Diane. Well, I don't want to be a wet blanket, but I hope you're not having you-know-who and her dizzy boy friend. They're a scream! And, as for food, please skip the franks and beans. Let's have hamburgers and onions, etc., etc.
Marge. Enough said. This party will be strictly different. Wait till you see. I've got to go now.

Diane. Okay, small fry. See you later, alligator.
Marge. In a while, crocodile!

Better

Diane. Hello! This is Diane.
Marge. Diane, this is Marge. I am having a little get-together at my house on Saturday and would like you to come. Can you make it?

Diane. What's the occasion? Somebody's birthday? Tell me more!
Marge. No, nothing special, just a group to have some fun: a little dancing, some sandwiches and drinks, and a few games.

Diane. Sounds good. Nice of you to ask me. Who else is coming?
Marge. You know them all: Valerie and Tom, Dorrie and Ward, Connie and Fred, you and Pete, and Don and I.

Diane. That's fine. Count me in, and we'll talk about it some more tomorrow during lunch. Thanks a lot for calling. So long, Marge!
Marge. See you tomorrow. Bye, now!

3

A *phone call* is an intimate and candid picture of *you*. Your voice and your attitude go along with the message because **your** whole personality speaks louder than words.

SUGGESTIONS FOR PROPER USE OF THE TELEPHONE

Receiving Calls

1. Pick the receiver up promptly when your phone rings.
2. Begin by telling the caller your number or name. This saves time.
3. Get the name of the caller correct. If in doubt, say: "Will you please spell it?"
4. Listen carefully to the message. If it is intended for someone else, say: "Just a minute, please. I'll see if I can get him for you." If the person is out, make a brief memorandum of the date, time, person, and number to call back.
5. End by saying, "Thank you for calling!"
6. Replace the receiver on the hook.

Making Calls

1. Be sure you know the right number. If in doubt, look it up in the telephone directory. Write it down on a piece of paper. If you can't find the number in the directory, dial 411 for information. You should keep a record of numbers you call frequently.
2. Lift the receiver off the hook and wait for the dial tone (a humming sound). If you are making the call from a pay booth, deposit the proper coin in the box, and wait for the dial tone.
3. Dial the number carefully. Do not confuse zero (0) with the letter (O). If you make a mistake, hang up and start again.
4. If you get the busy signal (buzz-click-buzz), wait a few minutes before trying to dial the number again.
5. Complete your call promptly. An open wire allows other calls to be made or an urgent message to get through.

Telephone Courtesy

1. When your telephone rings, answer it promptly.
2. Give your name promptly. Avoid such annoying phrases as "Guess who" or "Don't you remember me?"
3. Remember that the call is really a personal conversation; be polite and friendly.
4. Don't repeat things or drag out the conversation aimlessly. Others may be waiting to make a call. Be considerate; be brief!
5. Be a good listener. Don't talk the whole time; give the other person a chance.
6. Live up to the motto: "The voice with a smile wins."

EXERCISE

PROBLEMS IN TELEPHONE CONVERSATION

Choose a pupil as partner and prepare a two-minute telephone conversation according to one of these situations.

1. Call the box office of your neighborhood movie to find out what films are being shown tonight, the time that the main feature begins, the price of admission, etc.

2. Call your classmate to ask for the homework assignment that you missed when you were absent from school because of illness.
3. Call the dentist to make an appointment to examine your teeth and to fill out the required dental note for your school nurse.
4. Call the public library to ask whether a certain book (give author and title) is available for borrowing and find out what hours the library will be open.
5. Suppose you have been baby-sitting and the youngster keeps crying. Call the mother for suggestions as to what to do.
6. Assume you are working as delivery boy in a grocery store and the owner asks you to take an order that a customer wants to give over the telephone. Write it down neatly.
7. A friend of your father calls while your father is out. Take the name, phone number, and message correctly.
8. Invite your favorite aunt (or uncle) to come to your graduation exercises. Be sure to tell her (or him) the exact date, time, and place. (Will you mail the ticket?)
9. Assume you have had a minor accident at school and the teacher has given you permission to notify your parent. Describe what happened (without alarming your mother) and pay attention to her advice.

 # PREPARING A SHORT TALK OR REPORT

Do you get "butterflies" in the pit of your stomach when you are asked to give a two-minute talk to the class? Then, you are perfectly normal. Stop worrying and get to work!

GETTING MATERIAL READY

1. Pick a topic you already know something about. If you raise tropical fish as a hobby, there's your answer.
2. Talk to others about your topic. You can get some new point of view or additional information.
3. Look in recent magazines for pictures or stories dealing with your topic. The librarian will help you.
4. Think about the material and organize it in advance. Never wait till the last minute.
5. Plan with your "audience" in mind so you can hold their interest.
6. Write the whole thing out in full in your notebook, and then prepare a brief outline on small 3 × 5 cards.
7. Read your notes before going to bed the night before you are to recite. Your memory will work on it for you.
8. If possible, bring to class something to show. If you are explaining how to build a model plane, take an actual sample to show the class while you talk.

The secret of a ***successful speaker*** is simply this: He has confidence in himself because he has prepared well and knows what he is going to say.

SUGGESTIONS FOR OUTLINING

MAKING SOMETHING	TELLING A STORY
1. Material and equipment needed.	1. Time, place, persons mentioned.
2. Process, step by step, in doing it.	2. Keep the happenings in clear order of time or place.
3. Some cautions for safety, or problems to face.	3. Build up to a climax, or most exciting part.
4. How it works, or what results to expect.	4. Keep the ending in suspense till the closing sentence.

EXERCISE

TOPICS FOR SHORT TALKS

Prepare a short talk (two minutes) using one of these topics.

1. How I earned my first dollar
2. The first time I got lost
3. How to rescue a drowning person
4. The happiest day in my life
5. My first ride in an airplane

6. A mistake I made
7. My favorite short story
8. The best show on television
9. How to make a book shelf
10. And then we became good friends

INTERVIEWING A FRIEND OR OTHER PERSON

WHAT IS AN INTERVIEW?

An interview is a personal meeting between two or more persons in order to ask questions and obtain information. You have probably watched Ed Murrow interview well-known persons on his television show, *Person to Person*. You yourself may have had an interview with your principal about your plans for high school. A formal interview is a prepared question-and-answer kind of conversation to get information directly, face to face. Pupil-to-pupil interviews may be informal give-and-take.

PREPARING FOR AN INTERVIEW

Make arrangements in advance as to the time and place of the meeting so that you will have a definite appointment with the one you wish to interview. Be there promptly.

Prepare in your notebook a brief list of questions you would like to have answered so that you will not waste time. For example, if you are about to interview a new teacher for an article in your school newspaper, ask such questions as these:

1. What college did you go to? Special course taken?
2. What are your favorite sports? Hobbies? Other interests?
3. Have you ever taught in any other school? Where?
4. What are your first impressions of our students here?

DURING THE INTERVIEW

Keep notes during the interview so you will be able to remember the main points for your writing later. Use tact in not asking embarrassing questions. Be courteous in listening with attention. Watch the time so that you will not take too long. Thank him politely for his kindness.

MAKING A GOOD IMPRESSION WHEN APPLYING FOR A JOB

1. Be neat and tidy in your personal appearance!
2. Organize the facts about your school and special training.
3. Learn about the field in which you seek to work and be prepared to show interest in and some knowledge of the job.
4. Be able to give reasons why the person should hire you.
5. At the end, thank him for his consideration.

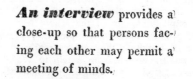

An interview provides a close-up so that persons facing each other may permit a meeting of minds.

EXERCISES

INTERVIEWING OTHER PUPILS

A. Select a member of the class and conduct a personal oral interview to find out various kinds of information as suggested by the problems listed below.

1. A pupil has a large stamp collection. Ask him how he got interested in this hobby; how long he has saved stamps; stories about foreign stamps; cost and present value; local stamp club, if any; swap stamps; etc.
2. A pupil came to this country from abroad a year or two ago. Find out where he came from; how he made the trip here; how he used to go to school; kinds of games played abroad; special customs; his impressions of us; etc.
3. A pupil is captain of the school traffic squad. Find out how many members work under him; what duties they perform; what service credit they receive; special problems they are currently facing; suggestions for improvement; etc.
4. A pupil returned from a trip to Washington, D. C. Question him regarding famous buildings visited; national shrines; Congress at work; souvenirs brought home; any exciting incidents during the trip; etc.
5. A pupil is running as candidate for president of the school. Interview him regarding his qualifications for the office; his experience in any other position; his participation in school activities; his scholarship record; his platform or campaign promises; etc.

INTERVIEWING SOMEONE OUTSIDE OF CLASS

B. Choose a member of the class as your partner and prepare a series of questions in advance for a "mock" interview which you can conduct at the teacher's desk.

1. Assume you are the neighborhood grocer and your partner comes to apply for a part-time job to deliver orders on Saturday morning. Find out his qualifications, etc.
2. As class representative you approach your partner who acts as the traffic policeman near your school and you ask him for suggestions for better cooperation by the pupils.
3. As a member of the school clean-up squad you ask your partner, acting as a neighborly homeowner, how the pupils can assist in keeping the community clean.
4. Assume you have been asked by your classmates to interview the school custodian regarding careless damage to school property and ways of tidying up the play area.
5. Suppose you are to interview the school nurse or doctor about proper eating habits for building strong bodies and keeping healthy.

10

D | ORGANIZING A DISCUSSION OR DEBATE

A *debate* is the presentation of arguments on both sides of a question in order to convince the listeners to support either side. A *discussion* is a more rambling kind of give-and-take of facts and ideas in order to air opinions without trying to persuade the listener.

SELECTING A TOPIC

Probably the best way to arrive at a topic is to have each member of the class bring in a suggestion. These may be listed at the board and voted upon by the pupils. The topic receiving the largest popular vote will attract more interest and volunteer speakers. Make sure there are at least two sides to the problem so that the speakers will have equal opportunity to find material and prepare arguments.

GATHERING MATERIAL

Depending on the kind of topic, you may have to interview people who know about it, or read current magazines, or write to agencies for information. For example, regarding the topic "Should homework be abolished?" you may do the following:

1. Get statements from classmates, teachers, the principal.
2. Interview parents, businessmen, community leaders.
3. Read magazine articles suggested by the teacher or librarian.

CHOOSING SIDES OR TEAMS

A debate is really a contest. Just as in sports, you should elect a captain for each team and at least two or three other members for each side. The *affirmative* side upholds the question as stated. The *negative* team takes the opposite side of the question. A pupil chairman or the teacher may call on the speakers, one from each side, to give the arguments in favor and against. A timekeeper will limit each speaker to no more than two or three minutes as agreed in advance. Good sportsmanship requires speakers to obey his signal (tapping a pencil) to stop. At the end, the class may vote on the question or join in an open discussion.

CLASS VOTING

In a debate, as in any contest, one side should win. However, the judging should be based not on whether you think the team is on the right side of the question, but whether you feel that the winning team has done a better job in gathering material and a better job in presenting it to the class.

EXERCISE

TOPICS FOR DEBATE OR DISCUSSION

Two pupils acting as captains select two additional members each to form a team for debate on one of these topics. One team chooses the affirmative side and the other team the negative side.

1. Should teenagers be given a regular allowance?
2. Should the school require uniform dress by pupils?
3. Should school lunch be provided free?
4. Should television commercials be discontinued?
5. Should comic books be banned?
6. Should the president's term of office be six years?
7. Should immigration quotas be abolished?
8. Should pupils be allowed to get regular work permits at 15 years?
9. Should military service be dropped during peacetime?
10. Should hydrogen bomb tests be outlawed?

E | CONDUCTING A CLUB MEETING OR COMMITTEE WORK

GROUP DISCUSSION — A DEMOCRATIC PROCESS

Part of your training in oral English should consist in group discussion which gives you a chance to share ideas and opinions with your classmates. Perhaps your teacher occasionally organizes a Club Day on which you exchange views on current events or talk about books or movies. Such a friendly gathering is on a small scale similar to the important councils held in adult life.

The United Nations admits delegates from the smaller nations as well as the large powers so that the whole world may participate in the discussion. To make this possible, certain rules of order have been established. Therefore, you should become acquainted with some of the simple rules of parliamentary procedure to help you in carrying on a class discussion and to understand how the world's work is done.

> **The democratic ideal** of freedom of expression means that the timid or weak as well as the bold or strong will be heard.

LEARN THESE TECHNIQUES — TAKE AN ACTIVE PART!

These are some of the activities which you should be able to do: Learn to preside at a program meeting or informal discussion; conduct the class as a club, including simple business meetings; elect a chairman and a secretary; make motions; address the chair; keep minutes; be recognized before speaking; make announcements; introduce participants in a program; keep the meeting moving smoothly; and adjourn a meeting.

WORTHWHILE BENEFITS — SOCIAL AND PERSONAL

Some of the values which you can gain from club activities and group discussion include: (1) good social habits through emphasizing the need for courtesy, consideration for others, and a sense of responsibility for the orderly and efficient conduct of business of concern to the group as a whole; (2) ability to select and organize fact and opinion bearing on a problem; (3) improved speech through a genuine desire to participate in a project of interest to all; (4) the habit of expressing an opinion, fact, or suggestion in a single, clear-cut sentence or two, rather than in rambling chatter.

HOW TO ORGANIZE AND CONDUCT A CLUB

1. Elect a chairman and a secretary.
2. State and discuss the purpose of the meeting.
3. Make a motion to organize the group or club.
4. Call the meeting to order.
5. Have the secretary read the minutes, if any.
6. Hear reports or other business presented by the members.
7 Introduce the program and speakers for the day.
8. Discuss any of the matters presented.
9. Adjourn the meeting.

ORDER OF BUSINESS FOR A COMMITTEE MEETING

1. **Call to order.**
   Chairman raps for attention and says, "The meeting will please come to order."

2. **Call the roll.**
   Chairman requests the secretary to do this: "The secretary will please call the roll."

3. **Read the minutes.**
   Chairman requests the secretary as follows: "Will the secretary please read the minutes of the last meeting?" ("Any corrections or additions? If not, they stand approved as read.")

4. **Hear reports.**
   "Are there any committee reports ready?"

5 **Finish old business.**
   "Is there any old business to consider?"

6. **Introduce new business.**
"Is there any new business to take up now?"

7. **Present the program for the day.**
"At this time I shall turn the meeting over to the program chairman." (or: "I am happy to present the speaker for today.")

8. **Adjourn the meeting.**
"A motion to adjourn is now in order." (No second is required.)
"All in favor, say *aye!*" (pronounced *eye*) "Meeting is adjourned."

CORRECT FORMS OF EXPRESSION

1. "Nominations are now in order." (teacher or temporary chairman)
2. "Mr. Chairman, I nominate (name of candidate)."
3. "I move that nominations be closed."
4. "All in favor, please say *aye*."
5. "Any opposed, please signify in the usual manner (say *no*)."
6. "Mr. Chairman, I make a motion that (state the motion)."
7. "Will someone second the motion?" (chairman asks group)
8. "I second the motion."
9. "The meeting will please come to order." (rap on desk)
10. "The secretary will please read the minutes."
11. "I am happy to introduce today's speaker (name)."
12. "Thank you very much." (at the end of the talk)
13. "Is there any discussion?" (addressed to the class)
14. "Ladies and gentlemen, what is your pleasure?" (inviting a motion or a vote)
15. "I move that this meeting be adjourned." (close of program)

For sample minutes of a club meeting, see page 45.

EXERCISES

PARLIAMENTARY PRACTICE

A. Following the rules of parliamentary procedure, select one of these situations and work it out in class.

1. Organize an Oral English Day as a club meeting with a pupil chairman, a secretary, and assigned speakers.

2. Hold a speech dinner or luncheon in the cafeteria. Invite parents, teachers, and the principal to attend, if possible.
3. Hold a special meeting of the Student Council to discuss proposals for a class outing, graduation, or yearbook.
4. Organize a "mock" Class Reunion as if it takes place ten years after graduation. The class president may serve as toastmaster to introduce "guests," make plans, etc.
5. Plan a "mock" Publishers Meeting to discuss the standards proposed by the class for better textbooks, magazines, comic books, etc.
6. Hear and discuss reports of students who have made trips to historical places or attended sessions of the town board, city council, state legislature, Congress, or the United Nations Assembly.
7. Have the Senior Class meet to discuss and plan such activities as Senior Day, Student-Faculty Ball Game, Prom, etc.
8. Organize the class as the Motion Picture Awards Committee to discuss winners for the best films of the year ("Oscars").
9. Plan a class discussion to prepare a set of rules for class behavior or establish a Student Court.
10. Have a committee report on a survey of the Student Handbook to suggest revisions for the next edition as a guide to newcomers.

B. Select the answers that correctly complete the following statements:

1. *Read the minutes* means (a) to tell the speaker his time is up (b) to announce the official treasurer's report (c) to narrate what happened at the previous meeting as recorded by the secretary.
2. *Motion to adjourn* refers to (a) the date of the next meeting (b) an ending of official business (c) a quiet and orderly exit.
3. *Question of privilege* requires the chairman to decide on (a) the rights of a member or the group (b) the suspension of dues (c) the exact meaning of a resolution.
4. *Point of order* requires the chairman (a) to correct a mistake in parliamentary order (b) to restate the issue under discussion (c) to take a general vote on a motion.
5. *Move the question* requires all discussion on a motion (a) to stop (b) to continue (c) to be interrupted by the chairman.
6. *Take recess* provides for (a) different group discussions of a topic (b) a brief relaxation before voting (c) an unofficial closing of old business.
7. *Motion seconded* means (a) another member supports the motion presented by someone (b) someone disapproves of the motion (c) the motion has been put to a vote for the second time.
8. *Lay on the table* means (a) put off all discussion of a main motion (b) rest the gavel on the desk (c) collect dues from members.
9. *Corrections and additions* refers to (a) errors in previous minutes (b) current bank balance (c) introduction of new members.
10. *Majority vote* refers to (a) a vote by two-thirds of the members (b) a vote by more than one-half of those present (c) a unanimous vote.

C. Select the answers that correctly complete the following statements:

1. *Come to order* marks (a) the end of useless discussion on a motion (b) the beginning of an official meeting (c) the notice for the next meeting.

2. *Limit debate* serves (*a*) to control the time for discussion (*b*) to allow anyone to filibuster (*c*) to present only one side of an issue.
3. *Defeat a motion* refers to (*a*) an affirmative vote (*b*) a negative vote (*c*) a split vote.
4. *Out of order* refers to a motion made (*a*) by a show of hands (*b*) while a previous motion is under consideration (*c*) by an absentee officer.
5. *Refer to committee* means the chairman may (*a*) table a motion (*b*) appoint members to study a motion (*c*) overrule a motion.
6. *Postpone indefinitely* means the motion has been (*a*) put to a vote (*b*) amended somewhat (*c*) put off without any date.
7. *Motion to amend* means (*a*) set a time to adjourn the meeting (*b*) have the secretary correct the minutes (*c*) change the motion as proposed.
8. *Pass a motion* refers to (*a*) tabling a motion (*b*) adopting a motion (*c*) dropping a motion at the chairman's request.
9. *Voice vote* signifies a decision to be reached by (*a*) a show of hands (*b*) a number of aye and no answers (*c*) a standing vote.
10. *Have a quorum* means (*a*) enough members are present to carry on business (*b*) start a free-for-all debate (*c*) take recess.

F GUIDE TO STANDARD PRONUNCIATION

DICTIONARIES

The correct way of saying English words may be found in any standard dictionary. The most often used dictionaries are:

Merriam-Webster: *New International Dictionary*
Funk and Wagnalls: *New Standard Dictionary*
Winston: *A Dictionary of the English Language*
Jones: *English Pronouncing Dictionary*

Dictionaries contain a record of the way words are spoken by cultivated speakers. When more than one way is acceptable, the first pronunciation given is called the *preferred* form; the second pronunciation is called the *alternate* form. For example, *abdomen* may be said "ab do' men" (preferred), or "ab' do men" (alternate)

PRONUNCIATION KEY

The pronunciation key is a series of common words showing the sounds of vowels and consonants. This key is usually printed at the bottom of the page in the dictionary to serve as a guide to the meaning of the diacritical marks. Since these key words are a guide to the pronunciation of all other words, it is important to learn how to say them correctly.

The first place to look for the correct pronunciation of a word is the dictionary. Learn to use the *key* to better speech!

In Webster's dictionary, the following sixteen words provide the key to the chief vowel sounds. (Learn to recognize those little marks!)

Pronunciation Key for Vowels

ā — ale	ē — eve	ō — old	o͝o — foot
ă — add	ĕ — end	ŏ — odd	ū — cube
ä — arm	ī — ice	ô — orb	ŭ — up
á — ask	ĭ — ill	o͞o — food	û — urn

STANDARD PRONUNCIATION

Since English is spoken in all parts of the world, some differences in sounds and stress (or accent) have naturally come about. Thus, the British say "gar' age" (rhyming with *carriage*), while the Americans say "gar age' " (rhyming with *mirage*). Such national differences are approved by usage and tradition. On the other hand, it is wrong and slovenly to pronounce *library* as "lĭ' bêr ĭ" because this omits an *r* sound; the right way to say it is "lĭ' brĕr ĭ." The nasal kind of *a* in *candy* is wrong; it should be the short ă as in *add*. Omitting the strong *g* in finger (mispronounced "fing' er" with one *g*) is also incorrect; the right way is "fing' ger" (said with two *g*'s).

The point we are trying to make is that national differences in speech may be accepted, but careless errors should be avoided.

EXERCISE

100 WORDS COMMONLY MISPRONOUNCED

Use the dictionary to find the correct pronunciation of each word below. Practice saying the correct form aloud and use it in your own speech.

absolutely	direct	interesting	romance
address	employee	iodine	roof
admirable	entire	kerosene	route
aerial	envelope	laugh	routine
after	etiquette	legend	says
alias	experiment	leisure	schedule
allies	exquisite	lingerie	secretary
amateur	faucet	longer	statistics
apparatus	February	luxury	stronger
athlete	fiction	margarine	supreme
aunt	film	matinee	theater
aviator	forehead	medieval	thirty
ballet	futile	menagerie	tragedy
because	garage	menu	unanimous
biography	genuine	mischievous	vase
bouquet	government	museum	vehicle
caramel	grievous	naphtha	width
catch	guarantee	often	window
cement	hangar	omelet	with
cleanliness	horizon	perspiration	won't
colonel	hospital	pianist	xylophone
coupon	humane	picture	younger
courtesy	ideal	probably	youth
depot	influence	recognize	youths
diamond	inquiry	ridiculous	zoology

G RULES FOR SYLLABICATION

Syllabication means dividing words into syllables to indicate either pronunciation or word-division at the end of a line.

Do

1. Use a hyphen at the end of the line to show division of syllables.

   EXAMPLE: Our school made a contribution of one hundred dollars.

2. Divide a word only at the end of a syllable.

   WRONG: conveni-ence   RIGHT: conven-ience
   WRONG: is-thmus   RIGHT: isth-mus

3. Divide a word so that the part before the hyphen suggests the entire word.

   POOR: rev-erence   BETTER: rever-ence
   POOR: fla-voring   BETTER: flavor-ing

4. Divide compound words between their main parts.

   EXAMPLES: text-book, house-keeper, rail-road, flash-light

5. Divide prefixes and suffixes from the rest of the word.

   EXAMPLES: (prefixes) contra-diction, inter-national, super-human
   (suffixes) geol-ogy, complica-tion, peace-able

Don't

1. Don't divide a word containing only one syllable.

   EXAMPLES: strange, through, strength, train, reign

2. Don't divide ordinary contractions or possessives.

   EXAMPLES: isn't, can't, don't, James's, Mary's, Joneses'

3. Don't divide words of two syllables unless the word contains six letters or more.

   POOR: be-gin, end-ed, fe-ver, re-ly, in-ner
   RIGHT: en-trance, thor-ough, con-fess, fren-zied

4. Don't divide a word so that a single letter is left either at the beginning or the end.

WRONG: a-cross, heav-y, e-lect, bod-y

5. Don't divide a word so that only two letters are left either at the beginning or the end, except when such a division is unavoidable.

POOR: se-cretive   BETTER: secre-tive
POOR: deposit-ed   BETTER: depos-ited

Whenever possible, avoid breaking up a word. If you *must* divide, look it up in the dictionary, and make the separation so clear and logical that the reader may easily follow the reading without false impressions.

EXERCISES

SYLLABICATION

A. Assume that the following words come at the end of a line and because of lack of space you must divide them. Show how you would correctly separate them. Use the dictionary to check your answers!

1. amusement	11. adventurous	21. measurement
2. unavoidable	12. biographical	22. illustration
3. interestingly	13. communication	23. particular
4. television	14. introductory	24. occurrence
5. regulations	15. civilization	25. independently
6. inexperience	16. headquarters	26. mountainous
7. underestimate	17. fingerprint	27. recommendation
8. impoliteness	18. fundamental	28. broad-mindedness
9. specification	19. enthusiastically	29. explanatory
10. environment	20. requirements	30. insignificant

B. Show how the following words should be divided into syllables:

1. approximately	11. equipment	21. international
2. advertisement	12. extraordinary	22. improvement
3. broadcasting	13. embarrassed	23. inconvenient
4. bungalow	14. entertainment	24. intelligence
5. beautifully	15. furniture	25. judgment
6. behavior	16. favorable	26. lieutenant
7. correspondence	17. graduation	27. locomotive
8. consideration	18. gymnasium	28. membership
9. development	19. gasoline	29. occupation
10. disappointment	20. happiness	30. opportunity

II   TRAINING IN WRITTEN EXPRESSION SKILLS

What did Adam say to Eve when she offered him the apple in the Garden of Eden? What did Jonah say when he found himself inside the whale? We do not know because their words were not written down. On the other hand, we all know the courageous words spoken by great men of the past because they have come down to us preserved in writing. John Paul Jones aboard the *Bonhomme Richard* said, "I have not yet begun to fight!" Abraham Lincoln in his speech at Gettysburg said, "Government of the people, by the people, and for the people shall not perish from the earth." The point is clear: speech is important, but writing is more enduring.

It is well to remember that written expression is the last and most difficult of the language arts that we learn. First, we listen; then, we speak. Later, we read; and, finally, we write. We need the greatest amount of training in writing because it includes weighing ideas, organizing them, choosing effective words, and expressing thoughts in acceptable style. This does not mean that every bit of writing deserves to be chiseled into marble forever. It does mean, however, that both factual writing for everyday needs and creative composition for self-expression require a conscious effort. Clear, direct letters as well as imaginative stories demand work. They do not come easily. Yet, you can acquire a satisfactory degree of skill—if you study this section carefully!

A   FACTUAL WRITING

This kind of writing requires the writer to be clear, brief, accurate, and courteous. The main emphasis should be on getting the facts down as concisely as possible. The *message* counts most. Later on when you study Creative Composition, you will be concerned with style and imagination. But here your aim is simple directness.

22

▷ WRITING FRIENDLY LETTERS

A FRIENDLY LETTER IS A PERSONAL VISIT

The writing of friendly letters or social notes is the art of bringing together two persons for a little while. When rightly done, a letter can help to cement a casual acquaintanceship into a lasting friendship. Be natural and express yourself in as lively and interesting a way as you can.

Some helpful questions to aid you in judging the merit of the content of a letter are: Have I made the point of the letter clear? Have I written as I would talk with this person? Does the beginning draw attention and catch the reader's interest? Are the parts of the letter in good order? Is the closing effective?

Show your friend the same courtesy and sincerity in a **social note** as you do in a personal visit. Write as you would talk with this person if he were standing before you.

FIVE PARTS OF A FRIENDLY LETTER

1. Heading	Your address: number, street, city, zone, state The date: month, day, year
2. Salutation	Greeting, friendly style— Dear (name of person),
3. Body	The message or content of the letter
4. Closing	The closing phrase: Sincerely, or Cordially yours,
5. Signature	Your name written below the closing phrase

SAMPLE FORMS FOR THE LETTER AND ENVELOPE

Friendly Letter and Envelope — Indented Form

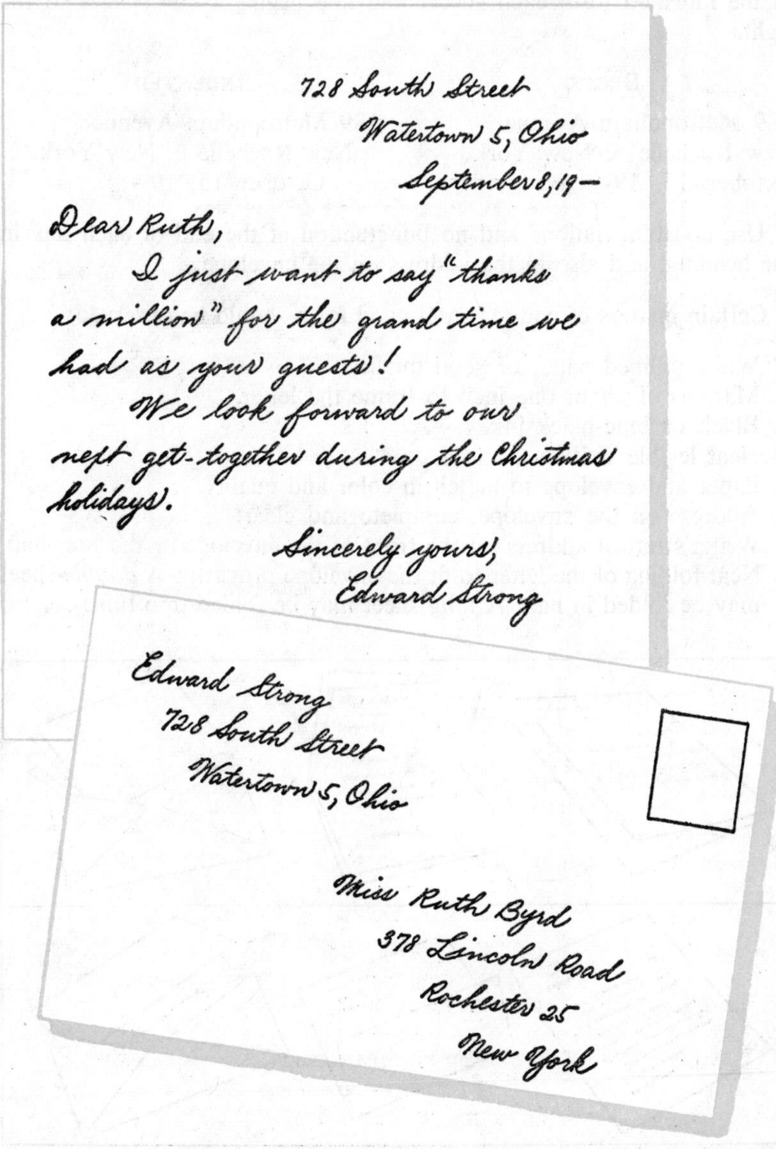

728 South Street
Watertown 5, Ohio
September 8, 19—

Dear Ruth,

I just want to say "thanks a million" for the grand time we had as your guests!

We look forward to our next get-together during the Christmas holidays.

Sincerely yours,
Edward Strong

Edward Strong
728 South Street
Watertown 5, Ohio

Miss Ruth Byrd
378 Lincoln Road
Rochester 25
New York

Either the *block* or the *indented* form may be used in friendly letters. Handwritten letters, however, usually follow the indented form. In the block form, each line begins directly below the previous line, whereas in the indented form each succeeding line begins a few spaces to the right.

BLOCK	INDENTED
189 Metropolitan Avenue	189 Metropolitan Avenue
New Rochelle 6, New York	New Rochelle 6, New York
October 15, 19--	October 15, 19--

Use no abbreviations and no punctuation at the end of each line in the heading, and also in the address on the envelope.

Certain matters of courtesy and good form should be observed:

1. White unlined paper of good quality.
2. Margins of about one inch to frame the letter.
3. Black or blue-black ink.
4. Neat legible writing.
5. Paper and envelope to match in color and quality.
6. Address on the envelope, complete and clear.
7. Writer's return address on the front of the envelope or the rear flap.
8. Neat folding of the letter to fit the envelope properly: A *double* sheet may be folded in half. A *long* sheet may be folded into thirds.

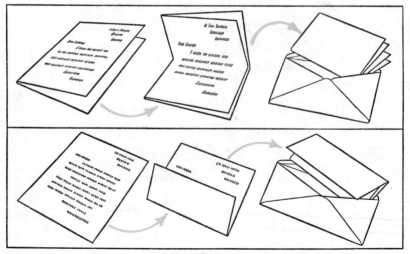

MODEL FRIENDLY LETTERS

1. To a Close Friend

256 Bement Place,
Seaford, Long Island
August 8, 19—

Dear Johnny,

I have just heard Dad phone your father about a beach outing at Jones Beach for next Sunday. That's why I have to write this note.

Listen! Bring along your underwater goggles and fins. Also be sure to carry your portable radio so that we can hear the ball game. If you can borrow some cash, we can visit the Indian Village. We're going to have lots of fun, boy.

Eagerly,
Stephen

754 Stanhope Street
Ridgewood 27, New York
May 24, 19—

Dear Mr. Smith,

I want to thank you very much for all the extra help you gave me in order to prepare for the entrance examinations at Brooklyn Technical High School.

You were patient with me in solving those tricky problems in mathematics and you gave me enough confidence to try the real thing. Whether I passed or failed, I know how much I owe you for your efforts in guiding and teaching me. Thanks a lot!

Sincerely yours,
Frank Bell

EXERCISES

SOCIAL NOTES

A. Rewrite these faulty letters in accordance with the rules of courtesy, good form, and natural friendly tone. Include correct heading, closing, signature, etc.

235 Lincoln Lane
Atlantic City, NJ
April 18, 19--

Dear Kathy—

You know what happened in school today? Well, we had a quiz on current events in the form of a "bee" between two teams of "experts." The boys beat the girls because they really know what's going on in the world of affairs. The question that knocked me out of the line up was, "Who is the president of the French Republic?"

Now, let's get back to you, Kathy. How do you feel? I hope you are getting better day by day and will soon be back in School.

So long for now!

Your Friend,
Marge

41 Boise Blvd.
Hartford 1, Conneticut
July 15, 19--

Uncle Lou:

I'm writing to you because I'm in a bit of a jam. You see this is the end of the first marking period at School and my report card has too many red circles around my marks. Mother and Dad have decided to cancel my hunting trip until I can show some improvement. Meanwhile, you know we have all the plans made, food bought, equipment ready, and no place to go! Isn't it terrible? Besides, Mother ordered me to scrub the kitchen, and Dad wants me to wax the car, and nobody cares what happens to me. Your my only hope. So come soon.

Your prisoner at home,
Vincent

1211 Springfield Avenue.
Emmitsburg 3, Maryland,
June 10, 19--

Hi, Pal!

What do you say about coming along with me to see the new Auto Show next week? All you need is carfare and the price of a ticket. Maybe some nice grownup will see to it that we are admitted. I'd like to see the sports models and some of the recent station wagons in order to try to get Dad to buy a second car for our growing family. Of course, we can also use it for our scout trip next summer. Have you entered your plastic and wood carved model in the club contest? You've got a good chance to win a prize!

Your's truely
Paul

B. Write the following social notes. Then draw a rectangle to represent the envelope in which the letter is to be sent and address this envelope for mailing.

1. Suppose a cousin who is about your age is to spend the summer with you. Write him (or her) a letter expressing your pleasure at his coming and telling him enough of your plans for the summer to make him eager for his visit.
2. Suppose that you have a relative or friend in the armed forces. Write a letter telling him the local and family news.
3. Suppose a friend is visiting you. You plan to have a party in your friend's honor. Write a letter to another friend, inviting him or her to attend the party. Give all necessary details.
4. Suppose you were the friend who received the invitation (question 3) and could not accept. Write a letter expressing your regret at not being able to attend.
5. Suppose that you have just returned from a weekend visit with a friend or relative of your own age who provided you with a very well-planned and pleasant time. Write a letter to him or her, recalling some of the activities that you enjoyed together and expressing your appreciation for the fine time you had during the visit.
6. Suppose that your class is planning to hold exercises on Friday, June 23. Write a letter to a friend or relative inviting him or her to attend. Tell in your letter the time, the place, and the other plans that your class is making for your program.
7. Suppose that you had a friend visiting you last Easter and that you two started to build a clubhouse to use during the summer months. Write a letter to your friend about the progress you have made on the project. You might also tell something about your plans for using the clubhouse.
8. Write a letter to a friend or relative whom you have just visited. Express the pleasure that your visit has given you and courteously request the return of an article which you carelessly left behind.
9. Write a letter inviting a friend to join your hobby club. Tell him (or her) why you think he (or she) will enjoy collecting stamps, building models, painting pictures, or some other hobby.
10. The joy that we feel when a friend has met with success makes us want to congratulate him. Suppose a girl or boy has just been given some honor or won a prize. Write a letter of congratulation to show that you are pleased at his or her good fortune.

11. Suppose you had planned to visit your cousin last weekend but at the last minute could not make the trip. You sent him the following telegram:

James Cousin, Neartown, N.Y.
Cannot visit you Saturday. Something unexpected happened. Letter follows.

Write a letter to James, expressing your regret and explaining the circumstances that made it impossible for you to make the visit.

12. Suppose that the coach of your school baseball team has had to leave for military service before the end of the season. Write him a letter telling the news of interest to him, especially how the team finished the season.

13. Suppose you have received an unexpected gift, such as a bicycle, from a friend or relative. Write a thank-you letter in which you tell why you were pleased with the gift and describe some of your experiences with it.

14. Suppose that you have just received a letter from your cousin, part of which is given below. Write an answer to your cousin in proper letter form.

My parents are making plans for an automobile trip to Florida during the Easter vacation and have given me permission to invite a companion of my own age. I know that you and I would enjoy the trip, so I am writing this letter to ask you to go with us. We plan to leave on the Wednesday before Easter and return on the Sunday after Easter.

Please talk it over with your parents and write me soon. If you want to know what things to take, ask about them in your letter. I will find out the details and write you later.

It sounds exciting to me and I know we shall have fun. I look forward to hearing from you.

 # WRITING BUSINESS LETTERS

A BUSINESS LETTER COMES RIGHT TO THE POINT

Business letters differ from friendly letters in tone and content. They are formal and direct. No time is wasted in getting to the point. You must take care in stating things exactly because any error will involve delay and unnecessary correspondence. Before you start to write a business letter make sure you have at hand all the necessary facts: name of firm, address, catalog number, meter reading, size of article, price, check or money order, actual date of purchase, sales slip, etc. State in your opening sentence whether you are ordering goods, requesting information, complaining about service, returning an item, etc.

Be courteous and businesslike in setting forth the purpose of your writing. Be brief, but include all necessary details. If you are applying for a position, give full particulars about yourself, such as age, education, experience, references, salary desired, and request for an interview.

SIX PARTS OF A BUSINESS LETTER

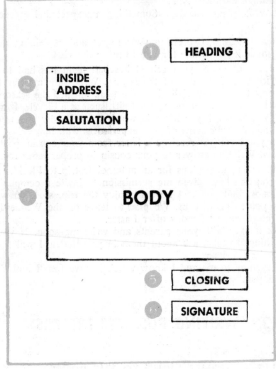

1. Heading	Your address: number, street, city, zone, state
	The date: month, day, year
2. Inside address	Name and address of business firm or person to whom you are writing
3. Salutation	Greeting, formal style— Gentlemen: or Dear Sir:
4. Body	The message or content of the letter
5. Closing	The formal closing phrase: Very truly yours,
6. Signature	Your name written in ink in full below the closing phrase

SAMPLE FORMS FOR THE LETTER AND ENVELOPE

Business Letter and Envelope — Block Form

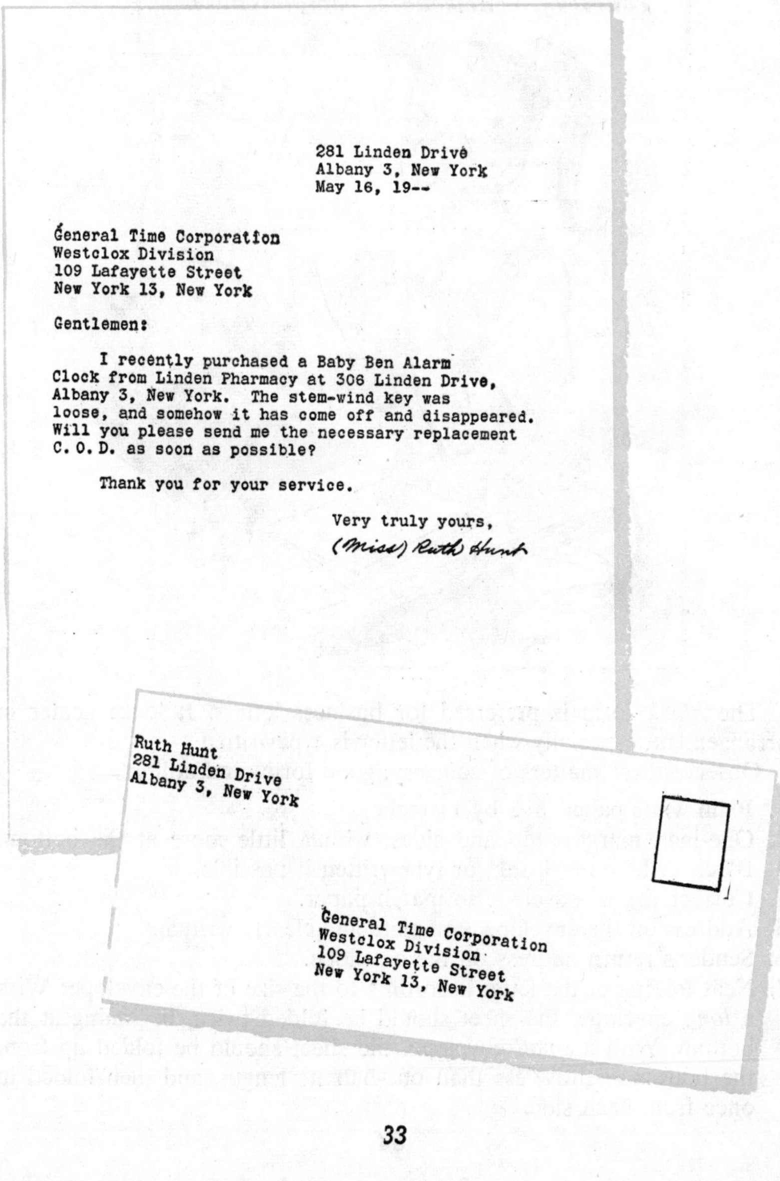

281 Linden Drive
Albany 3, New York
May 16, 19--

General Time Corporation
Westclox Division
109 Lafayette Street
New York 13, New York

Gentlemen:

    I recently purchased a Baby Ben Alarm
Clock from Linden Pharmacy at 306 Linden Drive,
Albany 3, New York. The stem-wind key was
loose, and somehow it has come off and disappeared.
Will you please send me the necessary replacement
C. O. D. as soon as possible?

    Thank you for your service.

               Very truly yours,

               (Miss) Ruth Hunt

Ruth Hunt
281 Linden Drive
Albany 3, New York

General Time Corporation
Westclox Division
109 Lafayette Street
New York 13, New York

When writing a business letter, let the three C's be your guide:

courtesy, conciseness, completeness.

The *block* form is preferred for business letters. It looks neater in arrangement, especially when the letter is typewritten.

Observe these matters of courtesy, good form, and utility:

1. Plain white paper, 8½ by 11 inches.
2. One-inch margins top and sides, with a little more at the bottom.
3. Black or blue-black ink, or typewritten if possible.
4. Correct size of envelope to match paper.
5. Address on the envelope, complete and clearly written.
6. Sender's return address on the envelope.
7. Neat folding of the letter according to the size of the envelope: With a *long* envelope, the sheet should be folded twice, beginning at the bottom. With a *small* envelope, the sheet should be folded up from the bottom slightly less than one-half its length, and then folded in once from each side.

269 Elizabeth Street
New York 17, New York
July 2, 19--

Herald Tribune Fresh Air Fund
230 West 41 Street
New York 36, New York

Dear Sir:

I am writing this note to tell you how much I
appreciated the two weeks vacation away from the crowded
city. This was the first time in my life that I spent
in a summer camp, and I shall never forget it. The food
was fine, the counselors were friendly, and the swimming
and other activities out of this world. Please give my
deepest thanks to all those kind people whose contributions
made it possible. Thanks a lot to you for selecting me
as one of the lucky ones.

Sincerely yours,

Walter King

275 Stockholm Street
Brooklyn 27, New York
December 16, 19--

Manager
World-Telegram & Sun
215 Bleecker Street
New York City

Dear Sir:

   I am interested in the job advertised (above) as newspaper
delivery boy after school. I am at present in the eighth grade at
J. H. S. 162 and have just passed my fourteenth birthday. My parents
are willing to sign the application for part-time working papers.
The principal will recommend me for satisfactory work, conduct,
effort, and attendance. Will you please consider me for a vacancy in
or near Ridgewood since I am well acquainted with this neighborhood.
I shall be glad to come for an interview at your convenience.

                                        Very truly yours,

                                        Carl Raymond

36

EXERCISES

BUSINESS LETTERS

A. Rewrite these faulty letters in accordance with the rules of courtesy, conciseness, and completeness. Include correct heading, closing, signature, etc.

1. LETTER OF COMPLAINT

> 1890 Bryant Street
> Buffalo 12, N.Y.
> August 3, 19--

Time Magazine
540 N. Michigan Av.
Chicago 11, Ill.
Dear Gentlemen,
   My aunt Betty told me she ordered 52 issues of your magazine as a gift for me. Well, it's all a big mistake. I really want Popular Science, so send me the money back. I don't like to read about news. I like to see pictures of the latest cars and other hobbies. You don't have to tell aunt Betty about this because she will get pretty mad. Just mail me the cash.

> Trully Your's
> Larry

2. LETTER OF APPLICATION

> 43 Latham St.,
> Hempstead, New York
> May 2, 19--

Dear Mr. Green,
   I saw your ad asking for a helper to work in your greenhouse after school and on Saturdays. That's just the job for me. I'm tired of doing chores around the house for nothing and will be glad to make a few easy bucks watering flowers. I hope there ain't no dust around because I get asthma attacks and start wheezing. Next Saturday we're playing ball against the district champs, so please excuse me for not coming to work. Just drop me a card when you need me to start and I'll be right over before you can sneeze. So long, now.

> Thanking you,
> Chuck

37

3. LETTER OF INVITATION

141 Fifth Street
New Rochelle 2, N.Y.
June 5, 19--

Mr. Albert Warner
City Hall
Richmond, N.Y.
Gentlemen:

Our class voted to have you come and speak at our graduation next week. We know your a busy man but also a public figure. We really want somebody big to dress up the occasion, but we hope you will not talk more than two or three minutes, and give us a message. And make sure you come with a police escort because we love to see the motorcycle cops and hear the sirens.

Respectively yours
The Committee

B. Write the following business letters. Then draw a rectangle to represent the envelope in which the letter is to be sent and address this envelope for mailing.

1. The regular subscription price of the *Defense Digest* has been reduced to one dollar for men in the military service of the United States. Write a letter to the *Defense Digest,* Cartersville, New York, ordering subscriptions for two of your friends, one a lieutenant in the 113th Cavalry at Camp Bowie, Texas, and the other a cadet at the U. S. Naval Air Station, Jacksonville, Florida.

2. Suppose that there are to be some contests for boys and girls in your community. Each boy who competes is to make a model airplane and each girl who takes part is to knit one pair of socks. Write to the Atlantic Novelty Company, 123 Andrews Street, Albany, New York, ordering the materials you will need in order to enter the contest.

3. Suppose that the Amerco Seed Company of 130 First Avenue, Seedtown, New York, is offering a $3.50 Victory Seed Packet for boys and girls, at the special price of $2. You must promise to raise a garden in order to get the packet at that special price. Write a letter asking for the packet as offered.

4. Write a letter of application, answering the following advertisement:

   Wanted: A boy or girl over 14 years of age to deliver newspapers every afternoon after 4 p. m. Must have a bicycle and be acquainted with the community. Apply by letter to County News, Ourtown, New York.

5. Suppose a group of eighth-grade pupils have decided to form a Salvage Club whose business it will be to collect scrap metal and paper during the summer. Write a letter to the Editor of Local News, Nearbytown, New York, telling him of your plans and asking him to help you promote the club, especially by news stories about the club.

6. Suppose you have just read in the newspaper about a boy or girl of your own age who will be confined to bed for many weeks. The article states that the boy or girl would appreciate having letters from people of his (or her) age. Write a letter that would interest him (or her).

38

7. Suppose that you had ordered "Youthtime Magazine" for one year beginning last month and as yet you have not received your first two copies. Write a letter to Youthtime Publishers, Anytown, New York, explaining your action and requesting that mailing of the magazine be started as your subscription stated.

8. Suppose you have been selected by your class to arrange for a speaker for your Arbor Day activities. Write to Mr. Henry Carter, 126 Chestnut Street, Oldtown, New York, telling him of your plans and inviting him to be the speaker. Mr. Carter is well known for his interest in nature, especially trees and plant life.

9. Suppose that there is to be a "Letter to the Editor" contest conducted by *Ourtown News*, Ourtown, New York, in which each contestant is to tell why he is proud and happy to be an American. Assume that you are entering the contest and write a letter of 75 to 100 words expressing yourself on the subject.

10. Suppose that Teencamp, Inc., Evergreen, New York, is offering a three-week camping trip with all expenses paid for the boy or girl who can write the best letter telling why camping is a worth-while activity for teen-agers. Write a letter of no more than 100 words to Mr. Bob Man, Director, giving your ideas on the value of camping.

11. Suppose that you have just lost your puppy. Write a letter to Mr. John Brown, Police Department, Ourtown, New York, asking him to have the police try to find the puppy. Include a description of the puppy and any other details that may help in the search.

12. Suppose you wanted a job and saw these advertisements in your local paper. Write a letter of application in answer to one of the advertisements:

   (1) *Wanted*—Gardener's Helper. Boy to help gardener in greenhouse after school and on Saturdays. Write R. M. Green, My-Own-Greenhouse, Ourtown, N. Y.

   (2) *Wanted*—Girl to take care of two children Saturday nights. Write Mrs. Miles Brown, 421 Elm Street, Mytown, N. Y.

13. Suppose that your citizenship education class, which is studying the present foreign policy of the United States, has chosen you as its secretary. Write a letter to the United States Government Printing Office, Washington 25, D. C., requesting four copies of *Our Foreign Policy*, which is Department of State Publication 3972. Identify yourself as secretary of the class and explain why your class is interested in receiving the booklets. Also mention that you are enclosing a money order for one dollar to cover the charge for the four booklets.

14. Write to John H. Miller, Executive Secretary, Chamber of Commerce, Yourtown, New York, asking him to send you information about the chief industries of Yourtown.

15. Suppose that you want to apply for *one* of the jobs described in the advertisements below. Write a suitable letter of application.

   BOY—To deliver messages and small packages. Bicycle needed. References required. Brown and Co., Ourtown, N. Y.

   GIRL—To care for small child after school and Saturdays. References required. Mrs. Charles Carlson, 24 Gorton St., Ourtown, N. Y.

③ SCHOOL CORRESPONDENCE

Occasionally, you are required to bring a note to your teacher or principal requesting permission, explaining absence or lateness, or for any other reason. Be careful to use correct form and appearance, as well as to state clearly the purpose of the note. Make sure your parent or guardian signs, too, indicating approval.

Absence Note

Class_____

October 18, 19--

Dear (Name of Teacher):

Will you please excuse my absence from school on October 15, 16, 17. I had to stay home because of a severe cold and upset stomach.

Approved: Very truly yours,

_____   _____
Parent's signature   Pupil's signature

EXERCISE

SCHOOL CORRESPONDENCE

Good letters serve a purpose in each of the following situations. Write notes using correct form and content. Be polite!

1. Ask the teacher to excuse your lateness caused by a delayed school bus.
2. Thank the principal for selecting your essay to be entered in a prize contest.
3. Request permission to leave school one hour earlier in order to accompany your parent to a doctor's office for an examination.
4. Apologize to the teacher for making an unkind remark about another pupil in the class.
5. Ask your teacher to give you the homework assignments you have missed because of illness.

6. Request the principal for an appointment to interview him for an article in the next issue of the school newspaper.
7. Inform your teacher that your family has moved to a new address.
8. Ask your teacher to excuse your absence on account of a religious observance.
9. Notify your teacher that you promise to pay (in weekly installments) for a textbook you have lost.
10. Suggest to the principal an assembly program including students and parents in a forum dealing with teenage problems.

 ## SUMMARIZING NOTES FOR STUDY

The art of study includes the ability to keep a notebook in which important ideas are briefly summarized for review or as a refresher for the memory. This is especially valuable in preparing for tests and serves as an outline for classwork and readings in the textbook. Some pupils use index tabs or divider sheets to separate their notebook into handy sections, such as ENGLISH, SCIENCE, ARITHMETIC, GEOGRAPHY.

A tidy notebook is a sign of an orderly mind.

Here are two sample pages taken from pupils' notebooks. The first was written by a girl during her home economics class in cooking. The other page was written by a boy in his general science class on a topic in biology. Notice the clear arrangement of notes in outline form. Each main heading has a series of subheadings or illustrations which help to expand the statement or definition. Each page of notes may well represent several full pages of print in a textbook or the results of a recitation period. The value of summarizing notes for study is readily apparent, both in the organization of the material and in the fact that these pupils earned honor roll ratings in these subject areas. Does *your* notebook look like this?

Home Economics Notes

SAFETY IN THE HOME

I. *In the Kitchen*

Suitable clothing for the kitchen.
Wear washable dresses with short sleeves for kitchen activities.
Protect the dress with a clean apron.
Wear a cap or hair net which covers your hair completely.
Tie back long hair.
Use a small hand towel (not Turkish or fringed).
Keep an adequate pot holder in your apron pocket.

II. *The Stove*

Directions for lighting top burner.
1. Strike a match away from you on a closed box.
2. Turn the gas on full.
3. Apply match to the burner nearest to you.
4. Blow out match and dispose of it in a suitable metal container.
5. Adjust the flame.

III. *Fire Prevention*

Extinguish with salt or sand a fire caused by burning grease. Do not use water.
Keep inflammable liquids in approved fireproof containers. Use only in a well-ventilated room or out of doors. Keep them away from fires.
Keep oil rag or wax cloth in metal containers. If your clothing catches fire, do not run. Roll on floor. Call for someone to bring an asbestos blanket, rug, or heavy coat. Roll on floor in fire blanket.

Biology Notes

1. Bacteria—are the smallest living plants.

2. Most of the bacteria are not harmful; some are of benefit to man:
   - *a.* tanning of leather
   - *b.* give butter taste
   - *c.* needed to make linen from flax
   - *d.* dispose of dead plants and animals by feeding on them

3. The three shapes of bacteria are:
   - *a.* rod shaped ⬭ bacillus (bacilli)
   - *b.* ball shaped ∘∘∞ coccus (cocci)
   - *c.* spiral shaped ∿ spirillum (spirilla)

4. Bacteria cause—
   - *a.* a type of pneumonia
   - *b.* tuberculosis
   - *c.* typhoid
   - *d.* diphtheria

5. Viruses—are the smallest living things that can be seen only with an electron microscope.

6. Viruses cause—
   - *a.* influenza
   - *b.* smallpox
   - *c.* measles
   - *d.* the common cold
   - *e.* a type of pneumonia

7. Fungi—are tiny plants, most of which are larger than bacteria.
   - *a.* Some fungi like yeast and mushrooms are of benefit to man.
   - *b.* One fungus, penicillium, produces penicillin used to cure such diseases as bacterial pneumonia.
   - *c.* One fungus causes athlete's foot.

8. Protozoa—are very tiny animals seen only with a microscope. Protozoa cause malaria and African sleeping sickness.

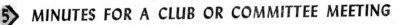

5 MINUTES FOR A CLUB OR COMMITTEE MEETING

The *minutes* are an official written record of the proceedings of any club or group. They are kept by the secretary and must be read and approved by the other members at the next meeting. They are important because they serve as a kind of running history of the activities of the club, as well as a permanent source of reference as to matters approved or disapproved by the group. The minutes should be neatly written (or later typed) and should include the following information:

Obeying the rules

gets things done.

A free-for-all

gets nowhere.

1. Whether it was a regular or special meeting.
2. The name of the club or committee.
3. The date on which the meeting was held.
4. The place in which it occurred.
5. The name of the presiding officer.
6. An account of the proceedings: including reports made, matters discussed, motions approved, and program of the day.
7. The date scheduled for the next meeting.
8. The name of the secretary or other person who prepared the minutes.

SAMPLE MINUTES FOR A CLUB MEETING

A regular weekly meeting of the Scribblers Club of Willoughby Junior High School was held on February 14, 19-- in room 209. The president, Constance C——, presided and the secretary and members were present, together with the faculty adviser, Mr. H——. The minutes of the previous meeting were read and approved.

Mr. H—— introduced the guest speaker for the day, our librarian, Mrs. B——. She congratulated us for showing such an interest in creative self-expression and invited us to explore the poetry section in the school library. She suggested we ask the General Organization to donate $10 to purchase recordings of poets reading their own verse, such as Robert Frost, Carl Sandburg, and Edith Sitwell.

Our president thanked the speaker for coming to our meeting, and then suggested we hold a writing session for ten minutes to try to complete some limericks. We read our poems aloud and had a lot of fun.

Pat F—— made a motion to send a copy of a poem entitled "Courage," written by Constance, to the Industrial Home for the Blind. The motion was carried.

Paul M—— made a motion that the members of the club enter the Citywide Poetry Contest sponsored by the Board of Education. The motion was postponed to the next meeting.

Joseph L—— made a motion that we request a Scribblers Club Corner in our school newspaper to publish selected verses written by club members. The motion was adopted. Then the president appointed Joseph as a committee of one to present the idea to the editor of the school paper as soon as possible and to report back to the group.

The meeting was adjourned at 4:30 P.M. after setting the date for our next session on February 21.

Respectfully submitted,
Lena A——, Secretary

⟨6⟩ REPORTING ON RESEARCH WORK

Pupils working on a problem no longer use a single textbook to supply the answer. They refer to several books, magazines, pamphlets, newspapers, government bulletins, encyclopedias, and other library resources. Sometimes they interview businessmen or visit factories and other community resources. These activities may be carried out by the class as a whole or by committees. Such research by individuals involves gathering information and organizing it in the form of notes for a special report to the group. For problems related to school or family life, the research may be done quite readily because the materials lie close at hand.

Research means finding answers to problems, and that is the way you learn to become self-reliant.

For broader problems in social studies, science, or literature, the library and the community must come into play. In any case, there are two main jobs: collecting facts and organizing them into a written report. For example,

"How Has Big Business Made the United States a World Leader?"

STEPS IN COLLECTING INFORMATION

1. Make sure you have a clear understanding of the question or problem for research, and your particular phase of it.
2. Go to the school or public library for printed materials related to the topic. The librarian stands ready to help.
3. Jot down the titles of reference books you use and make brief outlines of important facts.
4. Interview persons who may know something about the problem and note their opinions or ideas.
5. Collect newspaper clippings, magazine articles, etc.

STEPS IN ORGANIZING INFORMATION

1. Prepare a skeleton outline of the topic so that you know the general direction of your research:
   a. Natural resources of the U. S.
   b. Development of agriculture in the U. S.
   c. Growth of the factory system in the U. S.
   d. Effect of science and invention on the U. S.
   e. Transportation and communication in the U. S.
   f. Big business corporations in the U. S.
   g. World trade and U. S. leadership.
2. Divide these seven subtopics among separate committees for investigation and keep notes on facts as discovered.
3. Have each committee pool its information in order to select what is to be included and discard what is to be omitted.
4. Draft a combined committee report, under the direction of the chairman, bringing the seven subtopics together for the central problem.
5. Assemble the report in the form of a scrapbook containing:
   a. The problem for research.
   b. The members of the committee.
   c. The typewritten body of the report.
   d. A list of sources or reference books consulted.
   e. Neat paste-ups of clippings, pamphlets, etc.
6. Present the report to the class for discussion and evaluation.

EXERCISE

RESEARCH WORK

1. *Prepare a history of the school:* how it got its name; date of opening; former principals; special rooms, shops, etc.; outstanding graduates; present staff members; rules and regulations; picture of the school; clippings from the school paper; clippings from local newspapers; etc.
2. *Make a survey of pupils' television habits:* chart of hours spent viewing telecasts per week; favorite programs; effect on homework and school ratings; etc.
3. *Famous American men and women:* pioneers and explorers; presidents and statesmen; scientists and inventors; artists and musicians; captains of industry and labor leaders; generals and heroes; writers and actors; other categories (sports, etc.).
4. *The UN and world peace:* origin of the UN; organization of General Assembly, Security Council, etc.; agencies (UNESCO, UNICEF, etc.); record of UN in settling international problems; current world affairs; include newspaper clippings, bulletins, pamphlets, etc.

STUDENT REPORT ON RESEARCH WORK

OUR SCHOOL HISTORY

Willoughby Junior High School was opened in December, 1909 as an elementary school with classes from kindergarten through 4B. The principal, Mrs. Moriarity, and a number of teachers were transferred here from P.S. 86. There were about 30 teachers and about 1000 pupils in the school. From 1913 to 1947, the upper grade classes (7A-8B) were for girls only, and remained that way until 1947 when the school became a co-ed junior high school (7A-9B) with no elementary grades.

For many years, P.S. 162 was a special school with many special classes. It had the first class in Brooklyn for blind pupils. It had several classes for handicapped children and many pre-vocational classes for girls in the upper grades. Visitors came from all over the country to see the work done by pupils in this school.

Long ago, the community surrounding the school, including Suydam Street and Willoughby Avenue from St. Nicholas Avenue to the car barns, was farmland. Some of the handicapped children came to school in stagecoaches drawn by horses! Today, it is a community of apartment houses and attached houses and there is little land that is not used. (We could use some of that farmland right now, if we could get it! We need more play space.)

Willoughby Junior High School now has a principal, three assistant principals, three clerks, 65 teachers and over 1400 pupils. It has 6 vocational shops, 3 home making rooms, and a typewriting room—in addition to 30 regular classrooms. It has a cafeteria capable of serving three or four hundred pupils per hour.

7 KEEPING A DIARY OR AUTOBIOGRAPHY

A *diary* is a day-by-day record of events. It is usually a confidential personal account. The best known writer of a diary in English, Pepys (pronounced *peeps*), kept his record in a secret shorthand system so that nobody else could pry into his private life and thoughts. Some teenagers like to keep a little notebook or buy a printed diary book, just for their own use. Naturally, the entries are frank and realistic comments on people and things, written in brief "thinking aloud" style.

An *autobiography* is a life story or character sketch of a person written by himself. You probably have read or heard about such books as Helen Keller's *The Story of My Life,* and Charles Lindbergh's *We;* or Agnes de Mille's *Dance to the Piper,* and Bob Feller's *Strikeout Story.* Here you can learn about a blind author, a pilot, a dancer, and a baseball player. On your own level of experience, you can write a sketch about yourself, using 200 words rather than 200 pages to tell the highlights of your career.

There are certain *values* in writing a diary or autobiography. It gives you a chance to review your own past and to size up yourself. In what have you succeeded? or failed? and why? It also provides an opportunity for expressing thoughts in clear sentence form. With a bit of honesty and discretion you can make this an interesting experience.

STUDENT DIARY

MY FIRST WEEK IN A JUNIOR HIGH SCHOOL

Monday. I met Mary and took the bus to the annex where all newcomers were waiting in the play yard. We went to our home room and were welcomed by our new teacher. I paid a dollar for the G.O. and got my program card. We studied English and social studies and math in the annex. Then we had lunch and went to the main building for a double period of art. Everything is so exciting and I enjoy changing classes every period better than in the elementary school.

Tuesday. I was elected class treasurer in our home room. The boys went to shop and we went to cooking class. We had general science, and health education in gym. I'll have to buy sneakers and a gym suit.

Wednesday. We had group guidance today and discussed the Pupils' Handbook. In the afternoon, we visited the school library. I love the magazine section. Joan was lucky to find her lost bracelet.

Thursday. As part of our introduction in social studies, Miss C—— had us tour the school building from the cafeteria in the basement to the apartment on the top floor. We had music today, and I volunteered for the Glee Club. We're going to have some fun!

Friday. We walked over to the main building for our first assembly in the school auditorium. The principal spoke to us and then upper classmen told us how we can get into various school activities. At three o'clock, we met Frank and John and went to the Freshman Dance in our after-school recreation center. This has been a wonderful week!

STUDENT AUTOBIOGRAPHY

Instead of beginning by telling you that I was born in Brooklyn fourteen years ago, I'll tell you about myself according to places I've been, people I've met, and things I've learned. I want to be different!

From Brooklyn, my dear home town, we have traveled to New England and Canada on our way north during the summer. I particularly liked the beach at Cape Cod and the cathedral of St. Anne de Beaupré in Quebec. We went south to Washington, Richmond, and Virginia Beach. I'll never forget the Lincoln Memorial and the Smithsonian Institution. They are really impressive!

People I remember most include Sister Rosalita from St. Mary's Parochial School and her brass bell calling us in to school; Doctor Cotter who removed my tonsils; Uncle Myles who treated me to my first ride in the parachute at Coney Island; the nameless lifeguard who pulled me out of the surf at Jones Beach; the college boys who waited at the table down in Williamsburg.

What have I learned so far? Well, I have an interest in playing the piano, studying slides under the microscope, going to parties with friends, swimming in the ocean, playing tennis and badminton, and loafing in front of a T.V. set. I hope I'm normal. I know I have just started to live.

EXERCISE

WRITING A DIARY OR AUTOBIOGRAPHY

1. Have each member of the class interview another boy or girl and write a character sketch about each other, omitting names. Then, read these aloud and "guess who." Give actual details to fit the person.
2. Prepare a diary for a week's trip to a point of interest (Niagara Falls, etc.). Be specific.
3. Write an imaginative account of a boy or girl living in England (or other place) 100 years ago. Give actual facts and conditions.
4. Keep a daily record of errors in English that you read, see, or hear in class, on the bus, in the lunchroom or play yard. Call this a "Diary of Common Errors." (Bring it to class for discussion!)
5. Keep a log of your daily habits of eating, sleeping, playing, studying, listening to radio or TV, etc. Call this a "Time Log of My Schedule for a Week."

 GIVING DIRECTIONS OR INSTRUCTIONS

Have you ever followed someone else's directions for finding his house in a different part of town? Then you know how easy it is to get lost, unless the directions are accurate and clear. Words alone are not enough at times; a map or sketch may be necessary, too.

In the following pages you will find two samples of written directions and instructions prepared by pupils. Study them carefully to observe whether they are so clear that you could follow them without trouble.

In general, written instructions for *making things* should:

1. Be arranged logically, step by step.
2. Include itemized lists of materials needed.
3. Explain each process clearly from beginning to end.
4. Contain a sketch to illustrate the things to be done.

Similarly, written directions for *going places,* should:

1. Start from a known location; end with a certain destination.
2. Proceed clearly to each point, labeling turns properly.
3. Indicate landmarks or other road markers.
4. Provide a map (or sketch of the route) for the traveler.

Starting from Brooklyn, take the Belt Parkway or Shore Road to 69 Street. Take the 69 Street Ferry across the Narrows to Staten Island. At the ferry landing, turn left along Bay Street for two miles to Victory Boulevard. Turn right into Victory Boulevard and continue for three miles to Forest Avenue. Turn right on Forest Avenue (near Clove Lakes Park) and continue for seven miles to the Goethals Bridge. Take the bridge over to Elizabeth, New Jersey, and follow the road signs to the Garden State Parkway entrance (about two miles south). Enter the Garden State Parkway South and continue for about 90 miles to the exit marked Absecon Drive. Leave the Parkway at this point and go east to approach Atlantic City seashore. Total distance from Brooklyn = about 110 miles. Total traveling time = about 4 hours.

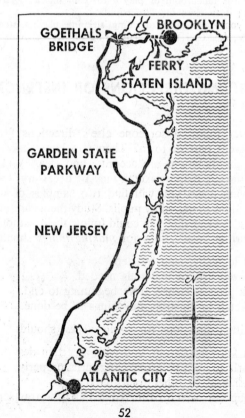

Directions for Making Tomato and Cheese Pizza (on Muffins)

Have all these ingredients ready before you start:

4		English muffins (sliced)
2	oz.	butter or margarine
4	oz.	can of tomatoes (whole)
8	oz.	mozzarella cheese (sliced)
2	oz.	Parmesan cheese (grated)
4	tsp.	olive oil
1	oz.	salt and pepper
1	oz.	oregano or basil (spices)

Split the English muffins by opening them gently with your fingers. Spread a little butter or margarine on the cut sides. Toast them in the oven under the broiler for a few minutes until they are lightly browned.

Remove them from the oven and cover each muffin with 2 tablespoons of canned tomatoes (pulp and juice). Top each muffin with a slice of mozzarella cheese. Then, sprinkle over each pizza, in the order listed below, these items:

½ teaspoon olive oil
½ teaspoon grated Parmesan cheese
a few grains of salt and pepper
a few crumbled leaves of oregano or basil

9 FILLING IN BLANK FORMS

To save time and to organize information, most business people use printed blank forms. Part of your training in factual writing includes the ability to supply accurate and complete information in a neat, readable style on such forms as pupils' program cards, health records, attendance cards, etc., in school. Then, too, you should be able to fill out order blanks, applications for working papers, telegrams, accident reports, and any other printed materials.

The best way to learn is by doing. Collect samples of blank forms and paste them neatly into your notebook. You may get some from the Sunday papers, magazines, your teacher, local stores and businesses, and so on.

Last Name   (Print)   First

Address   (Number—Street—Floor)   Telephone

New Address   Telephone

New Address   Telephone

Father's Name   Mother's Name

Class										
Date										

ALPHABETICAL INDEX CARD

Street   Number   Floor

....

....

....

Name...

Family Name   Given Name

Telephone...

Date	Class	Room	Time	Date	Class	Room	Time	Date	Class	Room	Time

PUPILS' ADDRESS CATALOG CARD

Date_____

For this term, I should like to join the following club:

1st choice_____

2nd choice_____

3rd choice_____

Pupil_____

Teacher_____

Class_____

_____

(Date)

To the Principal of Public School_____

I respectfully request that my son (daughter) _____

of Class _____ be permitted to take part in the extracurricular

activity indicated by my initials below:

( ) Excursion on _____ to _____.

( ) Attend Field Day at athletic field.

( ) Participate in games and athletic program at field.

( ) Assist in monitorial duties as member of the Service Squad.

( ) Serve on Safety Squad at street posts.

( ) Class demonstration at _____.

( ) Attend meeting of after-school _____ club.

( ) _____

( ) _____

( ) _____

Very truly yours,

Date:_____ Signature:_____

Parent or Guardian

Address:_____

POST-OFFICE FORMS TO FILL IN

CHANGE OF ADDRESS ORDER
MAIL OR DELIVER TO POST OFFICE OF OLD ADDRESS

This order provides for the forwarding of first-class mail, parcel post and books, unless you or the sender direct otherwise.

CHECK IF:

FORWARDING POSTAGE IS GUARANTEED FOR
- ☐ ALL MAIL
- ☐ NEWSPAPERS & MAGAZINES
- ☐ CIRCULARS

CHANGE FOR
- ☐ ENTIRE FAMILY OR FIRM
- ☐ INDIVIDUAL SIGNER ONLY

CHANGE IS
- ☐ PERMANENT (Expires after 2 years— not renewable)
- ☐ TEMPORARY UNTIL (Give date)

Orders to forward general delivery mail (at delivery offices) expire in 30 days unless renewed.

ENDORSEMENT OF CLERK OR CARRIER	DATE ENTERED

Postmaster

_____
(City and state)

AFFIX
TWO-CENT
STAMP
HERE WHEN
MAILED

COMPLETE OTHER SIDE

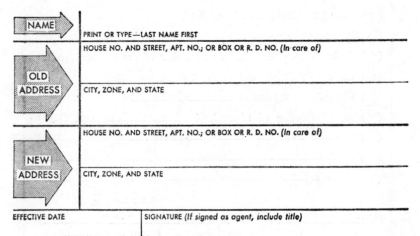

NAME — PRINT OR TYPE—LAST NAME FIRST

OLD ADDRESS — HOUSE NO. AND STREET, APT. NO.; OR BOX OR R. D. NO. (In care of)

CITY, ZONE, AND STATE

NEW ADDRESS — HOUSE NO. AND STREET, APT. NO.; OR BOX OR R. D. NO. (In care of)

CITY, ZONE, AND STATE

EFFECTIVE DATE	SIGNATURE (If signed as agent, include title)

COMPLETE OTHER SIDE

WORKING PAPER APPLICATION FORMS

THIS IS NOT AN EMPLOYMENT CERTIFICATE

BOARD OF EDUCATION CITY OF NEW YORK	APPLICATION	BUREAU OF ATTENDANCE

I HEREBY APPLY FOR:—(CHECK ONE)

STANDARD EMPLOYMENT CERTIFICATE	☐	VACATION WORK PERMIT	☐	FARM WORK PERMIT	☐	STREET TRADES BADGE	☐	CERTIFICATE OF AGE	☐

SIGNATURES

CHILD OR MINOR   PARENT OR GUARDIAN

RESIDENCE	HOUSE NO.	STREET	BORO.

SCHOOLING RECORD: REQUIRED ONLY FOR MINORS APPLYING FOR STANDARD EMPLOYMENT CERTIFICATES. IF THIS MINOR IS UNDER 17 YEARS OF AGE HE IS REQUIRED TO ATTEND CONTINUATION SCHOOL.

THE RECORDS OF	SCHOOL NO. OR NAME	LOCATED AT			CITY OR TOWN	STATE
		NUMBER	STREET	BORO.		

SHOW THAT THE MINOR IN THE FOREGOING APPLICATION OF PARENT

WAS BORN_____19___		YES ☐ NO ☐
	GRADE REACHED	GRADUATED

TO THE DEPARTMENT OF HEALTH:
KINDLY MAKE A PHYSICAL EXAMINATION OF THIS MINOR AND SEND US A RECORD OF THE EXAMINATION.
DATE........................195............   SIGNATURE................................Principal

THE DEPARTMENT OF HEALTH WILL COMPLETE THE ENTRY BELOW

195

PHYSICAL EXAMINATION INITIATED AT	MO. DA. YR.

(TO BE COMPLETED BY CERTIFICATING OFFICER)

TRANSCRIPT OR COPY OF EVIDENCE OF AGE

BORN:
19

FAMILY NAME OF CHILD	GIVEN NAME	BIRTHPLACE OF CHILD	MO. DA. YR.
NEW YORK CITY BIRTH CERTIFICATE No._____	NATURE OF DOCUMENT SUBMITTED OTHER THAN NEW YORK CITY BIRTH CERTIFICATE	No.	

ORIGIN OF EVIDENCE OF AGE	LOCATION
19	

MO. DA. YR. MADE OR ISSUED	NAME OF PERSON BY WHOM MADE OR ISSUED	OFFICIAL TITLE OF PERSON

1. APPLICATION OF PARENT	☐	2. CERTIFICATE OF PHYSICAL FITNESS	☐	3. SCHOOLING RECORD	☐	4. EVIDENCE OF AGE	☐	5. PLEDGE OF EMPLOYMENT	☐

HAVE BEEN EXAMINED. ALL PAPERS HAVE BEEN APPROVED
A CERTIFICATE HAS BEEN ISSUED. ALL PAPERS HAVE BEEN FILED.

19 MO. DA. YR. ISSUED	NO. OF CERTIFICATE	SIGNATURE OF CERTIFICATING OFFICER

BOARD OF EDUCATION   **PLEDGE OF EMPLOYMENT**   BUREAU OF ATTENDANCE

(IT IS UNLAWFUL TO EMPLOY A MINOR UNDER 18 YRS. WITHOUT A CERTIFICATE OR PERMIT)

FAILURE ON THE PART OF THE EMPLOYER TO FILL IN THE REQUIRED DATA WILL DELAY THE ISSUANCE OF THE EMPLOYMENT CERTIFICATE.   MAKE ALL ENTRIES IN INK.

SECTION 3212 COMPULSORY EDUCATION LAW.

NO PERSON SHALL MAKE A FALSE, ORAL OR WRITTEN STATEMENT IN OR IN RELATION TO ANY EMPLOYMENT CERTIFICATE OR OTHER PAPER REQUIRED BY PART I OF THIS ARTICLE AS TO ANY MATTER REQUIRED TO APPEAR THEREIN.

(CHECK ONE)

| FOR STANDARD EMPLOYMENT CERTIFICATE | ☐ | *FOR VACATION WORK PERMIT | ☐ | *A VACATION WORK PERMIT IS VALID ONLY OUTSIDE OF SCHOOL HOURS AND ON DAYS WHEN SCHOOL IS NOT IN SESSION. |

I, WE (NAME OF FIRM OR CORPORATION)	LOCATION (PLACE OF EMPLOYMENT)	BORO

WHO CONDUCT (CHECK ONE)

| A FACTORY | ☐ | MERCANTILE ESTABLISHMENT | ☐ | IF OTHER ENTERPRISE, STATE TYPE OF BUSINESS_____ |

EXPECT TO EMPLOY

NAME OF MINOR	RESIDENCE	BORO	Born Mo. Day Yr. To be Verified by Certificating Officer
			19___

IN THE CAPACITY OF	TO DO THE FOLLOWING SPECIFIC WORK	STARTING ON MO. DA. YR.
		19___

HOURS PER DAY	DAYS PER WEEK	HOURS PER WEEK	TIME WORK BEGINS A.M.	TIME WORK ENDS P.M.

SIGNATURE OF EMPLOYER OR REPRESENTATIVE	TITLE, AS MANAGER, ETC.	TELEPHONE NO.

PLEASE ATTACH YOUR BUSINESS CARD OR LETTERHEAD TO THIS STATEMENT AND RECORD THE CLASSIFICATION OF YOUR BUSINESS AS LISTED WITH THE NEW YORK STATE DEPARTMENT OF LABOR

———————→ **NOTICE TO EMPLOYERS** ←———————

A VACATION WORK PERMIT IS NOT VALID FOR EMPLOYMENT IN OR IN CONNECTION WITH A FACTORY, INCLUDING THE OFFICES THEREOF IF OCCUPYING THE SAME PREMISES.

A MINOR OVER 16 YEARS OF AGE MAY BE EMPLOYED IN A FACTORY, FULL TIME OR PART TIME IF HE OBTAINS A STANDARD EMPLOYMENT CERTIFICATE.

A MINOR UNDER 16 YEARS OF AGE MAY RECEIVE A STANDARD EMPLOYMENT CERTIFICATE ONLY IF HE IS A GRADUATE OF A FOUR YEAR HIGH SCHOOL COURSE.

A MINOR UNDER 17 YEARS OF AGE IS REQUIRED TO ATTEND CONTINUATION SCHOOL IF HE IS NOT A GRADUATE OF A FOUR YEAR HIGH SCHOOL COURSE.

MO. DA. YR. ISSUED	NO. OF CERTIFICATE	SIGNATURE OF CERTIFICATING OFFICER

CREATIVE COMPOSITION

A watch tells us not only time but something about the watchmaker: he likes orderly and precise movements. Whatever we make tells something about us; for example, a stained glass window reveals a craftsman's love of beauty and sense of reverence. An artist, Van Gogh, painted not only sunflowers, cypress trees, and vegetable gardens, but also painted his own love for brilliant color and motion. So, too, an author, Thoreau, wrote about brooks, and trees, and quiet woods; he also told us that he liked peace and quiet and solitude. In other words, a person puts part of himself into anything he does. Even in a small way, a bit of verse written by a pupil may show a sense of humor, whereas another pupil's short-story may indicate a liking for mystery and terror.

Creative refers to "making," and *composition* means "putting together." Therefore, creative composition means the putting together of the topic and the person to make a subject come alive in writing.

The art of creative composition depends on this ability to express yourself in writing. But, it is not an unconscious outpouring of words and ideas. Rather, it is a conscious and controlled *ex-pressing* (giving out) of personal views, moods, opinions, and interpretations of things —because it is orderliness that gives shape and meaning to written composition.

◆▷ WRITING THE LONG COMPOSITION

As in all skills, writing requires practice and the desire to improve yourself. When you make up your mind that you are going to dive better, or skate better, or write better, you have already taken an important step in learning. Then, you need some expert guidance or advice and some good models which you can imitate. The *purpose* of this section is to stimulate you to write more effectively and to show you how to do it.

Notice the word *purpose* in the previous sentence. That is the key to all kinds of writing. Just as the notes on a musical scale may be arranged to compose a gay dance, a solemn march, or a dreamy lullaby, so, too, the words in a piece of writing may be arranged to fit the author's purpose. Compare these two statements of the same idea:

1. "Fourscore and seven years ago, our fathers brought forth upon this continent a new nation, conceived in liberty and dedicated to the proposition that all men are created equal." —Lincoln: *Gettysburg Address*
2. "Eighty-seven years ago, a new country was started; its motto was 'Liberty and Equality.' " —Paraphrase of Lincoln's idea

The purpose in (1) was to suggest the Divine guidance that shaped the United States; the arrangement of words had the rhythm and imagery of the Bible. On the other hand, the purpose in (2) was to state the thought in a simple, direct, matter-of-fact way. Which stirs your emotion when read aloud?

STANDARDS FOR RATING STUDENTS' COMPOSITIONS

The rating of students' compositions takes into account two main factors: *thought* and *expression*. Some teachers give separate marks for the thought content and the mechanics of expression; then, the two marks are averaged together for a final rating of the paper.

THOUGHT	EXPRESSION
1. clear grasp of topic	1. correct usage of language (grammar)
2. good development of topic	2. clear sentence structure
3. orderly organization of ideas in paragraphs	3. freedom from errors in spelling
4. smooth transitions between paragraphs and sentences	4. proper punctuation and capitalization
5. adequate illustrations or facts to prove one's point	5. correct usage of words (diction)
6. sensible conclusion to round out the topic	6. acceptable format and handwriting

EXERCISE

RATING STUDENTS' COMPOSITIONS

Student I

Rating: Thought 100 plus expression 90 = 95%.

Comments: This essay is definitely superior because it reveals maturity in outlook and expresses a personal interpretation of the topic in a well-organized series of paragraphs. The strong opening sentence and the excellent conclusion help unify the composition. Sentence structure shows variety and smoothness. Minor errors include two misspelled words and two instances involving use of the wrong word. Approximate perfection of technic is indicated by use of transitions and specific examples. The wholesome philosophy makes this an effective piece of writing.

If you can enjoy yourself and make the most of what you have, then, and only then, is life worth living.

Life isn't really as complicated a thing as some people like to think it is. It isn't like the "Class System" of long ago when people were born and died without having the chance to better themselves. We now have the privlege of trying to make the world a better place for our families and ourselves to live in.

We have more leisure time then our grandparents and their parents before them did. We have numerous luxuries such as television, and the radio to fill up some of our leisure time. The rest of this newly found time is being used to further many ambitions and increase knowledge. It is now possible to travel almost anywhere within a number of hours because of automobiles, planes, trains and ships which play a big part in our lives today.

Long ago, when people were sick, they were isolated from everyone and left to die. Today, we are working on many new cures to help the sick. For those who can't be cured, we have many fine institutions and hospitals.

The people of America are a wonderful kind of people. They lend many helping hands to all who ask for them. In our country, all kinds of people live and work together. They send their children to the same schools and enjoy their recreation hours together. Yes, my country is truly a great one and the things in it really make our lives enjoyable and worth living.

Student 2

Rating: Thought 95 plus expression 85 = 90%.

Comments: This student shows clear grasp of the topic from start to finish and good command of style. The picturesque phrases contribute force and humor. The specific examples taken from personal experience give sincerity, strength, and originality. Development of the topic is orderly and adequate, except in paragraph three which rambles a bit. The closing sentence provides an interesting final comment. There are a few technical errors in idiom and punctuation and a sentence fragment.

My Family Is Something Special

We are a close-knit family. As a herd of yaks stand with their tails to the center, and their horns facing outward against their common enemies, my parents and brother join with me in meeting my challenges. Sometimes this assistance is too efficient for my age and scholastic level, since I'm struggling to pass plane geometry, and not higher mathematics.

Last year my brother was preparing for college entrance and state scholarship examinations. My father and mother studied every week-end in order to prepare themselves to prepare my brother for his tests. This proved successful since he was accepted into every college to which he applied, and also won "the family" a state scholarship. My father and mother were very proud of themselves, with some pride left over for brother David.

When they heard of my current assignment to write a paper for English, my family pitched in and started on several drafts simultaneously. It was necessary to leave the house in order to write it on my own. After all, I must find for myself if I'm a moron, a genius, or something in between. This year my father feels that he must pass geometry for the third time. First for himself, then for my brother, and now for me. My mother is reviewing her French so we can get a better mark than last year.

Dear reader, if you are still wondering why my family is something special count how many four-headed girls are students at our school.

Student 3

Rating: Thought 95 plus expression 75 = 85%.

Comments: This student used actual personal experience as a basis for writing. He showed maturity by using broad generalizations to introduce each of the first two paragraphs. The brief closing paragraph served to emphasize the continuity of the story. He enlarged the scope of the topic from *first dollar* to *first job,* a sensible extension. The style is marked by fluency, vigor, good choice of details. The main weakness lies in paragraph structure. To strengthen the sequence of thought in major divisions, combine paragraph 3 with paragraph 2. Other faults include some errors in tense, spelling, punctuation.

How I Earned My First Dollar

Many young people are confident of becoming millionaires, but not many of them do something about it. During the past summer I earned my first dollar and gained great experience at the same time. I had worked for my father in his law office doing many odd tasks such as filing, preparing client files, running errands and going into court. This experience gave me a better understanding of legal processes, as I wish to become an attorney. My salary was not very high, but gave me a chance to buy what I always wanted—stocks in a company. The work was difficult and I worked during very uncomfortable weather.

It is a common assumption that all work is an effort and difficult, but that is not always true. Working in a great metropolis affords social outlets. I met more people working in the past summer than I have at any other time.

My job has brought me into Municipal Court and the Appelate Court. I have read books on laws of accidents, laws of real property and the processes involved in proving civil legal cases. I have met several judges and have visited their chambers.

This is all a part of the story of "How I Earned My First Dollar."

Student 4

Rating: Thought 100 plus expression 60 = 80%.

Comments: This is a good example of the long composition full of worthwhile ideas strongly stated but marred by weaknesses in use of English. The student shows a fine sense of social awareness and real power of thought. His material is clearly divided into three unified paragraphs, each convincingly setting forth a phase of the main topic. The weaknesses come from two sources: (1) the verbose style leads to overdeveloped sentences and occasional wrong use of long words; (2) the rambling sentence structure includes many sentence fragments and overlong involved expressions. With judicious pruning of unnecessary detail and tightening of sentence structure, this would become a superior composition!

IF I HAD THREE WISHES

If I had three wishes my first wish would be that bestial men and dictators such as Hitler and Khruschev would be abolished from this world I want. I would like to look up upon this earth as a place where stars above shine down on a land of plenty and a land of beauty. A land on which there is no fear of warlaords, no evil nearby. Where people may walk the paths and ride on high with little fear of crashing. A place where people and children can walk and play without fear of atomic bombs to carry them away. A world united under one flag of all nations not only one. An earth in which the Jews, Christians, Moslems black, yellow and white can live together without holding prejudices against each other in a land of health and happiness.

My second wish would be that from this day on their would be no death, sickness, fights among friends and pain to any human being. That there will be no more dolorous feelings among people who have just had a sad or frightening experience because there will be no sad things happening. There will also be no more maniacal and despicable people who at times cause a chaos but instead these same people will be blithe and fervent to neighbor, friend and stranger alike! In this wish I would include that even though friends shouldn't fight there is still no reason why other friendships can't be made.

My last wish is that I would come into great wealth, monetary and things money cannot buy. The most important things which money cannot buy are love, happiness, health and friendship; things most important to any human being on this earth. Under the monetary part I could donate some of my great wealth to charity, hospitals, and health foundations so they could find cures for people with diseases such as cancer, leukemia, muscular dystrophy and cerebrel palsey or preventives for people who might get these diseases. It would go to work such as that which Dr. Salk was working on. With this money and the help of great men like Jonas Salk we could maybe prevent with vaccines all diseases and maybe cure the sick. Aside from fighting disease it might also help us to find other necessary scientific data. This part of wish three would only be necessary if wish two could not be granted, but the next part of wish three has nothing at all to do with the second wish. The next part of this wish is that with my money slums can be torn down and beautiful new and modern apartment houses could be built on a low rent scale. It would also put up schools in neighborhoods where they are needed. This money would go to the building of recreational places so that children do not roam the streets to grow up as juvenile deliquents but as decent, well-liked people of their communities.

Student 5

Rating: Thought 90 plus expression 60 = 75%.

Comments: This student has taken his own slant on the topic by selecting three types of *strange* people. In a well-organized series of paragraphs he describes each type clearly, using imagination in labeling the unusual qualities of each person. Paragraphing reveals clear structure with smooth transitions. The general tone seems a bit cynical in attempting to be funny. What makes the style fall below passing is the careless and extensive number of errors in spelling, grammar, punctuation, word usage, agreement, and capitalization.

People I Have Met

Up to now, I have been living for 15½ years and have come across the wierdest people you can ever anticipate. In my opinion and theorys, I believe all people to be wierd in their own little ways. There are many different types of wierd people, and I would like to mention a few to you.

One of these types are the "interlectual sociaty group". These people actually believe themselves to be superior to the common man. Most of them would not even speak to their hired servants. They have interlectual conversations about politics and art works, when they really don't know the first thing they're talking about.

In another type, which I call "the people with the split tongues", there are people that may talk to you for an hour about the lack of proper music education for children, and then go to one of those rock & roll shows.

Last but not lest, there are "women". For centurys, men have been trying to figure them out. Unfortunately they have not yet been successful. These "women" have a tendency to do the unexpected. They may go shopping for a dress and go through the entire stock of at lest 10 stores, and then go back to the first store & buy the first dress they saw. There are many other strange things about "women" that I doubt man will ever be able to figure out.

There are many other types of people that appear to be wierd. Take yourself for instance. Try to figure out certain things that you do and if you don't have a reason for these actions, you will understand what I mean.

Student 6

Rating: Thought 80 plus expression 60 = 70%.

Comments: The real topic discussed in this composition appears to be not the one stated at the head of the paper, but rather "Life today is better than it was 400 years ago." There are some good ideas on progress, science, and education, but somehow they lack a sharpness of definition in relation to the theme. At two places, this leads to major defects: (1) exaggerated statement (paragraph 3); (2) weak ending (closing paragraph). The style suffers from too many errors in spelling, punctuation, word usage, tense, run-on, etc., resulting in awkward and inept expression.

Ever since the world began people have been trying to make the work of every person easier, either by machinery, or by do it yourself kits. Right now in the 20th century you have ten times better living conditions then in the 16th century. Take one item in a home that is a necessity now that we didn't have in the 16th century. That necessity would be electricity. Electricity is so important now that if people don't have it they will be lost. Just name more living conditions, you have better factories, better offices, and twice as good hospitals.

Going on in this world we have travel agencies. If someone you know is dying in Florida and you have to go see them but you can't afford it they have fly now-pay later offers. Another wonderful thing that they have now are trains and buses that take you anywhere you want to go.

Going on we also have better schools and colleges. If a person is extra smart in science there are special scholarships to different schools in or out of the State. Every day more schools are being built than homes.

The last thing that I am going to write about would be the life span of people. Years ago when a person had a disease that nobody knew about they left him to die. But now cures for all kinds of diseases are being experimented on. In about thirty years there will probably be a cure for almost every kind of disease.

I think that life is worth living because you always have something to look forward to, and all the mistakes you make or made would be left behind in your life.

Student 7

Rating: Thought 65 plus expression 65 = 65%.

Comments: This composition is superficially correct but deserves only a passing rating because of two major factors: (1) it expresses a childlike fantasy on a selfish level rather than coming to grips with the topic on a level of social maturity; (2) it is oversimplified in structure, offering a series of questions and answers which are monotonous and repetitive. The overlong introduction and numerous slips in punctuation and spelling further weaken the thought and expression.

This story is very hard to believe, but I know it is true because it happened to me.

Last week, while sitting in my room, feeling low I heard a voice. The voice was very low at first then it became loud and clear. I jumped up. I could't imagine where this voice was coming from. These things only happen in fairy tales.

This lady or fairy, what ever she was came into view. She was beautiful. "I have come to make your life a happy one", she said. "Just say three wishes that you desire and they will be granted".

Well, you can imagine, how I felt. I could't believe my eyes or my ears. I thought I fell asleep and that I was dreaming all this."

Now came the big moment. She said in a soft voice, "I'm waiting, what are your three wishes"?

My first wish is that, the people I love the most have a bundant supply of health and wealth.

"It is granted." she said.

My second wish is that I make a squad in school service.

"It is granted". she said

My third wish is that I may suceed in my life's role. I should be successful in what ever I undertake.

"It is granted". She said.

WRITING ON FACTUAL TOPICS

Do you have a ready fund of information based on experience and wide reading? Do you prefer to write on one of these topics?

> Building model airplanes
> Why we plant trees
> American citizenship—its duties and privileges

Then you should be able to write on factual topics.

Firsthand information, good sense, and orderliness—these are the three essentials for developing a factual topic. To make your explanation of ideas, processes, and situations clear, you must know how to organize your points in an orderly way so that the reader will find it easy to understand. Much of your material will be based on nonfiction and informative articles in magazines. Develop "the inquiring mind," the will to know, and the ability to think through a problem.

For example, what thoughts come to your mind as you dwell upon the topic, "Heroes of the Present?"

First: Who is a hero? How does one become a hero? Are there different kinds of heroes? What makes a hero perform his deeds?

Second: Can you name some outstanding heroes of today? What special action did each contribute? Are there any "unsung" heroes in other fields? Can you tell what they have done?

Third: How long will their reputation last? Can you name some living heroes who have already become almost forgotten? Why should we honor our heroes? Why are heroes such an inspiration to the young?

You might jot down ideas using this simple outline:

(Outline A) HEROES OF THE PRESENT

I. The making of a hero in different fields of activity
II. Some known and unknown heroes and what they have done for man, for country, and for God
III. The debt we owe to heroes for inspiring us to better things

Another way in which you can organize your paragraphs might be:

(Outline B) HEROES OF THE PRESENT

I. Military heroes who have served our country with outstanding physical courage—
  A. Leaders (Doolittle, Eisenhower, MacArthur, etc.)
  B. Men in the ranks (winners of the Purple Heart, etc.)
II. Scientific heroes who have worked to improve the conditions of life through outstanding moral courage—
  A. Dr. Fleming and penicillin
  B. Dr. Fermi and others in the atomic experiment
III. Humanitarian heroes who have dedicated their lives to assist their fellowmen all over the world—
  A. Wendell Willkie and "One World"
  B. Dr. Albert Schweitzer in Africa

Obviously, such a factual topic requires a breadth of knowledge of a variety of fields—war, medicine, politics, etc. Instead of loose rambling talk, you must be able to give names and tell what each hero has done to deserve fame. This is a challenging assignment. To devote the whole composition merely to one or two war heroes would be to miss the wider significance of the term *hero*. To include men and women from other fields would show a mature grasp of the subject. Can you write the composition now? Try it!

EXERCISE

OUTLINING

Choose the topic that you know best and prepare an outline with at least three main topics or subdivisions.

1. Progress in transportation in the twentieth century
2. Safety precautions in the home
3. Opportunities for character training in school
4. The latest scientific helps for curing illnesses
5. Active ways of making friends
6. Nutrition habits and good health
7. Weather and its influence on people's disposition
8. Shopwork as a preparation for future jobs
9. The three most important dates in world history
10. How to get a job for the summer vacation

WRITING ON IMAGINATIVE TOPICS

Some pupils have a refreshingly individual quality about their compositions. This springs from originality and keenness of observation.

Do you like to write about topics dealing with yourself—your opinions, your personal struggles, your private imaginings? Can you describe these intimate facts and fancies with frankness and humor?

Things I can do without
I wash dishes
My most embarrassing moment

The personal element, the individual touch, the human side—that's what an imaginative topic calls for. You must be the sort of person who likes to share his emotions of pleasure, surprise, hope, etc. You must be willing to reveal your likes and dislikes, your dreams and your disappointments, your real and your possible reactions to the little things that make life endlessly interesting.

EXERCISES

IMAGINATIVE TOPICS

A. To develop your imagination, try to write an original theme based on one or more of these suggestions:

1. A newspaper headline that suggests an experience
2. A news item that may recall a similar or contrasting experience
3. A slogan or proverb applicable to real life
4. Names for characters in a play or movie
5. Names for characters in a story or radio program
6. A picture that carries you away
7. A pictorial design that stimulates contemplation or recall
8. A word that stimulates thought or recalls experience
9. A group of words suggesting a situation or an action
10. A report of an observation or experience you have heard

B. To obtain material for imaginative expression, you need (1) alertness of observation, and (2) association or insight. Here are some suggestions for training your imagination.

First, a specimen activity to increase your alertness of observation; this particular type of exercise trains you to watch for and identify characteristic details in a situation:

Discuss how we can tell from *observation* alone, that—

1. A train is due at the station
2. The morning is very cold
3. The lady has lost something
4. A storm is brewing
5. The tree has long been exposed to strong winds from one direction

Now, another specimen activity which promotes insight and *liveliness of association:*

1. Take an experience like "hearing an echo" and discuss what an echo reminds you of; to what it can be compared; what imaginative or fanciful things you can say about it.

Do likewise with other items from your experience—

2. A halo around the moon
3. The white surf rolling upon a rocky beach
4. A swinging lantern seen at a distance
5. The north wind blowing in a desolate spot
6. A meteor falling on a summer's night

PREPARING SIMPLE OUTLINES

It is as necessary to plan a composition as to plan how to build a model plane or how to cut material for a dress. Even a rough sketch will give better results than no plan at all. At least you will know where you are going from beginning to end. An outline is a plan to guide writing. You usually begin simply by *jotting down ideas* on a given topic. By *careful rearranging,* make sure that everything is in good order. An outline makes you think before you write and avoids a composition made up of a rambling mass of disconnected statements. Let's take a sample topic and get to work.

GOOD TEENAGE ACTIVITIES

Jotting down ideas

Roller skating party at a nearby rink
Picnics at the lake on weekends
Movies on a rainy afternoon or evening
Horseback riding when we have money
Club meetings after school
Dances and house parties
Taking part in church services and activities
Playing games like baseball, tennis, ping-pong, etc.
Making things in a workshop at home
Exploring things in the attic
Radio programs for stories, music, and news
Trips to museums, parks, showplaces
Boatrides up the Hudson or sightseeing around the harbor
Visit to Radio City and a bus ride up Fifth Avenue
Helping Dad wash the car, mow the lawn, etc.
Helping Mother with the cooking and cleaning
Opening a book once in a while to relax and read
Sunbathing on the beach
Visiting a friend who is not feeling well
Eating ice cream at the soda fountain
"Swapping" stories and gossip with the "gang"
Doing odd-jobs for "pin money" after school
Practicing music lessons sometimes
Collecting stamps, coins, or knick-knacks

Arranging ideas

Take some of the 24 activities listed previously and organize them into two or three paragraphs under such headings as these—

(Outline A) GOOD TEENAGE ACTIVITIES

I. At home (workshop, attic, radio, reading, music, stamps)

II. In my neighborhood (skating, movies, clubs, church, games, jobs)

III. Further afield (Fifth Avenue, museums, parks, beach, sightseeing)

Or, you might group some of these activities under different headings:

(Outline B) GOOD TEENAGE ACTIVITIES

I. Having fun at home (collecting stamps, making things, exploring attic, etc.)

II. Going places (house parties, church services, visiting a friend, Radio City, etc.)

III. Doing things outdoors (horseback riding, playing games, sunbathing, etc.)

Once you have decided on the three main headings, you can select whatever items you wish to include and omit whatever you feel is trivial or irrelevant. These main headings will serve as pigeonholes into which you pack your thoughts. Then, when you are ready to write the composition, these headings will become the main topics for your three paragraphs. Indeed, you can change these into topic sentences by adding a few words:

Topic sentences

I. When the weather keeps us teenagers indoors, we can find many ways of having fun at home.

II. We especially like going places, seeing things, and meeting people.

III. But, best of all, we enjoy doing things outdoors because we love action and sports.

Notice how naturally the topic is developing. First, you jot down ideas. Then you arrange these ideas under a few main headings. These headings become topic sentences. You are now ready to build the paragraphs for the composition. Follow the simple outline as carefully as a pilot follows a map or chart to make sure he reaches the right destination.

OUTLINING TO ORGANIZE IDEAS AND HAPPENINGS

The purpose of an outline is to arrange materials in good *order* so that the reader can follow them easily. An outline is a plan to guide writing. It is a brief and simple pattern making clear the general story or the direction of your thinking. You know that you can build a better bookshelf with a sketch, or cut a dress more accurately with a pattern. So, too, you can prepare a series of paragraphs for a composition more intelligently if you make an outline first.

You have learned two ways of correctly preparing simple outlines in the form of either (1) a *topical* arrangement of material, or (2) a *sentence* arrangement of material. These traditional methods are approved and useful as *formal guides to structure*. There is another approach to outlining based on the relationship between ideas and happenings that might be called *logical guides to thinking*. Here, the arrangement of the items in the outline follows the steps in the ladder of thought—according to *time, place, importance, cause and effect*.

They all emphasize *order* in a clearcut, logical process. Let's get acquainted with some of these so that you can use whichever fits best, depending on what kind of topic you plan to write about. Remember that the only purpose of an outline is to make things orderly.

1. Order of Time

This sequence keeps you from wandering. Start from the beginning, continue with smooth transitions such as "First, . . ." "Then, . . ." "Next, . . ." "After that, . . ." and end clearly with a closing word like "Finally, . . ."

2. Order of Place

Keeping a definite point of view prevents mix-up as you describe the scene. Put yourself at a spot; then, pretend you are a camera and rotate with "the seeing eye" from left to right, from bottom to top, or from back to front. This is ideal for any kind of description of a place.

3. Order of Importance

Build up to a climax by stating the less important facts first and add more particulars or details until you reach the most important idea or conclusion. Use transitions such as "In addition . . ." "Furthermore . . ." "Another . . ." "Therefore . . ."

4. Order of Cause and Effect

State the origin or reason for each main topic and tell what effect or result follows. This helps to make the three paragraphs unified and clear. This is especially useful in argument or debate topics. "If this is true . . . then this must follow . . ."

In all writing, plan clearly with the chief stress on *logical process*.

Let's begin with a single paragraph first to see whether we can work out the proper order of sentences. If you can organize a series of sentences into a unified paragraph, then you will more readily understand how to build a series of paragraphs into a unified theme or composition. Here is a sample, jumbled style. Can you rearrange these five sentences in good order?

The fire engines came out of the firehouse. There was a fire on our block. The engines finally arrived, and the firemen put out the fire. Someone turned in the alarm at once. As one engine was turning a corner on the way to the fire, it skidded into an automobile.

(*Answer:* The proper order of sentences should be 2-4-1-5-3.)

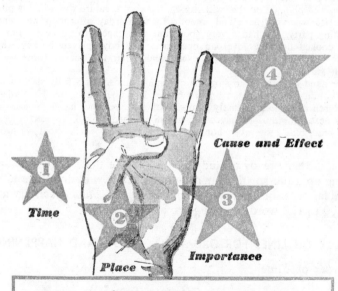

Think it out! Decide which way will make the theme most effective. Follow the order of time, place, importance, or cause and effect. Your writing will then have clarity and unity.

EXERCISE

PROPER ORDER IN A PARAGRAPH

The sentences in the following paragraphs are not arranged in their proper order. Rewrite the paragraphs, arranging the sentences in proper order. Do not change the wording of the sentences.

1. Without a moment's hesitation, Abraham waded across the stream and rescued the dog. After they had crossed, Abraham noticed that their dog had not followed them. When the Lincoln family were once moving from one farm to another, it was necessary to ford a river much swollen by heavy rains. When Abraham overtook the family, he was a very wet, but a very happy boy. Afraid to plunge into the swift stream, the poor creature was whining piteously.

2. The ice was very hard and smooth. Last Saturday afternoon we went on a skating party. We had a very good time and expect to go again. For supper we cooked hot dogs over an open fire. The boys played hockey while the girls watched and cheered for every goal. After the hockey game we skated with partners.

3. One hand is upraised to stop the oncoming autos. He is fully six feet tall and well-built. The policeman on our corner is a striking figure. He smiles at us children as he sees us safely across. With his free hand he motions us to pass. His neat, blue uniform gives him a distinguished look. His cheerful smile and his kind, blue eyes prove him our friend. It is no wonder that we are proud of him.

You are now ready to study the outlines for three or four paragraphs making up a full-length composition. Notice how each outline follows a particular order of *time, place, importance, cause and effect.* Try to write the 100 to 150 word compositions, as outlined.

SAMPLE OUTLINES FOR ORGANIZING IDEAS AND HAPPENINGS

1. Order of Time

A Camping Trip

   I. Preparations we made (including food, supplies, equipment, etc.)
  II. Getting there by means of train or bus and locating a suitable camp site
 III. Activities we took part in (including games, sports, hikes, etc.)
 IV. Our return home and fun on the way back

2. Order of Place

I. The special corners for storing tools, painting, class library, mock-ups, and work exhibits

II. The floor arrangement for work-benches in aisles for safety and convenience

III. The wall exhibits, including the shop duty assignments, daily attendance record, pupil project charts, safety rules, etc.

IV. The teacher's demonstration table and blackboard sketches of jobs to be done

3. Order of Importance

MY REASONS FOR WANTING TO BECOME—
(engineer, teacher, nurse, etc.)

I. My understanding of the duties and responsibilities of such a job or career (visiting places of work, parent's advice, school guidance counselor)

II. My own interests and qualifications for this vocation (based on hobbies, reading, related experiences)

III. The personal satisfactions it will bring (salary, promotion, service to others, etc.)

4. Order of Cause and Effect

THE UNITED NATIONS AND WORLD PEACE

I. The end of World War II—the feeling of great waste and the desire to create an agency for settling disputes

II. The membership among nations of the world—and the feeling of security among the smaller countries as well as the big nations

III. The problems and functions of the major agencies—and the attempt to help build up backward regions with assistance from powerful allies

IV. Recent affairs involving trouble spots in the world—the development of a UN police force and strong world opinion as pressures against war

EXERCISE

PREPARING OUTLINES

Choose one of the following topics and prepare an outline for three or more paragraphs for a composition. State whether you follow the order of *time, place, importance,* or *cause and effect.*

Summertime on the farm	Road maps
When my shoelace broke	Teenage heroes I admire
Pictures I enjoy	Popular fashions in dress
Our graduation plans	My favorite comics
Entertaining an out-of-town guest	The greatest events in history
What puzzles me	The zoo parade
A brave deed	An adventure at home
Looking forward to high school	How to become a "shutterbug"
Learning to swim	The right way to tell a joke

Suggestion: Take your outline as a guide and write the full-length composition. Does it "hang together" better, a bit more clearly, than if you had merely started to write? Practice makes perfect. As you learn the art of organizing ideas *in advance,* you will find that planning becomes not a chore but a real stimulus to thinking.

ORGANIZING MATERIALS INTO PARAGRAPHS

A paragraph is to the composition what a room is to a house: it is a large unit forming part of the whole. Just as passageways connect the various rooms, so too the orderly flow of ideas connects the various paragraphs. You can drop your thoughts into a composition in the same way that a truck dumps a load of bricks on the pavement into a jumbled pile. Or—you can lay down sentence after sentence, paragraph after paragraph, with the neat architecture of a mason who places a corner-stone here, an arched doorway there, a window another place, to build a modern home. What kind of worker-with-words are you?

Ask yourself these questions to check your organization of materials within a paragraph:

1. Do I have a *clear idea* of what I am trying to say?
2. Does my *topic sentence* offer an interesting introduction? Does it *attract attention?* Does it prepare for what follows?

3. Have I *arranged the points* so as to aid the reader in following the ideas? Are they smoothly connected?
4. Does my *clincher sentence* round out and reinforce the idea? Does it leave the reader with something to think about?
5. Does the paragraph have a *unity of purpose* or final impression? Does it "hang together?"

Depending on the materials, you usually have to emphasize some things more than others. You may be telling a story, describing a place, explaining how something works, or arguing about a question.

1. Narrating

Short narratives of action should usually deal with only one incident. Begin with a strong introduction to arouse interest. Work up to a climax and a quick conclusion. Follow the sequence of time by using such expressions as: "at first, slowly, a little later, just as, before, then, after a while, finally, at last."

2. Describing

Description of persons, places, or objects should aim at a central impression. Take a point of view and state your general impression. Then give the three or four prominent details which help to create that impression.

3. Explaining

In explanations of ideas, processes, situations, and operations, the main aim is clearness so that the reader will understand. Give sufficient details to make the subject clear to the uninformed. Arrange these details in logical order of relationship.

4. Arguing

In arguing about a question, aim at convincing the reader. State your point of view forcefully and set down all the reasons, facts, examples, authorities, evidence, etc., that you can give. Try to anticipate any possible objections and answer them. Work toward an inevitable climax or conclusion that satisfies the mind.

REVISING THE COMPOSITION

The last step in writing a composition is called *revision*. Revision comes from the Latin *re,* meaning "again" + *vis,* "to see"; it means to look over what you have done in order to change and correct whatever is necessary. This does not mean a hasty glance to dot an *i,* or cross a *t,* but a careful rereading to improve the content and to check the form. As an aid to finding weaknesses and errors, you should have a guide list. This procedure is so valuable that it is a regular part of the way things are done in the world outside the classroom. For example, a special committee checks the exact wording of every bill to be submitted to Congress. Every word in your insurance policy means dollars and cents in terms of coverage. All publishers of books, magazines, and newspapers engage experts to do the proofreading of manuscripts. Get the habit of careful revision and you will improve the ratings you receive for composition.

The following chart is an aid to discover weak spots in your writing.

Composition Chart for Checking Your Writing

I. CONTENT (Organization and expression of ideas)

A. The Thought

1. Is it expressed with clearness?
2. Is it expressed with sufficient fullness?
3. Are all ideas relevant?
4. Does the thought hold the attention?

B. The Vocabulary

1. Do the words convey the exact idea intended?
2. Does any word convey a wrong meaning?
3. Is there variety in the choice of words?
4. Is the language stilted?

C. Organization

1. The composition as a whole
   a. Does it show evidence of planning?
   b. Are the thought divisions correctly indicated?
   c. Is there proper sequence of paragraphs?
2. The paragraph
   a. Is the topical idea evident?
   b. Are sentences in proper sequence?
   c. Is there a good opening sentence?
   d. Is there a good closing sentence?
   e. Is there variety in form and structure of the sentences?

II. FORM (Appearance and technical matters)

A. Arrangement

1. Is the title centered?
2. Has each paragraph been indented one-half inch?
3. Have one-inch margins been left at each side of the page?

B. Grammatical Usage

1. Is the English correct?
2. Are there sentence fragments?
3. Are there run-on sentences?
4. Are there rambling sentences?
5. Are there involved sentences?
6. Is slang used?
7. Are foreignisms used?

C. Spelling

D. Capitalization

E. Punctuation

F. Penmanship

EXERCISE

100 COMPOSITION TOPICS

Write a well-planned composition of at least 100 words on a topic.

1. Tracking animals
2. The greatest surprise of my life
3. Stalled in the snow
4. If I could have one wish
5. A funny dream that I had
6. My baby brother (or sister)
7. The winter sport that I like best
8. A visit to a place of historical interest
9. The person I should like to be
10. A day of mishaps
11. The family garden
12. Just in time
13. High school ahead
14. Sharing with others
15. Safety first
16. Window shopping
17. The atomic age
18. How to make a snow man
19. A great American

20. A teenager looks at the world.
21. How I won the prize
22. My favorite game
23. We can learn from animals.
24. To the rescue!
25. A lost child
26. New friends
27. How I make a kite
28. An exciting play in a game
29. A kind act
30. How to raise a pet
31. Hunting game with a camera
32. My hobby
33. News of the day
34. I'll never forget _____.
35. A teenager's place in his home
36. I wish someone would invent a
_____.
37. "Asleep at the Switch"
38. Circus day
39. The lonely house
40. Summer fun
41. Saturday at my house
42. When the car broke down
43. Something I'll never do again
44. Our fire department on the job
45. My life story
46. What will the next half century
bring?
47. A trip to _____
48. A funny experience
49. A birthday party
50. Trapped
51. An unexpected guest
52. Friendly people
53. A bicycle trip
54. A good radio program
55. The best day of the year
56. A fire in the neighborhood
57. The work of the Boy Scouts (or
some other club)
58. Why we are trying to preserve
our forests
59. My favorite comic strip
60. Our old automobile

61. New York City—World Capital
62. Getting along with one another
63. Treasure hunt
64. My dog seemed to understand.
65. The future of aviation
66. Ways of living in early colonial
America
67. A new boy or girl in our school
68. I'll be wiser next time.
69. Our celebration
70. It took courage to do it.
71. "Grandma"
72. Boys should learn to cook.
73. Naming our pet
74. Playmates
75. The boat suddenly started to leak.
76. Poison ivy
77. How I finally caught that mouse
78. A story for the newspaper
79. Fun in my community
80. Money of my own
81. How I may help in civilian defense
82. The things a dog can learn
83. Amusing the baby
84. My hero
85. Fair play
86. I wash the car
87. A good game for a stormy day
88. A strange journey
89. I just couldn't believe it.
90. If I could talk to the weather man
91. Good teamwork
92. An important news event
93. What the flag means to me
94. Why we plant trees
95. How I keep informed
96. Should we believe all that we
hear?
97. Why democracy will win
98. Should young people talk about
world affairs?
99. My most embarrassing moment
100. Advantages of living in the city
(or country)

THE CLASS NEWSPAPER

A class newspaper gives every youngster a chance to break into print. It is a wonderful way to write with sincerity and freedom and enjoyment. Local events, daily happenings, friendly interviews, harmless gossip, bits of verse, word puzzles, cartoons—all these minor items add up to lively class spirit. A mimeographing machine or any duplicating device will give the class "scandal sheet" a dressed-up look. Pupil typists and pupil editors can organize and proofread the contributions by the members of the class. It can be lots of fun if everyone does his share!

Suggestions

	be mean or "catty" in remarks about others.
	give nicknames that will hurt your friends.
DON'T	repeat rumors or malicious gossip.
	use too much slang or "secret" codes.
	refer to "guess who was seen with so-and-so."

	be "newsy" and alert to happenings.
	be friendly and praise good deeds.
DO	talk about things that interest the class.
	include a touch of humor and clean fun.
	try to brighten the page with sketches or drawings.

STUDENT ARTICLES FROM A CLASS NEWSPAPER

IT'S DESSERT TIME

(Jello Milk Shake or Soda)

Both pretty and refreshing for young folks and grownups.

MILK SHAKE SODA: Place 1 tablespoon of Jello (any flavor) in a tall glass. Add about 2 tablespoons of very hot water and stir to dissolve. Then fill the glass (gradually) with cold milk or ginger ale, stirring well to blend. Add spoonfuls of ice cream, if so desired.

PUNCH: For a pitcher of punch, dissolve 1 package of Jello in 1 cup of hot water. Then add a cup of cold water. Cool. Stir in gradually 1½ quarts or more of chilled milk.

THE LITTLE CHURCH

Oh little church, that stands so clear,
The people worship in you year by year.
They pray to God in heaven above,
To protect the ones they love.
This weakened world would not be worth living in,
If there were no church that we could go in.
Let's all go to church and pray,
To thank the Lord for every day
There is peace on earth and may it stay.

THE CLASS VISITS LEVY'S BAKERY

On Tuesday, November 15, our class went to visit Levy's Bakery. Our guide first took us to the mixing room, and we saw the dough from its earliest stages of being mixed to the final mixing. We then went into the room where they allow the dough to rise. Do you know why it takes rye bread dough only 30 minutes to rise and white bread dough about 3 hours? The sour base in rye bread dough causes the dough to rise quickly.

Next, we went to see the bread being kneaded and molded into loaves. After the final shaping, the bread goes on a conveyor belt and is sent to a machine where it is automatically timed for 10 minutes of rising, and then on to be shaped for baking. The loaves are removed from the conveyor belt and placed in pans. From there they are placed in a very warm room to finish rising. The bread is then baked, sliced, packaged and packed for delivery to stores.

On the whole, it was very interesting, especially to those of us who had never seen the workings of a bakery. Before our class departed, we were given a loaf of white bread and a comic book.

THE SCHOOL NEWSPAPER

A school newspaper has a style more literary than that of a class newspaper, especially if it appears in regular printed form on slick paper with pictures, etc. The articles contain more general news and views, yet retain local flavor. Often, the articles combine straight reporting together with personal comments. A well-written and lively school newspaper helps to build fine school spirit. The staff of pupils works under the direction of a teacher and makes sure that there is a variety of content as well as correctness of expression. Here, too, there is room for originality as well as directness in recording the happenings and describing the personalities that *make* a school.

Read some of the sample articles on the pages that follow and then try to write an article for your own school newspaper.

Suggestions

1. When quoting a teacher, get permission first.
2. When referring to events, check all the facts.
3. If you try to be funny, make sure no one gets hurt just to get a laugh for others.
4. Omit anything that may harm the reputation of the school.
5. Include personal reactions to guest speakers at assemblies or unusual programs.
6. Make sure your style is acceptable "journalese" in tone and grammatically correct.
7. Remember that "a boost" is better than "a knock."

STUDENT ARTICLES FROM A SCHOOL NEWSPAPER

ROCKET TO THE MOON

"Spaceport 162 calling all passengers for them to assemble in space ship 204 to don their space suits."

Good afternoon, I am your space guide, here to help you to assemble your gear and ready you for your forthcoming flight. While making your preparations, permit me to brief you on a few interesting facts about the moon.

Some of the precautionary measures you must take are: never go outside without your oxygen tank or your space suit, for on the moon there is no atmosphere. This is because it is so much smaller than earth, too small to hold an atmosphere. Instead of having an even temperature, it goes from one extreme to the other. For instance, today it will be over 212° (boiling point); tonight it will be lower than 200° below zero on the Fahrenheit thermometer.

As you explore the moon, you see in the sky not only the sun and many stars, but also the earth. You will notice none of the living things you see on earth. All the plants and animals we are familiar with must have water and oxygen. Remember, too, the temperature changes on the moon are greater than living things we know could stand.

On our tour of the moon, as far as the eye can see, only mountains, craters and dull gray plains are on the horizon.

The lack of a dense atmosphere means you are running a risk as you walk about in the bright sunshine. The sun sends out ultraviolet rays which are deadly in large amounts. Enough of these rays might kill you, if it were not for your space suit.

The girls taking home economics and hygiene will have a chance to be models in the spring fashion show, "Fashion Bouquet for the Modern Miss," to be presented by the Simplicity Pattern Company on Thursday, April 26 at 10:00 A.M. Simplicity's educational stylist will make the presentation.

Though the clothes to be modeled cover every teenager fashion favorite, from summer separates to prom dresses, all can be made right in our sewing class. The Simplicity Patterns from which they are made feature a special group of simple-to-make fashions designed for beginners in sewing.

Carrying out the "Fashion Bouquet" theme of the show will be a group of flower prints: a carnation print blouse worn under a red linen jumper, a border print shirt that's a circle of daisies, a long-torso, full-skirted dress in a pretty poppy printed cotton, and the rose-scattered sheath dress you saw on the cover of the January issue of "Seventeen."

One of the highlights of the show will be the ensembles, the coat-and-dress fashions so popular for spring. They will be shown in both slim and full-skirted versions. There will be many sheaths, too, in jumpers and in jacketed dresses and styles pointing up the Oriental influence.

Simplicity's stylist will be commentator for the show and can help answer any questions on how students can "make and model" these fashions for themselves.

WILLOW-BEE WINS THIRD PRIZE IN CONTEST

We are happy to announce that our wonderful school magazine, the "Willow-Bee," has won third prize in the Columbia Scholastic Press Association Contest. We received 711 points out of the potential 1000. Below is a list showing how our magazine was rated.

	Maximum	Rating
1. Editing, Make-up	300	254
2. Content	375	255
3. Reporting of School Activities	175	80
4. Advertisement	50	47
5. General Consideration	100	75
Total	1000	711

Many comments were enclosed which will aid in the make-up of this year's "Willow-Bee." If you are interested in seeing the award, it can e found in the showcase on the first floor.

ORIGINAL SHORT-STORIES FOR SCHOOL PUBLICATIONS

Does your school publish a literary magazine or yearbook? Such a publication provides an outlet for creative composition in many ways, especially for budding short-story writers. The formula for a short-story is simple; there are three elements—plot, setting, and characters. Stick to persons, places, and happenings that are familiar to you. Choose a *single* situation, involving *one* main character, and a *local* background. This will be easier to handle than an imaginary trip by rocket ship to the moon! A good device for getting started is to pool ideas from the class. Each pupil prepares three slips of paper (size 3″ x 6″) labeled separately (character, situation, scene) and fills in each slip as follows:

1. Give the name of a *character* and describe him or her briefly: age, dress, traits, likings, dislikes, chief interest or problem in life, etc.
2. Invent a possible *situation:* a lost letter, a mistake in identity, a stolen car, a hidden treasure, an accident on the road, a sports contest, etc.
3. Describe a local *scene:* the neighborhood bank, the police precinct, a doctor's office, the school play yard or lunchroom, a public park, etc.

The teacher collects these three slips from each pupil and puts them into three separate cartons or piles according to each element—character, situation, scene. Then, she gives each youngster one slip from each carton and he tries to write a short-story suggested by these items. Try it!

STUDENT SHORT-STORY

THE KILLER AND THE SNOW

It was snowing. From inside the brightly lit house came a blood-curdling scream. A few minutes later a man in a uniform came out. In his hand was a razor covered with blood. On the back of his jacket were the words "State Institution for the Criminal Insane."

No one had heard the woman scream. The howling wind had taken care of that. Now he had to get out of town. He had plenty of food. "Old Fanny," the miser, didn't have any use for it now. The guards would never know he was gone until morning.

The snow was coming down harder. He could hardly see his hand in front of his face. He stumbled suddenly and fell into a brook. He lay there motionless, too stunned to move. His food sank slowly to the bottom. Now there was only one end in sight—DEATH!

No! He wasn't going to freeze to death. He'd walk, but he couldn't. He was too tired. Suddenly he remembered—the razor. One quick cut across the neck and it would be all over. Of course. That was it. Slowly he drew the blade across his throat. NOTHING HAPPENED.

The blood on the knife was frozen solid. He'd melt it. He took out his matches. They were soaking wet.

"No! No! Not freezing to death." "Hey, quiet down in there!" He looked around at the padded walls of his cell. It was all a dream. Of course it was. Then he stopped in horror as he heard the guards talking.

"Did you know 'Old Fanny' was killed this evening?"

"How did it happen?"

"Slashed to death with a razor. The police say it's the work of a maniac."

Yes it was a dream, or was it? The snow had stopped; the wind was calm.

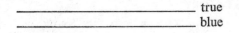 **WRITING VERSE FOR FUN**

If you have a rhyme or two
Running round your head, please do
What we'd like to try today:
Write some verse for fun, this way!

You see, there's really nothing to it. Just begin with a few rhyming words and a little rhythm and a single idea to carry through to the end. The easiest kind is a *couplet,* or two lines rhyming thus: *a, a.*

_____ true
_____ blue

Next, try a *quatrain,* or four lines rhyming like this: *a, b, a, b.*

_____ moon
_____ star
_____ June
_____ far

Those with more talent or courage can try a humorous *limerick,* or five lines rhyming like this: *a, a, b, b, a.*

There was a small boy from Quebec
Who was buried in snow to his neck.
When they asked, "Are you friz?"
He said, "Yes, I is—
But we don't call this cold in Quebec!"

A New Friend

Tired and sleepy, one Sunday morn
I looked out the window at my front lawn.
There was a bird all wet with rain
Pecking at my window pane.
I opened the window and in he flew
A beautiful picture of jet black and blue.
He perched on my shoulder, and held on real tight,
Hungry and cold and shaking with fright.
I fed him some bread crumbs and wrapped him up tight.
He slept through the day and a part of the night.
And in the morning when the new day was born
I opened the window and, flash, he was gone.

Parents

There never were such loving parents,
I'm sure that it is true.
To show how much I love you,
What can I do for you?

I'll do my best in school
And keep the Golden Rule.
I'll be kind and polite in every way
And make you proud of me each day.

Sweet mother dear, I love you so.
Much more than you will ever know.
Daddy dear, you are so kind,
A treasure like you I'll never find.

How can I show my love for you two?
A million ways are still too few.

5 PREPARING CHARACTER SKETCHES

A character sketch is an attempt to describe a person in words so that he will come alive as in a snapshot. You already know from your experience in taking pictures with a camera that you get better results when you "compose" the person or subject in relation to the background. Proper focus makes a good candid shot. So, too, in writing you must first focus your attention on a definite plan so that your sketch will reveal character. Here is a sample outline:

1. Begin with a strong central impression of the person.
2. Tell some anecdotes, or experiences he has had, that build up this main quality or impression.
3. Include some contrasting personality traits to help round out the picture; both good and bad points.
4. Mention some of his likes, dislikes, hobbies, interests, favorite subjects, sports, jobs, friends, etc.
5. Close with a look into his future by predicting what you think he will become someday.

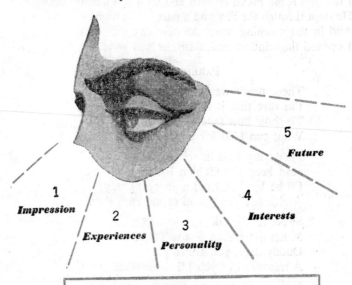

1
Impression

2
Experiences

3
Personality

4
Interests

5
Future

The eyes are the windows of the soul. They reveal much about a person, but they may also conceal even more! True character is the result of living, of both good and bad qualities. A *character sketch* must give a balanced picture without distortion.

My Mother Is My Hero

I'm very proud of my mother. When I was born, during World War II, my city was bombed. My mother saved my life many times at the risk of her own.

I was born in 1942 and only three months old when my house was destroyed by a bomb. My mother and I were in it at the time. I was lying in a carriage; a big stone was about to fall on me. My mother grabbed me and ran out of the back door, because the front of the house was already bombed out. She ran out to the street with me in her arms. The enemy was shooting at us, but my mother took shelter in time. My mother was very frightened, but she thought only about me. My mother took all the responsibility because my father was fighting in the war.

My grandparents were the only ones we could turn to; their home had not been bombed. After a couple of months when the Russians came, my grandparents wanted us to stay, but my mother took me with her on an open truck to a different city.

We rode on the truck for days and days; we didn't have any food or clothing, but somehow my mother managed to take care of me. We had many hard years, especially my mother. When I was one year old my father was killed in the war. My mother started on a job in an airplane factory. I was always sick because of the war.

Now I'm here in the United States. I'm the happiest girl in the world with a mother, a new father and baby sister. My mother is a very courageous woman.

What Is a Teenager?

A teenager is half man, half child. . . .
He is in the state of adolescence,
And the foolish things he does are blamed on this.
He is undecided about the future and,
Not sure of the present.
He will sometimes think as a man would think,
And act as a child would act.
He will completely ignore girls at one moment and—
He will think nothing but girls at the next moment.
He will come home looking like a coal-miner,
And then, spend half an hour combing his hair just right.
There is something strange about a teenager,
But cheer up—it happens to the best of us . . .

WHAT IS A TEACHER?

A teacher is a person with eyes in back of his head, ears all over, and a sixth sense.

He has the difficult job of teaching the youth of America right from wrong. The teacher is the backbone of America. Some students dislike teachers but without them we would be lost.

As the pupil grows physically and mentally, the teacher has a more difficult job. The pupil is not satisfied with reading, writing and arithmetic any more. Now the teacher must guide the pupil into the right high school and later into the right type of work.

When the pupil graduates, the teacher's job is completed with this pupil, but it starts all over again with a new pupil.

 # WRITING A BOOK REPORT

We read books for enjoyment and information. Talking about books stimulates further interest in reading. Preparing a written report helps us to remember what the book is about. In general, we can classify most books as either *full-length books* (a novel, a biography, a travel story, etc.), or as *collections* (short-stories, poems, essays, one-act plays). A book report should give at least an idea of the main contents together with the reader's personal comment.

OUTLINE FOR A FULL-LENGTH BOOK REPORT

(Novel, Biography, Travel Story, Long Play, etc.)

1. Title of book: *Treasure Island*
2. Author's name: Robert Louis Stevenson
3. Kind of book: adventure novel
4. Background or setting: England and South Sea Islands
5. Main persons or characters in the story: (at least five)

   a. Jim Hawkins, a daredevil boy who became the hero
   b. Long John Silver, a clever one-legged pirate chief
   c. Dr. Livesey, a hot-headed leader of the expedition
   d. Billy Bones, an old sailor who had Flint's map
   e. Captain Smollett, the grim captain of the *Hispaniola*
   f. Ben Gunn, the maroon who found the treasure

6. Highlights of the story: Some exciting scenes include the raid by Blind Pew and his men against the Admiral Benbow Inn; the spying by Jim hidden in the apple barrel; the bombardment of the stockade; the finding of Ben Gunn on the island by Jim; the digging for the buried treasure by Silver's crew; the escape of Silver on the voyage back to England.
7. Personal reaction: I enjoyed this story very much because there were many surprises and plenty of action. It held my interest by creating suspense regarding the map and the search for buried gold on Treasure Island. I particularly liked that clever rascal, Long John Silver, and that lucky boy, Jim Hawkins.

Note: A book report should not be a long and complete re-telling of the *whole* story. This would not only spoil the listener's interest but also destroy the reader's pleasure. The write-up may take the form of an original "book-jacket," including a sketch, drawing, or picture on the outside cover and a series of three paragraphs including the material outlined above.

STUDENT BOOK REPORT ON A BIOGRAPHY

THOMAS JEFFERSON
by Clara Ingram Judson

This story will take its place among those I want to read again because it tells the true life of Jefferson to its smallest detail. It tells of his sorrows, hardships, beliefs and loves. We learn of his dream for Monticello, his family and friends. Judson read Jefferson's writings, and she visited Monticello before undertaking the writing of this book. I thoroughly enjoyed it and would recommend it to anyone. It is the story of the "Champion of the People" come to life.

Thomas Jefferson lived to be 83 years; in those years he acquired many skills that few men have equaled. He was a lawyer, architect, musician, botanist, farmer, politician, and philosopher, the greatest creative genius of his time.

Thomas Jefferson was born on April 13, 1743. The summer that Tom was 14, disaster came to his happy family. Peter Jefferson, a strong, vigorous man of 50, was taken sick, and died. It was that day that Tom realized that his boyhood days were over. His father had made careful plans for his future. He was sent to some good schools, and at 21, was given his choice of property.

Thomas met Martha Skelton in the summer of 1770. Martha was a very beautiful, talented and wealthy widow. He fell in love with her and they were married in 1772. Jefferson took his bride to Monticello, his dream home. The house was started in 1768, and was inspired by Palladio, a 16th century Italian architect that Jefferson admired.

Jefferson had two daughters, and when the third one, Lucy, was born, Martha did not regain her strength, and later died. He was then heartbroken. The eldest daughter, Patsy, finally roused him by talking about the outdoors. He slowly regained his interest in life, in his children, and in beautiful Monticello.

On the morning of March 4, 1801, Jefferson took the oath of office as third President of the United States. He served for eight years and tried to give his country the best he could.

Jefferson spent the last years of his life at Monticello with his grandchildren. He had enjoyed good health most of his life, but having passed his 83rd birthday, he sensed his work nearly done. His life ended on the day he always said was more important than his own birthday, July 4th.

OUTLINE FOR A REPORT ON A COLLECTION

(Short-Stories, Poems, Essays, One-Act Plays, etc.)

1. Title of collection: *Selected Stories*
2. Author's name: Edgar Allan Poe
3. Kind of book: tales of mystery and terror
4. Background or setting: usually fantastic and romantic places, haunted with horror
5. Cross section or sampling: (at least three)

   a. Story of *atmosphere:* "The Fall of the House of Usher" told how Roderick and his sister Madeline met death in a strange haunted house that was struck by lightning after he had buried her alive.

   b. Story of *detective work:* "The Gold Bug" described how Legrand figured out the location of buried treasure by deciphering a code or cryptogram.

   c. Story of *horror:* "The Masque of the Red Death" painted a gruesome picture of a gay masquerade ball at which all guests perished when they discovered that the fatal disease they tried to escape was present in disguise at their party.

6. Personal comment: All of Poe's stories deal with weird and strange places, sudden death by suicide or murder, beautiful ladies and odd

men. Everything seems supernatural; nothing is commonplace. Even the language is unusual in choice of long, extraordinary words. The stories are fascinating but terrible and should not be read in a dark lonely house!

Note: If the collection contains works by *several* authors instead of a single writer, then mention at least three *different* authors in order to show the variety in the book.

If it is a collection of *poems,* a suitable quotation of several lines will serve to show the kind of poetry found in the book: narrative, lyric, or dramatic; another classification may be humorous, serious, tragic; or else nature, love, patriotism, or other themes.

Similarly, for a collection of *one-act plays, essays,* or *brief selections,* give a cross section of the contents to show the range of materials.

STUDENT REPORT ON A NONFICTION BOOK

WE, THE AMERICAN PEOPLE
by Marguerite Ann Stewart

This book is about how people came to America; how they settled, and what they did for the country.

It tells how the people worked together and why we should all get along with each other. Here are a few ways people from other nations helped America grow: The Chinese worked in mines and brought to America their skill in laundering. And they opened restaurants where Chinese food was served. They also helped in the building of railroads.

With the Germans came Peter Zenger. He struggled bitterly for freedom of the press. The Germans brought to America hot dogs, hamburgers, pumpernickel, sauerkraut, pretzels, liverwurst, picnics and bowling alleys. The Germans also brought about the spreading of education in America. They helped in the development of chemicals, toolmaking, musical instruments, and in baking and brewing.

The Italians brought artists, farmers, stuffed ravioli, minestrone soup and many other Italian dishes. Toscanini, a great conductor, and Fermi, a scientist, both came from Italy.

We can strengthen our democracy by working together peacefully and by not being prejudiced against people of different color or religion. People of different nationalities have all helped to make America one of the wealthiest countries in the world.

I liked this book because it told about different people and their ways of living.

Movies and television programs provide many opportunities for entertainment and relaxation. You enjoy films dealing with many topics: western adventure, mystery thrillers, Bible stories, family comedies, world travel, musical comedies, and cartoons. Such memorable movies are: *The Ten Commandments, The King and I, Shane, Oklahoma, The River, Bambi, Snow White and the Seven Dwarfs.* Television offers many worthwhile shows, such as documentaries, drama, science fiction, current news, comedies, live music, quiz contests, sports events, and others. Some topnotch TV shows include: *Person to Person, Science Fiction Theatre, Omnibus, Meet the Press, Victory at Sea,* and so on.

Learn to use television, not to be abused by it.

Writing a review of a movie or television program helps to develop a better sense of values. You learn to look for such things as good acting, appropriate dialog, effective scenery or background, truth to life, mood music, suspense, final outcome or ending. You develop better taste in selecting movies and television programs by reading the columns of professional critics in the newspapers and magazines. As a result, you can prepare your own Movie Guide or TV Log for a balanced schedule, including something for fun and something for instruction.

STUDENT REVIEWS OF MOVIES

Here are some sample reviews written by pupils. Do their opinions agree with yours?

Love Is a Many Splendored Thing

I think that *Love Is a Many Splendored Thing* is the best movie I have ever seen. The stars are William Holden and Jennifer Jones. It takes place in Hong Kong, China.

This is the story of an American war correspondent's love for an Eurasian woman doctor. William Holden tries to explain his love to Jennifer Jones, but she believes she has a duty towards her country, and also he was a married man and it could just never be. Their lives were in different patterns. It goes on that they fall in love with each other. He asks his wife for a divorce but she refuses to give it to him. So they both decide to wait and he would ask her again. While time goes by, he is called to Korea to cover a story. She continues her work at the hospital, until one day she reads in the paper that he has been killed. She is completely heartbroken, but she recalls what he has always told her. I think that was one of the most heartwarming and most beautiful stories I have ever seen.

Good Morning, Miss Dove

Good Morning, Miss Dove starring Jennifer Jones and Robert Stack is a beautiful, tender story of a smalltown school teacher. It shows how she helps mold the lives of her pupils and what happens after they leave her guidance in school. Jennifer Jones as Miss Dove, the old-maid school teacher, gives a beautiful performance. It is in Color and Cinemascope.

STUDENT REVIEWS OF TV PROGRAMS

CHILDREN'S THEATER

Children's Theater is an entertaining and educational program for children and adults. It shows how products are made. Its films cover science, history, and the customs of many different people all over the world. They show such films as "Water Pygmies," "Lake Side Dwellers," "The Story of Time," "How People Live in Mexico" and even how spaghetti and macaroni are made. During the program, they have cartoons for the younger children and you'd be surprised how amusing they are. One program, the story of time, proved to be very interesting. First came the sundial that kept time in the day. At night they used a fire clock, a sand clock or an hour glass.

Ray Forest, who is the narrator, makes this program more interesting because of his warm personality and the soothing quality of his voice.

NEW YORK TIMES YOUTH FORUM

The *New York Times Youth Forum* is on every Sunday evening at 6:30 P.M. on Channel 5. It is a panel of high school students and a well known and important guest. They sit in a semicircle and express their opinions. They discuss all topics from teenage problems to world affairs. Some discussions were "Music for Teenagers" and "Can We Make the World Safe for Mankind?" It is especially interesting for junior high school students because students in the audience have a chance to ask questions.

DISNEYLAND

Disneyland is on every Wednesday from 7:30 to 8:30 P.M. Each week Disneyland brings an exciting program for young and old. The stories vary from wild life to fantasy land. The four different lands are:

1. Tomorrowland is the future. A few weeks ago they described what the first rocket ship to the moon will look like.

2. Adventureland is about nature. One particular show described the Pacific moose. It shows the trail they took and how dangerous it was when they moved south to a warmer climate. The older moose go first, then the others follow. After the cold season is over, they go back north and each year they do the same.

3. Frontierland brings us adventures with the brave frontier men, Davy Crockett and Mike Fink. Their famous race down the Mississippi has become legendary.

4. Fantasyland is the happiest kingdom of all. It shows cartoons and animated figures that the children like most.

Can you tolerate commercials? I know I can't! But my kids go for the singing commercials on all the programs. One day I got a bright idea. I asked my wife to buy all the things that the kids sing about but actually don't like. When suppertime came around, their faces sagged and fell to the floor. When I told them what the brands of the foods were, they gobbled them down.

Yesterday my son told me, very seriously, that The Late Late Show would not be on for the next two weeks. Then he actually cried!

Since we've had that miserable contraption, I've very nearly been electrocuted nine times, stubbed my bare toe thirteen times on the T. V. table, and had to spend $15 on it for assorted tubes. Once I had to climb out on the roof during a blizzard to set the aerial upright.

I guess T. V.'s here to stay, but I don't have to be here to welcome it. I think I'll rig a room in the cellar with a radio, a light, some good books and become a hermit.

EXERCISE

PERSONAL ESSAYS ON FAMILIAR TOPICS

1. Describe a room and someone in it. Include details to show the special interest or taste or background of the person: whether rich or poor, neat or messy, young or old, etc.
2. Describe a scene outdoors with an animal or bird in it. Picture the setting and show its relationship with the creature you have selected: deer in the woods, trout in a brook, a sea gull near the shore, etc.
3. Tell us your first experience as a baby-sitter for a neighbor's youngster that you escorted to a park or playground. Describe your emotions: confidence, fear, surprise, relief, etc.
4. Relate your first visit to the dean's office in your school. Imagine your mental state as you notice each detail and tell the outcome of your interview.
5. Recall your first lunch in the school cafeteria. Tell about your new or old acquaintances at the table, the kind of food and drink served, the manners shown, the remarks by the teacher or dietitian, etc.
6. Describe the dentist who extracted your tooth, real or imaginary. Picture his manner, the various types of "horror" equipment, your relief at the end, etc.
7. Tell us the way your family behaves at breakfast time on a regular school day. Try to include sights, sounds, smells, cries, etc., that show the color and movement of real or imaginary happenings. Humor flavors life.

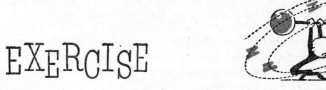

EXERCISE

MOVIE AND TV REVIEWS

1. Write a paragraph, about one full page, reviewing a recent movie or television program. Include these main points, as outlined:
   a. A *topic* sentence stating the title of the movie or TV show and the name of the chief person or "star" of the story.
   b. A brief *summary* of the plot or general nature of the film story or TV program in about 100 words.
   c. A *closing* sentence expressing some critical comment together with your personal reaction.
2. Write a paragraph comparing a movie with a similar television production and tell why you prefer one or the other. Mention the effect of color, sound, size of screen, advertising, length of show, choice of stars, or anything else you consider important.
3. Select two TV programs, one for entertainment and another for instruction. Write a short paragraph for each, telling why you like it.

 ## PERSONAL ESSAYS ON FAMILIAR TOPICS

Have you ever watched the hand of a clock quietly sweeping the seconds across the dial—and thought of your future hurrying too? Have you noticed a goldfish swishing around a glass bowl—and been reminded of your own lack of privacy at home or school? The first snowfall, a doorbell ringing, an unexpected letter in the mail, a face in a crowd, a crumpled dollar, a missing coat button—all these familiar things can suggest comedy or tragedy for someone. A personal essay is a written attempt to give a special meaning to the commonplace. It is your own interpretation of the ordinary things or events of daily living. It requires two abilities: *observation* and *imagination*. You see the last leaf on a tree in November and your mind turns to thoughts of —what? Winter, holidays, ice skating, toasting marshmallows, rabbit hunting, indoor parties, annual colds, storm windows, concerts, TV shows, school examinations—what? It all depends on your personal reaction.

Take something familiar right in the classroom; for example, *the teacher's desk*. Look at it—as if for the first time. Try to imagine the mystery it contains! Jot down some real or fanciful items:

1. Records of attendance and punctuality
2. Notes of excuse for absence, etc.
3. Tests and ratings for work done so far
4. Private reports on conduct of pupils
5. Objects removed from pupils for safekeeping
6. Ordinary supplies and equipment
7. Special cards for commendation
8. Textbooks and courses of study
9. Odds and ends of all kinds

Now, decide to select any *three* that appeal to your own imagination; for example, items 4-5-9. Think about these in terms of what they may mean to you. Include both actual facts and invented possibilities. Can you write about 100 words telling us your reaction to these familiar things? Try it. To help you get started, here are some *sample opening sentences* you may wish to borrow:

1. I was commended to the principal for exceptional work in connection with the Junior Red Cross Drive in March.
2. Teacher took my envelop containing one dollar because I should have delivered it to the main office for my transportation pass instead of toying with it.
3. I handed in a wallet I found on the way to school this morning, and they teased me about a reward.

As you can see, the mind of the writer notices a simple fact and adds to it some possible incident which is the result of imagination. The result should seem a natural outcome of the incident or situation. Build up the account with a few such items of personal interest and their probable effect on your life, conduct, or report card. Then, try to close with some general statement that ties all the loose ends together. You may use one of these *sample closing sentences:*

1. What a satisfaction it was to distribute the dressed up dolls in the children's ward of the local hospital!
2. Maybe the clerk will be good enough to give me a temporary pass until I can remember where I left the money.
3. After all, virtue is supposed to be its own reward, isn't it?

Imagination

Observation

Take an ordinary thing or commonplace event. Mix well with imagination. Stir the emotions. Then, pour carefully into a **personal essay.**

STUDENT PERSONAL ESSAY

I'm Cracking Up

Why did they have to invent television? In Abe Lincoln's day, people went to plays and operas, and in the days of F. D. Roosevelt, people went to the moving pictures. But today, in the second half of the Twentieth Century, we are plagued by the television set.

Please don't think that I'm a crank. Far from it! The truth is that millions of dollars are invested in millions of T. V. sets sold to millions of parents with children who are developing one track minds.

When we are able to tear ourselves away from the T. V. set and go visiting, my daughter wants to go to the nearby friendly ESSO dealer; my son demands to go to a MOBILGAS station. When we finally get to Aunt Henrietta's house, the children, instead of saying, "Hello," tell their aunt that her screen is too small. She has a twenty inch set.

TELLING PERSONAL EXPERIENCES, REAL AND IMAGINARY

We all live in two worlds: the world of fact and the world of fancy. Remember the story of Walter Mitty in the movies? Do you recall how while parked in a car outside a bank he would dream of himself as the hero stopping a bank robbery? Especially when you are young, the world is full of dreams, with you as the brave conquering hero or the beautiful heroine. Even now, that redheaded boy gazing out of the window may be thinking of himself as a captain on a pirate ship sailing the high seas! That golden girl near the door may be dancing in a starlit ballroom in silver slippers! Maybe it's the result of reading fiction, watching movies and television, or pure imagination. At any rate, it's normal.

How can you tell a personal experience in words so that others can share it? The problem is to make the reader see it, whether real or make-believe, just as clearly as you do.

SUGGESTIONS FOR TELLING A REAL EXPERIENCE

1. Begin with some commonplace, everyday happening or bit of conversation.
2. Describe normal, matter-of-fact persons and places that everyone recognizes as true to life.
3. Build up the mood, whether happy or sad, with realistic details.
4. Follow a clear time-pattern that naturally moves along in answer to this question: "What happened next?"
5. End with a definite incident or personal comment that leaves a feeling that the total account is believable because "It could have happened to anyone."

SUGGESTIONS FOR TELLING AN IMAGINARY EXPERIENCE

1. Begin with an unusual happening or strange and puzzling object that "starts the ball rolling."
2. Describe extraordinary creatures in normal surroundings, or ordinary persons in unearthly places.
3. Sustain the mood, whether wonder or surprise, with supernatural details or invent "fake" references that build up "atmosphere."
4. Keep the suspense as to the outcome till the very end in order to maintain interest.
5. End with a vague, indefinite conclusion that allows room for further imagination to roam into the unknowable: "I wonder what else happened?"

We live in the past by memory as we dwell in the future by hope. This mixture of fact and dream gives all our experiences a double quality. **Composition** reflects both!

SAMPLES OF PUPILS' PERSONAL EXPERIENCES

I Can Dream—Can't I?

The Spring we graduated from high school was a lovely one. I got my driver's license from the City and a car from my mother. A few weeks after graduation my cousin and I set out for California.

Believe it or not we had been looking forward to this vacation for years. My cousin Kate even brought her dog along for protection. He was a cute cocker spaniel.

We took turns driving and once we got out on the wide highways it was wonderful. Not until we got to the Middle West did we have any trouble.

We were in the midst of the desert area, miles from the nearest gas station when we discovered our gas tank read, EMPTY. As usual, Cousin Kate volunteered to walk back and get a can of gas. I wasn't overjoyed at the prospect of staying in the car which was out of gas in the middle of a desert, but there was no other choice.

I persuaded my cousin to take the dog with her. When she had gone, I looked around for something to do. I spied a book and started to read. All I read were words, words which didn't make any sense. By now the sun was beginning to set. Stars appeared here and there. It was getting cold and I was hungry and miserable. I was also beginning to worry about my cousin. What was keeping her? Had something happened?

Just as I was about to go in search of her, I saw headlights and heard a dog bark. My cousin had gotten a ride back. We filled the gas tank and set out once more on our way to California.

A Wish Come True

Have you ever dreamed of taking a long trip? My father made this wish come true one morning when he came to me and said, "Peter, would you like to go on a long trip?" My answer, almost before he could finish his question, was, "Yes, dad; where are we going?" "To Louisiana, son."

I was ten years old at the time and our home was in Virginia. For our trip we bought a covered wagon and in a few days we were packed and ready to go. Three days later, about ten o'clock in the morning, we left for the West, our hearts full of excitement and hope.

For the first two weeks, our trip was a very peaceful but bumpy one. Then, one morning, I heard strange sounds behind us. Looking back, I saw four painted Indians charging after us. "Dad!" I yelled,

105

"Indians!" My father began to whip the oxen to get more speed out of them. I picked up my rifle and began shooting.

Luck was with me. I managed to down three of the savages and the fourth Indian ran away. "Good work, my son," said my father. "I guess we're safe for the time being." My father's words made me feel very good.

Several weeks later, we reached our destination. We were very happy to be among the pioneers who were settling the fertile land of the Louisiana Territory.

EXERCISE

TELLING PERSONAL EXPERIENCES

The problem in writing about our experiences, whether real or imagined, is to make them sound believable and interesting to the reader. Select one of the topics below, and in a paragraph of about 100 words, tell a personal experience as convincingly and effectively as you can.

1. Pretend you are a historical figure (Lewis, Clark, Pocahontas, Barbara Frietche, etc.) and describe an incident as if it happened to you.
2. Make believe you are a character from fiction (Scrooge, Alice, Katrina Van Tassel, Rip Van Winkle, Jo, Tom Sawyer, etc.) and describe an incident as if it happened to you.
3. Put on your space helmet and tell us about your trip on a rocket ship to the planet Mars.
4. Assume you are a deep-sea diver trying to salvage the gold that sank with the liner *Andrea Doria* off Nantucket.
5. Pretend you are one of the explorers who first conquered the snowy summit of Mt. Everest.
6. Describe your experiences on the day you arrived at a summer resort or day camp during your vacation.
7. Tell us about something that happened in one of your lower grades on a "day you will never forget."
8. Narrate your recollections of the first time you were invited to a birthday party (not your own).
9. Tell an amusing experience on a shopping trip with a friend of yours in a supermarket or large department store.
10. Describe the most exciting part of a game or sports event you played in or watched.

LEARNING THE MECHANICS OF EXPRESSION

"Expression" is personal communication through spoken or written language. We refer to "creative expression" when we discuss thinking, imagination, and such qualities of composition as sincerity, vividness, and force. We use the phrase "mechanics of expression" to mean the *elements of form,* including choice of words, usage, grammar, and so on. Therefore, this part of the book contains a solid and valuable guide to develop strength in handling language.

We are human beings, not mechanical robots. Your expression is as personal and intimate as your own personality. Let your writing be *alive!*

Just as there are rules for playing football or any other sport, so there are rules for using language. Grammar is nothing more than the study of the rules of language. Learning grammar is an unconscious act when you begin to speak and to form language habits. Unfortunately, you sometimes acquire wrong habits in the process. Therefore, a brief systematic review of fundamentals will help you to handle language correctly to express your ideas. Remember that grammar is not just a classroom exercise; it is a valuable tool for building more effective sentences.

Your aim should be to develop improved style based on a knowledge of correct form. You will gain confidence by *study, imitation, and practice!*

According to the kind of work that words do in a sentence, all words are divided into eight classes called *parts of speech*. The eight parts of speech are: *noun, pronoun, adjective, verb, adverb, preposition, conjunction,* and *interjection.* To tell the part of speech of any word in a sentence, you must first determine what kind of work the word does. Ask yourself: "How is this word *used* to express an idea?"

Noun	a word used to name a person, place, thing, or quality. *boy, desk, teacher, girl, beauty, car* Then the *man* entered the *room* quietly.
Pronoun	a word used in place of a noun. *I, we, you, they, he, she, it* *You* should have told *her* that *it* was raining.
Adjective	a word used to describe or to limit a noun or pronoun. *red, blue, tall, short, beautiful, sad* *Faint* heart never won *fair* lady!
Verb	a word used to show action or to express a state of being. *study, play, rest, pray, dream, work* She *sang* while the orchestra *played.* (*action* verbs) We *are* happy to hear that you *feel* better. (*state-of-being* verbs)
Adverb	a word used to modify the meaning of a verb, an adjective, or another adverb. *quickly, slowly, skilfully, usually, extremely* He *suddenly* threw the ball. (modifying a *verb*) Honey is *very* sweet. (modifying an *adjective*) He ran *too* fast. (modifying another *adverb*)

Parts of Speech (Continued)

Preposition	a word used to show the relation between a noun or pronoun and some other word in the sentence. *to, in, by, at, under, over, near, before* Mother went *into* the store *for* some bread. (*into the store* and *for some bread* are prepositional phrases; *store* and *bread* are objects of the prepositions)
Conjunction	a word used to connect words, phrases, and clauses within sentences. *and, or, but, while, since, if, as, because* Bread *and* butter, crackers *and* cheese, coffee *and* cake, ham *and* eggs are favorite combinations. (*Words* are connected.) The sky in the morning *and* in the evening shows a remarkable change. (*Phrases* are connected.) Mary stayed home *because* she wanted to listen to a special broadcast. (*Clauses* are connected.)
Interjection	a word used to express sudden emotion or feeling; it has no grammatical connection with the sentence. *Oh! Ah! Lo! Alas!* (for *strong* feeling) *oh, ah, lo, alas* (for *mild* emotion) *Bah!* That sounds ridiculous to me. I tried to warn him, but, *alas,* he wouldn't listen.

Remember that the part of speech depends on the *use of the word in a sentence.* For example, *walk* may be used as a verb or as a noun, depending upon the idea expressed in the sentence:

We *walk* (verb) to school.

We took a *walk* (noun).

See the difference between *fast* as an adjective and as an adverb in these sentences:

The *fast* (adjective) horse won the race. (= speedy)

The horse ran *fast* (adverb) and won the race. (= speedily)

EXERCISES

PARTS OF SPEECH

A. Name the part of speech of each of the 10 italicized words below:

To city *dwellers*, the arrival of the postman is a daily occurrence, *but* to those *who reside* in rural areas, *it* is an important *event*, for *frequently* it is their *principal* contact *with* the *outside* world.

B. Write the part of speech of each italicized word in the following sentences:

1. The batter hit a long *drive* over the center field.
2. We *drive* more carefully on city streets.

3. They *wax* the floors regularly.
4. As the candle burned, *wax* dropped down.

5. He carved a *walking* stick out of a hickory limb.
6. *Walking* to school is good exercise.

7. Can you *cook* the way Mother does?
8. She is really an excellent *cook*.

9. We lost the written *guarantee*.
10. I *guarantee* this watch against all imperfections.

11. The plumber fixed the *break* in the pipe.
12. Be careful you don't *break* the plate.

13. Will you join our *club*?
14. The *club* sandwich has now grown larger into a hero sandwich.

15. This is an *iron* kettle.
16. *Iron* is very useful.
17. Did you *iron* this dress?

18. He dropped the *pin*.
19. *Pin* it on the wall.
20. The *pin* tray is very pretty.

C. Write the part of speech of each italicized word.

1. The *fast* train goes too *fast* for safety.
2. These luscious *strawberries* will make a good *strawberry* shortcake.
3. The postman *travels* many miles in his *travels* around the city.

D. Write all the words that illustrate the part of speech mentioned at the left.

Prepositions 1. As we went down the mountain, the sun rose before us.
Verbs 2. I want a copy of your paper.
Nouns 3. Some birds pull the down from their breasts to line their nest.
Adverbs 4. Down tumbled both boys, but quickly they scrambled up.
Pronouns 5. The coach told the boys who are to play in the game to report to him at one o'clock.
Conjunctions 6. Either syrup or honey is a good substitute for sugar.

E. Use each of the following words in original sentences according to the part of speech indicated at the left:

1. *noun* —football, book, radio, history, suit
2. *verb* —make, tell, assist, cooperate, refuse
3. *pronoun* —you, we, he, she
4. *adjective* —brave, honest, sincere, trustworthy
5. *adverb* —proudly, gratefully, kindly, willingly
6. *preposition* —besides, near, under, to, into
7. *conjunction*—but, or, and, while, because
8. *interjection* —well, oh, ah, say, alas

F. From the following paragraph, choose two examples of each part of speech listed below: [Do not include *a, an, the.*]

"Oh!" gasped the spectators as the fireman quickly climbed through an upper window and rescued the elderly lady. "Bravo," they exclaimed happily when he finally reached the foot of the ladder with the woman. By quick action the man saved her life.

| nouns | verbs | adverbs | conjunctions |
| pronouns | adjectives | prepositions | interjections |

G. From the following sentence, select an example of each of the parts of speech named below.

"Hurrah!" shouted the two small boys, as their lost companion and his dog suddenly appeared before them.

| noun | adjective | pronoun | preposition |
| verb | conjunction | adverb | interjection |

H. From the following paragraph, select an example of each of the forms named below. [Do not include *a, an, the.*]

The Indians told a curious legend about the "Old Squaw" of the Catskills. She supposedly resided on a high peak and controlled the weather of the region. Some residents still believe in her, because they plainly see her outline on a clear day.

| common noun | adverb | pronoun | conjunction |
| proper noun | verb | preposition | adjective |

SUBJECT AND PREDICATE

We express our ideas in the form of sentences. Usually, we talk about persons or things, and these words are called the *subject* of a sentence. We say something about the persons or things by means of verbs, which are called the *predicate* of a sentence.

Every sentence must have a subject and a predicate.

Simple subject	composed of a noun or pronoun without any modifiers.
	1. The subject usually precedes the verb.
	Harry called me today.
	2. To find the subject and predicate in an inverted sentence, change the word-order to subject followed by verb.
	On the first shelf were the *dishes.* (*inverted* order)
	The *dishes* were on the first shelf. (*normal* order)
	3. To find the subject and predicate in a question, turn the question into the word-order of a statement.
	What book are *you* reading? (question)
	You are reading what book. (statement)
	4. Sometimes the subject word follows the verb.
	Here is the *book* you ordered.
	There are the *winners* of the spelling bee.
	(*Here* and *there* are introductory adverbs; they are not the subjects.)
Simple predicate	composed of a verb or verb phrase without any modifiers.
	1. Frank *hit* a single. (verb)
	2. We *will go* with you. (verb phrase)
	(*go* is the principal verb; *will* is an auxiliary or helping verb. Other auxiliaries are *shall, can, do, may, have, had,* etc.)

Subject and Predicate (Continued)

Compound subject	two or more simple subjects connected by *and* or *or*. *Milk* and *cookies* are on the table. *Victory* or *defeat* comes at the end of every race.
Compound predicate	two or more simple predicates connected by *and* or *or*. The children *read* and *played* all afternoon. We *laugh* or *cry* as the spirit moves us.
Complete subject	the simple subject and all its modifiers. *The boy with the blue and white sweater* is a class-mate of mine.
Complete predicate	the simple predicate and all its modifiers. The frightened child *clutched her mother's hand tightly*.

Finding the Complete Subject and Complete Predicate

To determine the complete subject and the complete predicate:

Step 1. Find the simple subject and underline it once.

The <u>man</u> with the small boy is my neighbor.

Step 2. Find the simple predicate and underline it twice.

The man with the small boy is my neighbor.

Step 3. Continue to underline once the words that describe or tell more about the simple subject. (These are called *modifiers*.)

<u>The man with the small boy</u> is my neighbor.

(The words underlined once are the complete subject.)

Step 4. All the words that are not in the complete subject must be in the complete predicate. These words are underlined twice.

<u>The man with the small boy</u> is my neighbor.

114

To find the complete subject and complete predicate of interrogative and inverted sentences, rewrite the sentence to follow the normal word-order of statements.

> Where did you find my hat?
> You did find my hat where.
>
> Into the pool dived the two boys.
> The two boys dived into the pool.

EXERCISES

SUBJECT AND PREDICATE

A. Draw *one* line under the simple subject and *two* lines under the predicate verb:
1. The captain of the team quickly called a new play.
2. Bravely the small boy fought his way back to the capsized canoe.
3. Out of the box rushed the frightened rabbit.
4. The little dog, alarmed by the noise, crept under the sofa.
5. Mother, with John and me following, led the way.
6. The cat with her three kittens ran to the door.
7. Quickly four of the boys offered to collect the papers.
8. Tom, alert to every sound, cautiously approached the entrance to the cave.
9. Against the sky, the single elm was majestic in its beauty.
10. Down the street dashed the boys after the fire engine.
11. The pilot of the airplane inspected his machine thoroughly before starting.
12. Stealthily the intruder crept through the half-open door.
13. The poor woman with her five children sought shelter from the cold.
14. The puppy, frightened by the boy, hid under the chair.
15. Into the kitchen rushed the hungry children.

B. Draw a vertical line between the complete subject and the complete predicate.

[Example: A heavy rain | fell in the night.]
1. The current of the river was swift.
2. The logs floated down the stream.
3. They went to live in Alaska.
4. The sight of Old Glory thrills every heart.
5. The soldiers and sailors stood at attention.
6. The man in the house next door trimmed his lawn.
7. In his disguise, John looked like a stranger to us.
8. A bird with a broken wing was hopping along the ground.
9. My plaster model of the Eiffel Tower received special commendation.
10. Boys and girls together enjoyed the dance sessions held after school.

COMPLEMENTS OF A VERB

A sentence *must* have at least a subject and a predicate. Some sentences go further in expressing an idea. They have additional parts, called *complements,* or words used to complete the meaning of a verb or to enlarge the meaning of the subject.

Direct object	a noun or pronoun in the predicate that is the direct receiver of the action. We visited the *zoo.* I expect *her* today.
Indirect object	a noun or pronoun in the predicate that is the indirect receiver of the action. The indirect object is preceded by the preposition (*to*) understood and comes between the verb and the direct object. I gave (to) *him* my card. (*card* = direct object)
Predicate nominative	a noun or pronoun that completes the meaning of a copulative verb and refers to the subject. The most common copulative verb is *be.* Others are *become, act, seem, grow, appear, look, feel, smell, stay, remain, taste.* A copulative verb does not show action, but describes a state of being. Therefore, it does not have an object. Joe DiMaggio *was* a great baseball *player.* (*player* = predicate nominative; *was* = copulative verb)
Predicate adjective	an adjective that completes the meaning of a copulative verb and describes the subject. The flowers *smell sweet.* (*sweet* = predicate adjective; *smell* = copulative verb)

Complements

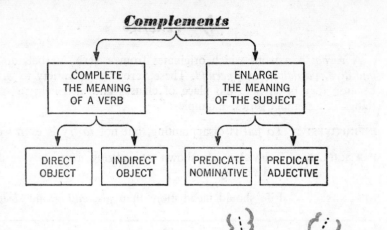

COMPLETE
THE MEANING
OF A VERB

ENLARGE
THE MEANING
OF THE SUBJECT

DIRECT
OBJECT

INDIRECT
OBJECT

PREDICATE
NOMINATIVE

PREDICATE
ADJECTIVE

EXERCISE

COMPLEMENTS OF A VERB

Find the complements in each of the following sentences. Label them correctly: *dir. obj., ind. obj., pred. nom., pred. adj.*

1. Election results showed that Harold remained president of the class.
2. In her hurry, she made an unfortunate mistake.
3. Because of his recent illness, he looked quite pale.
4. The doctor said it was he who gave him some vitamin pills.
5. Broiled hamburgers taste better on toasted rolls.
6. After serving in the Lower House, he became a Senator.
7. The policeman tied the stray dog to a nearby tree.
8. The tearful youngster thanked him for finding his pet.
9. Some hailstones seem marbles of ice.
10. Formica tabletops feel cool even on warm days.
11. She solved the problem all by herself.
12. The waiter handed him a check for the meal.
13. In a few months, he was the leader of the Scout troop.
14. With experience and training, he felt more confident.
15. He drove the car carefully into the garage.
16. It was she at the door.
17. We offered her a free ticket to the school show.
18. During the emergency, the intern acted the veteran doctor.
19. In spite of advancing years, he seemed younger than ever.
20. Will you please give me a glass of water?

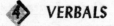 **VERBALS**

A *verbal* is a word which originates from a verb. Verbals are the *infinitive, participle,* and *gerund.* These verbals lend variety to writing because they often take the place of clauses and also help in saying things in a parallel series. Examples:

INFINITIVES: *To fail* is disappointing, but not *to try* is even worse.

PARTICIPLES: Television has shown us *waltzing* mice, *talking* dogs, and *skating* bears.

GERUNDS: Life should mean more than just *eating* and *sleeping.*

Infinitive	is preceded by *to* and is used as a noun, an adjective, or an adverb.
	To walk is good exercise. (noun; subject of *is*)
	They wanted *to eat.* (noun; object of *wanted*)
	Show me the way *to play.* (adjective; modifies *way*)
	The boys are ready *to leave.* (adverb; modifies *ready*)
Participle	ends in *ing* (and the past forms *ed, en, t*) and is used as an adjective.
	We bought a dozen *drinking* glasses. (modifies noun *glasses*)
	The *exhausted* runner could not continue the race. (modifies noun *runner*)
Gerund	ends in *ing* and is used as a noun.
	Singing is his great joy. (subject of *is*)
	I enjoy *dancing* in the evening. (object of the verb *enjoy*)
	Our team gives (to) *sliding* a great deal of emphasis. (indirect object; preposition *to* is understood)
	My sport is *swimming.* (predicate nominative after *is*)
	The boy was scolded for *lying.* (object of preposition *for*)

EXERCISE

VERBALS

Insert the verbal form (indicated in parentheses) next to the italicized verb:

1. There is no use *cry* (gerund) _____ over *spill* (participle) _____ milk.
2. Our country has always welcomed the *oppress* (participle) _____ people.
3. These immigrants have helped build America by *work* (gerund) _____, *struggle* (gerund) _____, and *become* (gerund) _____ worthwhile citizens.
4. It is more satisfying in the long run *discover* (infinitive) _____ one's real ability and *make* (infinitive) _____ the most of it.
5. When the *fish* (participle) _____ fleet comes in, the men are greeted by their *laugh* (participle) _____ children and wives.
6. Why must you avoid walking barefoot on *splinter* (participle) _____ wood or *break* (participle) _____ glass?
7. There is a time *eat* (infinitive) _____, a time *work* (infinitive) _____, and a time *play* (infinitive) _____.
8. How can a *work* (participle) _____ man raise a *grow* (participle) _____ family without *sacrifice* (gerund) _____ himself?
9. If you learn *obey* (infinitive) _____ your elders and *pray* (infinitive) _____ for guidance, you will be better able *succeed* (infinitive) _____.
10. Some baseball players are good in many activities: in *hit* (gerund) _____, *field* (gerund) _____, and base *run* (gerund) _____.

5 PHRASES AND CLAUSES

Phrases and clauses help to modify or round out the meaning of a sentence. A simple statement containing just a subject and predicate makes sense. But the same idea may be enlarged by the use of phrases and clauses in answer to the questions: how? where? when? with whom?, etc. Compare these statements as to the fullness of expression made possible by adding phrases and then clauses:

| We went home. |

PHRASES: After the game, we went home in a crowded bus with some friends.

CLAUSES: After the game was over, we went home in a crowded bus with some friends who were arguing about the last home run.

119

Phrase	two or more words having neither a subject nor a predicate.
	The prepositional phrase includes the preposition, the object of the preposition, and the modifiers of the object.
	The young girl *in the car* is Jane.
	(adjective phrase modifying the noun *girl*)
	(*in* = preposition; *car* = object of preposition; *the* = modifier of *car*)
	Dry your hands *with this towel*.
	(adverb phrase modifying the verb *dry*)
	(*with* = preposition; *towel* = object of preposition; *this* = modifier of *towel*)
Clause	a group of words containing a subject and a predicate.
	A **principal clause** (or **independent** or **main clause**) can stand alone to express a complete thought.
	I enjoyed last night's play.
	A **subordinate clause** (or **dependent clause**) cannot stand alone, but helps to express a complete thought when it is attached to a principal clause. (The subordinate clauses below are italicized.)
	She wondered *where you were*.
	(noun clause; object of the verb *wondered*)
	The girl *who used to live next door* is now married.
	(adjective clause; modifies the noun *girl*)
	I will not play today *because I have some homework to do*.
	(adverb clause; modifies the verb *will play*)

Connecting Words

Phrases begin with *prepositions:*		*Clauses* begin with *conjunctions:*	
to	about	why	what
in	as	when	if
at	on	where	either
by	between	how	neither
for	off	and	or
but	among	because	nor
from	except	since	for
under	into	while	but
above	through	after	so
after	upon	who	as
while	beside	that	although
within	like	which	though

Note: Some words may be used as either a preposition or a conjunction: as, after, while, for, but.

EXERCISE

PHRASES AND CLAUSES

Using the phrases and clauses given below, write 10 complete sentences. Make sure each sentence will contain a main clause and at least one phrase and one dependent clause to expand the meaning.

PHRASES	CLAUSES
for a while	who gave us wrong directions
to the street	when the player seized the ball
at his signal	where she used to live
in the morning	because someone made a mistake
from his pocket	after we had enjoyed the party
by surprise	if the storm had suddenly stopped
under the desk	although her coat had a high collar
after a slight delay	as we scrambled for the seats
within two weeks	since the wallet had disappeared
above her shoulders	why she was always to blame
between friends	what I should have guessed sooner
into the car	that it really made no difference
over the fence	how they all seemed excited

Diagramming is a useful way of showing the structure of a sentence. Lines are used to show the grammatical relationships of the various elements. This blueprint of words, phrases, and clauses helps you to visualize the proper connection between ideas. It clarifies meaning, too, because it analyzes the relation between the parts of a sentence.

A good diagram makes clear the design of a sentence, just as a floor plan guides the builder of a house.

Connecting Words

Phrases begin with *prepositions:*

to	about
in	as
at	on
by	between
for	off
but	among
from	except
under	into
above	through
after	upon
while	beside
within	like

Clauses begin with *conjunctions:*

why	what
when	if
where	either
how	neither
and	or
because	nor
since	for
while	but
after	so
who	as
that	although
which	though

Note: Some words may be used as either a preposition or a **conjunc-tion**: as, after, while, for, but.

PHRASES AND CLAUSES

Using the phrases and clauses given below, write 10 complete sentences. Make sure each sentence will contain a main clause and at least one phrase and one dependent clause to expand the meaning.

PHRASES	CLAUSES
for a while	who gave us wrong directions
to the street	when the player seized the ball
at his signal	where she used to live
in the morning	because someone made a mistake
from his pocket	after we had enjoyed the party
by surprise	if the storm had suddenly stopped
under the desk	although her coat had a high collar
after a slight delay	as we scrambled for the seats
within two weeks	since the wallet had disappeared
above her shoulders	why she was always to blame
between friends	what I should have guessed sooner
into the car	that it really made no difference
over the fence	how they all seemed excited

Diagramming is a useful way of showing the structure of a sentence. Lines are used to show the grammatical relationships of the various elements. This blueprint of words, phrases, and clauses helps you to visualize the proper connection between ideas. It clarifies meaning, too, because it analyzes the relation between the parts of a sentence.

A good diagram makes clear the design of a sentence, just as a floor plan guides the builder of a house.

Subject — Predicate — Complement

Every sentence must have a subject and a predicate (diagram 1), and may have a complement (2). The subject may be compound (3), or the predicate may be compound (4).

1. Prices tumbled.

| Prices | tumbled | subject | predicate |

2. The team won the game.

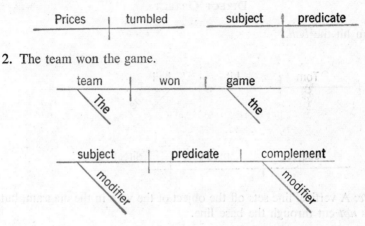

3. The *man* and his *wife* have gone home.

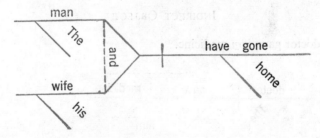

4. The men *saluted* the flag and *stood* at attention.

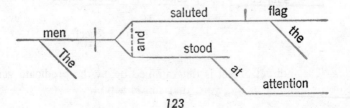

123

Kinds of Complements

There are four kinds of complements: the direct object (diagram 5), indirect object (6), predicate nominative (7), and predicate adjective (8).

DIRECT OBJECT

5. Tom hit the *ball*.

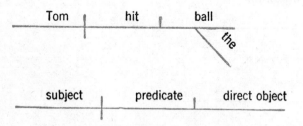

Note: A vertical line sets off the object of the verb in the diagram, but it does *not* cut through the base line.

INDIRECT OBJECT

6. The doctor gave *him* medicine.

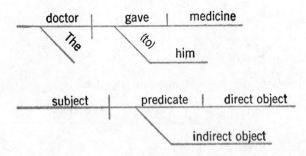

Note: The indirect object is diagrammed below the predicate verb to indicate its relation to the word that shows action.

7. Frank was a *hero*.

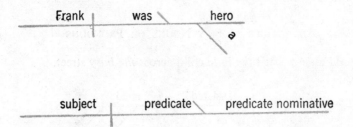

Note: The line placed before the predicate nominative in the sentence diagram slants toward the subject to show that its meaning refers to the subject.

PREDICATE ADJECTIVE

8. Lincoln became *famous*.

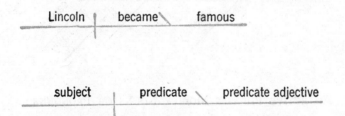

Note: The line placed before the predicate adjective in the sentence diagram slants toward the subject to show that it serves to describe the subject.

Modifiers of a Sentence

The modifiers of a sentence consist of words, phrases, and clauses which may be used either to enlarge or to limit the meaning of the subject, the predicate verb, or the complement.

ADJECTIVES MODIFY NOUNS OR PRONOUNS

9. *The tall* man assisted *the little* child across *the busy* street.

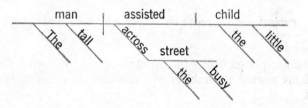

ADVERBS MODIFY ADJECTIVES, VERBS, OR OTHER ADVERBS

10. He *carefully* examined the *finely* carved statuette.

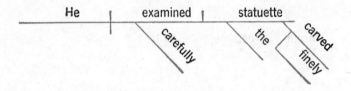

ADJECTIVE PHRASES MODIFY NOUNS OR PRONOUNS

11. The girl *in the train* waved to the lady *on the platform*.

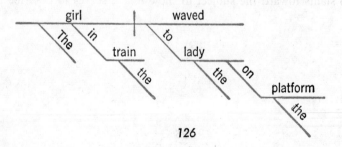

12. The fisherman rowed his boat *near the shore in the cool shade.*

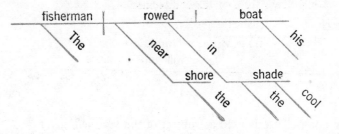

ADJECTIVE CLAUSES MODIFY NOUNS OR PRONOUNS

13. The girl *who sits near the window* looks drowsy.

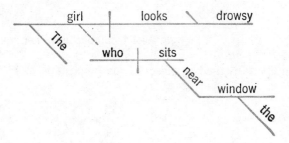

ADVERB CLAUSES MODIFY ADJECTIVES, VERBS, OR OTHER ADVERBS

14. The trained seal balanced the ball *while the band played.*

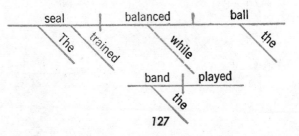

15. *Whoever finishes first* will get the extra piece of cake.

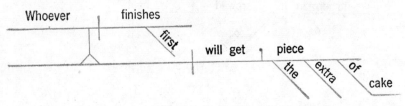

(The noun clause is used as subject of the verb *will get.*)

16. She gave the ticket *to whoever approached her.*

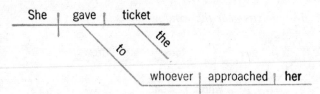

(The noun clause is used as object of the preposition *to.*)

EXERCISES

DIAGRAMMING

A. Write the full sentence form for the following diagrams:

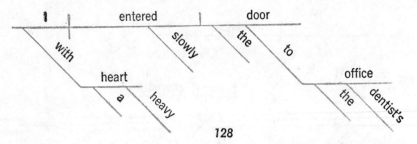

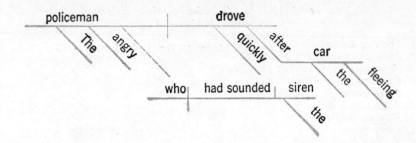

B. Insert the words from the sentences on the accompanying diagrams.

1. At last the steamer stopped at Bear Mt. and we rushed to the playground.

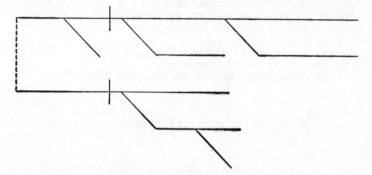

2. How do you expect to earn money if you just sit there lazily in the sun?

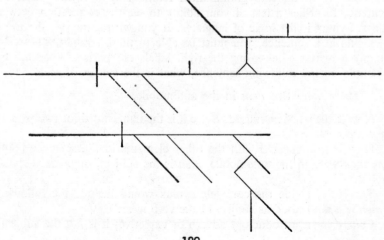

C. Following the models given in this section, carefully diagram the following sentences so as to make clear the relationship between parts.

1. The ship docked at noon.
2. Some mushrooms are poisonous.
3. Sportsmanship means fair play.
4. Good posture can be acquired.
5. I like mountain climbing.
6. What time is it?
7. How do you know?
8. Come in!
9. Tell me about yourself.
10. Is there a doctor in the house?
11. We traveled wherever we pleased.
12. I listen to the radio because it entertains me.
13. Since you returned, things seem brighter.
14. When it started to rain, we stopped the ball game.
15. I will not give you a book until you pay for it.
16. She wavered a bit and suddenly fainted.
17. We drove in and parked the car.
18. A young chorister played the organ and sang a hymn.
19. Mother and Dad always took care of us.
20. The coach and the team went on a tour over the holiday.

USE IN THE SENTENCE (SYNTAX)

Giving the syntax of a word, phrase, or clause means telling its part of speech and showing its relation to other elements in the sentence. This ability to indicate grammatical relationship between parts of a sentence furnishes a test of your ability to see the connection between ideas. Syntax is the logic of language. If you wish to master the use of elements in a sentence, you must be able to think straight. The rest is simply a matter of choosing the right labels or "parts of speech." For example, in the following sentence, what is the syntax of *men?*

There were two *men* in the automobile.

How is the word *men* used? Since it is the name-word for two persons, it is a noun.

How is it connected with the other elements in the sentence? Since the *men* were in the automobile, *men* is the subject, or persons spoken about.

Therefore, giving the complete syntax would include the following: "*men* is a noun used as subject of the verb *were*."

(*There* is an introductory adverb or expletive; it is *not* the subject!)

EXERCISES

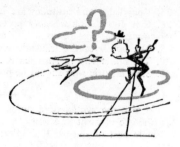

SYNTAX

A. Divide a page in your notebook into three columns; give the syntax of words as shown in this sample: "The bell rang."

WORD	USE	RELATION
the	adjective	modifies "bell"
bell	noun	subject of "rang"
rang	verb	predicate of "bell"

Write the syntax (use in the sentence) of the italicized words or groups of words in the following:

Words

1. Washington, the leader, was *very* brave.
2. Have you given *uniforms* to the players?
3. There were four *men* in the boat.
4. *John's* mother is calling him.
5. All the members *voted* for the new president.
6. Mary is a good *student.*
7. *Cellophane* wrappers keep candy fresh.
8. The dentist *distributed* toothbrushes as prizes at our assembly.
9. She understands the first few lessons in French *quite* readily.
10. The red ink corrections made the *composition* look messy.
11. *Ah!* Now I've got you where I want you.
12. His new tie-clasp slipped *under* the dresser somehow.
13. The morning shower feels *so* refreshing!
14. There is real pleasure in one of the *old-fashioned* rockers.
15. The proverb states: "Life is short, *but* art is long."
16. The two men stood *handcuffed* as a safety measure.
17. When the truck *delivered* the fuel oil, the snow had melted.
18. As the fog lifted, the ferries resumed their regular *speed.*
19. *I* always chop walnuts to make an ice-cream sundae.
20. She offered *me* her sandwich.
21. Do *your* parents stay up to see the Late Show?
22. *Wow,* look at that jet plane zoom across the sky.
23. Liver and onions are not so popular as ham *and* eggs.
24. Smile *if* you have courage to face the injection, sonny.

131

25. Knowledge and attitudes are important aims *of* education.
26. Can fluoridation *actually* prevent tooth decay in children?
27. Air parcel post *saves* time from coast to coast.
28. The *power* of the transmitter makes the broadcast clearer.
29. The *oldest* city in America is St. Augustine, founded in 1513.
30. Such historic *sites* should be preserved for generations to come.

PHRASES AND CLAUSES

To give the syntax of a phrase or a clause, take the whole group of words as a single element and consider its use and relationship the same as if it were a single part of speech. Examples:

In the evening, we relax as we watch television.
←— *phrase* —→   ←——— *clause* ———→

ELEMENT	USE	RELATION
in the evening	adverb phrase	modifies "relax"
as we watch television	adverb clause	modifies "relax"

31. The ship sank *in the river* during the storm.
32. The witness was murdered *because he knew too much.*
33. The pilot flew *over the mountain* as scheduled.
34. The light flashes *when anyone opens the door.*
35. All the members *of the team* received trophies.
36. *Under the desert sand* lay millions of barrels of oil.
37. *After he finished eating,* he tidied up the kitchen.
38. He tossed the paper *into the basket* on his way out.
39. *As he jumped for the ball,* his sneaker fell off.
40. The little boy *with the dog* is my neighbor's child.
41. The ambassador's daughter cried *when he kissed her.*
42. The floor *under the rug* was waxed and slippery.
43. She tripped *as she walked across the room* in the dark.
44. We parked the car outside *in the rain* for two hours.
45. Please tell us *why you did it.*
46. *At his desk* there is a small American flag.
47. *For a while* the visitors seemed to be losing the game.
48. I thank you from the bottom *of my heart.*
49. The ideal lunchroom has seats for all *who want to eat.*
50. He promised his parents *that his work would improve.*

B. The position of a word in a sentence may decide its use. Notice the changes in meaning as you give the syntax of the italicized words below:

1. *a.* Send *only* your name and address to this company.
   b. Send your name and address to this company *only.*
2. *a.* He finished *almost* everything he started.
   b. He *almost* finished everything he started.
3. *a.* Tooth decay is a *major* health problem in our city.
   b. *Major* tooth decay is a health problem in our city.

132

Good usage is an expression that means acceptable language according to the rules of standard English. It covers the right use of words, and grammatical correctness. Good usage requires language forms which are clear, correct, and effective. Usage really signifies the style of expressing ideas according to the current practice of the better writers and speakers.

A knowledge of **good usage** is the gateway to the world of communication. You move forward confidently to meet each new experience.

COMPARISON OF ADJECTIVES AND ADVERBS

The Degrees of Comparison

When we compare persons or things in order to see which contains more or less of a certain quality, we express this relationship in three ways:

1. The **positive** degree denotes the simple quality.
   Iris is a *pretty* child.
2. The **comparative** degree denotes a higher degree of the quality.
   Mary is a *prettier* child than Iris.
3. The **superlative** degree denotes the highest degree of the quality.
   Frances is the *prettiest* child of the three.

Forming the Comparison of Adjectives

1. Adjectives of ONE syllable, and adjectives ending in *y*, regularly form their comparative degree by adding *er,* and their superlative degree by adding *est.* (Remember to change *y* to *i* before adding *er, est.*)

POSITIVE	COMPARATIVE	SUPERLATIVE
brave	braver	bravest
lovely	lovelier	loveliest

2. Adjectives of TWO or more syllables regularly form their comparative degree by adding the word *more* (or *less*), and their superlative degree by adding the word *most* (or *least*).

POSITIVE	COMPARATIVE	SUPERLATIVE
beautiful	{ more beautiful { less beautiful	most beautiful least beautiful

3. Some adjectives are irregular and have different forms in the comparative and superlative degrees.

POSITIVE	COMPARATIVE	SUPERLATIVE
good	better	best
bad	worse	worst
some	more	most
little	less	least

Forming the Comparison of Adverbs

1. Adverbs are compared in a manner similar to adjectives by regularly adding the word *more* (or *less*) to form the comparative degree, and by adding the word *most* (or *least*) to form the superlative degree.

POSITIVE	COMPARATIVE	SUPERLATIVE
easily	{ more easily { less easily	most easily least easily
cleverly	{ more cleverly { less cleverly	most cleverly least cleverly

A few adverbs add *er* and *est,* or are irregular in form.

POSITIVE	COMPARATIVE	SUPERLATIVE
fast	faster	fastest
well	better	best
much	more	most
badly	worse	worst
far	farther	farthest

Errors To Avoid

1. Never use both methods of comparison together.

   The sky is *bluer* (not *more bluer*) today.

2. *a.* Use the comparative degree when comparing TWO persons or things.

   Paul is the *taller* (not *tallest*) of the *two* boys.

   b. Use the superlative degree when comparing MORE THAN TWO persons or things.

   Louise is the *tallest* (not *taller*) of the *three* girls.

3. When comparing members of a group, use *else* or *other* with the comparative, and *all* with the superlative.

   Ann is *taller* than anyone *else* in her class.
   Ann is *taller* than any *other* girl in her class.
   Ann is the *tallest* of *all* the girls in her class.
   Ann is the *tallest* girl in her class.
   Error: Ann is taller than anyone in her class.

EXERCISES

COMPARISON OF ADJECTIVES AND ADVERBS

A. In each of the following sentences, select the word in parentheses that makes the sentence correct:

1. Louise is the (more, most) beautiful of the three girls.
2. Henry is the (tallest, most tallest) boy in the class.
3. This book is the (less, least) interesting one of all.
4. My teacher is (more stricter, stricter) than yours.
5. My composition was the (bestest, best) in the class.
6. Of my two brothers, I like George (better, best).
7. Do you feel (weller, better) today?
8. We walked (more far, farther) today than yesterday.
9. My father caught the (mostest, most) fish.
10. This candy is (sweeter, more sweeter) than that.
11. Of the three, I like Jim (best, better).
12. Is Frank (more younger, younger) than Sam?
13. This is the (worst, worse) mark I have ever had.
14. Jack is the (least, less) ambitious of my four brothers.
15. Joan is the (most smartest, smartest) girl I know.
16. This is the (bestest, best) comedy I have seen for a long while.
17. Our house is the (most largest, largest) in the neighborhood.
18. Ed is a (more better, better) player than Bill.
19. I know she is the (less, least) studious in the class.
20. Ruth is the (oldest, older) of the three girls.

B. Some of the following sentences are correct, others incorrect. Rewrite those which are incorrect.

1. This is the most sweetest candy of all.
2. She is the more older of the two.
3. This is the worstest suit in the store.
4. Helen is the younger of the three girls.
5. The city is three miles farther.
6. This is the greenest grass I have ever seen.
7. Myrna is the smartest of the twins.
8. The ambitionest girl in the class is Louise.
9. Joan is the beautifuller of the two.
10. Martin is shorter than any boy in his class.
11. She is the most contented person I have ever known.
12. Alice is much taller now than a year ago.
13. Our school has the bestest football team in the state.
14. This is the sharper of all the knives.

136

15. Phil is the more better hitter on the team.
16. All the money was left to the eldest son.
17. Mother feels gooder than yesterday.
18. Since that day we quarreled, she has been more angrier than ever.
19. Her hair seems more redder when she becomes angry.
20. Do you feel weller today?

C. In each of the following sentences, write the correct form of the adjective or adverb. Some are correct as they are.

1. Our class has the bestest attendance record in the school.
2. George is the handsomest boy in the school.
3. Rose is the beautifuller of the two.
4. This is the most sweetest cake in the store.
5. Our house is about two miles farther.
6. She is the more taller of the two girls.
7. This one is the bigger of all the apples.
8. Marian is the more better tennis player on the club.
9. He is a better runner than any man on the team.
10. This is the worstest game I ever saw.
11. Today was the warmest day of the year.
12. We did lesser work yesterday.
13. Sam is the most brightest boy in the class.
14. Don't you think Joe hit betterer last season?
15. Fred has grown much taller since you last saw him.
16. Louise is the smartest of the twins.
17. He felt much weller after resting for a while.
18. She is more younger than he.
19. He is the most reliable boy in the class.
20. Frank is the taller of the three boys.

D. Write the comparative and superlative of each of the following:

1. tall	9. light	17. many	25. cold
2. sure	10. warm	18. wise	26. well
3. early	11. happy	19. lonely	27. sleepy
4. good	12. pretty	20. careful	28. clean
5. bad	13. friendly	21. sweet	29. recent
6. young	14. easy	22. great	30. sad
7. quickly	15. old	23. some	
8. smart	16. useful	24. lovely	

E. According to the meaning, write the correct degree of the adverb or adjective given before each pair of sentences.

1. *pretty* This picture is _____ than any other one in the exhibit. Indeed, it is the _____ of the group.

2. *quickly* Paul, hide _____! You must hide _____ than any other player if you want to win.

3. *well* John plays the game very _____. I believe he plays _____ than any other boy on the team.

4. *bright* The sun is _____ today than it was yesterday. I think it is the _____ I have ever seen it at this time of year.

5. *friendly* You should try to be more _____. Your sister is the _____ girl in the class.

137

ADJECTIVES AND ADVERBS SOMETIMES CONFUSED

---

1. Use adjectives after these verbs because they are used to qualify the subject: *be, look, taste, smell, feel, sound, appear, seem, grow, become.*

> This candy tastes *sweet* (not *sweetly*).
> I feel *bad* (not *badly*).

2. Use adverbs to describe action and qualify the verb. Adverbs answer the questions: how? in what manner?

> Ride your bike *carefully* (not *careful*).
> She walks *awkwardly* (not *awkward*).

3. Do not misuse the words *good* and *well.*

   a. *Good* is an adjective which follows the copulative verbs in 1 above.

   > The dinner looks *good* (not *well*).
   > This fur feels *good* (not *well*).

   b. *Well* is an adverb and describes action. It answers the questions: how? in what manner?

   > She skates very *well* (not *good*).
   > He plays tennis *well* (not *good*).

4. *Real, sure, most,* and *near* are adjectives which are commonly misused as adverbs.

   > I was *really* (not *real*) angry with Tom.
   > You were *surely* (not *sure*) early today.
   > He scored a basket *almost* (not *most*) every time he tried.
   > When the light turned green, I *nearly* (not *near*) missed the bus.

EXERCISES

ADJECTIVES AND ADVERBS CONFUSED

A. Select the word in parentheses that makes the sentence correct.

1. She spoke very (good, well).
2. The food looks (delicious, deliciously).
3. Did you notice how (beautiful, beautifully) the sky looked?
4. My, how (sourly, sour) this tastes!
5. The piano does not play (good, well).
6. How (strange, strangely) the noise sounded!
7. Accidents happen when people drive (carelessly, careless).
8. He has always done his work (well, good).
9. I take the bus (most, almost) every morning.
10. He (sure, surely) was glad to see me.
11. Mother handles the baby (carefully, careful).
12. I felt (bad, badly) when Mother scolded me.
13. Lemonade tastes very (sour, sourly).
14. New cars ride (smoothly, smooth).
15. The flowers smelled (sweetly, sweet).
16. Florence listened (attentively, attentive) to the music.
17. The sun made us feel (warm, warmly).
18. Don't you think fish smells (badly, bad)?
19. Arithmic problems must be done (accurately, accurate).
20. Jack does not swim as (good, well) as Fred.

B. Select the word in parentheses that makes the sentence correct.

1. Don't you think she speaks (well, good)?
2. The house looks (beautifully, beautiful).
3. I can't hear so (well, good) from here.
4. She feels (badly, bad) when you shout at her.
5. The radio does not sound so (good, well).
6. The sun appears very (strongly, strong) today.
7. Please do this test (carefully, careful).
8. Because of the fog, we (near, nearly) had an accident.
9. I am (really, real) sorry to have disturbed you.
10. Always do your work (good, well).
11. How (smoothly, smooth) this silk feels!
12. Father reads his paper (hurried, hurriedly).
13. The children listened to the story very (attentive, attentively).
14. My finger hurts; I can't write (well, good).
15. When Dad went out, Mother appeared very (angrily, angry).
16. Bob plays the piano very (badly, bad).
17. Ann plays tennis very (well, good).
18. Because she lost my sweater, she felt very (bad, badly).

Tense means time. Tense of the verb refers to the time of the action or state of being, or condition which is expressed in the sentence.

Simple Tenses

1. The **present** tense indicates present time; some action or condition is now going on or is in progress.

    I *am writing* my composition. I *write* my composition.

2. The **past** tense indicates past time; something happened or is already over or done.

    I *wrote* my composition yesterday.

3. The **future** tense indicates future time; something is expected to come or happen.

    I *shall write* my composition tomorrow.

Perfect Tenses

1. The **present perfect** tense indicates that the action is complete at the present time.

    I *have written* my composition and am ready for dinner.

2. The **past perfect** tense indicates a past action completed before some other past action.

    I *had written* my composition before Frank arrived.

3. The **future perfect** tense indicates an action that will be completed in the future before some other action in the future.

    I *shall have written* my composition before Frank will arrive.

Note: All the perfect tenses are formed by these two elements: an auxiliary verb and the past participle of the main verb.

Principal Parts of Verbs

1. The principal parts of verbs are the *present tense,* the *past tense,* and the *past participle.* These parts, together with auxiliary or helping verbs (*be, have, do, shall, will,* etc.), form all the tenses.

2. *a.* Verbs which form the past tense and past participle by adding *d* or *ed* to the present tense are **regular** verbs.

	REGULAR VERB	EXAMPLE
Present tense	laugh	I *laugh* at mistakes.
Past tense	laughed	I *laughed* too soon.
Past participle	laughed	I should not have *laughed.*

b. Verbs which form the past tense and past participle by irregular changes in vowel are **irregular** verbs.

	IRREGULAR VERB	EXAMPLE
Present tense	drink	We *drink* milk regularly.
Past tense	drank	We *drank* milk for lunch.
Past participle	drunk	We have *drunk* the milk.

Note: The past participle is the only principal part that requires an auxiliary or helping verb.

3. The irregular verbs cause trouble because of confusion between the past tense and past participle.

They have *done* (not have *did*) their best work.

After he had *blown* (not had *blew*) the whistle, the score was tied.

I shall have *spoken* (not shall have *spoke*) to John before Father returns home.

Principal Parts of 100 Troublesome Verbs

PRESENT TENSE	PAST TENSE	PAST PARTICIPLE
am	was	been
arise	arose	arisen
attack	attacked	attacked
awake	awoke	awaked
bear	bore	borne, or born
beat	beat	beaten
become	became	become
begin	began	begun
bend	bent	bent
bite	bit	bitten
bleed	bled	bled
blow	blew	blown
break	broke	broken
bring	brought	brought
burn	burned, or burnt	burned, or burnt
burst	burst	burst
catch	caught	caught
choose	chose	chosen
climb	climbed	climbed
come	came	come
creep	crept	crept
dig	dug	dug
dive	dived	dived
do	did	done
drag	dragged	dragged
draw	drew	drawn
dream	dreamed, or dreamt	dreamed, or dreamt
drink	drank	drunk
drive	drove	driven
drown	drowned	drowned
eat	ate	eaten
fall	fell	fallen
fight	fought	fought
flow	flowed	flowed
fly	flew	flown
forget	forgot	forgotten
forgive	forgave	forgiven

PRESENT TENSE	PAST TENSE	PAST PARTICIPLE
freeze	froze	frozen
get	got	got, or gotten
give	gave	given
go	went	gone
grow	grew	grown
hang (suspend a thing)	hung	hung
hang (execute a person)	hanged	hanged
hear	heard	heard
heat	heated	heated
hide	hid	hidden
hold	held	held
hurt	hurt	hurt
kneel	knelt	knelt
know	knew	known
lay (to put)	laid	laid
lead	led	led
lend	lent	lent
lie (to rest)	lay	lain
lie (to tell a lie)	lied	lied
light	lighted, or lit	lighted, or lit
lose	lost	lost
mean	meant	meant
mistake	mistook	mistaken
pay	paid	paid
prove	proved	proved, or proven
read	read	read
rid	rid	rid
ride	rode	ridden
ring	rang	rung
rise	rose	risen
run	ran	run
say	said	said
see	saw	seen
set	set	set
sew	sewed	sewed, or sewn
shake	shook	shaken
shine	shone	shone
show	showed	showed, or shown
shrink	shrank	shrunk

PRESENT TENSE	PAST TENSE	PAST PARTICIPLE
sing	sang	sung
sink	sank	sunk
sit	sat	sat
slay	slew	slain
slide	slid	slid
speak	spoke	spoken
spend	spent	spent
spit	spit, or spat	spit, or spat
spring	sprang	sprung
steal	stole	stolen
strike	struck	struck
swear	swore	sworn
sweep	swept	swept
swim	swam	swum
take	took	taken
teach	taught	taught
tear	tore	torn
throw	threw	thrown
wake	waked, or woke	waked, or woken
wear	wore	worn
weep	wept	wept
wind	wound	wound
wring	wrung	wrung
write	wrote	written

EXERCISES

TENSES OF VERBS

A. Select the word in parentheses that makes the sentence correct:

1. Larry has (drank, drunk) his glass of milk.
2. She has always (did, done) her best.
3. Please (sit, set) down.

4. Will you please (lay, lie) your book on the table?
5. Yesterday Dad (came, come) home early.
6. She has (went, gone) to the store for bread.
7. Someone has (lay, laid) the package on the floor.
8. The plate had (fallen, fell) to the ground.
9. Fred has (took, taken) two lessons already.
10. Have you (wrote, written) your letter yet?
11. Will you please (lie, lay) down for a while?
12. Have you (ate, eaten) lunch?
13. I have (did, done) my lessons.
14. The page was (torn, tore) out of the book.
15. I watched him as he (laid, lay) down for a nap.
16. Has John (went, gone) to work today?
17. I think Fred (did, done) it, Dad.
18. I noticed that she (lay, laid) the hat on the shelf.
19. Have you (forgotten, forget) to call Aunt Mary?
20. I was all (wore, worn) out after the day's work.

B. Select the word in parentheses that correctly completes each sentence:
1. The ship (sunk, sank) very rapidly.
2. My dog has never (bit, bitten) anyone.
3. I had (lain, laid) awake all night.
4. I (saw, seen) the car speeding down the road.
5. The men had (ridden, rode) over the same course.
6. He has (became, become) a skilled worker.
7. I am sure he (did, done) it.
8. The pen has (fallen, fell) into the water.
9. The boys (sung, sang) all the old songs.
10. I wanted to see if the sun had (rose, risen).
11. Mary has (drank, drunk) two glasses of water.
12. Was your picture (taken, took)?
13. Richard and Jerry have (went, gone) to the game.
14. Where did you (lay, lie) the book?
15. The girls (swum, swam) in the cold water.
16. Who (rung, rang) the bell?
17. We would not have been (beat, beaten) if George had been playing.
18. Tom said that he did not (chose, choose) to run again for the captaincy.
19. Has he (ate, eaten) all his lunch?
20. The old man (came, come) for the package.

C. Write the proper form of the verb in parentheses:
1. Have you (do) your lessons?
2. I thought he had (lay) the box here.
3. As soon as Father came home he (sit) down to eat.
4. Harold has just (go) home.
5. At an early age, he was (teach) French.
6. Have you ever (swim) to the other side of the lake?
7. The milk was (freeze) this morning.
8. Margaret has (take) her piano lesson.
9. Frances (drink) her tea and left.

145

10. They (sing) songs and then danced for a while.
11. Have you (eat) lunch yet?
12. My pencil (break) just as I started to write.
13. The ball was (throw) by the pitcher.
14. In the excitement, I (forget) my hat.
15. My eraser is all (wear) out already.
16. Have you (see) his new car?
17. She (lie) down and slept for an hour.
18. My, how tall she has (grow).
19. Have you (speak) to Mother about this?
20. He (ride) his new bicycle this morning.

D. Complete each of the following sentences by writing the proper form of the verb in parentheses:

1. I (see) a good picture last night.
2. The lady has (sing) several songs for us.
3. He has (begin) his work at the store.
4. The vase was (break) when it fell to the floor.
5. After he had (eat) his dinner, he went on his way.
6. Yesterday I (run) all the way to the post office.
7. Mary (swim) across the lake last summer.
8. Have you (forget) the pleasant times we had?
9. The pupils' faces (shine) with joy yesterday at the game.
10. He (do) his work well last term.
11. The boys have (eat) their lunch.
12. He has (know) me for a long time.
13. She (see) a beautiful sunset Saturday.
14. Jane was (teach) many pretty dances by her instructor.
15. The girl (lay) the book on the table when she left the room.
16. The doctor has (say) that I may go home tomorrow.
17. Yesterday she was (bite) by a dog.
18. Are you sure Bill has (go) home?
19. How tall Larry has (grow)!
20. He said he (lay) the book on the desk and left.

E. Complete each of the following sentences by writing the proper form of the verb in parentheses:

1. He always (speak) to me when we meet.
2. She (study) her lesson last night.
3. The boy (fall), if he is not careful.
4. Neither Gladys nor Jane (go) home.
5. Our cat was nearly (drown) yesterday.
6. I (do) all my work before the bell rang.
7. Mary (drink) two glasses of milk.
8. The dish has (break) into many pieces.
9. After I (run) three blocks, I lost sight of the man.
10. If you (come) sooner, I would have helped you.
11. The wind has (blow) hard today.
12. The pupils (bring) their skates to school yesterday.
13. Why have you (take) your books home?
14. He (lie) sleeping while we took the pictures.

15. The sailors (begin) to swim ashore as the boat sank.
16. We have all (eat) too quickly.
17. Mother came in just after I (set) the table.
18. I (see) him in the hall an hour ago.
19. She (bring) her books to school every day next week.
20. She (get) a better mark than I next time.

F. In each of the following sentences, change the verb from the present to the past:

1. We eat our lunch in the cafeteria.
2. With a shout of joy John throws down his baseball bat.
3. Mary drinks a quart of milk every day.
4. I see no possible solution to the problem.
5. Eagerly Harold goes to the door.
6. Jim climbs to the very peak of the hill.
7. The lion drags his prey into the cave.
8. In the spring the river rises rapidly to flood level.
9. The children run swiftly down the street.
10. The cat lies on the rug in the sunshine.

G. Cross out each verb that is incorrectly used and write the correct word that fits the meaning in each sentence:

1. Tim had did his work and had went away before I seen him.
2. Ain't it true that you was there before she set down?
3. Has Jack and Don came to learn us how to make that boat?
4. We had not drove far before we knowed that we had took the wrong road.
5. As the car striked a telephone pole, four people were hurted and tooken to the hospital.

H. Select the correct form of the verb in parentheses to complete the meaning of each of the following sentences:

1. We got up early, but John must have (rose, risen) at dawn.
2. She was tired from work, yet she could have (written, wrote) a short letter home to her parents.
3. Andrew looked bruised from fighting, but you should have (seen, saw) the other boy.
4. I wouldn't believe him even if he had (swore, sworn) on the Bible.
5. No nail could have (torn, tore) such a hole in your pants, son.
6. The noise at your party would have (waked, woke) the dead.
7. He was in a hurry and must have (mistook, mistaken) the door.
8. The cat might have (hid, hidden) the kittens under the porch.
9. The Pony Express riders must have (rode, ridden) dangerous trails.
10. How could they have (knew, known) the way over mountains?
11. A more expensive garment could not have (shrunk, shrank) in the laundry.
12. A slight opening in the surface of the earth has sometimes (shook, shaken) down many buildings.
13. You owe most to your family for having (given, gave) you encouragement and support.
14. The force of the collision alone could not have (sunk, sank) the vessel.
15. We arrived at the stadium just after the last half of the game had (began, begun).

AGREEMENT OF VERB WITH SUBJECT

1. A verb must agree with its subject in person and number.

   > There *were* (not *was*) two *pots* on the stove.
   >   (subject is *pots;* not *there,* which is an introductory adverb)
   > A *box* of oranges *was* (not *were*) sent from Florida.
   >   (subject is *box;* not *oranges,* which is the object of the preposition *of*)

2. Remember that *doesn't* is the contraction for *does not; don't* is the contraction for *do not.*

   > Frank *doesn't* (not *don't*) swim well.
   > Why *don't* (not *doesn't*) they come?

3. Always use *were* with the subject *you* (whether singular or plural).

   > *Were* (not *Was*) *you* late today?
   > All of *you were* (not *was*) marked present.

4. A compound subject joined by *and* requires a plural verb.

   > *John and Mary are* (not *is*) at home.

5. If two or more singular subjects are joined by *or* or *nor,* use a singular verb.

   > Either *Tom or Henry is* (not *are*) at fault.
   > Neither *Larry nor James has* (not *have*) written to me.

6. If two subjects are not in the same person or number, the verb should agree with the subject nearer to it.

   > Neither the *girls* nor *Fred is* (not *are*) at home.
   > Neither *Fred* nor the *girls are* (not *is*) at home.

7. The following indefinite pronouns are singular: *each, every, either, neither, one, everyone, anyone, nobody, each one, no one, someone, everybody, somebody, anybody.* They require singular verbs.

   > *Neither* of the boys *was* (not *were*) whistling.
   > *Every* man, woman, and child *is* (not *are*) welcome.

EXERCISES

AGREEMENT OF SUBJECT WITH VERB

A. Select the word in parentheses that makes the sentence correct.

1. There (were, was) a man and a lady in the store.
2. Each of the boys (look, looks) alike.
3. She (don't, doesn't) look very well today.
4. Everybody (was, were) asked to remain quiet.
5. Either Joyce or Ellen (was, were) here.
6. (Wasn't, Weren't) you absent yesterday?
7. (Do, Does) any of you boys live near the school?
8. A boy and a girl (were, was) here to see you.
9. It (doesn't, don't) seem so cold today.
10. Neither of the men (is, are) here yet.
11. That kind of apple (is, are) delicious.
12. (Is, Are) each of the boys ready to leave?
13. One of the girls (is, are) out of tune.
14. Neither he nor I (talks, talk) Spanish.
15. Each of us (play, plays) the violin.
16. Either George or Bob (are, is) wrong.
17. A corsage of flowers (were, was) sent to Ruth.
18. Either you or she (is, are) to be called upon.
19. One of the glasses (is, are) broken.
20. Everyone in the class (try, tries) hard to pass.

B. Select the word in parentheses that makes the sentence correct.

1. Neither Louise nor the boys (were, was) on time.
2. The box of apples (is, are) on the porch.
3. A pound of cookies (cost, costs) fifty cents.
4. Neither Jane nor Alice (swims, swim) well.
5. The package of books (is, are) in the office.
6. Nobody in the class (have, has) the answer.

7. The boxes of candy (was, were) placed on the table.
8. There (was, were) a dog and a cat in the chair.
9. He (don't, doesn't) speak very well.
10. Each of the girls (observe, observes) all the restrictions.
11. Everybody (was, were) asked to remain seated.
12. Civics (is, are) easy for Jane.
13. (Are, Is) each of the pies the same size?
14. (Doesn't, Don't) either of you girls want this?
15. Some members of the faculty (are, is) present.
16. Interesting news (is, are) what sells our paper.
17. There (is, are) a dog, a cat, and a bird in the garage.
18. A box of cigars (was, were) found on the porch.
19. A magazine and a book (was, were) lying on the floor.
20. Neither of you (seem, seems) to be paying attention.

5 AGREEMENT OF PRONOUN WITH ITS ANTECEDENT

1. A pronoun should agree in number, gender, and person with its antecedent. The antecedent of a pronoun is the word for which the pronoun stands.

   The *boy* lost *his* sweater.
   (*boy* is the antecedent of *his*)

   The *girls* did *their* best.
   (*girls* is the antecedent of *their*)

2. The following indefinite pronouns are singular and the personal pronouns that refer to them should be singular in number: *every, everybody, everyone, anyone, someone, each, nobody, either, neither, one, no one, a person, many a.*

   Everybody brought *his* lunch.
   Each of the girls wants *her* way.

   Note: Errors may be avoided by using a plural subject with a plural pronoun referring to it.

   All students must bring *their* books to class.
   All of the girls went *their* way.

AGREEMENT OF PRONOUN WITH ITS ANTECEDENT

A. Select the correct pronoun to complete the meaning of each sentence below:

1. If anyone cares to leave, (he, they) may do so now.
2. One of the boys forgot (his, their) book.
3. All the workmen brought (his, their) lunch.
4. Neither of them volunteered (his, their) services.
5. All the boys did (his, their) best work today.
6. Will everyone please serve (themselves, himself)?
7. Each of the women did (their, her) best.
8. Every pupil must do (their, his) own work.
9. Has everyone done (their, his) lesson?
10. Someone forgot to take (his, their) sweater.
11. Every student must bring (their, his) books.
12. Has either boy brought (his, their) skates?
13. One of the girls lost (their, her) books.
14. Helen and Jane did (her, their) best.
15. Each of the men did (his, their) duty.
16. Many a person has to earn (his, their) own living while in college.
17. Will everyone please open (their, his) own book?
18. Both Marie and Joan dressed (her, their) best today.
19. Each of the boys shines (their, his) shoes.
20. All the girls sewed (her, their) own clothes.

B. Select the correct pronoun to complete the meaning of each sentence below:

1. I expect everyone to pay (their, his) dues within a week.
2. Whichever of you has (his, their) money, may settle this now.
3. Each of the members will receive (their, his) card at once.
4. None of the unpaid members may request (his, their) privileges.
5. A person may conceal (their, his) true feelings, but not for long.
6. Many a lonely boy wishes (they, he) could find a good friend.
7. Every tribe has (its, their) own local customs and manners.
8. Some natives hide behind a tree when (they, we) eat a banana.
9. You must learn to respect the traditions of (others, another).
10. They should be careful not to hurt (theirselves, themselves).
11. Visitors entering a house remove (their, theirs) sandals.
12. When everybody minds (his, their) own business, no one gets hurt.
13. Neither of the boys admitted (their, his) share in the blame.
14. Let's measure (ourself, ourselves) by the Golden Rule.
15. Some girls dress (themselves, theirselves) up to look older than they are.

6 CASE OF PRONOUNS

All pronouns are divided into three cases according to their use in a sentence: nominative, objective, possessive.

	PERSON	NOMINATIVE	OBJECTIVE	POSSESSIVE
SINGULAR	First	I	me	my, mine
	Second	you	you	your, yours
	Third	he, she, it	him, her, it	his, her, hers, its
PLURAL	First	we	us	our, ours
	Second	you	you	your, yours
	Third	they	them	their, theirs

Note: Avoid the mistake of inserting an unnecessary apostrophe! Possessive pronouns are correctly spelled thus: yours, hers, its, ours, theirs.

Possessive Pronouns

RIGHT | WRONG

YOURS
HERS
ITS
OURS
THEIRS

YOUR'S
HER'S
IT'S
OUR'S
THEIR'S

Uses of the Nominative Case

1. Subject of a verb

John and *I* (not *me*) are friends.
  (compound subject)
Louise is more beautiful than *she* (not *her*).
  (. . . than she *is beautiful* is understood)

2. Predicate nominative (a pronoun occurring after any form of the verb *to be*)

It was *he* (not *him*) who called you.

3. Appositive (if the word with which the pronoun is in apposition is in the nominative case)

May *we* (not *us*) girls be excused now?
  (*we* is in apposition with *girls*)

Uses of the Objective Case

1. Direct object

Father scolded Iris and *me* (not *I*).
  (compound object after *scolded*)

2. Indirect object

I gave *him* his money back.
  [preposition (*to*) before *him* is understood]

3. Object of a preposition

We sent gifts to Sam and *her* (not *she*).
  (*Sam* and *her* is a compound object of the preposition *to*)

4. Appositive (if the word with which the pronoun is in apposition is in the objective case)

He invited both Mary and *me* (not *I*) to the party.
  (*me* is in apposition with *both*)

Uses of the Possessive Case

1. Before a gerund (a verbal noun ending in *ing*)

I do not approve of *his* (not *him*) crossing the street alone.

2. To show ownership

My friend gave *his* brother *our* tickets to the game.

Who and Whom

1. Use **who** as the subject.

    Who (not *Whom*) is your teacher? (subject of verb *is*)

2. Use **whom** as the object of a verb or object of a preposition.

    Whom (not *Who*) did you call? (object of verb *did call*)
    To *whom* (not *who*) did you write? (object of preposition *to*)

EXERCISES

CASE OF PRONOUNS

A. Select the word in parentheses that correctly completes each sentence.

1. Helen and (she, her) are friends.
2. Dad asked (we, us) boys to help him.
3. Mother took Joan and (me, I) to the theater.
4. Ann swims as well as (he, him).
5. This is to be divided between you and (he, him).
6. (Who, Whom) are you calling?
7. It is (her, she) who called.
8. (Us, We) boys are going to the game together.
9. Al is taller than (me, I).
10. It was (me, I) who wrote Aunt Mary.
11. Miss Young asked Joseph and (he, him) to carry the packages.
12. Who is (her, she)?
13. Frank went with Sam, Bernard and (I, me).

14. From (who, whom) did you receive this gift?
15. Lunch was left for you and (me, I).
16. Between you and (me, I), Louis is right.
17. Do you think (us, we) girls will beat the boys?
18. Many opportunities exist for you and (I, me).
19. It is (me, I) who called.
20. You must pay (him, he) what you owe.

B. Select the word in parentheses that correctly completes each sentence.
1. There is no prettier girl in the class than (she, her).
2. I gave it to you and (her, she).
3. May Frank and (I, me) go with you?
4. (We, Us) boys went to the game together.
5. Dad took Mary and (me, I) to the movies.
6. I am not so tall as (she, her).
7. I asked (her, she) to go with me.
8. When will (we, us) girls meet tonight?
9. We sent (they, them) a surprise package.
10. They invited Jack and (I, me) to the party.
11. The two girls, Joan and (her, she), went for a walk.
12. Either Ted or (me, I) will go with you.
13. Between you and (I, me), Fred is wrong.
14. (Who, Whom) do you think will win today's game?
15. In the cafeteria this morning sat Joseph and (I, me).
16. Neither Bob nor (she, her) is at home.
17. Does your mother approve of (your, you) staying out so late?
18. It was (we, us) who visited Aunt Ruth.
19. Louise is not so old as (me, I).
20. You and (me, I) should do this more often.

C. Select the word in parentheses that correctly completes each sentence.
1. In front of the house sat Sam and (he, him).
2. Francis is shorter than (he, him).
3. (Us, We) two boys are very close friends.
4. It was (they, them) who called.
5. Divide it between Jane and (him, he).
6. (Whom, Who) shall we invite?
7. May Mary and (me, I) go with him?
8. I don't know what I would do if I were (him, he).
9. Father criticized (me, my) doing my homework while playing the radio.
10. If I were (she, her), I would be ashamed.
11. Jerry and (him, he) are always together.
12. Between you and (I, me), I do not agree with Frank.
13. The teacher called upon two girls, Joan and (I, me).
14. The salesman sold (they, them) the car as advertised.
15. Did you want (her, she) to go with you?
16. They met Peter and (I, me) at the door.
17. Dad does not approve of (you, your) working so late.
18. (Whom, Who) are you writing to, Alice?
19. I am as good a player as (she, her).
20. To (we, us) pupils it was wonderful news.

7 DOUBLE NEGATIVES

Words like those below express a negative idea by themselves and do not require the use of *no* or *not* (or *n't*) with the predicate verb of the sentence. Avoid using double negatives!

Negative Words

never	no one	hardly
only	nothing	scarcely
none	neither	barely
nobody	nowhere	but (meaning *only*)

I don*'t* like *any* (not *none*) of these hats.
or I like none of these hats.

I could *not* go *anywhere* (not *nowhere*).
or I could go nowhere.

We did*n't* see *anybody* (not *nobody*).
or We saw nobody.

You *can* (not *can't*) *hardly* tell them apart.

We *were* (not *weren't*) *scarcely* able to hear.

EXERCISES

DOUBLE NEGATIVES

A. Select the word in parentheses that correctly completes each sentence.
1. I couldn't see (nothing, anything).
2. You (can, can't) scarcely tell the twins apart.
3. I hardly had time to do (no, any) homework.

4. The tear (was, wasn't) hardly noticeable.
5. Of all the dresses I saw, I did not like (none, any).
6. I was so cold I (could, couldn't) scarcely move.
7. Rose (could, couldn't) hardly talk.
8. He didn't hear (anything, nothing).
9. Didn't you see (none, any) of the boys?
10. Bob could not find his coat (anywhere, nowhere).
11. I (can't, can) hardly walk a block with this heavy package.
12. I couldn't find (any, no) pencils anywhere.
13. She (wasn't, was) not able to call me yesterday.
14. No, I did not see (any, none).
15. Don't you need (no, any) help?
16. Haven't you (any, none) left?
17. I couldn't see the girls (nowhere, anywhere).
18. I (wasn't, was) barely able to walk.
19. Mother did not leave (none, any) for us.
20. Didn't you hear (nothing, anything) then?

B. Some of the following sentences are incorrect and some are correct. Rewrite only those sentences that are incorrect.

1. I haven't nothing to read.
2. She didn't go nowhere today.
3. I don't have no money.
4. Laura hasn't written neither Barbara nor me.
5. Are you positive that you haven't forgotten something?
6. She couldn't hardly hear me.
7. I was not allowed to go nowhere.
8. I haven't no appetite today.
9. There was no time left to do the last question.
10. I've never seen no circus.
11. She hasn't nobody to play with.
12. Leonard hadn't never been to New York before.
13. She said she won't go nowhere this summer.
14. It wasn't hardly light when we left.
15. She hadn't never seen that man before.
16. Is he certain that he has not lost anything?
17. There isn't no homework to do.
18. Don't you like none of these?
19. I didn't see no one in the library.
20. We were so terrified we couldn't scarcely talk.

C. Copy the following sentences, making all necessary corrections. A few sentences are correct as they stand.

1. He doesn't have no paper.
2. I haven't nothing to sell.
3. They haven't nobody to play with.
4. I hadn't never seen him before.
5. I did not see him nowhere.
6. John didn't eat neither vegetable.
7. Are you sure you haven't lost anything?
8. I've never seen no rodeo.
9. I don't have no books to read.

10. Neil hadn't never heard of the book.
11. Mother couldn't hardly hear me.
12. I haven't no time for such things.
13. I have never seen any submarines.
14. There wasn't no opportunity to study.
15. I am sure I have not dropped nothing on the way.
16. He isn't hardly able to swim to shore.
17. I didn't find nobody at home.
18. I haven't any appetite, Mother.
19. I am sure he won't go nowhere.
20. She didn't like none of these.

8 FAULTY DICTION

By "faulty diction" is meant the wrong use of words. You must use words according to their recognized meaning. Since popular usage at times confuses one word with another, it is your task to learn and use the correct words to express your ideas.

1. **ain't** is not acceptable! Say *am not, isn't, aren't,* etc.

2. **all ready** means *everything is set,* or *everbody is prepared.*
   Are you *all ready?*

   already means *previously.*
   We have *already* studied these pages.

3. **all right** means *entirely correct,* or *perfectly well.*
   It is *all right* (not *alright*) for you to leave now.

   alright—this is not recorded in any standard dictionary and is to be avoided.

4. **almost** is an adverb meaning *nearly.*
   He *almost* (not *most*) drowned in the pool.
   Almost (not *Most*) everybody wore a flower.

   most is an adjective, the superlative of *some* (some, more, most).
   Most boys wore jackets today.

5. **among** is used to refer to more than two persons or things.
   The money was divided evenly *among* the five children.

   between is used to refer to only two persons or things.
   They kept it a secret *between* brother and sister.

158

6. **amount** refers to quantity in bulk.
   Cuba ships us a large *amount* of sugar.

   number refers to countable units (persons or things).
   Prizes were awarded to a *number* of graduates.

7. **anywheres**—no such word! Drop the *s*.

8. **as** is a conjunction, meaning *in a way that; as* introduces a clause.
   Please do *as* (not *like*) I say.

   like is a preposition, meaning *in the same manner,* or *similar to; like* introduces a phrase.
   He looks *like* a sailor.

9. **awfully** is not acceptable in the sense of *very*.
   That puppy looks *very* (not *awfully*) cute.

10. **beside** means *next to,* or *close to.*
    He stood *beside* the bed.

    besides means *in addition to.*
    Two players, *besides* the captain, received major letters in sports.

11. **bring** means carry *towards* the speaker.
    Please *bring* me a glass of water.

    take means carry *away from* the speaker.
    Please *take* my coat upstairs.

12. **can** expresses *ability*.
    Can you build a canoe?

    may expresses *permission*.
    May I go out now that the rain has stopped?

13. **different than** is not acceptable; say *different from.*

14. **fewer** refers to *number*.
    I have *fewer* friends than I used to have.

    less refers to *amount*.
    Less money was contributed than we needed.

15. **it's** is the contraction for *it is*.
    I think *it's* raining.

    its is a pronoun.
    The bird broke *its* wing and couldn't fly.

16. **learn** means *to gain knowledge or skill*.
    I would like to *learn* how to play chess.

    teach means *to give instruction*.
    I will *teach* you how to play the guitar.

17. **leave** means *to go away*.
    When will the bus *leave?*

    let means *to allow*.
    Let us take a walk to the beach.

18. **lots of** should not be used to mean *much, many, a good deal of,* etc.
    He still has *many* (not *lots of*) friends and *a good deal of* (not *lots of*) money.

19. **nowheres**—not acceptable! Drop the *s!*
    All of a sudden a plane seemed to come out of *nowhere* (not *nowheres*).

20. **of** should not be used in place of *have,* or the contraction *'ve*.
    You should *have* (not *of*) come home earlier.

21. **off, off of**—avoid using them in place of *from*.
    I borrowed a raincoat *from* (not *off* or *off of*) my brother.

22. **real** is an adjective.
    He is a *real* friend.

    really is an adverb.
    I am *really* (not *real*) glad to see you.

23. **somewheres**—drop the final *s!*
    Haven't I met you *somewhere* (not *somewheres*)?

24. **them** is a personal pronoun and should not be used to modify a noun; use *those*.

Don't talk to *those* (not *them*) girls.

25. **this kind** and **that kind** are correct singular forms; **these kinds** and **those kinds** are correct plural forms. Never say *these kind* or *those kind*. *Kind of* should not be followed by *a* or *an*.

CORRECT: I prefer *this kind* of book (or *this kind* of books).
CORRECT: *These kinds* of books are not to my liking.
WRONG: *These kind* of books are not to my liking.

26. **too** is an adverb; **to** a preposition; **two** an adjective.

The package is *too* (not *to* or *two*) heavy for him to carry.

27. **who** refers to persons.

The boy *who* (not *which*) was injured was rushed to the hospital.

which refers to things.

I lost the watch *which* my father gave me.

28. **who's** is the contraction for *who is*.

Who's (not *Whose*) going to the game with me?

whose is a pronoun.

Do you know *whose* (not *who's*) hat this is?

29. **you're** is the contraction for *you are*.

He thinks *you're* (not *your*) ready to leave.

your is a pronoun.

Where is *your* (not *you're*) other shoe?

30. Omit all unnecessary or useless words.

Do you think *this* (not *this here*) tie would be to Dad's taste?

We expect to see *that* (not *that there*) movie tonight.

Now I know what *kind of* (not *kind of a*) person you are.

Don't you think you *ought* (not *had ought*) to go home now?

None came *but* (not *but only*) Robert.

EXERCISES

FAULTY DICTION

A. Select the correct expression from the pair given in parentheses.

1. The reward (must have, must of) pleased them very much.
2. Why do you want to borrow the book (from, off) her?
3. I tried to lift the chest but it was (to, two, too) heavy.
4. I can't find my cap (anywheres, anywhere).
5. Mother, (may, can) I go to the movies?
6. I should (of, have) gone earlier.
7. I borrowed the pen (off, off of, from) my friend.
8. My father (teached, taught) me to fish.
9. He was not permitted to go (anywhere, anywheres).
10. You should (of, have) been in the assembly yesterday.
11. (Can, May) I take the book home?
12. Jane prefers (this, these) kind of apples.
13. My brother is (to, too, two) young.
14. (May, Can) I borrow your knife?
15. (Let, Leave) Joseph go first.
16. Do you like (that, those) kind of book?
17. I wish I could (of, have) gone to the game.
18. (This, This here) hat is mine.
19. He took the book (off of, from) me.
20. We could (of, have) taken the first train.

B. Select the correct expression from the pair given in parentheses.

1. That fine fruit came (from, off of) our farm.
2. The dog wagged (its, it's) tail.
3. (This, These) kind of shirts is very popular.
4. Please (let, leave) the kitten go.
5. Did you borrow the skates (from, off, off of) your brother?
6. (Who's, Whose) at the door?
7. The horse lifted (its, it's) head and snorted.
8. Mother divided the cake (among, between) the four boys.
9. (This, These) kind of material is difficult to find.
10. Don't touch (them, those) cookies.
11. (Can, May) I leave this package with you?
12. Sam tried (awful, awfully, very) hard to succeed.
13. What (kind of, kind of a) hat do you want?
14. Why won't you (leave, let) me go?
15. There (isn't any, ain't no) use talking to him.
16. Let's keep this a secret (among, between) you and me.
17. Is his sweater (different from, different than) mine?
18. There are (fewer, less) boys absent today than yesterday.
19. We (ought to, had ought to) start going home before the storm.

20. There was (a good deal of, lots of) debris in the room after the fire.

C. Select the correct expression from the pair given in parentheses in each sentence below.

1. I don't believe this watch is any (different than, different from) mine.
2. I don't suppose you know what (kind of a, kind of) animal this is?
3. Mr. Frank (taught, learned) us science last year.
4. (Nowhere, Nowheres) could we find the lost puppy.
5. We shall have (fewer, less) seats in the room now.
6. (That there, That) man is our English teacher.
7. You (ought to, had ought to) do your homework now.
8. Did you find my wallet (somewheres, somewhere)?
9. We have (lots of, plenty of) time before curtain call.
10. There (isn't, ain't) a job that doesn't require work.
11. Come to the picnic and (bring, take) along your brother.
12. Is that (your, you're) jacket on the floor?
13. Do you know the student (who, which) was elected president?
14. The captain of our team is (awfully, very) handsome.
15. You have (lots of, plenty of) time to do your work.
16. Our boat is (nowheres, nowhere) in sight.
17. (This here, This) shop opened for business last week.
18. (Who's, Whose) car is that?
19. When June comes, (its, it's) time to make plans for the summer vacation.
20. What (kind of, kind of an) insect would you say this is?

D. Correct the errors in diction in the following sentences:

1. Will you please learn me how to drive?
2. Can I please leave the room for a minute?
3. Ask your father if he will leave you join us.
4. I borrowed a dollar off of my father.
5. She likes to dress a bit different than others.
6. We ought to share it evenly between the four of us.
7. Who went there beside you and Mary?
8. I have less friends than I used to have before our family moved.
9. Don't you think you had ought to go home now?
10. I prefer these kind of books.
11. She made the cookies just like her mother told her.
12. Most every home has a television set nowadays.
13. All of a sudden a plane seemed to come out of nowheres.
14. He still has lots of time before the game.
15. When I need cash, may I borrow some off you?
16. We have hunted high and low, but the dog is nowheres to be seen.
17. I wish someone with patience would learn me how to drive.
18. The five children shared the sum of money equally between them.
19. You may say what you like, but it ain't right to spread gossip.
20. I tell you I saw her sitting there right besides me on the bus.

E. Correct the errors in diction in the following sentences:

1. Why must you try to do it different than the way I told you?
2. Most every family has a car today.
3. As he practiced typewriting daily, he made less errors per page.
4. These kind of vitamin pills help you grow stronger.

5. You really hadn't ought to walk home alone after dark.
6. I couldn't find it anywheres in the house.
7. The little puppy looks awfully cute.
8. It's perfectly alright to visit us any time during Open House.
9. No one else can do it but only Sam.
10. Anywheres you go, you will find schools and churches.
11. She would take advice from no one but only Miss Brook.
12. The cheering seemed awfully weak during the last half.
13. Just go away and leave me do whatever I want.
14. I borrowed a raincoat off of my brother.
15. We've been to that place lots of times before tonight.
16. If you don't mind, can I take another cookie, please?
17. Didn't the cheerleader look real cute in her outfit?
18. What kind of a pupil wins most of the graduation prizes?
19. He hurt himself real bad with that piece of broken glass.
20. Haven't I met you somewheres?

EXERCISES

REVIEW OF USAGE

A. Write the word or expression in parentheses that makes the sentence correct.

1. Peter and James (is, are) doing very well.
2. It (don't, doesn't) make any difference.
3. May (we, us) boys play a little longer?
4. Have you (ate, eaten) your lunch?
5. For a long time the dog (laid, lay) beside his master.
6. Don't you think we could have (went, gone)?
7. Would you like to buy some of (them, those) apples?
8. She expects each boy to do (his, their) work well.
9. How long (was, were) you sick?
10. I wonder (who's, whose) going to be at the party tonight.
11. She brought neither paper (or, nor) pencil with her.
12. The (larger, largest) of the two should go.
13. That boy has just (come, came) here to live.
14. I borrowed a book (off, off of, from) my cousin.
15. (Leave, Let) us go home early.
16. He (did, done) the best he could.
17. Neither Henry (or, nor) William went to the game.
18. We (brung, brought) our lunch with us today.
19. We could have (went, gone) with the team.
20. Paul ran (good, well) enough to win the race.

B. Write the word or expression in parentheses that makes the sentence correct.

1. I should (of, have) walked to school this morning.
2. Jane is the (older, oldest) of the two sisters.
3. They do not use (this, these) kind of pencils.
4. Father has (laid, lain) down on the bed.
5. We did not expect to get (nothing, anything).
6. The dessert tasted (delicious, deliciously).
7. All at once I (throws, threw) the ball across the field.
8. The man has (swam, swum) a long distance.
9. Do you want some of (them, those) cookies?
10. The boy (eat, et, ate) his dinner an hour ago.
11. The teacher distributed the books (between, among) the four boys.
12. (Was, Were) you in the room when the bell rang?
13. Each boy had (his, their) chance at bat.
14. Sally and (I, me) walked home.
15. (Who, Whom) did you see there?
16. Mother divided the cake between Helen and (I, me).
17. The bear had (its, it's) paw caught in the trap.
18. The man (who, which) was here has gone.
19. Jennie slipped (off, off of) the step.
20. Do you like (that, those) kind of peanuts?

C. Write the word or expression in parentheses that makes the sentence correct.

1. Shall we expect you and (she, her) at the party?
2. Daddy gave (us, we) boys a basketball for Christmas.
3. I (have not, ain't) heard a word from my friend.
4. A pile of apples (are, is) in the box.
5. Neither Jane nor my sister (like, likes) skating.
6. (Was, Were) you alone during the blizzard?
7. He jumped very (quick, quickly) into the hole.
8. Mary was (learned, taught) by her classmates.
9. We can't shovel snow (no, any) longer.
10. I could have (went, gone) with the family.
11. May we see (you're, your) collection?
12. Please pack my dishes (careful, carefully).
13. We (seen, saw) him come out of the building.
14. (Leave, Let) us get there on time.
15. She never says (nothing, anything).
16. Does your knife cut (good, well)?
17. I think we should (lay, lie) down for a rest.
18. May I borrow a quarter (off, from) you?
19. Does (that, that there) machine work?
20. There (go, goes) our last hope of victory.

D. Write the word or expression in parentheses that makes the sentence correct.

1. We are glad (your, you're) early today.
2. The boy (did, done) his report during his lunch hour.
3. One of the girls (was, were) in the library.
4. Each of the boys has (his, their) own skates.
5. We (saw, seen) that play in our school.

6. Will you turn in the money to John or (I, me)?
7. He would like to be (laying, lying) on the beach right now.
8. The team played (good, well) in the practice game.
9. The robin returned to (it's, its) old nest.
10. (Who's, Whose) at the door?
11. The ice had (broke, broken) in the skating rink.
12. A person never knows when (he, they) will be asked to help.
13. Many of the films (is, are) helpful in history class.
14. We do not know (who, whom) to invite to the party.
15. You would (of, have) enjoyed the assembly.
16. (Who, Whom) will be chosen as teenager-of-the-month?
17. We were (almost, most) home before it stormed.
18. Bill and (me, I) are very good friends.
19. I like pears (better, more better) than apples.
20. When (is, are) Helen and Alice leaving?

E. Write the word or expression in parentheses that makes the sentence correct.

1. Did you (let, leave) the dog go?
2. She will not need (no, any) help.
3. We all (saw, seen) the accident.
4. Mary has learned to write (good, well).
5. It is (he, him) whom we called.
6. He rides on the train (most, almost) every day.
7. I could have (went, gone) with them.
8. Shall (we, us) girls put the books in order?
9. Father divided the marbles (between, among) Joe and me.
10. (Its, It's) time to go home.
11. I like (that, those) kind of candies best.
12. The aviator's account of his battles (was, were) interesting.
13. He failed, even though he (did, done) his best.
14. John's letter was (real, very) amusing.
15. The children must (of, have) been at school.
16. Jane (don't, doesn't) know what the trouble is.
17. Neither George nor James (has, have) come yet.
18. I (says, said) that I would go at once.
19. Take the picture (off of, off) the wall.
20. Each of the boys carries (his, their) lunch.

F. Write the word or expression in parentheses that makes the sentence correct.

1. He has (drank, drunk) a quart of milk.
2. Lois usually (sits, sets) near me.
3. We saw the cat (lying, laying) in the sun.
4. Everyone who came brought (his, their) skates.
5. The boxes of candy (is, are) all wrapped.
6. Marie went to school with Jane and (I, me).
7. (Was, Were) you at the last basketball game?
8. We couldn't do (nothing, anything) with him.
9. Do you like chocolate or vanilla (better, best)?
10. May we have (you're, your) help?
11. I knew that it was (he, him).

166

12. How (sweet, sweetly) she sings!
13. Of the two players, John is (best, better).
14. The dog hurt (its, it's) paw.
15. John is more careless than (I, me).
16. Each pupil should do (their, his) work well.
17. Has she (spoke, spoken) to you about it?
18. In that respect, James is very little different (than, from) Jack.
19. (Us, We) boys raced down the street.
20. (Who, Whom) is your friend?

G. Some of the following sentences contain errors. If a sentence contains an error, rewrite the incorrect expression. If a sentence is correct as it stands, write C.

1. Whom are you calling?
2. He divided the apples between his three brothers.
3. The teacher learned us fractions.
4. Did you call me this morning?
5. It was us who refused to go.
6. My cousin don't like olives.
7. Her brother plays basketball good.
8. Will you go with Margaret and I?
9. I prefer these kind of apples.
10. John is a better student than me.
11. Shall we girls get your lunch for you?
12. I can't remember whose coming.
13. Every boy worked hard at their problems.
14. That tree is the largest of the two.
15. This room is smaller than any in the house.
16. The box had fell from the shelf.
17. The teacher called Sue and me.
18. The lion protected it's young.
19. I do not know whom is coming tonight.
20. Jennie she came into the house to say "hello."

H. In each of the following sentences there is an error in grammar. Select the incorrect word and give the correct word to fit the meaning of the sentence.

1. Who learned you all those tricks?
2. The dog hurt it's foot.
3. Yesterday I done that problem correctly.
4. You certainly can sing as good as Mary.
5. There isn't no gold in that mine.
6. The chair had been broke before I sat in it.
7. I have always liked these kind of stories.
8. I think that we have sang that song before.
9. I am not sure that it was him.
10. It must of been too stormy for the flight.
11. Does he have any gifts for you and I?
12. Why do you play with them big boys?
13. Three kittens were laying in the sunshine.
14. Did you hear that us fellows are going on a canoe trip?

15. One of the boys has not give a report yet.
16. We could of had a good time.
17. I think it was him at the door.
18. Joe was to my house when you phoned.
19. Peter don't want any.
20. The prizes were divided between the eleven players.

I. In each of the following sentences there is an error in grammar. Select the incorrect word and give the correct word to fit the meaning of the sentence.

1. We should have went on an earlier bus.
2. It's so foggy that we can't drive nowhere.
3. I thought them clowns were very funny.
4. It was so cold that we couldn't hardly stand it.
5. I didn't make no errors in using modifiers.
6. Do you recognize adjectives easy?
7. There are less pupils in class today.
8. Most people like those kind of stories.
9. It is not easy for us to set here.
10. Your answer is different than mine.
11. It is a matter of importance to Henry and I.
12. I know the man which owns this car.
13. The package of books have arrived.
14. The candy was for John and I.
15. I seen a boy driving a car.
16. Have you ate your lunch?
17. The robin hurt it's wing.
18. One of the girls were on television.
19. Divide it between the three of you.
20. Every boy brought their lunch to school.

J. Some of the following sentences contain errors. If a sentence contains an error, rewrite the correct expression. If a sentence is correct as it stands, write C.

1. I don't think he could of done it.
2. Mary is taller than me.
3. My bag of books are on the desk.
4. I like these kind of orange.
5. The weather is to cold for swimming.
6. John don't go skating any more.
7. Of the two girls Mary is the healthiest.
8. You can't hardly hear our radio.
9. Bring this paper to the man across the street.
10. Dick played the piano well.
11. If I were him, I would be a pilot.
12. I received a better mark than any student in the class.
13. Henry is the taller of the twins.
14. The cat licked it's paw.
15. Every player must do their best.
16. Mary could of been the leader.
17. We couldn't do nothing for him.
18. I borrowed a dollar off of my sister.

168

19. Paul and I are starting now.
20. Mother goes to the store most every day.

K. In the following paragraph, the boy who told the story made *twenty* mistakes in the use of words. Find each incorrect word in the paragraph and write the correct word in its place.

When John and me pushed our boat off the beach, it wasn't hardly daylight. There was two native fishermen who told John and I that they would leave us help them lift the net and would learn us how to find good fishing grounds. Its exciting to go on these kind of trip. John don't row very good, but he has a good head. He sets still when he's suppose to and he ain't noisy. We thought that we'd ought to pack some food, but the fishermen said we didn't need none. They promised to show us where we could ketch a good breakfast. Them men was right. We done just what they told us, and by dawn we were eating a breakfast of fresh fish. They tasted wonderfully to us boys.

L. Below is given a telephone conversation between two girls who are careless in the use of English. Write the correct form for each error.

Mary: Hello, Jane! Was you thinking about goin to the basketball game?
Jane: No, I ain't planning on it. Mother don't want me to go to no games until after the examinations.
Mary: That's too bad. I done my last test this afternoon. With who do you think I can go?
Jane: Leave me suggest Frances. She oughta be able to go, but I don't know where she is now.
Mary: Thank you. I'll see if she has came home from school. Goodbye, Jane.

M. In each of the paragraphs below, underline the 10 incorrect expressions. In each case write the correct form.

1. We use to live in Omaha Nebraska. Neither my brother nor I wants to go back. We can't scarcely remember how it was because we was to young at the time. Well, one day whom do you think comes to visit us. It was my favorite uncle, looking not one bit different than ten years ago.

2. When the stranger knocked on the door and walked in the room, I wondered who he wanted to see. Their was an empty seat besides me, so he set down without saying nothing to anybody. Everybody else minded their own business, so I turns to him and politely asked, "Can I help You?"

3. At graduation all the girls in white dresses looked real beautiful as they walked down the isle. The boy's wore light jackets and dark trousers in accordance with the custom. As the principle gave each one their diploma, he said, "congratulations!" Then he introduces a speaker who used to be a former teacher of our's. He said, "You cannot judge the full affect of education without you put it to the acid test of experience."

4. George was suppose to take a trip to Boston by plane. Being that he had never done no flying before, he was all excited. At the airport, who do you guess he met. It was an old school chum who could of helped him and gave him some good advice. If he would have known sooner, they could have planned things more pleasant. In my estimation, theres nothing like a friend.

5. In the middle of the game, someone started a fight. Once the referee had stopped the game and blew his whistle, the captain of each team rushed forward

to defend their side. You couldn't hardly make out what they said, but you could tell they were mad. "Leave him alone!" shouted one. "You had ought to soak your head in water!" answers the other. They were plenty rough. "I will penalize whomever deserves it," announced the referee. That settled it peaceful.

6. Owing to the unexpected company, she tried to bake muffins for dinner. Her mother warned she and I to be careful in reading the directions. After we had mixed the batter thorough, we put it into the pan. The oven was sure hot, but the dough did not raise the way it should of. Who's fault was it? "Why dont you and her go by some ice-cream instead?" her mother said.

7. Collecting autographs is one of my hobby's. Even at the expense of being a Bore, I hunt celebrities. Some day I will have a larger collection than any in the world I hope. Whenever a movie star or some famous persons visits our town nothing can't stop me going after the prized signature. Usually, they comply with my request quite willing. Its easy if you try.

8. Science has shown that there are no real differences between the races of mankind Size, color, and shape often depend upon climate, environment, and nutrition. Man is a creature composed of body and soul. Neither you nor me is perfect. Those with whom you argue with show narrow-minded. Except we all learn to live together this earth of our's will always be a battlefield. Now is the time for us to realize that all men are brothers. Tomorrow will be to late.

9. One day a box of oranges were sent to my brother and I by my cousin in Florida. Those kind of an orange taste sweeter being that it is fresh fruit. It don't seem possible that we could have drank a quart of juice apiece, but you should have been their and saw us that morning.

10. The salesman whom you said treated you discourteously is with this company for many years and has a record as good if not better than that of any salesman on our payroll. It is not for we ordinary salesmen to talk about other men, especially about him who we all admire. If I was in you'r place, I would not make no charges against him, for he got a fine record.

N. Write complete sentences using the following expressions correctly:

1. according *to* custom (not *with*)
2. accuse *of* the crime (not *with*)
3. acquitted *of* the charge (not *from*)
4. adapted *from* the original (not *by*)
5. adapted *to* (or *for*) the purpose (not *with*)
6. adverse *to* going (not *against*)
7. agree *to* a proposal (not *with*) = A THING
8. agree *with* the speaker (not *to*) = A PERSON
9. angry *at* the weather (not *against*) = A THING
10. angry *with* him (not *at*) = A PERSON
11. averse *to* action (not *against*)
12. blame him *for* it (not "blame it *on* him")
13. comply *with* your request (not *to*)
14. conform *to* (or *with*) the regulations (not *in*)
15. correspond *to* the right size (not *with*) = A THING
16. correspond *with* the editor (not *to*) = A PERSON
17. desirous *of* helping him (not "*to* help")
18. different *from* the other book (not *than*)
19. disappointed *in* the returns (not *with*)
20. disappointed *of* his hopes (not *with*)

SENTENCE STRUCTURE

Make it your business to say things in sentences, to shape thoughts into a sensible order of words. Each sentence must be *structured;* it must be built so that it states something clearly, or asks a question, or gives a command. The form of the sentence must follow the purpose or mood of the speaker or writer. This process of building sentences requires skill in arranging words to convey the meaning intended.

 BUILDING BETTER SENTENCES

Do you remember how you learned to speak? First, you pointed at things. Gradually, you imitated sounds to say single words. Finally, you learned how to put words together to say something. The sentence is the unit of expression because it is the statement of an idea. You can see the way a sentence is built by watching it grow from a single word. Let's take the word *go* and put it at the center of the black-board, or of a sheet of paper; thus:

> Go.

Now, let's add some words to show *who* is going.

> Will you **go** with me?

To round out the meaning, let's add the element of *time.*

> When we get out of school today,
> will you **go** with me?

To complete the sentence, let's add the *place.*

> When we get out of school today,
> will you **go** with me
> to the movies?

This process of expanding a word into a complete sentence will lend a game-spirit to your learning, if you try to do this with your buddy or classmates. Take any action-word as the center and build around it. Examples: play, dance, eat, work, run, write, sing.

171

Take a second look at the series and you will discover that each step is a complete sentence, but each enlargement helps to round out the thought.

1. Go.

This is an imperative sentence with the pronoun (*you*) understood. The verb *go* is the heart of the sentence.

2. Will you go with me?

This is an interrogative sentence. The subject is *you* and the predicate verb is *will go; with me* is an adverbial phrase.

3. When we get out of school today, will you go with me?

This is an interrogative sentence with a main clause *will you go with me,* and a dependent clause *when we get out of school today.*

4. When we get out of school today, will you go with me to the movies?

This is an interrogative sentence with a main clause, a dependent clause, and an adverbial phrase *to the movies.*

EXERCISE

BUILDING SENTENCES

Write complete sentences suggested by the following groups of words. Aim for variety in structure.

1. heroes of history
2. air conditioning
3. coming to school
4. listening to radio
5. art of losing friends
6. men of science
7. a funny happening
8. my favorite comedian
9. a woman's place
10. death on the highway
11. costume jewelry
12. "hot rods"
13. on being yourself
14. the flight to the suburbs
15. three men in a boat
16. preparing for a party
17. the day I missed
18. my pet storyteller
19. television habits
20. skill in making something

ELEMENTS USED IN ENLARGING THE SENTENCE

Since a sentence contains a subject and a predicate, some sentences are correct, but rather bare, when they consist merely of a noun or pronoun and a verb.

Sentences Using Individual Words

> He smiled. She nodded. They danced. Everyone applauded. They stopped. He bowed. She turned. The music ceased.

As you can see, such a series of short sentences lacks smoothness. They can be improved by adding phrases or combining them into clauses for longer sentences.

Here are the same sentences given above with the addition of phrases to round out the meaning a bit more fully.

Sentences Using Phrases

> He smiled *at her*. She nodded *toward him*. They danced together *for a while*. Everyone applauded *with pleasure*. They stopped *in surprise*. He bowed *for a moment*. She turned *to the orchestra leader*. The music ceased *at her glance*.

Notice how the use of phrases supplies important details regarding the actions of the persons and makes the series of sentences more meaningful. The next step in building sentences is to combine statements into clauses to show a better relationship between main ideas and dependent ideas, or to enlarge phrases into clauses.

Now, let's try to tell what happened by using clauses to express ideas in a more connected way.

Sentences Using Clauses

> He smiled | *as he approached her.* | She nodded | *as if she welcomed him.* | They danced | *while the others watched* | *until everyone applauded* | *because the exhibition was superb.* | They stopped | *as though they were surprised.* | He bowed | *while he whispered a polite "thank you."* | She turned to the orchestra leader | *at whose signal the music ceased.* |

Here you have the same sentences that were expressed so barely with individual words, now stated with the fullness of clauses and phrases to enlarge the meaning. You might compare this process of sentence building to the game in which you may take "baby steps" or "giant steps." As you grow up, you learn to stand more surely and walk more vigorously. So, too, as you improve in handling language, you move from individual words to phrases and clauses. Next time you write, will you take a few "giant steps" to say what you want? Try it!

EXERCISE

WRITING SENTENCES

Using the words, phrases, and clauses listed below, write 20 complete sentences. Select elements from different columns, not necessarily across the same line, and then add other words to complete the meaning.

WORDS	PHRASES	CLAUSES
car	in the morning	while the others cheered
dog	after school	because no officer was present
bicycle	at home	since this was a new toy
food	of all kinds	as if he had always known how
people	without a license	when real trouble began
work	until this week	after the company had left
eat	over the fence	why they relaxed as usual
play	with our friends	how the blueprint indicated
build	to the next one	where the enemy had attacked
sell	by pure luck	that makes the memories return
piano	beneath the tree	although we prefer peace and quiet
war	on the other side	than even strangers would allow
plane	during the evening	if the price is low enough
country	through many years	though there was no emergency
party	under our flag	because we all value our freedom
escape	about five times	when the skies looked clear overhead
listen	like a statue	while everybody expected a crackup
fly	into new places	after the whole thing had ended
enjoy	beside the neighbors	that we ought to plan better
love	from everywhere	since success follows effort

DECLARATIVE, INTERROGATIVE, AND IMPERATIVE SENTENCES

A sentence may make a statement, ask a question, or give an order. According to these three functions, a sentence may be *declarative, interrogative,* or *imperative.* These are indicated by means of punctuation at the end and also by word-order or position of subject and predicate. Learn these definitions!

Declarative sentence —makes a statement.	ends with a period and follows normal order of subject and predicate. Some boys can spell better than some girls. Television offers worthwhile educational programs.
Interrogative sentence —asks a question.	ends with a question mark and reverses the usual order of subject and predicate by beginning with an auxiliary verb or the predicate verb, or an adverb. Were you present when I called the roll? How can a candle burn without air?
Imperative sentence —expresses a command or strong feeling.	may end with a period to show a polite request or with an exclamation point to show strong feeling. It usually omits the subject noun or pronoun, which in this case is said to be (*you*) "understood." (You) Please come a few minutes earlier tomorrow. Class, (you) stand at attention! (You) Drop that, I say, or you will be hurt!

CHANGING ONE TYPE OF SENTENCE TO ANOTHER

To show change of mood, any sentence may be written in the form of a declarative, interrogative, or imperative sentence. Notice how the meaning changes!

John has finished his assignment.   (declarative)
Has John finished his assignment? (interrogative)
John, finish your assignment!   (imperative)

EXERCISE

DECLARATIVE, INTERROGATIVE, IMPERATIVE SENTENCES

Correctly label each of the following sentences according to type by writing *Decl.* for declarative sentence, *Int.* for interrogative sentence, *Imp.* for imperative sentence. Insert the correct punctuation at the end of each sentence.

1. Come into the garden, Maud
2. These are times that try men's souls
3. Awake and sing, O ye who dwell in dust
4. Wherefore art thou Romeo
5. Roll on, thou deep and dark blue ocean, roll
6. A thing of beauty is a joy forever
7. What men or gods are these
8. Heard melodies are sweet, but those unheard are sweeter
9. Swiftly walk over the western wave, spirit of night
10. She stood in tears amid the alien corn
11. When shall we three meet again
12. There is a pleasure in the pathless woods
13. If I should meet thee after long years, how should I greet thee
14. Hail to thee, blithe spirit
15. I bring fresh showers for the thirsting flowers
16. You know, we French stormed Ratisbon
17. What a hot day this was
18. Oh, what can ail thee, knight-at-arms
19. I must go down to the sea again
20. She walks in beauty like the night

SIMPLE, COMPOUND, AND COMPLEX SENTENCES

You have learned that a sentence is a group of words which says something. You can say whatever you have to say in short simple sentences, or in long compound sentences, or in various kinds of complex sentences. Each type serves its special purpose in conveying ideas. You should be able to handle each type in your own writing and speaking to give greater clearness and force to the messages you wish to convey.

Simple sentence	has one independent clause, consisting of one subject and one predicate.
	Swimming is my favorite sport. You will study after dinner.
Compound sentence	has two or more independent clauses, usually connected by *and, or, but.*
	I like all sports, *but* swimming is my favorite. The ball went out of the park, *and* everyone rose to cheer.
Complex sentence	has an independent clause and one or more dependent clauses. (Dependent clauses are italicized below.)
	Although I like every sport, I enjoy swimming most of all. I will see you *before you leave.*

EXERCISES

SIMPLE, COMPOUND, COMPLEX SENTENCES

A. Write S for simple sentence, Cx for complex sentence, Cd for compound sentence:

1. When she smiles, her eyes light up.

2. The missions do remarkable work in foreign lands.
3. A good magazine stimulates you, but a trashy one debases your mind.
4. Since you started the job, why not finish it yourself?
5. We have looked forward to your coming, and now we are happy to see you.
6. During a dull rainy day, I like to read a good story.
7. The trees shook and swayed as the storm lashed them.
8. You shall have to pay the bill, or else I will call an officer of the law.
9. Popular songs have catchy tunes, but the old favorites will outlast them.
10. It's an adventure story about a pirate and buried treasure.
11. Robert and Don printed the tickets and delivered them.
12. Wishing to see the principal, he went to the office and waited.
13. Defeat may bring discouragement but to the brave it brings a challenge.
14. The girls have sold but thirty tickets.
15. While I was at the game, I saw all the boys but Tom and Jack.
16. Throwing down the bat, I turned and smiled at the cheering crowd.
17. The Norwegians realized their danger very clearly but, like their Viking ancestors, they faced the perils of the sea with high spirits.
18. On the first of January, just before dark, the relief party arrived.
19. I finished the last question just as the bell rang.
20. At last the signal is given, the anchor is raised and slowly the ship glides away from the pier.

B. Classify each of the following groups of words by writing S for simple sentence, Cx for complex sentence, Cd for compound sentence, I for incomplete sentence:

1. Last night I visited Mr. Roberts, a friend of my father.
2. The doctor recognized the man who entered his office.
3. To disappear when he was most needed.
4. Automobiles are very useful but occasionally they need to be repaired.
5. We should learn to govern ourselves.
6. As I have often heard you say.
7. They came in quietly and seated themselves around the fire.
8. As he approached this fearful tree, Ichabod began to whistle.
9. I went to town yesterday, but my sister stayed home.
10. It is necessary to study in school.
11. I admire Mary's love of animals, Joan's happy spirit and Marjorie's loyalty to friends.
12. Slowly and quietly the snow covered the field and hill.
13. Some boys like hockey, that thrilling sport, but others prefer basketball, an exciting indoor game.
14. After the aviator had inspected his motor, he climbed into the cockpit and glided off.
15. Jane received many beautiful gifts for Christmas and she also made many friends happy by her thoughtful kindness.
16. Wash your hands before eating meals.
17. When the fruit is ripe, it will fall by its own weight.
18. Since chickens are sold in segments, no city child recognizes a dressed fowl.
19. Even if they successfully launch a satellite from the earth.
20. The world stands on the brink of war, and many persons are returning to religion today.

SENTENCE VARIETY

Some students wonder why they receive low ratings for compositions in which there are no sentence errors. The reason may be that, although they are correct, the sentences are monotonous repetitions of these three patterns:

- *a.* too often they begin every sentence with the subject and the predicate without any other introductory element,
- *b.* too many sentences are short and choppy, or
- *c.* too many sentences use *and* and *so* as connectives.

To obtain variety

in your writing, try to use more

than one type of sentence.

Begin your next composition with a *question.* End it with an *exclamation.* How does it compare with your usual style? Try it and see!

In order to make your writing a bit more forceful in expression, try to use some of these hints for obtaining variety in structure:

1. Use different *types* of sentences occasionally to change the *mood*.

   DECLARATIVE: My blood boils whenever I think of it.
   INTERROGATIVE: Why on earth did you have to do that?
   IMPERATIVE: For goodness' sake, turn on the lights!

2. Use different *forms* of sentences to change the *pace*.

   SIMPLE: We shall never forget that night.
   COMPLEX: When you mention murder, count me out.
   COMPOUND: The police rushed to the scene, but they found the victim dead on arrival.

3. Put some other element *before the subject* of the sentence to vary the *beginning*.

   ADJECTIVE: *Shiny* indeed, it was a newly-minted coin.
   ADVERB: *Suddenly,* a shot rang out in the dark.
   PHRASE: *In a moment,* the blue sedan roared away.
   CLAUSE: *While the dazed guests stumbled out of the house,* the host called the police on the telephone.

4. Change the normal *word-order* (subject, verb, object) to get greater *effect*.

   VERB FIRST: *Cried* a voice: "Help!"
   OBJECT FIRST: *Money* I would give freely, but not my life.

5. Condense *loose,* separate statements by using *shorter,* combined elements.

   LOOSE: Terry went swimming. Val went too.
   COMPOUND SUBJECT: *Terry* and *Val* went swimming.

   LOOSE: Jim hid in the barrel. He overheard the pirates.
   COMPOUND PREDICATE: Jim *hid* in the barrel and *overheard* the pirates.

   LOOSE: Last year we planted flowers. We also planted some vegetables.
   COMPOUND OBJECT: Last year we planted *flowers* and some *vegetables.*

6. Combine short sentences by subordinating minor ideas into dependent clauses.

    SEPARATED: The squad car dashed around the corner. The crowd parted to make room.

    COMBINED: As the squad car dashed around the corner, the crowd parted to make room.

    SEPARATED: We felt terrified. The siren shrieked. The headlights glared at us.

    COMBINED: We felt terrified when the siren shrieked and the headlights glared at us.

7. Use *verbals* instead of *clauses* for compactness and force.

    CLAUSE: He is a citizen who deserves honor.

    INFINITIVE: He is a citizen *to honor.*

    CLAUSE: As he ran down the court, he passed the ball.

    PARTICIPLE: *Running* down the court, he passed the ball.

    CLAUSE: She knew her lines. She acted with confidence.

    GERUND: *Knowing* her lines helped her act with confidence.

8. Use *appositives* in place of wordy clauses or short sentences.

    WORDY CLAUSE: Anthony who lives in the house near us has a cocker spaniel.

    APPOSITIVE: Anthony, *our next-door neighbor,* has a cocker spaniel.

    SHORT SENTENCES: Lindbergh was a young pilot. He flew from America to Europe.

    APPOSITIVE: Lindbergh, *a young pilot,* flew from America to Europe.

EXERCISES

SENTENCE VARIETY

A. Here are some practical ways to apply your knowledge of sentence variety:

1. Go over your last piece of *written work* and revise some of your sentences, especially the monotonous ones full of *and* and *so,* or the short choppy ones.

2. Analyze a piece of writing in your *literature* book (short-story, novel, biography, play, etc.) to discover the various kinds of sentence structure used by a professional writer.

3. Compare the sentences usually found in a *newspaper* article or story (simple, direct, declarative) with the sentences usually found in a *magazine* article or story (complex, verbals, appositives, inverted word-order).

B. Rewrite these sentences by changing the italicized part into the element suggested in parentheses.

Example: The lawyer, *who was a former judge,* made a dramatic appeal for the defendant. (appositive)

Answer: The lawyer, a former judge, made a dramatic appeal for the defendant.

1. The boy *who carried* the flag saluted sharply. (participle)
2. *Laughing* at trouble requires broad sympathy. (infinitive)
3. She bought a dress after *she had shopped* in several stores. (gerund)
4. Columbus, *who was the Admiral of the Fleet,* sailed in the Santa Maria as flagship. (appositive)
5. *After many days had passed,* the men grew weary of staring at the endless ocean. (phrase)
6. Three thousand miles of ocean did not discourage Columbus, *a brave and experienced navigator.* (clause)
7. *Joan of Arc claimed she had received miraculous visions.* She was burned at the stake as a heretic. (subordinate clause)
8. The raven *answered:* "Nevermore!" as the poet dreamed of his lost Lenore. (verb first)
9. *The English* were guilty of the martyrdom of Joan. *The French* were just as guilty. (compound subject)
10. Mother bought *new slip-covers for the chairs.* She also bought *new drapes for the windows.* (compound object)
11. Early in the morning, the boys *shoveled* the snow. They also *scraped* the ice off the walk. (compound predicate)
12. The virgin lands of the new country were settled by men *who had courage.* (phrase)
13. The women *that seemed weakest* proved to be the strongest in meeting hard times. (adjective)
14. The pilot *of the stricken airship* was able to make a safe emergency landing in an open field. (clause)
15. The painter worked *with great care* in coloring the details of the landscape. (adverb)
16. They decided to sell the *farmlands.* They also sold the *barn* and the *cattle.* (compound object)
17. There must be thousands of honest ways *to earn* a decent living in our country. (participle)
18. Jefferson decided *on purchasing* the Louisiana Territory from Napoleon for fifteen million dollars. (infinitive)
19. It is better to get into the habit of listening with attention and not *to make* excuses for inattention. (gerund)
20. George W. Carver *was a famous Negro scientist.* He suggested planting soybeans as another crop besides cotton. (appositive)

Now that you have developed your "sentence sense" and have learned how to write a variety of sentence patterns, you should study certain errors to avoid in sentence structure. Remember that, basically, sentence structure means thought structure. Think straight and you will write correctly.

Sentence Fragments

A **sentence fragment** is a group of words lacking a subject or a verb. It is therefore an incomplete sentence.	Supply the missing subject or verb to complete the meaning!

INCOMPLETE: Hoping to hear from you soon.
(subject and verb lacking)
COMPLETE: *I hope* to hear from you soon.
(subject and verb supplied)

INCOMPLETE: The young girl in an accident.
(verb lacking)
COMPLETE: The young girl *was injured* in an accident.
(verb supplied)

PERMISSIBLE NON-SENTENCE EXPRESSIONS

Certain words, phrases, or clauses may be used in *conversation* without forming complete expressions. These are acceptable because the listener supplies the missing words to complete the meaning. For example, we say:

Fine!	No, indeed.
Exactly right!	Any time you say.
Not at all!	Whenever you're ready.
What an idea!	As you wish.
Now, really?	Because he said so?

However, in *written* English, such as is required in formal letters, compositions, reports, examinations, and the like, we build complete sentences to make our meaning perfectly clear.

RUN-ON SENTENCE

COMMA BLUNDER

MISPLACED MODIFIER

To avoid sentence errors,

PRACTICE

PRACTICE

PRACTICE

EXERCISES

CHANGING FRAGMENTS INTO SENTENCES

A. Some of the following groups of words are permissible non-sentence expressions; others are sentence fragments. Change the fragments into sentences containing a subject and a predicate.

1. During Brotherhood Week, a special assembly with foreign-born pupils telling about customs in their own country.
2. What a delight! The music and singing of songs from Puerto Rico!
3. One group in colorful costumes representing the natives of Hungary and doing folk dances on the stage.
4. In spite of the applause, no time for extra numbers by some performers.
5. One boy, newly arrived from Finland, dressed in American style, a vivid account of his trip to this country and his impressions of our school.
6. And a refugee from Germany who escaped from the "iron curtain" and crossed the border into Austria at midnight.
7. Their holidays full of fun even though the families felt the pinch of hunger and poverty.
8. Humming the lilting melody of *The Hoya* as the swirling skirts of the dancers swung across the stage.
9. Someone with a good voice in a recitation of Emma Lazarus' poem written on the Statue of Liberty.
10. Not a melting pot, but a place where people are free to be different, so long as they respect the rights of others.
11. Good idea! Pen pals exchange friendly letters instead of bullets around the world.
12. After the pledge to the American flag, a parade of the flags of the United Nations.
13. Some exhibitions of games and stunts, like ju-jitsu from Japan.
14. A list of English words borrowed from other languages: piano, kimono, sauerkraut, tomato, and algebra.
15. We shared foods prepared by the mothers in foreign style. Delicious!
16. A brief talk on contributions to science by foreigners all over the globe.
17. Famous books which have been translated into English and are now on our own library shelves.
18. Movie stars who have recently come to Hollywood and have helped entertain us in current films.
19. How knowledge and acquaintance with other people gradually remove fear and superstition.
20. Excellent! That's the word used by our principal in praising the boys and girls who took part in the assembly program.

B. Write *S* for each of the following that is a complete *sentence* and *N* for each that is *not* a sentence:

1. We shall see the soldiers.
2. Do it now.
3. Having no time to go.
4. Especially where it is cold.
5. The children shouting loudly.
6. The officer gave a salute.
7. People riding on their bicycles.
8. The magazine called *Newsweek*.
9. We are building a dam.
10. A large one to hold water.
11. In God we trust.
12. Yes, we invited Kay but she could not come.
13. A beautiful valley beyond the mountain at the left of the road.
14. Do you know, Jane, when you will return?
15. The bird singing merrily from the tree.
16. How pleasant are the days in June!
17. Sometimes following tracks of animals through the woods.
18. On the table at the back of the room.
19. The boys, with their skates in hand, ran along the edge of the pond.
20. Quickly into the yard rushed the children, ready for play.
21. Drop it into the trash basket, please.
22. Women and small children in the store.
23. In baking, all measurements refer to level spoonfuls.
24. Sufficient unto the day is the evil thereof.
25. Hoping to meet you again in camp next summer.

Run-on Sentences

A **run-on sentence** consists of two or more sentences run together and punctuated as though forming one sentence.	Divide a run-on sentence into separate sentences or show the connection between the ideas by means of punctuation or a conjunction.

RUN-ON: Drive very slowly the road is icy.

CORRECT: Drive very slowly. The road is icy.
(Form two sentences.)

CORRECT: Drive very slowly; the road is icy.
(Punctuate with a semicolon.)

CORRECT: Drive very slowly *because* the road is icy.
(Insert a conjunction.)

EXERCISES

CORRECTING RUN-ON SENTENCES

A. Here is a sample of a run-on sentence written by a pupil who was in a hurry to keep going (and did not reread his work)! Can you cut this neatly into *four* sentences? (Omit unnecessary *and*'s and combine clauses.)

I went rabbit hunting with my uncle who let me use his gun in the woods and all of a sudden I saw a woodchuck and I aimed quickly but missed him so we waited till the noise died down and walked carefully until we noticed a pair of rabbit ears pointing through some grass and this time I took better aim and bagged him.

B. Divide the following paragraph into smaller complete sentences, omitting unnecessary *and*'s and combining clauses:

Every age has been marked with a symbol to show its place in history first there was the stone age, then the iron age, later the age of fire. As man developed tools and skill in using them, he was able to advance from cave-dwellings to huts, later to houses finally he built farms, villages, and cities. With progress in transportation and communication, gradually came the horse-and-buggy era and then began the age of sailing vessels which was in turn followed by the age of machines and steam power. Then, modern times saw the birth of the car age more recently the air age, with all kinds of flying machines in the sky. Today, we speak of the atomic age we learn a strange vocabulary of nuclear fission, automation, jet propulsion, and the wonders of miracle drugs and electronic computers like Univac.

C. Divide the following paragraph into smaller complete sentences, omitting unnecessary *and*'s and combining clauses:

Many years ago, maybe about thirty or forty years ago, boys used to go out and play and have fun with practically nothing, or just the odds and ends of things that they found lying in the street and in empty lots, or along a brook or in the ruins of an old deserted house. They spent a lot of time running around the block, and kicking empty tin cans, and chasing stray cats, and flying kites, or playing stick ball, or building tree huts, but nothing was fancy and everything was free and wonderful. When summer came, they used to swim in the nearest mudhole or dive off the docks, and sometimes went to a beach but hardly ever to a pool, and everybody learned how to swim and never asked whether the water was clean or polluted or safe for bathing. When winter came, they knew how to build forts out of blocks of snow and make fires out of fruit crates and how to cook potatoes in the middle of an igloo or cave shoveled out of a pile of snow pushed off the sidewalks. During the long springtime evenings, they played leap-frog and chase-the-white-horse and ran relays and when they were thirsty scrounged around delivery wagons for chunks of ice to melt in the mouth and told ghost stories under the dim street lamps until their parents yelled for them to go home and on hot nights slept on the rooftops. Life was exciting and boring and dangerous and dull and beautiful.

Comma Blunders

The **comma blunder** is the type of sentence error in which two or more independent clauses are wrongly separated by commas in a single sentence.	Divide the main ideas into individual sentences separated by periods; or subordinate some of the less important ideas to form a complex sentence; or change the blunder into a compound sentence.

BLUNDER: She played the piano, he sang songs, they were happy.

CORRECT: She played the piano. He sang songs. They were happy.

(Form separate sentences.)

CORRECT: When she played the piano and he sang songs, they were happy. (Change to a complex sentence.)

CORRECT: She played the piano while he sang songs; therefore, they were happy. (Change to a compound sentence.)

EXERCISE

CORRECTING COMMA BLUNDERS

Rewrite these sentences correctly by dividing the main ideas into *individual* sentences, or by subordinating some of the less important ideas to form *complex* sentences, or by changing them into *compound* sentences. Make appropriate changes in punctuation!

1. We are old enough now, we want an allowance, we know how to take care of ourselves.
2. Why must we be home by nine or ten o'clock, can't we have any fun at a party, may we stay till eleven just this once?
3. When you were young, you had crazy styles in dress and music, you have no right to make fun of things we like to do.

4. You should take care of your little sister, she is part of our family, someday she may help you.
5. What's the use of complaining, who's going to do your chores?
6. Silent waters run deep, you must be a sly one, you're so quiet!
7. Please move the table back, push the chairs under, smooth out the rug.
8. You set and serve, I'll clear away and wash, you dry the dishes.
9. Line up facing the windows, breathe in, breathe out, now be seated!
10. She bought a parakeet, the cat grew jealous, the goldfish looked sad.
11. We get up early, eat a good breakfast, get dressed in our Sunday best, go to church, and really feel good all day.
12. Why was he excused from homework, is he a privileged pupil, can't he make it up like the rest of us?
13. The ground thaws in the spring, the roots swell, the sap rises, and soon little flags of green appear on the earth.
14. Come in, have a seat, relax, your troubles are over!
15. I wish it were not true, I just can't forget, I lost my new watch.
16. See if you can guess who she is, she watches TV for a living.
17. She graduated from college, her first job was as society editor and general reporter for a newspaper in Connecticut.
18. This assignment took her to ladies' tea parties and luncheons, it also included such events as a fire, a midnight Army capture of the Merritt Parkway, and strange weddings.
19. Her next job was as a radio columnist for the *World-Telegram,* in those days the networks sent program transcriptions to the critics to be listened to at leisure.
20. Now she works as television critic for the same newspaper, she spends as much time as possible watching her set.
21. Most days, she gets up around noon and visits the studios, after dinner she watches TV till 10 or 11 o'clock, when she settles down to write her review of the programs.
22. About 2:30 in the morning, a messenger comes to pick up the copy, she then goes to bed for a well-deserved rest.
23. Besides her daily job of praising or blaming various shows, she serves as a good housewife and cook, she even collects cookbooks and copper casseroles for her kitchen.
24. She dislikes audience-participation shows, most daytime offerings, and old movies known as "re-runs," she likes good drama, spectaculars with real showmanship, documentaries, and stimulating panel shows.
25. Some of her readers write angry letters to her, many others write in with all sorts of praise for her comments.
26. Teenagers are the hope of the world, they are so full of energy, they have such a boundless optimism.
27. Girls spend hours before the mirror, making faces, curling their hair, they practice dance steps and admire their clothes.
28. Boys explore all kinds of gadgets, spring-winding toys, broken alarm clocks, they try to find out how such things work.
29. Some parents accuse teenagers of being selfish, lazy, careless, disrespectful, they hope and pray that they will soon grow up and get some sense.
30. Taken as a group, today's teenagers look healthier, dress more sensibly, know more about current affairs, and enjoy themselves more than previous generations, they merely have to learn a little more respect for elders and obedience for authority.

Short, Choppy Sentences

<table>
<tr><td>

Short, choppy sentences are loosely connected clauses strung along in a series of baby statements. Although grammatically correct, they show immaturity because there is a weak relationship in the sequence of thought.

</td><td>

Join several such short sentences by means of connectives to form larger thought units.

</td></tr>
</table>

CHOPPY: I have a friend. His name is Vincent. He likes to build model planes. He is especially interested in gasoline models.

SMOOTHER: I have a friend named Vincent who likes to build model planes, especially gasoline models.

CHOPPY: We spent last summer in Jackson. Jackson is in New Hampshire. There is a place with good food. Golfing, fishing, and swimming were all nearby. We enjoyed it.

SMOOTHER: We spent last summer in Jackson, New Hampshire. We enjoyed not only the good food, but the nearby golfing, fishing, and swimming.

EXERCISE

COMBINING SHORT SENTENCES

Combine the short sentences in each of the groups below into one smooth, well-constructed sentence:

1. Richmond was the capital of the South. It is located in Virginia. Grant captured it just before the close of the Civil War.
2. Evangeline and Gabriel lived in the French village of Grand Pré. Grand Pré was in Acadia. The British captured the village.
3. The Indians raised tobacco. They also raised maize. Sir Walter Raleigh took tobacco and maize back to England with him.
4. You must be up early in the morning. You will miss the trip. That would be a disappointment to all of us. We are going to Mt. Marcy.

5. Our mailbox is a long distance from the house. It is fastened to a post. The post is painted white. The post is at the side of the highway.

6. We left early in the morning for Albany. We left by automobile. Albany is the capital of New York State. It is located on the Hudson River.

7. Have you read *Evangeline*? It was written by Longfellow. It is a narrative poem. It is about the Acadians. Longfellow was an American poet.

8. A British bomber crashed in the North Sea. It sank in the North Sea. The crew managed to get off in a boat. The boat was made of rubber. This happened last week.

9. My aunt lives in the White Mountains. The White Mountains are in New Hampshire. I am going over to see her. I am going next summer. I expect to stay about three weeks.

10. Will you lend me a dollar? I want to buy a knife. Joe Smith wants to sell it. The knife has two blades.

11. The librarian told us a story. The name of the story was *Treasure Island*. The person who wrote is was named Stevenson. The story is about pirates and buried treasure.

12. Our parents had been to New York. They went down to buy Christmas presents. They traveled to New York by train. The presents were for the family.

13. My dog is my friend. He is loyal. He is my companion. He is a black dog. He is large. His name is Bob.

14. Children in America can go to school. They can play and be happy. Children should be glad that they are Americans.

15. Reading is a pleasant pastime. It also teaches us worth-while things. It is a valuable recreation. Many books carry us to other lands or past ages.

16. I enjoy ice skating. I like to go bobsledding. I like to make snowmen too. That is why I like winter.

17. Last Friday we had an assembly. The freshman class sang songs. The seniors sang too. Everyone enjoyed the program.

18. We have new members on the basketball team. There are four of them. None of them has had experience. They have promised to do their best.

19. *The Yearling* is a novel. It was written by Marjorie Kinnan Rawlings. It is a story about a boy and his pet deer.

20. Spintail is my dog. Last night he awakened me. It was a little after midnight. He was barking.

21. Did you see the bomber? It flew close to our school. It was here yesterday morning. It was a large one. It was painted gray.

22. My sister and I visited Grandmother. We visited her on New Year's Day. She showed us a beautiful old silk dress. She told us many stories. It was her wedding dress.

23. Food is wasted in America. The average family wastes it. A great deal is wasted. We cook too much food. Food is left uneaten on the plates.

24. Father and I attended a basketball game. It took place last week. It was an exciting game. Our team won. The game was held at our school.

25. I can't go with you. The reason is that I haven't finished my work. I should like to go very much.

26. I went to the circus. I went with my father. It was Bell's Mammoth Circus. It was held on the old fair-grounds. I enjoyed it very much.

27. General Braddock was the commander-in-chief of the army. His expedition set out to capture Fort Duquesne. George Washington went with the army as an aide to Braddock.

28. Careless driving of automobiles is dangerous. It is the cause of many collisions. Many persons are injured. Some are killed. It must be stopped.
29. I was spading in the garden. I turned over a clod of earth. I was hard at work. I found my lost knife.
30. Egypt is a strange land. It is in the midst of a desert. Rain almost never falls there. The Nile flows through Egypt.
31. Chum is my dog. One night he awakened me. It was a little after midnight. He was barking hard. He seemed to be warning me of danger.
32. I like winter. I like to play outdoors. I like to skate on the ice. I like to slide downhill on my skis or on our bobsled. My brother made a bobsled from our sleds and a long board.
33. *The Legend of Sleepy Hollow* was written by Washington Irving. It has its setting near Tarrytown. This place is in the southeastern part of New York State. The story has for its main character a schoolmaster. The schoolmaster's name is Ichabod Crane.
34. Last Saturday I watched a baseball game. It was an exciting game. Our junior team played. They played against older boys. They won the game.
35. "The Gold Bug" is a short-story. It is about buried treasure. The treasure was buried by pirates. It is an exciting story. It was written by Edgar Allan Poe.

Long, Rambling Sentences

A **long, rambling sentence** contains several ideas linked with *and, or, but,* often loosely related and padded with unnecessary details.	Such loose sentences should be broken up into more concise statements, with unnecessary details omitted.

RAMBLING: I turned the key *and* the car engine started, *but* it sputtered *and* suddenly died out because there was no gas in the feed line, *or* so I thought.

CONCISE: As I turned the key, the car engine started. Suddenly, it sputtered and died out because there was no gas in the feed line.

RAMBLING: We went to the garage *and* we asked whether we could use the telephone *and* we called Father, *but* no one answered *and* there we were stranded with no gas *and* no money.

CONCISE: We went to the garage to telephone Father. When no one answered, we realized that we were stranded with neither gas nor money.

EXERCISE

BREAKING UP LONG, RAMBLING SENTENCES

Rewrite these sentences by dividing them into more concise statements and omitting unnecessary details:

1. She used to love to go window-shopping along Fifth Avenue, and she would spend a whole afternoon just admiring articles she could never afford to buy, but she was happy, or so she said.
2. That's why it was so funny to see him dressed up like Mickey Mouse, and he was wearing one of those little black skull caps with big floppy earlaps, but best of all was his slim mustache painted on with burnt cork.
3. You should have seen the girl cheerleaders and watched them waving their white-gloved hands or swirling their short skirts and doing fancy somersaults in front of the grandstand as they encouraged the fans to yell for their team, team, team!
4. I tried all I could to please her and I worked on a special project after school, and I raised my hand to answer all her questions, but when the report cards were distributed, I still had the same mark, 85, as on the previous marking period.
5. Mother had prepared a few extra things because she was expecting company, but the little ones found the cookies, and candies, and fruits, and nuts, and had a grand time stuffing themselves before someone noticed what had happened.
6. Tom knew that he had to work to earn some money, so on Saturday morning he went to the supermarket manager and asked whether he needed a boy, but he didn't want any, so Tom went to the grocer's and made a dollar by cleaning out the basement.
7. When you read about the Battle of the Wilderness in 1864, you realize that both the Rebels and the Yankees were almost doomed to disaster because they could not see each other in the forest and the smoke of burning trees blinded them and the steady firing of muskets wounded thousands, but the opposing generals, Lee and Grant, kept fighting on.
8. Some cities in the United States have already tried to fluoridate their water systems in order to protect children's teeth against decay, but there are other cities in which the experts claim that the kind of food eaten and daily care of teeth are more important factors in preventing cavities.
9. Our school arranged a guided tour of the shops, both for boys and for girls, and invited all the fathers and mothers to visit them, and set up special demonstrations, such as repainting old furniture, changing a fuse, stopping a leaky faucet, or whipping evaporated milk, but the same faithful few parents appeared as at the previous meetings.

193

Dangling Participial Phrases

A **dangling participle** is a verbal usually ending in -*ing* or -*ed* which is set in the wrong place in the sentence or lacks a word to modify. Thus, the sentence meaning becomes either confusing or amusing. (A phrase introduced by a participle is called a *participial phrase*.)

Three ways of correcting this fault are: (*a*) change the position of the participial phrase so that it will be near the word it really modifies; or (*b*) change the participial phrase into a subordinate clause; or (*c*) insert the necessary word in the sentence which the participial phrase should modify.

DANGLING: I saw an automobile *walking down the street.*

CLEAR: *Walking down the street,* I saw an automobile.

DANGLING: *Coming into the museum,* the tomb of an Egyptian pharaoh may be seen on the main floor.

CLEAR: *As you come into the museum,* you will see the tomb of an Egyptian pharaoh on the main floor.

DANGLING: The lion was claimed by a hunter *shot dead by a stray bullet.*

CLEAR: *Shot dead by a stray bullet,* the lion was claimed by a hunter.

EXERCISE

CORRECTING DANGLING PARTICIPLES

Correct the faulty reference of participles in the following sentences and make the meaning unmistakably clear:

1. Flying around the room, I saw two birds.

2. A horse was purchased by a man weighing about 1300 pounds.
3. They hardly noticed the broken glass, enjoying an exciting game of hide and seek.
4. A fountain pen was lost by the boy filled with red ink.
5. We saw an automobile accident sitting in our front window.
6. Jimmy tossed bait to the fish standing on the river bank.
7. I saw a falling star the other night sitting on the front porch.
8. She missed the ferry boat dropping the wrong coin into the turnstile.
9. Cinderella is the poor girl dreaming of marrying a rich, handsome man dressed in rags.
10. You can watch the Easter Parade on a side street parked in a car near Fifth Avenue.
11. I found the fish strolling along the edge of the brook.
12. We noticed the plane take off standing in the cafeteria.
13. The bees stung the keeper swarming into the hive.
14. Dashing around the barn, a pile of hay tripped us.
15. Entering the revolving door, the elevator is very convenient.
16. Cutting the grass on the lawn, a robin's egg lay there.
17. The stagehands applauded the show hidden in the wings of the theater.
18. Lincoln's famous words were read by the tourists inscribed on the pedestal of his monument.
19. The wash on the line was hung there by a lady dripping wet.
20. Coming up the harbor, the Statue of Liberty greets the immigrants to America.

Confusion Due to Misplaced Modifiers

Sometimes the position of a single word may confuse or change the intended meaning of a sentence. The chief errors occur in using such common adverbs as *not, only, nearly, almost,* etc. Sometimes phrases or clauses that are misplaced may confuse or amuse the reader.

Make sure you place the word, phrase, or clause near the expression which it modifies to avoid misleading the reader or listener.

CONFUSING: Everybody *can't* do this trick.

This means that *nobody* can do this trick.

CLEAR: *Not* everybody can do this trick.

This means that *some,* but not all, can do this trick.

CONFUSING:	The dealer *nearly* made $200 on the sale of the car.
	This suggests that the sale may *not* have been made.
CLEAR:	The dealer made *nearly* $200 on the sale of the car.
	Here he made *almost* $200 on the sale of the car.
CONFUSING:	God can *only* make a tree.
	It implies He cannot *destroy* it or do otherwise.
CLEAR:	*Only* God can make a tree.
	It clearly states that He *alone* can make it.
CONFUSING:	I saw the circus passing *through my front window.*
	Here the *circus* went through the window. Impossible!
CLEAR:	*Through my front window,* I saw the circus passing.
	Now, it is clear that *I* looked through the window.

EXERCISE

CORRECTING MISPLACED MODIFIERS

Rewrite the following sentences, putting the misplaced modifiers in the correct position in the sentence:

1. He put his lunch on the shelf which he ate later.
2. I saw a man chopping wood through my window.
3. Servicemen receive air mail stationed at the North Pole by helicopter.
4. Let's buy something after the ball game at the lunch counter.
5. The dog belongs to our neighbor that we feed with bones.
6. There is a place where you can watch the boats sailing on the back porch.
7. The coat must belong to some little girl with red pockets.
8. Put the broom in the corner with the broken handle.
9. This plant is of great medicinal value with a peculiar odor.
10. Mr. Johnson advertised for boys to deliver groceries that have bicycles.
11. Take the dog to an animal hospital with a broken leg.
12. The goggle-eyed fish amused the boy in the glass bowl.
13. The man tipped his hat while passing Mrs. Brown with his right hand.
14. The meat came in a can which we immediately cooked for lunch.
15. The man climbed the ladder with a broken arm.
16. The fruit had been carefully wrapped in paper which we ate.
17. Take one of these powders on going to bed in a little hot water.
18. It is said that Lincoln wrote his most famous speech while he was riding to Gettysburg on a scrap of brown paper.
19. She went to bed after the company had left with the cat locked outside the house.
20. A baby-grand piano was requested by a woman with three wooden legs.

Ambiguous Pronouns

Avoid the repeated use of the same pronoun, especially when it does not clearly refer to any particular person.	It is better to (*a*) use direct discourse, or (*b*) insert the name of the person in place of the overused pronoun, or (*c*) restate the thought.

AMBIGUOUS: After Mary greeted Helen, *she* told *her* how happy *she* was that *she* was going to live next door to *her*.

CLEAR: After Mary greeted Helen, she said, "Helen, I'm so happy that you are going to live next door to me!"

AMBIGUOUS: *It* was dark and *it* started to rain when *it* crashed into a tree and that was the end of *it*.

CLEAR: It was dark and raining when the *car* crashed into a tree and turned into a *pile of junk*.

EXERCISE

AVOIDING AMBIGUOUS PRONOUNS

Rewrite the following sentences to make clear the relationships between persons and actions. Avoid the confusing repetition of pronouns.

1. Whenever they go on trips they behave better than when they stay in school.
2. He told him to hurry right over, and he said he would try; but he was delayed.
3. She asked her to meet her at her house, but she forgot her address.
4. It was an unavoidable accident when it skidded and crashed into it.
5. He invited him to meet his friend when he came to the party, but he failed to appear.
6. If they keep their word to them, they will have nothing to fear.
7. He worked at it until somehow it turned out better than it looked when he first bought it for him.
8. He told him to paint the ceiling first, and he asked him to use a flat-white color.
9. General Grant issued orders to the leaders of the armies to attack at dawn, but they somehow went astray and they suffered many casualties.
10. I laughed when I saw the keeper with the monkey eating peanuts from his lap.

Lack of Parallel Structure

A series of similar ideas should be expressed in similar form within a sentence; match words with words, phrases with phrases, or clauses with clauses.	You may use a series of phrases, clauses, participles, infinitives, or any other construction, provided that you keep the same kind of element in the sentence.

FAULTY: He played *checkers, chess,* and *golfing*. (2 nouns, 1 gerund)
PARALLEL: He played *checkers, chess,* and *golf*. (3 nouns)

FAULTY: She enjoyed *dancing* waltzes, *playing* the piano, and *to sing* oldtime melodies. (2 gerunds, 1 infinitive)
PARALLEL: She enjoyed *dancing* waltzes, *playing* the piano, and *singing* oldtime melodies. (3 gerunds)

FAULTY: I know *why the car should be waxed* and *the way to do it*. (1 clause, 1 phrase)
PARALLEL: I know *why the car should be waxed* and *how the job should be done*. (2 clauses)
PARALLEL: I know *why to wax the car* and *how to do it*. (2 phrases)

EXERCISE

CORRECTING FAULTY PARALLEL STRUCTURE

Rewrite the following sentences by expressing related ideas in parallel style:
1. I like eating and sleeping, but not to work!
2. The boxer advanced, side-stepped, lunged forward, and cleverly landing a blow right to the jaw.
3. This stuff cleans, waxes, and even polishing at the same time.
4. The tired troops came to a halt, dropped to the ground, and from sheer weariness almost falling asleep at once.
5. To dig, to plant, and watering all summer, paid off at last when we enjoyed eating the fresh tomatoes picked from the vine.

6. Some will help, and others will watch, but all involved in it somehow.
7. He explained which method to use and how much it would cost.
8. The salesman knows his product, knows his customers, and sometimes using the tricks of psychology in selling.
9. I approve your suggestion, admire your courage, but am really doubtful that you will succeed with it.
10. Nylon dresses wash easily, drip dry readily, and you can wear them right away.
11. Drain the fruit, boiling the juice, heating gently, and you may store the syrup in a cool place.
12. The waiter glanced at them, smiled knowingly, and he was leading them to a reserved table.
13. He collected foreign stamps, rare coins, and medals from old wars.
14. On land, in the air, even when you go under the sea, gravity pulls you down.
15. She prayed for her family, friends, relatives, and people she never knew.

EXERCISE

REVIEW OF SENTENCE ERRORS

In the selections given below, you will find three types of errors commonly made in composition: short, choppy sentences that should be combined into a single smooth, well-constructed sentence; long, rambling sentences that should be broken up; and parts of sentences that should be combined to make complete thoughts. Rewrite each selection in smooth, correct, well-constructed sentences. [Make any changes you think are necessary without destroying the thought.]

1. I have some new skates. They were given me for Christmas. Father gave them to me. I had wished for them for a long time. Because all the boys I play with have skates. And enjoy skating. The day after Christmas I set out to try my new skates. I was all alone. But I was not frightened. Having heard Father say the ice was a foot thick. I soon reached the lake, put on my skates and started to stand up all at once I fell flat on the ice. I heard a loud laugh. I saw Bob and Bill coming along the road. They are my chums. Who had stopped at my house to ask me to go skating with them. I had left home before they arrived and they helped me up and they put on their skates and showed me how to balance myself.

2. I visited a cousin. He lives in Vermont. It was last fall. One day I went out alone. To explore the surrounding country. I did not realize how far I had gone. Until I was ready to start back. Then the trouble began. I walked for miles over rough trails and it grew dark and I became cold and hungry and finally came to a road. I followed it to an unlighted farmhouse. There I pounded on the door with all my might. At last a window was raised. A man's voice

asked, "What do you want?" "I'm lost and I want to stay here all night," I said. The voice replied, "All right, stay there!" And the window banged shut. I walked slowly down the road, a car came toward me, it stopped. In it were my uncle and cousin. Who were looking for me.

3. One day last fall our principal called the pupils together. He made an announcement. That we were to have a parade and party. At the schoolhouse on Saturday, October 30. Everyone who came was to mask. Prizes being offered by the faculty for the most original costumes. All of us were delighted. All of us began to plan on the fun we should have. I was about to leave the schoolhouse. Tom called to me. He wanted me to join with him in planning costumes. I agreed. And every night we hurried home from school and we did our chores quickly and then we finished our homework. So that we could start work as soon as possible on our costumes. Intending to win those prizes. At last the day came and we arrived at the party and so did two other boys dressed exactly as we were!

4. Last week I received an invitation. It was to a treasure hunt. It was to take place on Friday night. The invitation told me to go to Mary's house. I was to go at seven o'clock. As soon as we had all arrived. Mary divided us into groups of four. Giving each group a list of directions for finding the treasure. My group was directed to walk east two blocks and then south to the schoolhouse, there we were to wait for a car. With a sign "Treasure Seekers." The car arrived. Mary's older brother was driving and he blindfolded us and he drove us around for ten or fifteen minutes, turning corners very often. At last he stopped. He let us out of the car. He led us to the door. He rang the bell. When the door was opened, I was led inside, my blindfold was removed, as my friends sang, "Happy birthday to you!"

5. We went hiking in the snow. It was cold. We went on Saturday. I wore high shoes. The other boys wore boots. I got lost. When I couldn't find the other boys I was frightened, and ran around a whole lot trying to find them but I only got more and more excited so finally I just stood still and tried to think about where we were when we were last together and just by luck I noticed a very tall tree that we had all remarked about as we walked past it, so I ran to that tree and found their tracks in the snow. I followed the tracks. I saw the boys. They had started a fire. They thought the smoke would help me locate them. Was I glad to see them! Next time, I'll be more careful. It's no fun to be lost.

6. Ever since the ice appeared on the pond. We had been planning a skating party. My two brothers and I had been planning it. My brothers' names are Harry and Joe. They are older than I am. For the first nice Saturday. The weather had been stormy. We did not have any party until last week. Saturday morning I woke up early and the sun was shining bright and I thought it would be a perfect day for a skating party and I called my brothers and dashed downstairs to ask if we could take a lunch and spend the day at Willow Pond. A favorite spot of ours for skating. Because we can walk there and back. Without getting so tired that it spoils all our fun. My brothers appeared at last. I had called them again. Telling them what a perfect day it was. We ate our breakfast. Mother made us drink all of our orange juice and eat every bit of our cereal and finish all of our toast and cocoa. Even though we were in a hurry to start. After having done our chores, we set forth for our day of sport.

7. Rewrite the following paragraph, dividing the sentences so that you will have a clear and well-constructed paragraph.

I read all about the eclipse that was to take place on the following morning and I made up my mind that I would see it and when I went to bed Friday night I told my father to call me early. Father called me bright and early and I was dreaming that the sun was a big lamp and the man in the moon put the light out and then everything grew cold and when I woke up I found the bed-clothes on the floor. I jumped out of bed shivering and dressed as fast as I could and then I got a piece of smoked glass and after I had eaten my breakfast I went up to the roof to see the eclipse. The black spot that everybody said was the moon grew larger and larger and you could see less and less of the sun so after a while you could not see the sun at all and it was as dark as it is at night.

8. Combine *each group* of sentences below into *one* smooth, well-constructed sentence. Then number your new sentences from one to five in the order they should follow to make a satisfactory paragraph.

Melvin took the ball. The crowd in the gymnasium became quiet. The goal might mean the winning point.

The ball shot through the air. It curved toward the basket. It balanced on the rim. For a moment it remained there motionless.

Then a deep sigh ran through the crowd. Everyone relaxed. The ball had dropped into the basket.

The referee's whistle blew. Melvin stepped forward. The referee handed him the ball.

Melvin stood before the goal. Every eye was upon him. Slowly and smoothly he tossed the ball.

9. Mark with C each of the following word groups that is a complete sentence and rewrite those that are incomplete, making complete sentences of them. Use such additional words as you find necessary.

a. The boys were not afraid to go into the room.
b. When the bell rang.
c. That the team would win this game.
d. He thought he knew all about the lesson.
e. If you will tell me where the room is.
f. Which I like very much.
g. Arrived home about six o'clock yesterday.
h. Boys and girls running and jumping.
i. My sister is studying chemistry, she hopes to become a famous scientist.
j. Wheat and corn are raised on our farm. Also potatoes.
k. My mother she went to the party.
l. The boy struggled slowly through the snow. Which seemed to grow deeper and deeper.
m. Hoping to hear from you soon.
n. You need not ask me to play with you any more.
o. The windows of our cottage were dark, I was scared, where was the rest of the family?

D VOCABULARY BUILDING

Word study is a fascinating hobby because words are full of endless surprises. Take a little word like *fix.* You will find that it has about fifty different meanings! Look up a word like *jewelry.* You will find that the British spell it jewellery! Many years ago, Lewis Carroll joined parts of two words (chuckle and snort) to make a new word: *chortle,* meaning to laugh through the nose. Recently, a ten-year-old boy on the *$64,000 Question* television show gave us a new word, *fantabulous,* by combining parts of two older words: fantastic and fabulous.

Vocabulary building combines fun with work when you study word-origins, word-groups, and word-families. Sharpen your wits by being curious about words and their ways in our language. This section will give you a good start. The rest is up to you!

▶ WORD STUDY

A WORD FOR EVERYTHING

Do you find the right word quite easily, or do you fumble through long explanations whenever you want to say something? You know that there is a word for everything. In Webster's *New International Dictionary* there are over 600,000 separate entries. Can you give the correct words that fit the following descriptions?

a. the little knob you turn on the radio set in order to change from one station to another?

b. the step upon which you put your weight in order to open the door of a bus automatically?

c. the man who plots the course and fixes the location of a plane while in flight and supplies this information to the pilot?

d. the lower part of the ear used by some girls to hang jewelry or ornaments?

e. the machine used in offices, schools, banks, etc., to clip sheets of paper neatly together with bent wire?

Of course, you probably guessed some of the right answers: (*a*) station-finder, or tuner; (*b*) treadle; (*c*) navigator; (*d*) lobe; (*e*) stapler.

Always be alert to observe and remember words wherever you meet them.

DIFFERENT LEVELS OF WORDS

Words may be divided into two large classes: *literary* and *conversational,* according to whether they occur chiefly in written or in spoken English. You will notice the difference in style by comparing some common expressions.

LITERARY	CONVERSATIONAL
portable television antenna	rabbit ears
Salk vaccine immunization	polio shots
step on the accelerator	give it the gun
deceased, or demised	passed away, or died

Style in language is like style in dress: the words must be suited to the time and place and person. In other words, you should use the expression that is acceptable, just the way you use trousers for going to church but dungarees for playing ball outdoors.

And now a caution regarding *slang:* Use slang very sparingly in your conversation. It sounds more polite to say "all right" than "okay," and it is better to avoid such low-level expressions as "nuts to you," "scram," and "park your carcass." Slang may seem funny the first time you hear it, but it grows very stale and dull after it has been repeated. Clean up your speech by using decent English always!

OLD FAMILIES AND NEWCOMERS

Many English words come from fine old respectable families, either Latin or Greek or French or what-have-you. For example, the Latin stem *duco,* meaning *lead,* has many offspring today: conduct, reduce, induce, viaduct, product, introduction, etc. The Greek stem *graph,* meaning *write,* has quite a few members of the family still living: graphic, autograph, biography, telegraph, monograph, lithography, etc. The French suffix *ette,* meaning *little,* is attached to such words as: cigarette (little cigar), chansonette (little song), layette (little garments for a baby), silhouette (little outline of a person or thing), etc.

Some newcomers or recent additions to our language are really interesting variations of old familiar words dressed up to fit modern times:

super, a Latin prefix meaning *over* or *above,* now means *bigger* and *better:* supermarket, superhighway, superman, supercolossal, supersalesman, etc.

orama, a Greek suffix meaning *that which is seen,* now means *broad new look:* cinerama (wide-screen movie), futurama (bigger design for automobiles), wonderama (new spectacular television show)

Of course, new things bring new words, too: jet planes, penicillin, televiewing, high fidelity, bookmobile, atomic bomb, the iron curtain, withholding tax, etc. Keep up to date!

USING THE DICTIONARY FOR DEFINITIONS

If you will examine the lists of words given on standard examinations in recent years, you will discover that the words you are required to define are chiefly of a literary nature. In other words, they are "bookish" in origin, the sort of expressions you meet in a piece of fiction, a magazine article, or a textbook. They may also include everyday, commonplace, or "bread-and-butter" terms. They serve to indicate the range of your vocabulary. Therefore, the definitions are usually on a literary level of usage.

Another interesting fact you will discover in analyzing the word lists is the occurrence of only three parts of speech: nouns, verbs, and adjectives. This may help you in figuring out the meanings. Now, if you will open your dictionary, you will observe that some words have a series of definitions. Which are you to select? Choose the meaning that fits the context.

For example, take the verb *to mimic,* as it might appear on a typical examination. The dictionary offers many definitions, among which are the following: to copy; to follow the example of; to use as a model; to reproduce or duplicate; to make a semblance of; to look like; to imitate; to mock; to ape; to counterfeit; to simulate; to impersonate; to resemble; etc. A sample sentence might be this: "The girl tried *to mimic* the gestures used by the actress in the movie." Answer: *to imitate.*

HOW TO INCREASE YOUR VOCABULARY

You can build up your knowledge of words in two ways: (*a*) by experiences in real-life activities, such as hobbies, studies, interests, travels, events, meeting persons, visiting places, etc.; and (*b*) by wide reading in books, magazines, and newspapers. In either case, you must be curious about new ideas and strange terms. You must develop the habit of jotting down new expressions and looking them up in the dictionary.

For example, you notice that there is an all-star variety show on television running for 24 hours around the clock in order to obtain contributions for a special fund. You learn a new word to describe this show: *telethon.* If you are a word-detective, you learn that the ending *thon* is a Greek suffix from the ancient *Marathon,* meaning a long-distance running race. Thus, you can guess the meaning of similar "long-distance" words, such as: walkathon, talkathon, dancethon, etc.

EXERCISES

VOCABULARY

In each of the sentences below one word is italicized. Underneath the sentence is a group of five words or expressions. From these select the word or expression that has most nearly the same meaning as the italicized word. [Example: The mechanic *welded* the broken parts.

        polished   <u>joined</u>   scattered   melted   scraped]

VOCABULARY EXERCISE 1

a. If he decides to *remain,* tell us at once.
    answer   hesitate   leave   move   stay
b. The reports of the election were *incomplete.*
    finished   not finished   answered   unpleasant   not classified
c. The dog began to *quiver* when his master appeared.
    bark   leap   run   stare   tremble
d. Some day you may *regret* your failure to study.
    be glad of   be sorry for   enjoy   look back on   reconsider
e. *Alert* policemen stood on every corner.
    uniformed   courageous   courteous   experienced   watchful
f. In one *instant* he put out the fire.
    glance   hour   moment   leap   motion
g. As he entered the court, the judge wore a *grave* expression.
    surprised   serious   smiling   kind   angry
h. Their mother's new hat, they thought, appeared *comical.*
    delightful   overdecorated   laughable   stylish   dainty
i. A dog is one of man's most *steadfast* friends.
    intelligent   gallant   faithful   wholesome   critical
j. Five doors opened into the *corridor.*
    courtyard   auditorium   passageway   tower   parlor
k. Several plans were *discarded* by the committee.
    drawn up   outlined   voted on   rejected   changed
l. The loser must *yield* the fort to the enemy.
    describe   disclose   deny   return   surrender
m. He has a tendency to *exaggerate* his problems.
    argue about   overstate   forget   avoid   laugh at
n. They planned to *duplicate* the Colonial costumes.
    copy   display   remodel   inspect   repair
o. The boy looked with *envy* at the motorcycle.
    disgust   fright   amazement   longing   suspicion

VOCABULARY EXERCISE 2

a. Do you think that was a fair *exchange?*
discovery   division   meaning   question   trade
b. The carpenters removed the *decaying* posts.
rotting   supporting   extra   splintered   oldest
c. The *mighty* army marched slowly toward the city.
allied   lawless   powerful   small   victorious
d. He *clutched* the rope as his feet began to slip.
loosened   shoved   stopped   grasped   twirled
e. There was a large *blur* in one corner of the painting.
smear   signature   figure   hole   image
f. That certainly looks like a *fierce* dog to me.
friendly   lazy   savage   outcast   unusual
g. The reporter gave a very *accurate* report of the meeting.
careless   correct   discouraging   confusing   long
h. He *ignored* the policeman at the corner.
insulted   disregarded   respected   greeted   signaled
i. Cinderella had never dreamed that such *bliss* could be hers.
companionship   distress   joy   hatred   warmth
j. They took a *conducted* tour through the museum.
guided   long   interesting   scientific   hasty
k. The results of the election *amazed* the candidates.
excited   pleased   enraged   astonished   disappointed
l. The letter was written in a very *commonplace* style.
humorous   unusual   fancy   forceful   ordinary
m. On the first day, they *encountered* an unfriendly tribe.
fled from   met   conquered   bargained with   visited
n. The boy felt very *conspicuous* in his red shirt.
noticeable   stylish   warm   untidy   guilty
o. The workman hastened to *fortify* the dam.
complete   modernize   strengthen   undermine   lower

VOCABULARY EXERCISE 3

a. The traveler carried *sufficient* money for the trip.
counterfeit   enough   less   too little   too much
b. He walked *hastily* to the counter.
angrily   often   quickly   seldom   slowly
c. I shall *conceal* the letter in the tree.
catch   find   hide   steal   throw
d. He prefers to *dwell* in the country.
build   picnic   rent   live   continue
e. There is no *certain* way of locating the treasure.
better   easy   familiar   private   sure
f. In *former* times life was more simple.
better   later   earlier   happier   calmer
g. The immigrant's arrival marked the *commencement* of a new life.
beginning   choosing   finishing   seeking   settling
h. The war brought the people much *misery.*
distress   distrust   toil   hatred   money

206

i. The teacher was *extremely* pleased with her students.
  seldom   often   sometimes   frequently   very
j. The trapper *indicated* the streams where fishing was best.
  described   kept secret   pointed out   retraced   walked along
k. The odd results of the experiment *perplexed* the scientist.
  decided   disgusted   helped   puzzled   surprised
l. The hostess greeted the guest *cordially*.
  unpleasantly   coldly   crudely   heartily   sentimentally
m. Do not *confuse* the audience when you speak.
  tire   bewilder   consider   criticize   forget
n. The *hostile* attitude of my neighbor frightened me.
  doubtful   friendly   indifferent   suspicious   unfriendly
o. How long do you think you can *endure* these conditions?
  await   bear   demand   escape   obey

VOCABULARY EXERCISE 4

a. The *timid* child surprised the class with her comment.
  beautiful   forward   lazy   shy   stupid
b. The forest offered the deer *security*.
  food   harm   imprisonment   pleasure   safety
c. There was a *terrible* moment after the explosion.
  costly   dreadful   steadfast   quiet   thoughtful
d. The noise did not *ruffle* grandfather; he continued reading as usual.
  disturb   please   puzzle   reach   satisfy
e. It is fun to *roam* through the countryside in the spring.
  drive   hunt   rush   search   wander
f. The most *skillful* workmen were asked to help.
  active   interested   handsome   expert   honest
g. Everywhere the army marched it left *ruin* behind it.
  crime   destruction   rage   trash   work
h. The Girl Scouts started *gaily* toward the lake.
  loudly   merrily   proudly   sadly   quickly
i. His not coming home to dinner was the cause of great *anxiety*.
  guilt   poverty   sickness   trouble   worry
j. The old sea captain had a *hoarse* voice.
  harsh   hearty   loud   mournful   musical
k. That white house has a good *situation*.
  decoration   direction   foundation   location   possibility
l. The *furious* storm tore the roof from our barn.
  bold   electric   fierce   huge   wicked
m. Such *industrious* workers are a pleasure to watch.
  busy   clever   contented   quiet   well-dressed
n. The simple farmer was a man of *noble* character.
  honorable   jolly   sensible   stern   stupid
o. The fumes from the science room were considered a *nuisance*.
  flare   annoyance   burden   carrier   tumult

VOCABULARY EXERCISE 5

a. It is dangerous to *pretend* that you are wise.
  boast   declare   forget   make believe   think

b. Please *mention* some of your friends who might be interested.
   describe   discourage   name   send   telephone
c. The firm kept its *surplus* coats in storage.
   expensive   extra   regular   useless   winter
d. The president expressed his *opinion.*
   criticisms   desire   plan of action   point of view   purpose
e. The *cargo* arrived at the port.
   automobile   engine   freight load   package   train
f. John *rarely* knows the answer.
   always   at once   constantly   frequently   seldom
g. The *ridiculous* costume won a prize.
   foolish   lovely   masquerade   practical   unwanted
h. He will *secure* a job at the plant.
   get   hold   plan for   save   work on
i. We *abandoned* the boat a few yards from shore.
   boarded   gave up   sank   slowed down   tipped over
j. The collision did not *disable* him.
   affect   alarm   bother   cripple   frighten
k. The coach of the team should always be *moderate* in showing enthusiasm.
   busy   extraordinary   loud   reasonable   uneasy
l. The manager was sometimes *insolent* while on duty.
   free   insane   polite   rash   rude
m. The place where the airplane landed seemed *dismal* to the pilot.
   evident   gloomy   peculiar   similar   strange
n. I saw them *promenade* along the garden path.
   clatter   hasten   stare   stroll   trip
o. The *amiable* doctor brought cheer to the patients.
   bewildered   lenient   lovable   particular   serious

VOCABULARY EXERCISE 6

a. *Perhaps* you misunderstood his instructions.
   at least   happily   maybe   of course   surely
b. Do you think the exhibit *merits* an award?
   deserves   gets   lacks   requires   wins
c. It was a very *unusual* day for April.
   cold   delightful   good   ordinary   rare
d. A single *fragrant* rose decorated his desk.
   late-blooming   rambling   sweet-smelling   wilted   yellow
e. The *glittering* bead attracted the crow.
   bouncing   colored   gleaming   pretty   rolling
f. Jack did *notice* the attractive child.
   believe   observe   overlook   speak to   write to
g. We are too fond of the *advantages* of civilization.
   benefits   changes   classes   powers   results
h. Accidents in the home may cause *injury.*
   danger   death   delay   grief   harm
i. The Spanish explorers found great *treasures* for their king.
   banks   chests   islands   riches   values
j. They prepared a great *banquet* for the returning general.
   ball   feast   gift   hall   surprise

k. We must learn to be *tolerant* of people different from ourselves.

    afraid   aware   careful   suspicious   **understanding**

l. His *ambition* caused him to go to night school.

    desire to succeed   fortune   hope of freedom   ignorance   **pride**

m. The frightened child ran to *embrace* her mother.

    call   escape   **hug**   scold   watch

n. *Actually* he did not know the man.

    now   often   **really**   suddenly   **then**

o. The hike up Mount Marcy was *strenuous*.

    disappointing   dull   pleasant   scenic   **vigorous**

VOCABULARY EXERCISE 7

a. The lane was *narrow* and led to a mountain lake.

    attractive   **not wide**   overgrown   rough   **without trees**

b. Blow the horn as you *approach* the gate.

    discover   leave   **draw near**   pass through   **unlock**

c. It was part of our *bargain* that you should wash dishes.

    agreement   debt   goal   plan   wish

d. I shall remember that little valley *forever*.

    often   yet   **always**   next   **no more**

e. The boy was *eager* to go on the trip.

    able   afraid   **anxious**   likely   **willing**

f. The children were having a *dispute* over the toy.

    conversation   crying spell   **disagreement**   performance   tantrum

g. The man was punished for his *brutal* act.

    bloody   **cruel**   deadly   defenseless   ugly

h. We *launched* our new business with great hope for the future.

    concluded   **started**   pursued   steered   watched

i. The two streets *intersect* at the edge of town.

    run parallel   change names   end   become thoroughfares   **cross**

j. She suffered from an *uncommon* disease.

    ordinary   painful   contagious   **rare**   new

k. The antique chair was very *fragile*.

    delicate   worn   beautiful   well-made   useless

l. They picked *edible* mushrooms.

    poisonous   well-formed   unusual   large   **eatable**

m. He found the reception at the airport very *gratifying*.

    surprising   deafening   **pleasant**   disagreeable   **impolite**

n. *Defective* brakes caused the mishap.

    old-fashioned   uneven   squeaking   unused   **faulty**

o. After a little *exertion* the box was moved.

    argument   delay   coaxing   **effort**   planning

VOCABULARY EXERCISE 8

a. The *rapidity* of the attack surprised us.

    power   effectiveness   possibility   strangeness   **swiftness**

b. She enjoyed *conversing* with her friends.

    meeting   laughing   **talking**   dining   traveling

c. There was a small *vent* near the end of the tube.

    cap   screw   **opening**   joint   pump

d. With great *caution* we opened the barn door.
care   fear   distrust   danger   difficulty
e. The old man's coat was *threadbare.*
spotted   tight   new   ill-made   shabby
f. I was sorry that I could not decide *otherwise.*
immediately   differently   favorably   positively   eagerly
g. The *gigantic* switchboard controlled all the lights in the theatre.
complicated   up-to-date   automatic   huge   stationary
h. The balls were made of *synthetic* rubber.
artificial   hard   cheap   imported   crude
i. He was *merely* a servant in the house.
occasionally   in no way   unhappily   formerly   no more than
j. The prisoner *conferred* with his lawyer.
argued   interfered   dined   sympathized   consulted
k. The soldier's *gallantry* went unnoticed.
strength   fright   disobedience   injury   bravery
l. The music was chosen for its *soothing* effect.
tuneful   calming   magic   exciting   solemn
m. The owners were advised to *reinforce* the wall.
rebuild   lengthen   lower   strengthen   repaint
n. They performed their duties with *utmost* ease.
noticeable   some   surprising   greatest   increasing
o. We picnicked near a *cascade.*
pond   camp   waterfall   trail   slope

VOCABULARY EXERCISE 9

a. The old soldier became a *trusty* watchman at the bank.
cordial   favorite   helpless   reliable   tough
b. The workmen will *produce* as many cars as possible.
destroy   hire   keep   make   sell
c. I hope that you will *notice* that boy at the right.
approve   greet   observe   recognize   search
d. The *captain* has outrun his companions.
engineer   fireman   leader   principal   seaman
e. The *midget* in the movie was the best actor.
cherub   dwarf   fairy   giant   nymph
f. The girl was clear and *honest* in her statements.
alert   fearless   lucky   thoughtful   truthful
g. The *enraged* man rushed out of the door.
angry   grave   impatient   skillful   unfortunate
h. His father was both wealthy and *distinguished.*
brave   famous   gentle   goodhearted   sociable
i. The woman's *despair* was shown in her face.
curiosity   hopelessness   poverty   power   sickness
j. Let us *cancel* the common factor in the fractions.
cross out   deal with   double   reduce   shorten
k. The trainer was *ever* kind to his animals.
always   helpfully   indeed   really   seldom
l. The *council* will decide the plans for next year.
adviser   banquet   board   commissioner   scouts

m. *Frequently* the chores were completed ahead of time.
  again   never   often   seldom   sometimes
n. The words on the page were *dimmed* by time.
  brightened   cleaned   colored   faded   smeared
o. The search for the documents was very *methodical.*
  disappointing   careless   orderly   far-reaching   **violent**

VOCABULARY EXERCISE 10

a. The chairman was anxious to *adjourn* the meeting.
  conduct   attend   start   address   close
b. The gown was made of a *glossy* fabric.
  shiny   embroidered   many-colored   transparent   **expensive**
c. An ocean voyage in a small boat can be very *hazardous.*
  thrilling   slow   dangerous   rough   tiresome
d. The weatherman predicted *variable* winds.
  drying   strong   cool   light   changeable
e. Not long after the play began, the children began to *fidget.*
  clap   move restlessly   cry   laugh aloud   shriek
f. That person has a habit of *meddling.*
  stumbling   interfering   playing jokes   cheating   **being late**
g. Young children are frequently *inquisitive.*
  curious   saucy   restless   shy   tearful
h. The *falsity* of the report was apparent at first glance.
  uselessness   untidiness   incompleteness   incorrectness   disagreeableness
i. Orders were given to *liberate* the prisoners by noon.
  question   transfer   free   sentence   fingerprint
j. She is *habitually* late for her dental appointments.
  usually   seldom   extremely   slightly   never
k. The soldiers were given *spacious* living quarters.
  pleasant   well-aired   crowded   well-furnished   **roomy**
l. The witnesses gave *straightforward* answers.
  hasty   frank   conflicting   helpful   serious
m. His income *exceeds* that of his brother.
  is less regular than   is greater than   is the same as   is less than
n. He *shunned* all of his neighbors.
  disapproved of   welcomed   quarreled with   avoided   insulted
o. Many of the natives are *illiterate.*
  unable to read   unclean   unable to vote   unmanageable   sickly

 # WORD GROUPS: HOMONYMS, SYNONYMS, AND ANTONYMS

Words are related in many ways. Sometimes they have similar sounds but different meanings, such as *steak* (= a slice of meat) and *stake* (= a piece of wood driven into the ground as a mark); these are called HOMONYMS.

Other words are closely associated in meaning, such as *victory* (= the defeat of an enemy) and *triumph* (= a brilliant victory); these are called SYNONYMS.

Certain words carry opposite meanings, such as *optimist* (= one who hopes for the best) and *pessimist* (= one who expects the worst); these words are ANTONYMS.

Learn to distinguish between homonyms in order to avoid confusion in spelling which will result in such "boners" as, "I feel a little *horse* today." (*horse* = an animal; *hoarse* = husky voiced)

Use a variety of synonyms to make your writing more vivid and colorful by avoiding the deadly monotony of sameness: "It was a *nice* party. We all had a *nice* time. I wore a *nice* dress and a *nice* pair of shoes."

Build up your vocabulary by learning the antonyms for a word whenever you consult the dictionary; for example, when you look up *revere*, you will find the following antonyms: *despise, defame, dishonor, revile*.

HOMONYMS

Two or more words that are pronounced alike but are different in spelling and in meaning are called *homonyms*.

1. to, too, two	26. there, their, they're
2. pail, pale	27. way, weigh
3. meet, meat, mete	28. blue, blew
4. road, rode	29. ring, wring
5. son, sun	30. bow, bough
6. know, no	31. plain, plane
7. some, sum	32. seen, scene
8. would, wood	33. course, coarse
9. hear, here	34. straight, strait
10. our, hour	35. mail, male
11. right, write	36. led, lead
12. break, brake	37. grown, groan
13. steel, steal	38. air, heir, ere
14. whole, hole	39. forth, fourth
15. red, read	40. principle, principal
16. great, grate	41. session, cession
17. sent, cent, scent	42. council, counsel
18. by, buy	43. patients, patience
19. eight, ate	44. hymn, him
20. peace, piece	45. stationary, stationery
21. pair, pare, pear	46. altar, alter
22. through, threw	47. compliment, complement
23. so, sow, sew	48. serial, cereal
24. sight, site, cite	49. rain, reign
25. capital, capitol	50. vain, vein

EXERCISES

HOMONYMS

A. Write a homonym for each of the following words:

1. mail	6. coarse	11. steel	16. piece
2. forth	7. wring	12. hear	17. threw
3. rode	8. strait	13. led	18. capitol
4. whole	9. ate	14. plain	19. site
5. heir	10. cession	15. patients	20. buy

B. Find a homonym for each of the words below, and then write a sentence using correctly the matching word:

1. doe	4. bare	7. rode	9. tide
2. night	5. kernel	8. reign	10. border
3. missed	6. plain		

C. Select the words in parentheses that make the sentences correct:

1. He received many (presence, presents).
2. The blood flowed from his (vein, vain).
3. The dog waited patiently (by, buy) the door.
4. Has the (pale, pail) been emptied yet?
5. Let them try to do it (there, their) own way next time.
6. We want to go to the movies (to, too).
7. The (principal, principle) cause for failure is excessive absence.
8. She asked the tailor to (altar, alter) the jacket.
9. The lawyer gave his client good (counsel, council).
10. Do you like the (sent, scent) of apple blossoms?
11. In order to have some (peace, piece), I had to give my little brother a (peace, piece) of the candy.
12. A large (some, sum) was contributed by (some, sum) of them.
13. The rope holding the (canvas, canvass) will (break, brake) if you (sees, seize) it (too, to) firmly.
14. The (stationary, stationery) is in the (principal's, principle's) office.
15. We walked (threw, through) the tunnel to visit the (capital, capitol) across the street.

D. One word in each of the following sentences has been incorrectly used in place of its homonym. Write the matching homonym that makes the sentence correct in meaning.

1. Ate small boys ran along the river bank.
2. James through the ball to Billy.
3. My mother makes good bread doe.
4. The ship sailed a true coarse.
5. He painted a beautiful winter seen.

213

SYNONYMS

If you will turn to some of the large department store advertisements in today's paper, you will notice that a dress is not always called a *dress*. You will find such synonyms as *frock, gown, house dress, party dress*, etc., which are more suitable to the different varieties of garments. In your own everyday speaking and writing, you may have fallen into the habit of overusing certain common words and expressions, such as *lots of, so, nice, swell*, etc. Make your sentences more lively by substituting other words and phrases. For example: Instead of "I liked it *immensely*," say, "I enjoyed every bit of it." Instead of "It's a very *interesting* movie," say, "It's the kind of movie that keeps you sitting at the edge of your seat." Use the larger-sized desk dictionary, or consult a book of synonyms. Your school library probably has one or more of the following reference books which you should learn to use to improve your oral and written expression:

Webster: *Dictionary of Synonyms*
Roget: *International Thesaurus of English Words and Phrases*
Fernald: *English Synonyms, Antonyms, and Prepositions*
Fowler: *Dictionary of Modern English Usage*
Crabb: *English Synonyms*

EXERCISES

SYNONYMS

A. A helpful way of improving your expression is to learn a variety of phrasings for a particular idea. Study the following groups of words and write original sentences containing them.

GROUPS OF SYNONYMS—I

1. denied, refused to admit, declared false
2. encouraged, spurred on, urged to greater effort
3. disliked greatly, had only contempt for, scorned
4. occurred frequently, happened often, took place repeatedly
5. unhurriedly, slowly, without haste, gradually

6. could easily be seen, was evident, seemed apparent
7. would not look at, refused to notice, ignored
8. was worthy of, deserved, had every right to
9. in vain, vainly, without success, uselessly
10. many a time, often, frequently, time after time

GROUPS OF SYNONYMS—II

1. thought, was of the opinion, held the belief
2. without doubt, surely, certainly
3. was the cause of, was the reason for, was responsible for
4. assumed, took for granted, believed likely, expected
5. the outcome was, the consequence was, as a result
6. had no interest in, was absolutely indifferent, showed disregard
7. was very angry, was in a rage, was most indignant
8. was uncertain, was not sure, was in doubt
9. was suspicious of, had little faith in, did not trust
10. appeared reluctant, seemed unwilling, hesitated

GROUPS OF SYNONYMS—III

1. not often, rarely, seldom
2. became careless, relaxed vigilance, grew negligent
3. was used to, was accustomed to, was in the habit of
4. after a time, after an interval, eventually
5. deliberately, without haste, carefully
6. instantly, at once, immediately, without delay
7. showed anxiety, was visibly concerned, seemed troubled
8. supposed, thought probable, had an idea that
9. concluded, brought to a close, put an end to, finished
10. did not doubt, was confident, was absolutely certain

B. Substitute a more vivid specific word for each italicized general word in the following sentences. Example:

(general) The *man looked* at the judge.
(specific) The *lawyer glanced* at the judge.

1. The *table* had a *dish* containing *fruit*.
2. The *boy* had three *dogs*.
3. The *car went* down the hill.
4. The *room* was full of *people*.
5. The *child gave* the *lady* some *flowers*.

C. Rewrite the following passages, using more colorful and original expressions to replace the italicized words.

1. "You mustn't go," *said* John.
   "Why not?" *said* Dick.
   "You'll get lost," *said* his friend.
   "I'm not afraid," *said* Dick, as he disappeared.

2. We had a *nice* time at Betty's party. Mother thought it was *nice* of you to bring us home. Wasn't Betty's dress *nice*? The refreshments were very *nice*.

3. It was a *great* day for the home team. There was a *great* crowd of watchers. Our pitcher surely was *great,* and all the fellows on the field gave him *great* support. The score stood tied in the last inning when one of our batters smashed a *great* drive over the outfielder's head. Amid *great* cheering, he came safely home. It was a *great* game, and we won.
4. We had a *grand* time at the picnic. The weather was *grand.* After eating our sandwiches and lying in the *grand* sunshine, we went for a dip. The swimming was *grand.* Everyone agreed it had been a *grand* experience.
5. I would like to get a *good* job. I mean a job with *good* hours and *good* pay. Of course, the next requirement would be a *good* boss, too. What's the use of working unless it's in a *good* place with *good* atmosphere and *good* co-workers? If I get a *good* job, I'll make *good.*

D. Vary the synonyms to help suggest color, size, manner, mood, etc. For each group of synonyms at the left, write the appropriate word selected from the list at the right.

1. robed, clad, garbed	*a.* old	
2. lass, damsel, maiden	*b.* new	
3. vision, trance, reverie	*c.* small	
4. recent, fresh, modern	*d.* light	
5. ancient, antiquated, antique	*e.* girl	
6. devoured, gulped, swallowed	*f.* dressed	
7. spied, gazed, observed	*g.* ate	
8. tiny, miniature, puny	*h.* horn	
9. glow, glimmer, twinkle	*i.* saw	
10. bugle, trumpet, cornet	*j.* dream	

ANTONYMS

Words opposite in meaning are called antonyms; examples: *asleep* and *awake, profit* and *loss, old* and *new, night* and *day, strong* and *weak.* A knowledge of antonyms increases your word-power and helps you to express ideas more readily, especially when you discuss comparisons and contrasts in experience. You have probably already noticed the numerous contrasts that make up the world and the people in it. Naturally, such contrasts or opposites as *birth* and *death, youth* and *age, work* and *play,* suggest the extremes of the pattern of living.

1. hard—soft	10. crooked—straight
2. easy—difficult	11. happy—sad
3. serious—gay	12. strange—familiar
4. greedy—generous	13. quick—slow
5. handsome—ugly	14. heavy—light
6. tall—short	15. empty—full
7. large—small	16. dull—bright
8. ignorant—learned	17. progress—retrogress
9. wise—foolish	18. advance—retreat

19. start—stop
20. first—last
21. stormy—calm
22. irritating—soothing
23. wound—heal
24. top—bottom
25. elementary—advanced
26. contract—expand
27. create—destroy
28. good—bad
29. buy—sell
30. near—far
31. together—apart
32. foremost—hindmost
33. beginner—veteran
34. consent—disagree
35. give—take
36. patriotism—treason
37. fear—courage
38. faith—disbelief
39. tell—ask
40. wet—dry
41. heed—ignore
42. war—peace
43. rich—poor
44. brief—long
45. plain—fancy
46. divide—unite
47. free—bind
48. loyal—treacherous
49. lazy—industrious
50. equality—partiality
51. simple—complicated
52. trivial—important
53. success—failure
54. gentle—cruel
55. increase—decrease
56. comfort—distress
57. silence—noise
58. superior—inferior
59. ally—enemy
60. delight—displease

61. dally—hurry
62. massive—slight
63. mix—separate
64. shout—whisper
65. laugh—cry
66. donate—accept
67. cautious—daring
68. harmless—dangerous
69. admire—ridicule
70. remember—forget
71. entrance—exit
72. certainty—indecision
73. protest—submit
74. declare—conceal
75. meager—abundant
76. definite—vague
77. odd—usual
78. increase—condense
79. hot—cool
80. praise—insult
81. ambiguous—clear
82. occupation—hobby
83. admit—deny
84. attack—defend
85. exaggeration—understatement
86. powerful—feeble
87. absence—presence
88. tardiness—punctuality
89. leader—follower
90. polite—rude
91. conspicuous—insignificant
92. aware—unconscious
93. keen—blunt
94. timid—forward
95. stained—spotless
96. lost—found
97. cheap—dear
98. help—hindrance
99. loosen—tighten
100. permanent—temporary

Note: Many antonyms may be formed by adding prefixes and suffixes which give words opposite meanings.

Examples: harm*ful,* harm*less* (suffixes)
*pro*motion, *de*motion (prefixes)

Whenever you use the dictionary, you will find at the end of the various definitions and synonyms for a certain word, a group of antonyms introduced by the abbreviation *Ant.*

Example: *repudiate* = to refuse to recognize. *Syn.:* disclaim, renounce, discard. *Ant.:* acknowledge, own, admit, keep.

EXERCISE

SYNONYMS AND ANTONYMS

Write a synonym and an antonym for each word listed below.

1. accurate	9. imprison	17. solemn	25. reliable
2. bold	10. justice	18. radiance	26. torrid
3. calm	11. knowledge	19. identical	27. defend
4. deceit	12. lament	20. talkative	28. divide
5. esteem	13. merge	21. difficult	29. peril
6. enhance	14. natural	22. prominent	30. adversary
7. genial	15. indolent	23. submission	31. renounced
8. habitual	16. delay	24. cautious	32. determined

 WORD FORMATION: PREFIXES, SUFFIXES, AND STEMS

From your study of the English language, you know that words may be built by using prefixes, stems, and suffixes. Therefore, a knowledge of these elements and their meanings will help you to understand English words more fully.

A *prefix* is an element placed at the beginning of a word to modify the basic meaning; examples: *trans, in, pro.*

WORD	PREFIX	STEM	SUFFIX

transportation → trans + port + ation
               (across)   (carry)   (act or state)
              [= act of carrying across]

invisible → in + vis + ible
            (not)   (see)   (able)
           [= not able to be seen]

promoter → pro + mot + er
        (forward)   (move)   (one who)
      [= one who encourages or forwards something]

Notice how prefixes can change the meaning of a word:

port = carry

ex port = carry *out*
de port = carry *away*
re port = carry *back*
im port = carry *into*

A *suffix* is an element placed at the end of a word to modify the basic meaning and to change the part of speech; examples: *ation, ible, er.*

Observe how the suffixes alter the meaning and change the part of speech of a word:

aud = hear

audi *ence* = hearers (*noun*)
audit *or* = hearer (*noun*)
audit *ory* = pertaining to hearing (*adjective*)
aud *ible* = able to be heard (*adjective*)
audit *orium* = place for public hearing (*noun*)

A *stem* is the central part of a word which remains unchanged although its meaning may be modified by the addition of prefixes or suffixes; example:

spect = see or look

in *spect* = to look at
pro *spect* = to look forward
spect acle = something to look at
spect ator = one who looks at

PREFIXES

Learn to recognize the following prefixes as used in forming English words. Observe the way in which the prefixes modify the original meaning in each case. Consult the dictionary to find more examples for each prefix.

PREFIX	MEANING	USED IN ENGLISH WORDS
ante	before	anteroom, antedate
arch	first, chief	archbishop, architect
anti	against	antislavery, antitoxin
bi	two	bicycle, bicameral
di, dis	apart, not	division, discomfort
de	down	describe, depend
e, ex	out of	export, exit
auto	self	autobiography, autograph
trans	across	transport, transfer
in	not	incomplete, insecure
inter	between	interrupt, interpose
super	beyond	supernatural, superior
semi	half	semicircle, semicivilized
sub	under	submerge, sublet
pro	forward	promotion, prospect
uni	one	uniform, united
mono	one, single	monoplane, monotone
re	again	return, regain
post	after	postpone, postscript
circum	around	circumference, circumstance
un	not	unable, unfriendly
se	apart	separate, secret
intro	within	introduce, introspective
a, ab, abs	from, away	avert, abnormal, abstract
mis	wrong	misdeed, mistrust
co, col, con	with, together	cooperate, collect, conspiracy

SUFFIXES

As explained before, suffixes are word-endings which modify the stem or root of a word and change its part of speech. For example: *liber* is a Latin stem meaning *free* in English; therefore, by adding suffixes these words are formed:

liber *al* = free-handed (*adjective*)
liber *ty* = state of freedom (*noun*)
liber *ate* = to set free (*verb*)

NOUN SUFFIX	MEANING	USED IN ENGLISH WORDS
ance	state of being	importance, attendance
ary	that which, place where	dictionary, stationary
ence	state of being	difference, independence
ery	that which, place where	creamery, stationery
ity	state of being	purity, simplicity
age	state of being	shortage, courage
an	one who	American, human
cy	state of being	infancy, constancy
ist	one who	dentist, dramatist
ism	state or quality	heroism, patriotism
ure	that which	posture, culture
tude	state of being	solitude, altitude
ation	action, condition	civilization, variation
ment	resulting state or condition	astonishment, contentment
ice	quality or state	service, justice
dom	power or state	kingdom, freedom
ling	diminutive	princeling, duckling
hood	state or rank	boyhood, womanhod
ship	state or quality of being	friendship, hardship
or	one who, that which	actor, supervisor, motor
er	one who, that which	baker, worker
ness	quality or state of being	kindness, goodness
ess	feminine ending	princess, goddess
ite	follower, descendant	Israelite, Brooklynite

221

ADJECTIVE SUFFIX	MEANING	USED IN ENGLISH WORDS
ous	full of	joyous, nervous
ious	full of	religious, delicious
al	pertaining to	legal, loyal
ic	pertaining to, like	geometric, comic
ical	pertaining to, like	classical, historical
il, ile	pertaining to	civil, juvenile
ory	pertaining to	auditory, introductory
some	pertaining to	winsome, tiresome
able	capable of being	lovable, unconquerable
ible	capable of being	forcible, perceptible
ive	relating to, given to	active, festive
en	of the nature of	wooden, golden
ish	of the nature of	foolish, childish
less	without	priceless, hopeless
fold	times (multiplied by)	twofold, hundredfold
ed	possessed of	dogged, wicked
ing	(present participle)	walking, dancing

VERB SUFFIX	MEANING	USED IN ENGLISH WORDS
fy	to make	magnify, fortify
ate	to make or do	dedicate, donate
ize	to make like	stylize, Americanize

ADVERB SUFFIX	MEANING	USED IN ENGLISH WORDS
ly	manner, like	attentively, gradually
er	more (in degree)	kindlier, sicklier
est	highest (in degree)	latest, kindliest
most	highest (in degree)	foremost, hindmost

STEMS (ROOTS)

Of course, the *stem* or *root* of the word is the basic element containing the central meaning of the word. Many English words contain stems borrowed from Latin and Greek. A few useful stems worth knowing are the following:

STEM	MEANING	USED IN ENGLISH WORDS
fer	to bear, to carry	transfer, refer, prefer
meter	measure	speedometer, thermometer
ped	foot	pedal, pedestal, impediment
fort	strong	fortify, fortress, fortitude
clud, clus	to shut	include, exclude, recluse
cred	to believe	creditable, incredible
sta	to stand	stationary, statue, static
struct	to build	construct, instruct, structure
ten, tain	to hold	retain, contain, detention
tele	far away	telephone, telegraph, television
cur, cour	to run	current, courier, course
flect, flex	to bend	deflect, genuflect, inflexion
fin	to end	final, finish, infinite
pater	father	patriot, patriarch, paternal
equ	equal	equality, equity, equation
grad, gress	to step	graduate, progress, transgress
pos	to place	position, repose, compose
scrib, script	to write	subscribe, describe, postscript
voc, vok	to call	vocal, vocation, revoke

EXERCISES

PREFIXES, SUFFIXES, STEMS

A. Using a different prefix in each case, write a word formed from each of the following words:

1. appear
2. commend
3. proper
4. scribe
5. take
6. arrange
7. expensive
8. marine
9. ordinary
10. important

B. Using a different suffix in each case, write a word formed from each of the following verbs:

1. begin
2. act
3. know
4. please
5. appear
6. intend
7. approve
8. disappoint
9. superintend
10. speculate

C. Using a different prefix or suffix in each case, write a word formed from each of the following:

1. notify
2. secure
3. known
4. perfect
5. hard
6. rare
7. enclose
8. conduct
9. complete
10. pray

D. Using the lists of suffixes, prefixes, and stems given on the preceding pages, build word-families. For example, *bene* (Latin) = well + *fic, fit* = do:

benefit	beneficiary	beneficially	beneficently
beneficent	benefited	beneficiaries	benefice
beneficial	beneficence	benefiting	benediction

E. Build three words from each of the following *prefixes:*

1. semi
2. sub
3. de
4. anti
5. un
6. dis
7. inter
8. re
9. pro
10. mono
11. ex
12. post
13. mis
14. super
15. circum

F. Build three words from each of the following *suffixes:*

1. ment
2. able
3. ism
4. ity
5. ery
6. less
7. ible
8. ic
9. ness
10. fold
11. ly
12. ous
13. tude
14. fy
15. ate

G. Prefixes meaning "not" or "the opposite" are: *un, im, in, il, ir, dis, mis.* Change the meaning of each of the words below to the exact opposite by adding a prefix. Examples of antonyms:

happy, *un*happy   legal, *il*legal
perfect, *im*perfect   regular, *ir*regular
active, *in*active   please, *dis*please
direct, *mis*direct

1. important
2. correct
3. reliable
4. approve
5. ability
6. possible
7. rational
8. fair
9. agree
10. patient
11. comfort
12. sure
13. complete
14. sincere
15. interesting
16. legible
17. pure
18. continue
19. understand
20. logical
21. advantage
22. state
23. literate
24. responsible
25. mature
26. action
27. necessary
28. appear
29. proper
30. sufficient

H. Write an adjective and its corresponding adverb formed from each of the following words: [Do not use the ending -ing for the adjective form.]

WORD	ADJECTIVE	ADVERB
[Example: play	playful	playfully]
1. cheer		
2. please		
3. agree		
4. courage		
5. obey		
6. care		
7. succeed		
8. hope		
9. speed		
10. service		

I. Change each of the words below to mean "a person" or "one who" by adding er or or. Examples:

dream, dreamer   instruct, instructor

1. sail	9. hit	17. paint	25. retail
2. fight	10. clean	18. operate	26. dictate
3. row	11. wash	19. plant	27. profess
4. orate	12. educate	20. win	28. play
5. edit	13. farm	21. inspect	29. print
6. wait	14. press	22. direct	30. sit
7. act	15. buy	23. sell	
8. wrap	16. bat	24. swim	

J. Change each of the words below to mean "a person" or "one who."

1. library	9. drug	17. shoe	25. electric
2. science	10. magic	18. type	26. chemistry
3. piano	11. humor	19. humanity	27. guard
4. pharmacy	12. colony	20. poetry	28. engine
5. drama	13. mathematics	21. physics	29. essay
6. senate	14. surgery	22. police	30. philosophy
7. grammar	15. comedy	23. philanthropy	
8. biology	16. fire	24. novel	

K. Write the proper adjective that corresponds to the proper noun.

1. Ireland	9. Norway	17. Mexico	25. Turkey
2. France	10. Sweden	18. Spain	26. India
3. Scotland	11. England	19. Peru	27. Israel
4. Russia	12. America	20. Brazil	28. Switzerland
5. Poland	13. Egypt	21. Australia	29. Korea
6. Hungary	14. Italy	22. Portugal	30. Austria
7. Greece	15. China	23. Finland	
8. Denmark	16. Japan	24. Wales	

FORMING PLURALS OF NOUNS

The first rule concerning the formation of plurals of nouns in English is, "Consult the dictionary." This is necessary if you wish the kind of accuracy that avoids guesswork. As you become familiar with everyday nouns, you will grow more certain of the spelling. Here are some suggestions that will aid you in fixing some regular spellings in mind. The irregular nouns you must memorize; luckily, there are not very many.

RULES FOR THE FORMATION OF PLURALS

1. Regular nouns form their plurals usually by adding *s* or *es* to the singular.

chair—chairs	box—boxes
tree—trees	church—churches
book—books	tomato—tomatoes
house—houses	potato—potatoes
car—cars	bench—benches

2. The plurals of nouns ending in *y* preceded by a consonant are formed by changing *y* to *i* and adding *es*.

city—cities	lady—ladies
liberty—liberties	prophecy—prophecies
variety—varieties	monopoly—monopolies
necessity—necessities	company—companies
country—countries	pony—ponies

3. The plurals of nouns ending in *y* preceded by a vowel are formed by adding *s*.

essay—essays	journey—journeys
holiday—holidays	survey—surveys
monkey—monkeys	attorney—attorneys
donkey—donkeys	buoy—buoys
key—keys	toy—toys

To form the plural correctly, or to guess carelessly—that is the question! The **dictionary** will give you the right answer every time.

Rules for the Formation of Plurals (Continued)

4. The plurals of most nouns ending in *o* are formed by adding *s*.

piano—pianos
radio—radios
solo—solos
folio—folios

proviso—provisos
canto—cantos
ratio—ratios
patio—patios

Exceptions: Add *es*.

potato—potatoes
tomato—tomatoes
cargo—cargoes
echo—echoes

veto—vetoes
motto—mottoes
embargo—embargoes
hero—heroes

5. The plurals of most nouns ending in *f* are formed by adding *s*.

brief—briefs
proof—proofs
belief—beliefs

staff—staffs
sheriff—sheriffs
chief—chiefs

Exceptions: Change *f* or *fe* to *v* and add *es*.

life—lives
wife—wives
knife—knives
leaf—leaves
shelf—shelves

half—halves
thief—thieves
wharf—wharves
loaf—loaves
wolf—wolves

6. A few everyday nouns form their plurals by means of a change in spelling, instead of by adding *s* or *es*.

foot—feet
tooth—teeth
mouse—mice
louse—lice
child—children

ox—oxen
man—men
woman—women
oasis—oases
goose—geese

7. A few nouns occur usually in plural form and are rarely singular.

scissors
riches
spectacles
athletics

proceeds
clothes
trousers
politics

Rules for the Formation of Plurals (Continued)

8. Compound nouns form their plural by adding *s*.

mouthful—mouthfuls	roomful—roomfuls
cupful—cupfuls	standby—standbys
spoonful—spoonfuls	potful—potfuls
teaspoonful—teaspoonfuls	boatload—boatloads
handful—handfuls	textbook—textbooks

9. Hyphenated nouns form their plural by adding *s* to the principal word (*not* at the end of the phrase).

mother-in-law—mothers-in-law
brother-in-law—brothers-in-law
sister-in-law—sisters-in-law
father-in-law—fathers-in-law
editor-in-chief—editors-in-chief
court-martial—courts-martial

10. A few irregular nouns have the same spelling for the singular as for the plural.

Singular	*Plural*
trout	trout
sheep	sheep
species	species
deer	deer
salmon	salmon
series	series
moose	moose

Note: By common usage, a noun which is plural in form is used in a sentence as though it were singular; for example:

Mathematics is my favorite subject in school.
Civics was more interesting with last term's teacher.
Politics is a field occupied chiefly by lawyers.

EXERCISES

PLURALS OF NOUNS

A. Write the plural for each word listed below.

1. battleship
2. airplane
3. baseball
4. brother-in-law
5. lily
6. ox
7. potato
8. story
9. spoonful
10. life
11. Englishman
12. Negro
13. valley
14. mission
15. church
16. plateful
17. mouse

18. echo
19. football
20. foot
21. siren
22. oasis
23. berry
24. species
25. editor-in-chief
26. handbook
27. bus
28. knife
29. goose
30. cupful
31. tomato
32. sheep
33. cargo
34. attorney

35. company
36. radio
37. passer-by
38. peach
39. father-in-law
40. proof
41. wolf
42. tablespoonful
43. anchor
44. woman
45. scissors
46. buoy
47. donkey
48. journey
49. monopoly
50. court-martial

B. Fill the blank space with the plural of the noun in parentheses.

1. The (woman) _____ bought two bushels of (potato) _____.
2. The (box) _____ were sent to many different (city) _____.
3. The (goose) _____ were kept in a pen which was twenty (foot) _____ long.
4. We saw several (deer) _____ and (ox) _____ in the field.
5. Each of the (passer-by) _____ stopped to watch the (player) _____.
6. In many (place) _____ (sheep) _____ are raised.
7. At the (party) _____ many (dish) _____ were used.
8. The (mother-in-law) _____ took the younger (child) _____ for a walk.
9. The (pony) _____ made many rides around the track during the (holiday) _____.
10. The (chief) _____ were talking among (himself) _____.

C. Preceding each sentence there are two singular nouns. Fill the blanks in the sentences with the correct plural forms in the given order.

1. (fox, bush) We saw two _____ running through the _____.
2. (hero, radio) Many of the disabled _____ did not have _____.
3. (leaf, cliff) The _____ of the trees along the _____ are red.
4. (brother-in-law, car) The _____ watched the men drive the _____ away.
5. (monkey, mouse) We saw many _____ and white _____ in the zoo.

D. Rewrite each of the following sentences, changing the singular subject to the plural and making any other change necessary to make the new sentence correct: [Do not make any unnecessary changes.]

[*Example:* The boy runs fast.
The boys run fast.]

1. From his post, the officer is watching the prisoner.
2. The man has gone to the city.
3. The mouse was caught in the trap.
4. The tooth needs to be filled.
5. Does he plan to study history next year?
6. An oasis is a cheerful sight to a traveler in the desert.
7. A potful of gold may be found at the end of the trail.
8. In the northern regions, the wolf prowls for his prey at night.
9. The sentry walks with measured pace on duty.
10. A monopoly of any industry is forbidden by federal law.

E. Rewrite each of the following sentences, changing each singular noun **and** pronoun to the plural and making any other changes necessary to make the **new** sentence correct.

1. I am glad the hunter carried the moose back to camp.
2. His wife fought hard to beat her opponent at cards.
3. She said that a scarf and a handkerchief are easier to iron.
4. The lawyer offered his brief as proof of his client's innocence.
5. The plaintiff claims his journey was really a business trip.
6. A democratic country is proud of its liberty.
7. The company gave a bonus in ratio to employee's salary.
8. A spoonful of medicine requires a mouthful of water.
9. The commander-in-chief met the staff-officer.
10. The baker put the fresh loaf on the top shelf.

F. Rewrite each of the following sentences, changing the singular subject to the plural and making any other changes necessary to make the new sentence correct. Do not, however, make any unnecessary changes.

1. There is a book on her desk.
2. The man lost his money.
3. Does she intend to go to the party?
4. The child has gone to school.
5. In his home was found a picture of the fort.
6. From the window, the child is watching the bird.
7. The mechanic repaired the radio.
8. Our sister went to the school dance.
9. My pen needs a refill of fluid.
10. Will she study her lesson for tomorrow?
11. My cousin is planning to spend his holidays with me.
12. I am pleased to be able to offer my help.
13. Early in July, he, as well as some other men from the office, took his vacation.
14. Naturally, I was disappointed to be the only one left at home.
15. My sister has invited me to go with her.

FORMING THE POSSESSIVE CASE OF NOUNS

The possessive case of nouns shows possession or ownership.

Possessives offer some students a lifetime of trouble. Yet, the main rule is very simple, and it fits most of the cases you will meet in your own writing. Learn this: "To form the possessive of any singular noun, add an apostrophe and an *s*." Of course, there are other points you should know, but at least 90% of the time you will feel on solid ground—if you remember the above rule.

RULES FOR THE FORMATION OF POSSESSIVES

1. To form the possessive of any **singular** noun, add an apostrophe and *s*.

SINGULAR NOUNS	POSSESSIVE CASE
boy	boy's hat
friend	friend's book
child	child's toy
James	James's mother

2. To form the possessive of a **plural** noun which does not end in *s*, add the apostrophe and *s*.

PLURAL NOUNS	POSSESSIVE CASE
men	men's clothes
women	women's handbags
mice	mice's tails
sheep	sheep's wool

3. To form the possessive of a **plural** noun ending in *s,* add the apostrophe alone (') after the *s*.

PLURAL NOUNS	POSSESSIVE CASE
girls	girls' lockers
ladies	ladies' dresses
students	students' projects
players	players' averages

4. To show the possessive case for two or more **nouns** in a series, put the apostrophe and *s* after the last noun.

   Jack, Bob, and Henry's tennis shoes are in my locker.

5. To form the possessive of a compound hyphenated noun, put the apostrophe and *s* after the last word.

    brother-in-law's   editor-in-chief's

6. To form the possessive of a non-living thing, use a phrase with *of.*

    color of the hat   (not *hat's color*)

Note: Possessive pronouns (*ours, yours, hers, theirs, its*) do NOT require an apostrophe since they are already in the possessive form. Examples:

That boat is *ours* (not *our's*).   I saw *theirs* (not *theirs'*).
These books are *yours* (not *yours'*).   Her hair lost *its* (not *it's*) gloss.
That dog is *hers* (not *her's*).

EXERCISES

FORMING THE POSSESSIVE

A. Write the possessive form of each of the following words:

1. women	11. Texas	21. she	31. our
2. it	12. their	22. Bess	32. Frank
3. John	13. girl	23. he	33. farmer
4. America	14. me	24. tree	34. towns
5. friends	15. Henry	25. states	35. they
6. city	16. your	26. boy	36. sister
7. country	17. roof	27. Keats	37. umbrella
8. firemen	18. dog	28. men	38. sentence
9. who	19. dress	29. teacher	39. Burns
10. Louis	20. ladies	30. bird	40. package

B. Complete the following sentences, correctly forming possessives:

1. We develop loyalty when we feel that the school is (our) _____.
2. Youngsters claimed that the football was (their) _____.
3. He has a new job selling (men) _____ shoes.
4. There was a special sale on (ladies) _____ hats.
5. When you are successful, the world is (your) _____.

6. The catcher misunderstood the (pitcher) _____ signals.
7. Why are (boys) _____ games more exciting?
8. We were allowed to walk on the (captain) _____ deck.
9. Please don't count me any longer as a friend of (her) _____.
10. Recent candidates tried to capture the (women) _____ vote.
11. I helped enter the marks into the (teacher) _____ book.
12. Maybe you can earn a dollar by washing (Dad) _____ car.
13. Most pictures show the (saints) _____ haloes painted with gold.
14. The veterinarian easily snipped off the (puppies) _____ tails.
15. Are you afraid of the other (team) _____ winning?

G SPELLING

Spelling is a personal problem. You *can* learn to spell! Most errors are the result of carelessness. Stop telling yourself that it is only a small matter. It is a serious handicap in school, on the job, among friends, and everywhere in life. Who will take pity on those careless blunderers who write such misspellings as these: *dosen't, childern, freind, sliping, shure,* and so on? You might be excused for stumbling over unusal words like *physician* and *meteorology;* but you should know easy, everyday substitutes for these hard words: *doctor* and *weather.* Spelling rules and word lists can help you become conscious of troublesome cases and give you a degree of confidence.

▷ SPELLING RULES AND WORD LISTS

SPELLING RULES

1. A consonant at the end of a one-syllable word is *doubled* when adding a suffix beginning with a vowel.

stop	stopped, stopping, stopper
run	running, runner
hit	hitting, hitter
put	putting
get	getting
swim	swimming, swimmer
plan	planned, planning, planner
win	winning, winner
wet	wetter, wettest, wetting
slip	slipped, slipping, slipper, slippery

Spelling Rules (Continued)

Exception 1. If the final consonant is preceded by *two* vowels, the single consonant is retained before adding a suffix beginning with a vowel.

sail	sailed, sailing
kneel	kneeled, kneeling

Exception 2. If the final consonant is accompanied by another consonant, no doubling of the consonant occurs before adding a suffix beginning with a vowel.

talk	talking, talked
stock	stocking, stocked

2. A consonant at the end of a word containing two or more syllables is doubled when adding a suffix beginning with a vowel (as *refer, referred*), unless the consonant—

    a. is preceded by two vowels: *contain, contained.*
    b. is accompanied by another consonant: *enlist, enlisted.*
    c. is an unaccented syllable: *benefit, benefited.*

DOUBLE THE FINAL CONSONANT

prefer	preferred, preferring
compel	compelled, compelling
occur	occurred, occurring, occurrence
transfer	transferred, transferring
expel	expelled, expelling
regret	regretted, regretting, regrettable
permit	permitted, permitting
commit	committed, committing, committee

DO NOT DOUBLE THE FINAL CONSONANT
(because the last syllable is unaccented)

benefit	benefited, benefiting
cancel	canceled, canceling
credit	credited, crediting
debit	debited, debiting
label	labeled, labeling
limit	limited, limiting
model	modeled, modeling
offer	offered, offering

You should develop a conscience about spelling, a feeling of right and wrong; and then check your doubts with a dictionary.

Spelling Rules (Continued)

3. Words ending in silent *e* drop the *e* when adding a suffix beginning with a vowel.

DROP THE FINAL *E*

move	moving, movable
desire	desiring, desirable
force	forcing, forcible
write	writing
take	taking
use	using, usable
argue	arguing, arguable
reduce	reducing, reducible
debate	debating, debatable

C AND *G* KEEP THE FINAL *E* BEFORE *A* OR *O*

Words ending in *ce* and *ge* keep the final *e* before adding a suffix beginning with *a* or *o*.

trace	traceable
service	serviceable
notice	noticeable
outrage	outrageous
manage	manageable
exchange	exchangeable
peace	peaceable
courage	courageous
advantage	advantageous

4. Words ending in silent *e* keep the *e* when adding a suffix beginning with a consonant.

care	careful
complete	completeness
engage	engagement
resource	resourceful

Exceptions. Drop the final *e* in these words:

true	truly
due	duly
argue	argument
acknowledge	acknowledgment
judge	judgment

Spelling Rules (Continued)

5. Final *y* preceded by a consonant is changed to *i* before any suffix except *ing*.

	CHANGE *Y* TO *I*	EXCEPT *ING*
carry	carried, carrier	carrying
sky	skies	
lady	ladies	
icy	icily, iciness	
satisfy	satisfied	satisfying
hurry	hurried	hurrying
reply	replied	replying
try	tried	trying

Exceptions. Keep the final *y* in these words:

shy—shyness
dry—dryness

6. Final *y* preceded by a vowel is not changed before a suffix.

	KEEP *Y*
annoy	annoyed, annoying
journey	journeyed, journeying
employ	employed, employing
delay	delayed, delaying
obey	obeyed, obeying

Exceptions. Change *y* to *i* in these words:

day	daily
drowsy	drowsiness
lay	laid, lain
pay	paid
say	said
dry	drier, driest, drily

7. Words ending in *c* must be followed by *k* before adding an ending beginning with *e, i,* or *y*.

colic	colicky
frolic	frolicked, frolicking
mimic	mimicked, mimicking
panic	panicky
picnic	picnicked, picnicking, picnicker

Spelling Rules (Continued)

8. Put *i* before *e* except after *c*, or when sounded like *ay* as in *neighbor* and *weigh*.

IE		EI		EXCEPTIONS	
relieve	chief	receive	conceive	neither	weird
believe	brief	deceive	perceive	either	leisure
piece	yield	receipt	ceiling	financier	foreign
gaiety	grief	deceit	conceit	seize	ancient
achieve	relief	weigh	neighbor	species	conscience

EXERCISES

SPELLING

A. Some of these words are correct as they stand. Write *C* next to the correct words. Other words require one or more letters to become complete. Insert the missing letters in the spaces provided. Aim for 100%.

1. stop—ed
2. swim—ing
3. sit—er
4. get—ing
5. prefer—ed
6. occur—ed
7. commit—ee
8. benefit—ed
9. profit—ing
10. permit—ed
11. desir—able
12. forc—ble
13. writ—ing
14. debat—ble
15. lov—ing
16. notic—able
17. peace—able

18. courag—ous
19. advantag—ous
20. servic—able
21. complet—ness
22. stat—ment
23. tru—ly
24. argu—ment
25. judg—ment
26. stud—ing
27. merc—ful
28. accompan—ed
29. bus—ness
30. salar—ed
31. heav—est
32. satisf—ed
33. repl—ed
34. dr—ness

35. hurr—ing
36. journ—ed
37. obey—ed
38. dai—ly
39. dri—est
40. mimic—ing
41. picnic—ing
42. frolic—ed
43. panic—ky
44. bel—ve
45. conven—nt
46. rec—ve
47. for—gner
48. l—sure
49. ach—vement
50. handkerch—f

B. Below you are given a complete word and a suffix. Combine the two into one correctly spelled word. In some instances, however, you are to fill the blank by writing either *ei* or *ie*.

1. drop-ed	11. rec--ve	21. dine-ing
2. bel--ve	12. manage-able	22. service-able
3. lazy-ly	13. get-ing	23. bag-age
4. hit-er	14. occur-ed	24. th--f
5. admire-able	15. slam-ed	25. lonely-ness
6. swim-ing	16. agree-able	26. choose-ing
7. rel--f	17. store-age	27. prefer-ed
8. lovely-ness	18. fit-ed	28. lucky-ly
9. courage-ous	19. n--ghbor	29. dance-ing
10. have-ing	20. busy-ly	30. charge-able

C. Add the following suffixes wherever possible to these words ending in silent *e: ing, ed, er, ate, ary, al, able, ty, ly, less, ment*. Be careful of those words in which you drop the final *e*.

1. advance	9. argue	17. peace	25. complete
2. use	10. love	18. notice	26. choose
3. fortune	11. safe	19. continue	27. arrange
4. desire	12. refine	20. advise	28. trade
5. encourage	13. change	21. adverse	29. antique
6. hope	14. judge	22. sincere	30. commence
7. please	15. fierce	23. move	
8. immediate	16. announce	24. extreme	

HELPFUL SUGGESTIONS IN SPELLING

1. There are only three verbs in the English language ending in *ceed*. All other verbs with that sound end in *cede*.

CEED	CEDE	
succeed	secede	accede
proceed	recede	cede
exceed	intercede	precede
	concede	supersede

2. There is only one word in English ending in *full;* it is the adjective *full*. All other adjectives end in *ful*.

cupful	hopeful	graceful
spoonful	healthful	masterful
careful	teaspoonful	spiteful
cheerful	tablespoonful	resentful
forgetful	wakeful	handful

240

Helpful Suggestions in Spelling (Continued)

3. The letter *q* is followed by *u* in a word.

   queen   queer   quiet   quite   quiz   quarter

4. Adverbs are formed from adjectives. Notice the endings carefully; some end in *ly*, others in *ally*.

LY	*ALLY*
accurately	occasionally
separately	accidentally
respectively	finally
respectfully	practically

5. All the subjects taught in school are spelled with *small* initial letters, except the names of languages, which are capitalized.

arithmetic	geography	English
reading	history	French
writing	science	Spanish
spelling	music	Latin

6. Possessive pronouns are *never* written with an apostrophe because they are already in the possessive case form.

   its   theirs   yours   hers   ours   mine

ADVERBS FORMED FROM ADJECTIVES

Add *ly* to the following words, making any other necessary change in spelling.

1. full	9. careful	17. neat	25. clear
2. sure	10. final	18. right	26. sad
3. haste	11. dreamy	19. idle	27. joyful
4. awful	12. wrong	20. warm	28. successful
5. graceful	13. quick	21. tearful	29. short
6. pure	14. hopeful	22. true	30. playful
7. shy	15. speed	23. quiet	
8. bright	16. clean	24. angry	

Review Word List

All words found in this review list have been taught in the elementary school. They include Jones' 100 Spelling Demons, Fitzgerald's 222 Demons and other words that have special characteristics that tend to make them troublesome to many pupils. There are 351 words in the list. These words should be reviewed in grades 7, 8 and 9 and retaught as necessary. They are sometimes misspelled by adults. They are important words since research shows that they are used repeatedly in all kinds of writing, and are misspelled more often than any other words in the language.

about	because	could	father
absence	been	couldn't	favorite
ache	before	country	Feb.
address	beginning	cousin	February
advice	believe	cupboard	fierce
advise	believed		fine
afternoon	birthday	daddy	first
again	blue	dairy	football
all right	bought	day	for
along	boy	dear	forty
already	boys	Dec.	fourth
although	break	decorate	Friday
always	brother	desert	friend
am	brought	didn't	friends
among	built	disease	from
an	business	doctor	fuel
and	busy	does	fun
answer	buy	dog	
any		done	getting
anything	can	don't	goes
anyway	cannot	down	going
appreciate	can't		good
April	children	early	good-by
are	chocolate	Easter	got
arithmetic	choose	easy	grade
aunt	Christmas	effect	grammar
awhile	close	elevator	guard
	color	enough	guess
baby	come	every	
balloon	coming	everybody	had
basketball	cough	exercise	half

*This word list is reproduced from *The Spelling Program*, Grades 7, 8 and 9, issued by the University of the State of New York.

Halloween	lose	please	stationary
handkerchiefs	lots	poison	stationery
has	loving	practice	store
have		practicing	straight
haven't	made	pretty	studying
having	make	principal	sugar
he	making	principle	summer
hear	many	probably	Sunday
heard	maybe		suppose
height	me	quarter	sure
hello	meant	quit	surely
her	medium	quite	surprise
herd	minute		surprised
here	Miss	raise	surrounded
him	morning	read	swimming
his	mother	ready	
home	Mr.	receive	
hope	Mrs.	received	teacher
hospital	much	receiving	teacher's
hour		religious	tear
house	name	remember	temperature
how	necessary	right	terrible
how's	neither	rough	thanksgiving
	nice	route	that's
I	nickel		the
I'll	niece	said	their
I'm	ninth	sandwiches	them
imagine	none	Santa Claus	then
immediately	Nov.	Saturday	there
in	now	saw	there's
instead		says	these
isn't	o'clock	scarce	they
it	Oct.	scene	they've
it's	off	school	think
I've	often	schoolhouse	though
	on	seems	thought
Jan.	once	send	through
jealous	one	sent	time
just	original	separate	tired
	our	several	to
knew	out	shoes	today
know	outside	similar	together
knowledge		since	tomorrow
	party	sincerely	tonight
laid	patient	skiing	too
latter	peace	skis	toys
lessons	people	snow	train
letter	physical	some	traveling
like	piece	something	trouble
likes	play	sometime	truly
little	played	sometimes	Tuesday
loose	plays	soon	two

until	waste	we're	won't
used	we	when	would
usually	wear	where	write
	weather	whether	writing
vacation	Wednesday	which	wrote
valuable	week	white	
very	weigh	whole	you
	well	will	your
waist	went	with	you're
want	were	women	yours
was			

EXERCISE

REVIEW WORDS

In each of the following lines, one word is misspelled. Find the word and spell it correctly.

1. Wensday, haven't, used, Tuesday
2. shoes, grammer, been, since
3. busy, ache, fourty, half
4. always, whether, sure, seperate
5. amoung, instead, believe, knowledge
6. country, writing, docter, choose
7. enough, Febuary, often, whole
8. friend, easy, women, buisness
9. again, meant, begining, tonight
10. minute, straight, coming, truble
11. appreciate, stationary, imagin, vacation
12. loveing, practice, having, surrounded
13. balloon, bought, scarce, imediately
14. decorate, neccessary, neither, niece
15. built, chocolate, guess, sincerly
16. temprature, waist, tear, schoolhouse
17. stationery, sometimes, recieved, traveling
18. principal, lessons, arithmitic, father
19. Easter, getting, fierce, valueable
20. swiming, cousin, nickel, religious
21. weather, remmember, desert, poison
22. baloon, surprise, rough, medium
23. loose, hieght, piece, through
24. favorite, would, scarce, physiccal
25. suppose, friends, everey, probably

CORE VOCABULARY LISTS

The words found in the core lists for grades 7, 8 and 9 are new words offered in addition to the 3000 basic words studied in the elementary school. These additional words, 400 or fewer for each year, have been selected from the best research available.

Grade 7—New Basic Words

accurate	code	distributed	frontier
active	coin	dock	fry
acts	colonial	doctors	funniest
adding	colonist	dreaming	
alive	commission	dreams	gained
ambition	communication	drunk	gaining
amounts	companies	dull	germ
amusements	compare	dusk	girl's
announce	compared		gladly
area	concern	earliest	glance
attack	concerning	ease	glee
attempt	concrete	effects	globe
available	conducted	efforts	goal
avoid	connections	enclose	good-by
	consent	enclosed	graceful
bag	considerable	enclosing	grandmother's
bars	contained	ending	greet
based	containing	enforce	guilty
battery	content	engines	
bean	convenience	enormous	happier
bearing	copies	errand	happiest
bears	corners	eve	hauled
became	counter	exact	hidden
beneath	crawl	experiment	hides
breaks	criminal	explore	highly
breeze	cure	export	hiked
broad	cuts	extended	hiking
bundle		extent	hobbies
	dam		holds
calm	decision	faint	hoped
carbon	declare	faith	
causes	degrees	fare	icy
checked	delight	fertile	idle
civic	depends	fir	impatient
civilization	deposits	firm	import
civilized	develop	fixing	improved
clouds	discouraged	floating	include
coarse	discover	fried	included
cocoa	discovery	fright	includes
coconut	diseases	frighten	income

increase	merchants	precious	scale
increasing	messages	pressure	scarlet
innocent	mild	prevention	scheme
inquire	military	prisoner	scrap
inquired	millions	produced	scream
insect	minds	produces	seaport
insisted	mineral	producing	seasons
instance	mines	product	sections
invalid	mining	promote	select
investigate	moist	prove	selected
inviting	moisture	provide	sells
irrigated	mornings		sensible
irrigation	mosquito		series
		quality	session
		quantity	severe
jacket	nerve	quart	shadow
jam	nerves		shelf
jewelry	No.		shirts
jewels	notify	rail	shout
jobs	numerous	railroads	shouted
joint		railway	signal
	occupation	reaching	skill
knit	occur	rear	skillful
knitting	occurred	receives	soda
	odd	recent	speaker
lame	odor	recovered	speaks
largely	opens	recreation	spoken
lasted	operations	refreshments	sports
latest	oxygen	refuse	springs
laughter		related	stated
legislature	pal	relation	stations
lighting	pale	relations	steak
limit	peak	relative	steamer
limited	pears	relatives	steer
lined	percentage	remained	stem
liquid	perfectly	remains	stones
logs	phoned	remarked	subway
lord	picnics	reported	suffer
loyal	pioneer	republic	suffering
	pioneers	require	suited
machines	pitch	requires	supplied
magazines	pity	resigned	swam
major	plains	resources	swift
manage	planes	review	swiftly
managed	player	richest	
maple	players	rod	
mass	pockets	romantic	task
matters	poet	rotten	tavern
medal	political	ruin	teams
meetings	portion	ruined	telescope
meets	postage	ruins	tells
men's	poultry	rushing	tenth
merchant	powers	rye	terms

thanked	tube	victory	wires
thorough		views	woman's
thoroughly	uncles	vine	worker
tickled	unhappy	voyage	workers
toboggan	uniform		
ton	upright	wasted	year's
tone		waters	yield
tons	vacant	wells	younger
touched	variety	width	
tower	vice-president	wine	
troops	vicinity	winning	zone

EXERCISE

SEVENTH GRADE WORDS

Find the one misspelled word in each line and spell it correctly.

1. anounce, convenience, happiest, concrete
2. pioneer, yield, mineral, visinity
3. acurate, connections, increase, jacket
4. frontier, jewelery, knitting, discover
5. stations, rushing, politicle, tavern
6. railroads, shadow, victry, toboggan
7. telascope, younger, percentage, millions
8. workers, resources, tickled, militery
9. laugther, irrigation, cocoa, enormous
10. refreshments, postage, width, prisioner
11. precious, thorough, sensable, republic
12. colonial, maggazines, impatient, criminal
13. civilazation, innocent, funniest, medal
14. available, fertile, expiriment, legislature
15. decision, machines, commission, develope
16. investagate, occupation, included, limited
17. ambition, deseases, girl's, irrigated
18. battery, managed, numorous, insect
19. considerable, distributed, producing, uniform
20. companies, extended, pioneers, invallid
21. maple, concern, amusments, based
22. oxygen, adding, merchant, recieves
23. errand, thancked, instance, coarse
24. messages, player, occured, rotten
25. delight, unhapy, moist, bundle

247

Grade 8—New Basic Words

ability	clearly	eager	horrible
aboard	closely	educated	humorous
accidents	collecting	electrical	
activities	command	engaged	ideal
admire	companion	enjoyable	illness
admit	composed	entering	image
admitted	conclusion	enters	imagination
advance	connect	entrance	imagined
advised	connection	equally	independence
affair	constant	equipped	informed
affairs	constantly	escaped	inn
agreeable	construction	evil	instrument
agreement	convinced	exercises	intelligent
amended	correctly	experiences	interfere
amendments	courteous	expression	international
annual	created	extreme	introduce
appears	credit		introduced
approved	crept	fame	invention
arrival	crew	familiar	inventor
atmosphere	curious	farewell	issued
attending	custom	fashion	
	customer	feature	judges
baggage	customers	features	jury
ballot	customs	federal	justice
barely		fewer	justify
beating		fifteenth	
belief	darkness	flesh	killing
belonged	dawn	founded	kings
belonging	debt	fully	kissed
benefit	deck	funds	knelt
bitter	delegates	furs	knob
blown	delicious		
bodies	delightful	gathering	leads
borrowed	demand	glorious	lean
boss	democracy	grant	lightning
brilliant	democratic	granted	liking
burnt	desire	grateful	lips
	determined	groups	liquor
capture	diameter	guests	loaded
carols	disappointment		locate
celebrated	discuss	handsome	location
chairman	discussed	happening	locked
charged	discussion	headed	losing
chiefly	disgusted	hearts	lovable
choice	distinct	heating	loveliest
citizenship	domestic	here's	lover
claimed	drawer	historical	
claims	dreadful	hitting	magic
cleared	dusty	holly	majority

248

manufactured	peculiar	reserve	strain
marched	permit	respected	stranger
mate	permitted	restaurant	streak
mathematics	phrase	rested	strict
mayor	plainly	resting	strikes
meals	planet	restless	stroke
meantime	pointed	retired	stronger
meanwhile	policy	returned	strongest
memories	politics	revolution	strongly
merely	port	rights	struggle
merrily	ports	rising	students
methods	positive	roam	stumbled
mission	possession	roar	suffered
mist	possibly	root	sunset
moments	powerful		surrender
monument	prefer	sailing	
moonlight	preparing	salesman	tale
motion	presence	scenes	tariff
movement	presented	selfish	tears
murder	priced	senate	temple
mystery	pride	sentences	territory
	prince	services	theft
nations	prints	serving	thoughts
natives	probable	shack	thousands
naturally	proceeded	shelter	thrill
nearby	profit	shock	thrilled
Negroes	promptly	shops	thrilling
nineteenth	proposed	shorter	thunder
	protected	shortly	tickets
objects	providing	sigh	title
obtain	provisions	signature	tongue
offices	purchased	signs	tough
official	purposes	silence	tracks
officials		sizes	trading
O.K.	qualities	slavery	trained
ornaments	quarrel	slight	treatment
overcome	quarters	slightly	treaty
owners		smiling	trial
owns	ragged	smoking	tribes
	range	somewhat	trips
pain	rates	sorrow	troubles
parted	realized	sorts	trout
partly	register	sounded	twelfth
partner	relief	sour	twenty-one
passage	rented	source	types
passenger	repair	sources	
passes	repeated	spirits	uncle's
patience	represent	spite	unit
paying	representative	spoiled	unusual
pays	representatives	stopping	
peaceful	reservation	stops	various

vast	wages	waves	wounded
verses	wander	wealth	wreck
veto	wandered	wealthy	
vitamins	warn	weary	youth
voted	warned	world's	you've
votes	warning		

EXERCISE

EIGHTH GRADE WORDS

In each of the following lines, one word is misspelled. Find the word and spell it correctly.

1. distinct, heating, retired, extream
2. signiture, passage, ability, brilliant
3. celebrated, delicious, posession, suffered
4. amended, arrival, choice, majority
5. belief, familiar, democracy, greatful
6. independance, mathematics, connection, quarrel
7. admitted, glorious, curteous, disappointment
8. patience, benifit, delightful, memories
9. desire, borrowed, feature, loseing
10. experiences, meanwhile, baggage, excercises
11. hansome, monument, electrical, historical
12. mystery, resturant, thousands, provisions
13. twelfth, policy, tarriff, smiling
14. unusual, revolution, wandered, prescence
15. ornements, surrender, wealthy, proceeded
16. struggle, citisenship, wounded, tongue
17. preparing, spirits, vitemins, territory
18. services, realized, treatment, pecular
19. ninteenth, officials, strongest, movement
20. selfish, lightning, representitive, silence
21. knelt, compannion, weary, priced
22. warned, imagination, shack, corectly
23. releif, international, customs, headed
24. ragged, farewell, temple, loveable
25. construction, stranger, naturaly, annual

250

Grade 9—New Basic Words

absolutely
abundance
abundant
abuse
accomplish
accused
accustomed
acknowledge
acre
actually
additional
adjust
adjustment
advertising
advisable
advising
agricultural
alas
allowance
ample
amused
amusing
angle
anxiously
apologize
application
applied
approach
approve
approximately
arise
arrange
arrangement
artificial
assigned
assist
assistant
assume
assure
athletic
attorney
attraction
audience
authority
automatic
aware

backward
barber

bargain
basis
beautifully
beloved
bid
blessing
bluff
bond
bridle
brief
budget

cable
campaign
cancel
candidate
capable
capacity
cape
career
ceased
centuries
cereal
chamber
circulation
clearing
closet
colleges
column
combined
committed
communism
complaint
compound
conclude
conference
confidential
congratulate
congratulations
consideration
consisted
consists
contracts
convenient
cordially
creature
credit
crude
curiosity

curve

debate
deduct
deducted
deduction
deeds
deeply
defeat
defective
defense
definite
definitely
delicate
demonstration
deposit
deserve
desirous
desperate
destination
devote
devoted
diet
difficulty
digest
digestion
dined
discontinue
dispose
disposed
disposition
distant
distinguished
document
drama
dread
dreary

economical
economy
educational
engagement
elements
eliminate
employees
engineers
entertain
entitled
essential

establish
established
estate
estimate
estimated
evidence
evident
examined
exceedingly
exception
exclusive
executive
exhausted
exist
existence
expression
extend
extensive

failure
faithful
faithfully
fame
fate
favors
filing
fitted
fixtures
forces
formerly
frankly
frequently
furnishes
furthermore

garbage
generation
generous
genuine
gloomy
gorgeous
governed
gown
graduated
graduation
grind

handy
healthful

hearth
heavens
heavier
hesitate
honored
hopeful
household
humor
hurriedly

impression
incident
inclined
inconvenience
indicate
individual
industrial
industries
influence
insert
insist
installment
instantly
instructions
insult
insurance
intention
interior
interrupt
interrupted
interview
introduction
issue

judgment

laboratory
laundry
lease
legal
license
likewise
loan
locally
loses

magnificent
mainly
majority
manly
mansion
marvelous

maximum
mechanical
medical
mend
mercy
mere
mess
midst
minimum
mirror
mislaid
misunderstanding
mountainous
mysterious

naming
neglect
neglected
noble
normal
northeastern
northwest
northwestern

objection
occasion
offense
official
opera
originally
outstanding

payment
permanent
personality
persuaded
platform
pleasing
pledge
poisonous
possibility
practical
practically
preference
prepaid
pretend
prevented
previous
primarily
primitive
principles
privilege

probability
proceeds
prominent
prospect
prosperous
publish
published

racing
range
rank
rapid
rare
reasonable
recognition
recognize
recognized
recommend
recorded
reduce
reducing
reduction
referee
reference
referred
refrigerator
refund
regard
regarded
release
reliable
removed
replacement
reporter
represents
requesting
rescue
reservation
reside
resignation
resort
respectable
respected
response
retain
routine
rural

saddle
sake
salary

savings
scarcely
schedule
scratched
scrub
secured
securing
seized
selection
senior
sentiment
shame
simply
situated
sleet
society
sole
solution
southwest
specific
specifications
specified
specify
spray
starch
steadily
steady
stenographer
storage
straighten
strain
strictly
substance
substitute
suggesting
suggestion
sufficient
supreme
surrounding
sympathy

tackle
theme
theory
thrifty
tomato
tropical
twentieth

unconscious
unfortunate

unnecessary   velvet   warrant   witness
unpaid   visible   welfare   worthy
unreasonable   volume   wherever

EXERCISE

NINTH GRADE WORDS

In each of the following lines, one word is misspelled. Find the word and spell it correctly.

1. intention, majority, distingwished, conclude
2. reconize, locally, prospect, specific
3. pleasing, unnecessary, objection, prosperus
4. assume, abundent, agricultural, garbage
5. reside, unconscious, previus, educational
6. capasity, artificial, discontinue, graduation
7. interrupt, wherever, perminent, supreme
8. individual, simpathy, document, deserve
9. consideration, disposition, routine, priviledge
10. congradulate, eliminate, committed, frequently
11. column, generous, candadate, desirous
12. allowance, definitly, hesitate, response
13. possibility, atheletic, conference, impression
14. occassion, reliable, senior, volume
15. resignation, privilege, inconvience, specifications
16. marvelous, visible, minimum, reccomend
17. extensive, gorgous, automatic, estimated
18. attorney, digestion, ingeneers, demonstration
19. economical, humor, communism, excedingly
20. hopefull, favors, genuine, exhausted
21. substance, tomatoe, accomplish, distant
22. primitive, scarcely, warrant, nameing
23. wellfare, employees, bargain, pretend
24. official, acknowlege, seized, economy
25. storage, ceased, anxiously, proceeds
26. beautifuly, neglected, advisable, maximum
27. judgment, digest, racing, conveniant
28. tropical, personallity, assure, referred
29. cereal, essential, secureing, insert
30. mountainus, incident, witness, schedule

253

TECHNICAL VOCABULARY IN CITIZENSHIP EDUCATION

Grades 7, 8 and 9

There are 321 words in this list. These are the words that citizenship education teachers should help their students learn to spell. Two hundred seventy-eight of these citizenship education words are so important that they also appear in the core lists of words that everyone needs to write frequently. The other words will probably not be taught as spelling words except by the citizenship education teachers. These words are starred for identification.

abundant	cattle	crime	employer*
acre	center	crops	enforce
act	century	cultivate*	establish*
administration*	chain	current	event
agent	channel *	customs*	executive
agriculture	citizen		expedition*
alfalfa	civic	dairy	explore
altitude*	civil	dam	export
amendment*	civilized	debt	
ancient	class	decision	factory
annual	clay	demand	federal
area	climate	democracy	fertile
article	cloth	dense*	flood
assembly	coal	department	flour
atmosphere	coast	deposit	forces
	cocoa	desert	foreign
ballot	coconut	development	forest
basin*	coffee	diamond	freedom
bay	colony	direction	freeze
beach	commerce	discovery	freight
belt	communication	distance	frontier
bill	communism	distribution*	frost
blizzard	community	district	fruit
border	company	divide	fuel
boundary	conference	dock	
breeze	constitution	document	gas
bureau*	continent	domestic	gasoline
business	convention	draft	globe
	copper	duty	goods
cabinet	corn		government
camel	corporation*	earth	governor
campaign*	cotton	east	grain
canal	country	economic	granite*
candidate*	county	education	grant
cape*	court	election	grapes
capital	credit	employee*	grazing*

* Do not appear in New York State basic spelling lists for elementary and for junior high schools.

254

hail
harbor
harvest
herd
hide
high
highway

import
income
industry
internal *
invention
iron
irrigation
island
issue
ivory*

journey
judge
jury
justice

labor
language
lead
league
leather
legal
legislature
level
liberal *
liberty
lightning
local
location
lumber

machinery
manufacture
map
marble
market
measure
metal
migrate
mills
mine

mineral
minister
mist
modern
moisture
motion
mountain
mouth
movement
mud

nation
native
Negro
north

official
oil
olives*
orchard
ore

pasture
peace
peak
peninsula*
petition*
pioneer
plain
planet
plantation*
plateau*
platform
point
pole
policy
politics
population
port
potatoes
poultry
president
pressure
primary
privilege
produce
production
property

race
railroad
railway
raise
ranch
range
region
reindeer
representative
republic
reservation
resolution*
revolt*
revolution
rice
rights
route
rubber
rural
rye

salmon
salt
savage*
seal
seaport
season
secretary
section
senate
senator*
session
settlement
shallow
shelter
shipping
shower
silk
silver
slave*
society
soil
sound
source
south
spring
state
steel
steep

storm
stream
strike
supply
surface

tariff *
tax
tea
telegraph
telephone
temperature
territory
testimony*
thermometer*
ticket
tide*
timber
tin
tobacco
trade
traffic
traitor*
transportation
travel
treasury*
tribe
tropical
trust

union

valley
vapor*
vegetables
vessel *
village
vote
voyage

wealth*
weather
welfare
west
wheat
wine
witness
wool

yield

TECHNICAL VOCABULARY IN MATHEMATICS

Grades 7, 8 and 9

There are 159 words in the mathematics list. These are the words that mathematics teachers should help their pupils learn to spell. One hundred thirty-six of them are so important that they also appear in the basic core list of words which everyone needs to spell frequently. The other words are peculiar to the field of mathematics education and are needed and used so frequently that pupils should learn to spell them for mathematics. These are starred for identification and will be taught only by mathematics teachers.

add	credit	half	origin*
addition	customer	height	
amount		high	pair
answer	daily	hour	payment
apiece	day		peck*
average	deep	inch	penny
	degree	income	percent
balance	difference	independent	pint*
bank	discount*	insurance	plot*
bargain	distance	interest	plus*
base	divide	issue	point
bill	division		policy
borrow	dollar	length	positive
bushel *	dozen	less	pound
business	drive	loan	power
	due	long	premium*
cancel			price
capacity		maker*	principal
capital	eliminate	market	profit*
carry	exchange	measure	property
cases	expense	members	purchase
cash	expression	mile	
cent		minus*	quantity
center	factor*	minute	quart
century	feet	month	quarter
change	fifth	multiplication*	quotient*
check	figure	multiply	
circle	foot		rate
collect	fourth	net	receipt
company	fraction*	nickel	reduce
constant	funds	note	remainder*
contain		number	retail *
corporation*	gain		root
count	graph	order	row

* Do not appear in New York State basic spelling lists for elementary and for junior high schools.

sale	square	times	weigh
savings	stock	ton	weight
second	substitute	total	wholesale*
security*	subtract*	trade	wide
share	subtraction*		width
side	sum	unknown	worth
sign	surface		
size		value	yard
solid	term	volume*	year
space	thick		
speed	third	week	zero

TECHNICAL VOCABULARY IN SCIENCE

Grades 7, 8 and 9

These 104 words are words that science teachers should help their pupils learn to spell. Fifty-six of them will also be found in the basic core list of words which everyone needs to spell frequently. The other words are peculiar to the field of science and are needed and used so frequently that science students should learn to spell them. These words are starred for identification, and will be taught only by the science teachers.

acid *	conservation*	experiment	matter
alcohol *	contract	explode*	metal
alfalfa	copper	extension*	mineral
altitude*	crops		mixture*
atmosphere	current	fertilizer*	moisture
atom	cycle*	flame*	molecule*
attraction		fluid *	moss*
	decay*	force	motion
bacteria*	degree	friction*	motor
balance	depth*	fuel	
base	dew*		negative*
battery	diamond	gas	nitrogen*
bulb*	digestion	gases*	
	discharge*	germ	oxygen
calcium*	dissolve*	gravity*	
carbon	draft		
cell *		horizon*	petals*
charcoal *	electricity	humidity*	petroleum*
charge	element*	hydrogen*	poisonous
chemical *	energy		pole
coal	erosion*	insect	positive
composition	evaporate*		preserve*
compound	exert*	laboratory	pressure
conductor	expand *	liquid	pump

257

rays*	salt	substance	vapor*
refrigerator	silver		volume*
resistance*	soil	temperature	
root	solid	thermometer*	
rotation*	solution	tissue*	weather
rust*	steam	tube	weight

EXERCISE

TECHNICAL VOCABULARY
(Citizenship, Mathematics, Science)

In each of the following lines, one word is misspelled. Find the word and spell it correctly.

1. agraculture, economic, session, salmon
2. deposit, goverment, tropical, village
3. gasoline, abundant, vegatables, society
4. harbor, temperture, president, platform
5. country, executive, custumer, property
6. forest, frontier, unknown, posative
7. labortory, conference, zero, measure
8. witness, electrisity, capacity, century
9. shallow, convention, eliminate, conducter
10. weight, boundary, quanity, motion
11. surface, insurence, silver, diamond
12. democrasy, governor, alfalfa, carbon
13. principal, pressure, foriegn, weather
14. degree, atom, liquid, factary
15. experiment, priviledge, lightning, quarter
16. composition, current, atmostphere, substitute
17. lenghth, ancient, independent, balance
18. solution, district, business, diference
19. poisenous, document, amount, division
20. substance, education, refridgerator, multiply
21. motion, candadate, source, cycle
22. calcium, testimony, blizzard, campain
23. irriggation, retail, plantation, business
24. receipt, distanse, coconut, ballot
25. channel, remainder, expence, thick

② ABBREVIATIONS

Abbreviations or shortened forms for words and phrases have passed into everyday use, whether at school, at home, or in the wider areas of human affairs. Therefore, you must know how to spell these abbreviated forms correctly and be able to give their meanings. For example, *C. O. D.* = cash on delivery. Abbreviations require *periods*. However, abbreviations of the names of government agencies and departments, radio and television stations, and some well-known organizations may be written without periods. Examples: NLRB, CBS, AFL-CIO.

The United States

Ala.	Alabama	Mont.	Montana
Alas.	Alaska	N. C.	North Carolina
Ariz.	Arizona	N. Dak.	North Dakota
Ark.	Arkansas	Nebr.	Nebraska
Cal.	California	Nev.	Nevada
Colo.	Colorado	N. H.	New Hampshire
Conn.	Connecticut	N. J.	New Jersey
D. C.	District of Columbia	N. Mex.	New Mexico
Del.	Delaware	N. Y.	New York
Fla.	Florida	O.	Ohio
Ga.	Georgia	Okla.	Oklahoma
Ia.	Iowa	Oreg.	Oregon
Ida.	Idaho	Pa.	Pennsylvania
Ill.	Illinois	R. I.	Rhode Island
Ind.	Indiana	S. C.	South Carolina
Kans.	Kansas	S. Dak.	South Dakota
Ky.	Kentucky	Tenn.	Tennessee
La.	Louisiana	Tex.	Texas
Mass.	Massachusetts	Ut.	Utah
Md.	Maryland	Va.	Virginia
Me.	Maine	Vt.	Vermont
Mich.	Michigan	Wash.	Washington
Minn.	Minnesota	Wis.	Wisconsin
Miss.	Mississippi	W. Va.	West Virginia
Mo.	Missouri	Wyo.	Wyoming

Continents of the World

Af.	Africa	**N. A.**	North America
Eur.	Europe	**S. A.**	South America

Government "Alphabet" Agencies

ICC	Interstate Commerce Commission	**NLRB**	National Labor Relations Board
CAA	Civil Aeronautics Authority	**TVA**	Tennessee Valley Authority
FCC	Federal Communications Commission	**AEC**	Atomic Energy Commission

Weights

oz.	ounce	**cwt.**	hundredweight
lb.	pound	**t.**	ton

Measures

in.	inch	**mi.**	mile
ft.	foot	**pt.**	pint
yd.	yard	**qt.**	quart
rd.	rod	**gal.**	gallon

Quantities

pr.	pair (2)	**q.**	quire (24)
doz.	dozen (12)	**rm.**	ream (500)

Time

B.C.	Before Christ	**hr.**	hour
A.D.	Anno Domini	**da.**	day
a.m.	morning	**wk.**	week
p.m.	afternoon	**mo.**	month
sec.	second	**yr.**	year
min.	minute	**cent.**	century

Business

acct.	account	**Corp.**	Corporation
adv.	advertisement	**div.**	dividend
amt.	amount	**dr.**	debit (or debtor)
approx.	approximate	**ea.**	each
assn.	association	**enc.**	enclosure
atty.	attorney	**est.**	estimate
aud.	auditor	**est.**	established
bal.	balance	**f.o.b.**	free on board
B/E	bill of exchange	**frt.**	freight
B/L	bill of lading	**fwd.**	forward
bbl.	barrel	**Inc.**	Incorporated
bldg.	building	**int.**	interest
Bros.	Brothers	**inv.**	invoice
B/S	bill of sale	**Ltd.**	Limited
C/B	cashbook	**mdse.**	merchandise
chgd.	charged	**memo.**	memorandum
c/o	care of	**mfg.**	manufacturing
C.O.D.	cash on delivery	**P. & L.**	profit and loss
con.	consolidated	**rec.**	receipt

Printing

ital.	italics	**ms.**	manuscript
b.f.	bold face	**ff.**	following pages
d.	delete	**cf.**	compare
l.c.	lower case	**sp.**	spelling

School

Prin.	Principal	**att.**	attendance
Asst. Prin.	Assistant Principal	**abs.**	absent
Tchr.	Teacher	**l.**	late
I.Q.	intelligence quotient	**P.S.**	Public School
Reg.	register	**H.S.**	High School

Grammar

n.	noun	**sing.**	singular
pron.	pronoun	**pl.**	plural
v.	verb	**syn.**	synonym
adv.	adverb	**ant.**	antonym
adj.	adjective	**sp.**	spelling
prep.	preposition	**cap.**	capitalization
conj.	conjunction	**masc.**	masculine
interj.	interjection	**fem.**	feminine

Days

Sun.	Sunday	**Thurs.**	Thursday
Mon.	Monday	**Fri.**	Friday
Tues.	Tuesday	**Sat.**	Saturday
Wed.	Wednesday		

Months

Jan.	January	**Aug.**	August
Feb.	February	**Sept.**	September
Mar.	March	**Oct.**	October
Apr.	April	**Nov.**	November
Jun.	June	**Dec.**	December
Jul.	July	(Note: **May** has no abbreviation.)	

Titles of Persons

Dr.	Doctor	**Hon.**	Honorable
Rev.	Reverend	**Pres.**	President
Mr.	Mister	**Gov.**	Governor
Mrs.	Mistress	**Gen.**	General
Messrs.	Messieurs (Gentlemen)	**V.P.**	Vice President
Mlles.	Mademoiselles (Ladies)	**Adm.**	Admiral

Miscellaneous Abbreviations

Electrical
a.c.	alternating current
d.c.	direct current
kw.	kilowatt

Television
N.B.C.	National Broadcasting Company
C.B.S.	Columbia Broadcasting System
A.B.C.	American Broadcasting Company
B.B.C.	British Broadcasting Corporation

Rank
V.I.P.	very important person
Jr.	junior
Sr.	senior

Ratings
A.1.	first class
n.g.	no good
O.K.	acceptable

Directions
N.	north
E.	east
S.	south
W.	west

Phrases
e.g.	for example
i.e.	that is
etc.	and so forth
viz.	namely

Addresses
Rd.	Road
Ave.	Avenue
St.	Street
Blvd.	Boulevard
Pkway.	Parkway

Transportation
S.S.	steamship
R.R.	railroad

Books
p.	page
pp.	pages
chap.	chapter
bibliog.	bibliography

EXERCISES

ABBREVIATIONS

A. Write the full spelling for the words represented below:

1. P.O.	6. Rev.	11. Aug.	16. Treas.
2. Inc.	7. Secy.	12. B.C.	17. sing.
3. e.g.	8. i.e.	13. C.O.D.	18. oz.
4. Pres.	9. Jr.	14. Supt.	19. W.
5. S.S.	10. Thurs.	15. Col.	20. f.o.b.

B. Write the abbreviation for each of the following:

1. yard	9. Principal
2. and so forth	10. Gentlemen
3. page	11. Incorporated
4. sergeant	12. chapter
5. number	13. Rural Free Delivery
6. United States of America	14. Governor
7. inch	15. New York
8. namely	16. feminine

C. For each item in column *A*, give in column *B* the word which represents the equivalent expression. Then write its abbreviated form in column *C*.

	Column A	Column B	Column C
Example:	12 inches	foot	ft.

COLUMN A	COLUMN B	COLUMN C
1. 16 ounces		
2. 36 inches		
3. 5,280 feet		
4. 4 quarts		
5. 24 sheets of paper		
6. 60 seconds		
7. 12 months		
8. 24 hours		
9. 7 days		
10. 2,000 pounds		

D. In each of the following sentences there are certain words that can be abbreviated. Write the correct abbreviation.

[Example: <u>Mister</u> Smith bought a <u>pound</u> of butter.]
       Mr.   lb.

1. We get two quarts of milk daily and a dozen eggs each Saturday.

2. Doctor Johnson will move to 10 Main Street on August 15.
3. General Sherman will arrive Wednesday.
4. Last November, President .... received a vote of confidence from the people of the United States.
5. On Liberty Street in New York City you will find a branch of the Bell Corporation.

③ CONTRACTIONS

Contractions are shortened forms of words by the omission of letters (*B'klyn* = Brooklyn) or by combination (cannot = *can't*) in order to economize space or time. Contractions always require an *apostrophe* to indicate the missing letters. Contractions may be used in friendly letters, but not in formal compositions or in business letters.

CONTRACTION	MEANING	USE
n't	*not*	with the following verbs: is, was, have, do, can, has, had, did, does, should, are, will, would, could
isn't	is not	
wasn't	was not	
haven't	have not	
don't	do not	These two words are misspelled every day by pupils as "dont" and "cant." Remember the *apostrophe* before the *t*.
can't	cannot	
hasn't	has not	
hadn't	had not	
didn't	did not	
doesn't	does not	
shouldn't	should not	
aren't	are not	
won't	will not	
wouldn't	would not	
couldn't	could not	

265

CONTRACTION	MEANING	USE
'm	*am*	with the pronoun I
I'm		I am
've	*have*	with the pronouns I, we, you, they
I've		I have
we've		we have
you've		you have
they've		they have
'	*v*	with the words never, over, ever
ne'er		never
o'er		over
e'er		ever
'll	*will, shall*	with the pronouns I, we, you, he, she, it, they
I'll		I will or shall
we'll		we will or shall
you'll		you will or shall
he'll		he will or shall
she'll		she will or shall
it'll		it will or shall
they'll		they will or shall
's	*is*	with the words it, that, what, he, she, who, there, where
it's		it is (don't confuse this with *its*)
that's		that is
what's		what is
he's		he is
she's		she is
who's		who is (not *whose*)
there's		there is
where's		where is

CONTRACTION	MEANING	USE
're	*are*	with the pronouns we, you, they
we're you're they're		we are you are they are
't	*it*	with the verbs is, was, were
'tis 'twas 'twere		it is it was it were
'd	*would, should*	with the pronouns I, we, you, he, she, it, they
I'd we'd you'd he'd she'd it'd they'd		I would or should we would or should you would or should he would or should she would or should it would or should they would or should

Note: Whenever a word is shortened in form, you may use either the period at the end, or the apostrophe to show missing letters. You should not use both. Compare the two shortened forms for each word below.

WORD	CONTRACTION (*Apostrophe*)	ABBREVIATION (*Period*)
brothers	bro's	bros.
department	dep't	dept.
secretary	sec'y	secy.
continued	cont'd	contd.
manufacturer	m'f'r	mfr.
general	gen'l	genl.
special	spec'l	specl.
delivery	del'y	dely.
package	p'k'ge	pkge.
limited	l't'd	ltd.

YES
Abbreviations require a *period.*

YES
Contractions require an *apostrophe.*

NO!
Never use *both* the period and the apostrophe!

EXERCISES

CONTRACTIONS

A. Write the commonly used contracted form for each of these expressions.

1. I am
2. they have
3. we are
4. should not
5. over
6. who is
7. will not

8. could not
9. he is
10. do not
11. we shall
12. it is
13. it was
14. you will

15. she is
16. is not
17. have not
18. we have
19. they would
20. they are

B. Fill each blank space with a contraction of the expression in parentheses:

1. I (cannot) _____ go with you.
2. (She will) _____ give you your books if (they are) _____ ready.
3. We (are not) _____ able to decide (who will) _____ play on the team.
4. Sally (does not) _____ know either.
5. I wonder (who is) _____ knocking at the door.
6. (They will) _____ be safe if kept in the vault.
7. (It was) _____ the night before Christmas.
8. We (have not) _____ seen the missing wallet.
9. The long war is (over) _____ at last!
10. He (must have) _____ met his friend next door.

C. In each group of sentences below fill each blank with the correct word or form from the parentheses preceding the group:

1. (its, it's)
   The cat sank _____ claws into the tree.
   Mary says that _____ going to rain.
2. (Whose, Who's)
   _____ going skating with us?
   _____ hat is this?
3. (your, you're)
   I think that _____ the one to decide.
   Please hang up _____ coat.
4. (Their, There, They're)
   _____ the best players in the school.
   _____ classmates are proud of them.
   _____ they are by the door.
5. (you'll, yule)
   Then, I hope _____ remember next time.
   The _____ log is an old German tradition.

269

WHY DO WE NEED PUNCTUATION AND CAPITALIZATION?

Read this sample of ordinary prose.

jules vernes classic around the world in 80 days has been made into an unusual film phileas fogg a sober calm and clever englishman is matched against the wide eyed amazement and merry pranks of his valet master and servant pursue their headlong way by balloon steamer train ostrich elephant and chinese junk through such dramatic scenes as snatching a beautiful indian princess from a burning funeral pile and a last minute cavalry rescue of the valet from the deadly sioux all this has been spoofed into a supreme triumph of farce who will not remember cantinflas plucking a handful of snow from a nearby mountain to cool his masters champagne as their balloon floats past who can forget the constant delightful surprises as fifty famous stars contribute their bit roles

Now, try it *this* way. Is it clearer? Why?

Jules Verne's classic, "Around the World in 80 Days," has been made into an unusual film. Phileas Fogg, a sober, calm, and clever Englishman, is matched against the wide-eyed amazement and merry pranks of his valet. Master and servant pursue their headlong way by balloon, steamer, train, ostrich, elephant, and Chinese junk through such dramatic scenes as snatching a beautiful Indian princess from a burning funeral pile and a last-minute cavalry rescue of the valet from the deadly Sioux. All this has been spoofed into a supreme triumph of farce. Who will not remember Cantinflas plucking a handful of snow from a nearby mountain to cool his master's champagne as their balloon floats past? Who can forget the constant, delightful surprises as fifty famous stars contribute their "bit" roles?

◊ PUNCTUATION

Punctuation means the separation or division of words and sentences by means of recognized marks for the sake of clearness. Punctuation is a very important part of sentence structure because it signals the reader when to pause or make a full stop in getting the meaning. For example, a missing comma makes this sentence absurd: "After eating the children were put to bed." To avoid this blunder, give the reader the correct signal to pause; thus: "After eating, the children were put to bed."

END PUNCTUATION: THE PERIOD, QUESTION MARK, EXCLAMATION POINT

End punctuation at the close of each sentence separates the main thoughts so that the reader can get the meaning of a series of ideas. As you noticed on the previous page, when a paragraph runs along without any end punctuation to separate its sentences, the meaning becomes obscure. The period, or question mark, or exclamation point serves to give form to writing. Punctuation directs the reader's attention as surely as road signs lead the driver along a highway. Use end punctuation properly and the reader will never get lost.

RULES FOR USING END PUNCTUATION

Use the Period [.]

1. At the end of declarative and imperative sentences.

 Today we will go home.   Please come back soon.

2. After most abbreviations.

 U.S.A.   lb.   ft.   N. Y.   pron.

3. To indicate decimals, and to separate dollars from cents.

 .01   3.1416 $2.98 $3.75

Use the Question Mark [?]

1. At the end of a sentence which asks a direct question.

 Who are you?   Where are you going?

2. At the end of a formal request.

 Will the witness please take the stand?

 Note: No question mark is used in a business letter when you are making a polite request; a period ends the sentence.

 Will you please mail me a copy as advertised.

Use the Exclamation Point [!]

1. At the end of a sentence to show strong feeling, surprise, disgust, or any other powerful emotion.

 Look at the way he is diving with his feet tied!
 Go away, you scoundrel!

2. After a short interjection charged with strong feeling.

 Oh! I am delighted to know you.

271

EXERCISE

END PUNCTUATION

Place the correct punctuation after each of the following sentences and state whether the sentence is declarative, interrogative, imperative, or exclamatory:

1. May I go with you
2. A violent tornado almost destroyed the town
3. Please close the window carefully
4. Mary, the house is afire
5. Were many people hurt
6. I am planning to go
7. I saw a recent movie based on the life of Moses
8. Why do we spend so much time wishing for things
9. In case of fire, walk—don't run—to the nearest exit
10. Tell it to the judge, Mister
11. Where are the buses that used to meet the trains
12. May all your dreams come true
13. Congratulations to you! You really deserved the prize
14. If you want to know the truth, I can't dive
15. Close your eyes and jump into the water like this
16. When the snow melts, the streets get slushy
17. Wipe away those foolish tears and try harder next time
18. Do you think my lateness will be excused
19. The story of Icarus and his attempt to fly is a Greek myth
20. Hats off! The flag is passing by

INSIDE PUNCTUATION: THE COMMA, SEMICOLON, COLON, ETC.

Inside punctuation refers chiefly to the uses of the comma and the semicolon as a means of separating words, phrases, and clauses within the sentence. In contrast to the style of writing that prevailed about 50 to 100 years ago, there is a tendency today toward using *less* inside punctuation. For example, compare a page taken from a short-story by Poe or Twain with one by a modern writer like Edna Ferber or Ernest Hemingway. In place of the slow, leisurely manner of the older writers, there is a lean, cleancut, less involved style today.

RULES FOR USING THE COMMA

Use the Comma [,]

1. To separate words in a series of three or more expressions.
   For breakfast we had bread, butter, eggs, and coffee.
   Note: The comma before *and* may be omitted.

2. To separate a direct quotation from the rest of the sentence.
   He said, "Let there be light!"

3. To separate the main clauses in a compound sentence of some length.
   In the morning we usually relax on the lawn, but after lunch we take a dip or row across the lake.
   Note: When the main clauses are short, no comma is necessary.
   He knocked on the door and she opened it.

4. After a long introductory clause.
   If there is any question about tonight's assignment for homework, please raise your hand now.

5. To set off words used in direct address (= person spoken to).
   Tell the truth, John.

6. To set off words, phrases, or clauses used in apposition.
   Staten Island, an island between New York and New Jersey, lies in the entrance to the harbor.
   Note: Appositives which have become closely associated need no comma.
   Paul the Apostle   My brother Jack

7. To separate a non-restrictive clause (= a clause which may be omitted without changing the meaning of the sentence) from the rest of the sentence.
   General Eisenhower, who was commander-in-chief, was familiarly called "Ike."

8. To separate a contrasting expression introduced by *not only . . . but also.*
   The airforce not only penetrated far behind the enemy lines, but also paved the way for the infantry.

273

Rules for Using the Comma (Continued)

9. To set off absolute constructions (= noun + participle).
   My friend being ill, I visited him last evening.
10. To separate dates and addresses.
    August 10, 19--   Tuxedo, New York
11. After the salutation in a friendly letter.
    Dear Dorothea,   Dear Albert,   Dear Ann,
12. After the closing of both friendly and business letters.
    Sincerely yours,   Very truly yours,   Cordially,
13. To separate transitional words used in a sentence.
    Therefore, we had to leave the dog outside.
14. To mark off groups of three digits in numbers.
    1,000   2,000,000   3,000,000,000

EXERCISE

THE COMMA

Insert the comma (or commas) wherever required to make the meaning clear.

1. Please include a hammer a saw a screw driver a pair of pliers and a wrench.
2. A balanced breakfast consists of fruit juice eggs toast butter and milk.
3. Sharon why don't you come with us to the skating rink?
4. Elias Howe the inventor of the sewing machine helped industry.
5. Please give your ticket to the doorman the one stationed in the lobby.
6. The night being cold we stayed home and watched television.
7. When you are in the middle of an experiment the bell rings.
8. You are entitled to say what you want but we don't have to agree.
9. In the beginning God said "Let there be light!"
10. We need not only prayers and sacrifice but also good works to enter heaven.
11. The common outfit for fishing includes line pole hook sinker and bait.
12. Since we have collected funds for the Red Cross let's send a check today.
13. You boys near the window stop glancing outside during the lesson.
14. I think it was Perry who said "We have met the enemy and they are ours."
15. Miami a well-known winter resort has become quite commercialized.
16. Safety in driving depends on drivers pedestrians brakes and road courtesy.
17. One company advertises "The tastiest cereal in the whole wide world."
18. The term ending early in June we planned an outdoor picnic for the class.

RULES FOR USING QUOTATION MARKS

Use Quotation Marks [" "]

1. To set off the exact words of the speaker.

> Stephen Decatur said, "My country, may she always be in the right; but, right or wrong, my country."

2. To indicate titles of *individual* short-stories, poems, magazine articles, essays, songs, etc.

> "The Red Headed League"   "The Highwayman"

Note: Current practice is to set off titles of *full-length* books, magazines, newspapers, and plays in italics in printing. In handwriting or typewriting, they are underlined.

> *David Copperfield*   *The New York Times*
> Treasure Island   Popular Science

3. To set off a word or phrase for emphasis; for example, the definition of a word, or a bit of slang.

> What is a "flat-top"? It is an aircraft carrier.

Note: Single quotation marks are used to enclose a quotation or a title within another quotation.

> The witness shouted, "Your honor, he called me a 'liar' before!"

EXERCISE

QUOTATION MARKS

Copy each of the following sentences, changing the punctuation marks in such a way as to change the speaker:

[Example: Mary said, "John is late."
"Mary," said John, "is late."]

1. The boy said, "Father is going to hoe the garden."
2. "Then, Henry," said Coach, "how do we work the next play?"
3. The girl said, "Her friend borrowed my umbrella."
4. "Tom Smith," said Frank Harris, "is the funniest man I know."
5. "Oh, Marion," called Marge, "please come into the parlor."
6. The policeman stated, "The driver is to blame."
7. "Stop, Bill," cried Joe, "the bottom of the boat is leaking."
8. Bob Hope exclaimed, "Jack Benny, you're the oldest comic on TV!"

275

RULES FOR USING THE APOSTROPHE

Use the Apostrophe [']

1. To show the possessive case of nouns and indefinite pronouns (one, everyone, anyone, nobody, somebody, someone).

    The man's hat was in somebody's coat.

    Note: Never use the apostrophe with possessive pronouns.

    its, hers, yours, ours, theirs

2. To show the omission of certain letters in a contraction.

    B'klyn (Brooklyn), Att'y (Attorney), don't (do not)

3. To form the plural of figures, letters, short words, etc.

    five 10's   3 A's   too many and's

EXERCISES

THE APOSTROPHE

A. Rewrite correctly those words which require an apostrophe.

1. My brothers car was damaged.
2. The meeting will be at Louis house.
3. Arent there too many ands in your sentence?
4. Is this yours or Alberts?
5. Wouldnt you like to see James toys?
6. Its too bad its raining today, isnt it?
7. Have you read any of Scotts poems?
8. This store sells mens and boys suits.
9. What is the sum of three 5s and two 10s?
10. Doesnt he know its lost?
11. These are yours, arent they?
12. Nobody elses children seem so clever as hers.
13. Dad bought a mans umbrella and two pairs of womens boots.
14. Shouldnt we share one anothers joys?
15. Hasnt the childs dog been found yet?
16. This is the Navys newest ship.
17. My two sisters children came to the house last night.
18. Are these skates yours or Johns?

19. Charles home is in New York, but Jacks is in Albany.
20. Lets go to Bills house tonight.

B. Rewrite correctly those words which require an apostrophe.

1. My cousins watch was lost.
2. The directors office has been redecorated.
3. Marys health is much improved.
4. Where is Thomas composition?
5. Is this Lewis book?
6. This new plane is the Armys pride.
7. Did you use yours or Helens?
8. Charles home is in Ocala, while Joes is in Rochester.
9. Werent you tired last night?
10. Wouldnt you like Phils books?
11. Whats the matter?
12. Its too bad that the dog hurt its foot, isnt it?
13. Give me a nickels worth of candy and two cents worth of gum.
14. On her report card, she received four As and two Bs.
15. The boys carried the girls packages for them.
16. Did you get three weeks pay for a months work?
17. Dont you want a real boys hat?
18. This is ours, not Johns.
19. The days work was soon begun.
20. He hung up a deers head.

RULES FOR USING THE SEMICOLON

Use the Semicolon [;]

1. To separate the main clauses in a compound sentence when no conjunction is used between the clauses.

   The road was jammed with traffic; long lines of cars stood waiting for hours.

2. To separate the main clauses in a compound sentence when the main clauses already contain elements punctuated by commas.

   Whenever there is some fixing to be done around the house, Robert disappears; but, knowing his favorite haunts, Mother always manages to get him back in time to do the work.

3. To separate the transitional word or phrase in a long compound sentence.

   Although he may hesitate at first, he yields in the end; otherwise, nothing would ever be accomplished.

RULES FOR USING THE COLON AND THE DASH

Use the Colon [:]

1. To introduce a list of particulars or a number of details.

> Churchill promised the British people three things: blood, sweat, and tears.

2. After the salutation in a business letter.

> Gentlemen: To Whom It May Concern:

3. To introduce a long quotation (several sentences).

> He addressed the jury as follows: "Gentlemen, I ask no mercy for the defendant. I beg you only to consider his wife and children. I move for acquittal."

Use the Dash [—]

1. To show a sudden shift in thought in a sentence.

> I have tried to forget and forgive—but I can't.

2. To introduce a summary after a series of expressions.

> Friends, position, money, respect—all these he wanted.

EXERCISES

PUNCTUATION

A. Insert the proper inside punctuation marks needed to make the meaning clear in each of the following sentences:

1. I want the radio turned off I just can't do any work.
2. We try to run a nice motel nothing fancy you know with tidy rooms and quiet atmosphere.
3. Did you hear anything else say any unusual sound after you locked the door?
4. You are testifying under oath sir another man's life is at stake.
5. My favorite subjects are these social studies science and mathematics.
6. Pope wrote the famous line "To err is human, to forgive divine."
7. These are the first signs of spring snowdrops crocuses and mud.
8. This is my favorite breakfast fruit juice eggs toast and coffee.
9. His absence from school was excused on account of illness you may check with the doctor's note on file in the office.

10. I saw the car ahead pull to the right just as I started to pass him on the left suddenly there was a crash.
11. A falling body accelerates at 32 feet per second per second according to the Law of Gravity.
12. She left her money to several heirs her nieces nephews and housekeeper.
13. He has an excellent record of attendance work conduct and effort therefore I recommend him with confidence.
14. Boris Karloff is really a gentle person yet he usually acts the part of a cruel monster.
15. Your honor, his past record has nothing to do with this case we are considering only the facts regarding this alleged crime.

B. Insert the punctuation needed to make the meaning clear.

1. While I was shaving my mother-in-law prepared breakfast.
2. Patterson said Robinson is the best boxer in the ring.
3. Throw the monkey the one in the cage a banana.
4. After we had eaten the dog enjoyed the scraps.
5. In short novels give us an introduction to persons and places.
6. The escaping convict staggered and dropped a bullet in his leg.
7. Directly as he had aimed the arrow split the apple in two.
8. The teacher came in on his face a smile in his hands our test papers.
9. This salt runs freely when it rains it pours.
10. Jones signaled Robbins bunted Brown slid home.

C. Tell how the punctuation changes the meaning in each case below:

1. (a) Nobody entered this room?
   (b) Nobody entered this room!
2. (a) Try our coffee and roll downstairs.
   (b) Try our coffee and roll, downstairs.
3. (a) Not more than five girls knew the answer, all told.
   (b) Not more than five girls knew the answer; all told.
4. (a) She left him feeling like a fool.
   (b) She left him, feeling like a fool.
5. (a) Which is the best work?
   (b) Which is the best, work?

D. Insert the punctuation needed to make the meaning clear.

1. This reference book experts agree is the best on the market
2. My mother replied the girl is the sweetest person in the world
3. He collected everything stamps coins medals and souvenirs
4. Selling buying managing appraising these are an agent's jobs
5. They served many flavors of ice cream vanilla chocolate strawberry pistachio
6. Come early if you can so we can chat awhile in private
7. He knew and trusted everyone therefore everybody trusted him
8. How much insurance should a wage earner carry today
9. She smiled how shall I say just a bit too easily and often
10. After she had put out the lights the door squeaked open slowly
11. We missed the train however we arrived before the end of the act
12. What a life these television comedians must lead
13. Why are schooldays black-letter days on the calendar

14. Save your money during good times spend your savings wisely
15. She is a darling if you don't cross her otherwise she can be an imp
16. Step into my parlor said the spider to the fly
17. When the lion had eaten the zoo keeper tossed him a bone
18. Have you ever read Franklin's Autobiography or Pepys Diary
19. Such shows as Omnibus Dragnet Medic and Caesar's Hour have high ratings
20. While Rome was burning Nero fiddled so they say

E. Punctuate the following sentences correctly:

1. What is the dogs name Mary
2. Hurrah There he is now
3. The painting a mass of colors did not appeal to me
4. Ellen Betty and George arrived on time
5. He bought several kinds of fruit oranges tangerines and bananas
6. I hope Bob said that I may go too
7. Well Mother said where were you
8. The night cool and clear made us unwilling to go home
9. Bring the following books papers and maps
10. They live at 145 Melrose Avenue St Petersburg Florida
11. He said Where are you
12. Where he said are you
13. Where are you he said
14. To make so many mistakes is bad enough but not to correct them is worse
15. You have been told often Frank yet you dont seem to understand
16. My what a day
17. Whos at the door Frances
18. Give it to Florence the girl in the front seat
19. We dont usually need heavy clothing here but this year we surely do
20. I was so frightened Mary admitted when I yelled I did it

F. Punctuate the following sentences correctly:

1. I gave him the following books David Copperfield Treasure Island and Call of the Wild
2. My best friend Rose Edwards won first prize in the beauty contest
3. Paul havent you had lunch yet
4. He was born in Albany New York on July 7 1942 at 815 p m
5. How is your sister Miss Gordon asked
6. Will you please go to the store for me Mother asked
7. When I met Ed yesterday he said he hadnt seen George for several days
8. Why didnt you go Jane Martha asked
9. Mary have you read Ivanhoe
10. Please bring the following bread cheese milk and cream
11. Just as you left the house with Alice Florence called
12. Clarence Brown the captain of the team moved to Buffalo New York
13. Bill will you please hand me the shovel
14. Louise Barbara and I decided that we wont go to camp this year
15. By the time Mother finished washing the dishes it was too late to go
16. I visited Ellen on Monday Tuesday and Thursday
17. I caught five flounders I replied
18. Mr Brown my brothers employer lives in this house
19. The big game is scheduled for Saturday November 18 at 200 oclock
20. Father asked Alfred why dont you do your homework now

WHY DO WE CAPITALIZE CERTAIN WORDS?

A capital letter is a mark of distinction. It serves to show importance, rank, or dignity. It helps the reader to locate principal ideas or names of persons and places more easily in a line of writing or print. A capital letter puts a special emphasis or highlight on official titles, quotations, and sentence openings. In the old days of beautiful handwriting, before the invention of the printing press, the monks in the monasteries used to pay devoted attention to capital letters by decorating them with artistic designs in gold and color. Only fifty years ago, the sign of culture was the Spencerian script, with curlicues embellishing each capital letter. Today, capitalization is purely a convenience in reading and a clue to the reader that certain words have an importance beyond the run-of-the-mill small letters. Capitals make sense—when properly used—by setting off key words visually.

CAPITALIZATION RULES

Capitalize:

A. Calendar Days

1. Days of the week
   Sunday, Monday, Tuesday, Wednesday, Thursday, Friday, Saturday
2. Months of the year
   January, February, March, April, May, June, July, August, September, October, November, December
3. Holidays and holy days
   New Year's Day, Easter, Fourth of July, Labor Day, Thanksgiving, Christmas

B. Nationalities

1. Proper nouns, such as the names of countries, races, etc.
   America, England, France, China, Russia
2. Proper adjectives, such as languages, etc.
   American, English, French, Chinese, Russian

Capitalization Rules (Continued)

C. Geographical Terms

1. Sections of the country, names of states, cities, towns, etc.

   the North, the East, the South, the West, Texas, New Hampshire, California, Connecticut, Omaha, Albany

2. Places, mountains, rivers, etc.

   Asia, the Atlantic Ocean, the Rocky Mountains, the Great Lakes, the Danube River, Niagara Falls

D. Famous Events and Places

1. Historical events

   the Crusades, the Treaty of Paris, the Magna Charta, the Battle of Lexington, the Atlantic Charter

2. Important buildings and structures

   the Empire State Building, the White House, the Congressional Library, the Tomb of the Unknown Soldier

E. Titles

1. Scriptures and the Deity

   the Bible, the Old Testament, the New Testament, the Psalms, God, Christ, Jehovah

2. The first and all the principal words in the title of a book, magazine, newspaper, poem, or article

   The Man Without a Country, The Saturday Evening Post, The New York Times, The Highwayman

F. Opening Words

1. The first word of each sentence

   We accept with pleasure your kind invitation.

2. The first word of each line of poetry

   Be not the first by whom the new is tried,
   Nor yet the last to lay the old aside.
   —Alexander Pope

   Note: Some writers of contemporary verse do not capitalize every line; for example, see "Fog" by Carl Sandburg.

3. The first word of each direct quotation

   Marshal Foch said, "They shall not pass!"

EXERCISES

CAPITALIZATION

A. Capitalize each of the words that should be capitalized:
1. we went to lake tiorati in the bear mountain region.
2. have you ever visited niagara falls from the canadian side?
3. abraham lincoln was born in kentucky on february 12, 1809.
4. margaret said, "please read me dickens' *a christmas carol.*"
5. the white house is located in washington, d. c.
6. down in texas there are large cities like san antonio and galveston.
7. miss young said, "grace, will you please face the class?"
8. the new testament contains the gospels of matthew, mark, luke, and john.
9. on labor day all the traffic comes pouring back into new york city.
10. i like christmas and easter because we always get vacations from school.

B. Capitalize the following titles of books, stories, poems, etc.:
1. the legend of sleepy hollow
2. king robert of sicily
3. the courtship of miles standish
4. the lady of the lake
5. the story of a bad boy
6. the ransom of red chief
7. the man without a country
8. the prince and the pauper
9. horatius at the bridge
10. the ballad of the harp-weaver

C. Rewrite the following letter with the proper capital letters as required by correct usage:

36 richmond terrace
staten island, new york
january 3, 19--

mr. louis goodwin
470 clove road
bloomfield, connecticut

dear sir:

i am interested in the offer you made in today's *herald-tribune* for the sale of your set of lionel trains and equipment. may i come to visit you some day next week to inspect the set with my father? we are both railroad hobbyists and would like very much to see whether we can make a satisfactory deal. our home telephone number is gibraltar 2-6125.

very truly yours,
leonard martin

D. In the following sentences, there are words that are not capitalized but should be. Write the words that should be capitalized.
1. we crossed the mississippi river three times.
2. the jamison company is having a sale.

3. we swim every sunday in the gulf of mexico.
4. providence street is the longest street in our city.
5. last night i met lieutenant franklin.
6. "my history paper is lost," said jane.
7. we listened with interest to sir james brown.
8. i listened while he read a passage from the bible.
9. the adirondack mountains are in new york state.
10. the all state club meets every monday.
11. his theme was entitled "the rights and wrongs done each day."
12. have you read *the trail of the lonesome pine*?
13. last night we listened to the president of the united states.
14. our neighbor, mr. crane, once lived in the west.
15. latin is as difficult as mathematics.
16. last week we studied the poem "on the road to vagabondia."
17. the hudson river lay before us.
18. we invited father duffy to attend our party on new year's day.
19. give the report to dr. harold j. evans.
20. i went north with mother and father last june.

E. In the following sentences, there are words that are not capitalized but should be. Write the words that should be capitalized.

1. i enjoyed the *tale of two cities*.
2. robert was born in august and larry in december.
3. when we went to the white house, we saw the president.
4. my english teacher is miss miller.
5. renee shouted, "your brother is looking for you."
6. we are going to uncle peter's farm in pennsylvania next sunday.
7. last august joe went south while i went west.
8. i met mother on state street.
9. the catskill mountains in new york are very beautiful.
10. we met captain harris at the corner of pine and vine.
11. in what state is lake okeechobee?
12. i went to the capital theater on sunday with ed and mel.
13. we visited the yellowstone national park in montana.
14. i expect to study spanish, french, and latin.
15. we are going to princeton, new jersey, to see my brother who is a student at princeton university.
16. i heard the army-navy game over station wor.
17. i received a bible from aunt ann.
18. "are you going to the football game this new year's day, dr. laws?"
19. she asked, "how many south american countries can you name?"
20. the rose bowl football game is played at pasadena, california.

F. In each of the following sentences there is one word which is not capitalized but which should be capitalized. Select the word and explain why it should be capitalized.

1. The south is mostly an agricultural region.
2. We plan to start on tuesday.
3. Part of New York State borders on lake Ontario.
4. Today, we are taking an examination in english.
5. Jane said, "my puppy is black."

284

6. I am proud to be an american.
7. He spent christmas with his grandparents.
8. The only doctor who lives here is doctor Brown.
9. How did you like the ending of *kidnapped*?
10. Benjamin franklin was a man of exceptional ability.

EXERCISES

PUNCTUATION AND CAPITALIZATION

A. Rewrite the following, using correct punctuation and capitalization:

While i was still dreaming of going to sea in a schooner to search for buried treasure we met squire trelawney dressed like a sea officer he was coming out of the door with a smile on his face

sir i cried when do we sail

we sail now shouted he

B. Rewrite the following in correct sentences, with proper punctuation and capitalization:

One day last summer we were camping out in the back yard sparks from our campfire blew against the tent and set it on fire you should have seen us run joe ran to the house for help and Father brought a pail of water the fire was soon out but there was great excitement while it lasted after inspection we found that one side of the tent was almost destroyed.

C. Rewrite the following, dividing it into sentences and using correct punctuation and capitalization:

thomas jefferson was president for eight years the nation was so well satisfied that his second election was nearly unanimous just after his second inauguration state legislatures began to pass resolutions urging him to become a candidate for a third term jefferson declined some limit to a presidents term he said should be fixed by custom or else the president may come to serve for life service for more than two terms may prove dangerous to the country.

D. Rewrite the following sentences so that each will be correct in punctuation and capitalization:

1. we should arrive in chicago illinois on decoration day
2. florence sit down and do your work quietly
3. ed my brothers friend had dinner with us this evening
4. have you read the book two years before the mast
5. i bought milk butter bread and cake
6. are you going to study french spanish or latin
7. because she didnt write me as she had promised i called her over the telephone

8. why dont you visit aunt martha mother said
9. my sweater the new gray one is missing
10. she answered yes i know the answer
11. will you be going to the dance on saturday gertrude
12. how are you feeling she asked
13. surely you know that trenton is the capital of new jersey
14. she sent william a present a pair of skates for christmas
15. last summer i went to the green mountains in vermont
16. while walking along the street with marge we met helen
17. phil went to the main street theater while i stayed home and read my book
18. the meeting is scheduled for december 8 at 200 oclock
19. ted why dont you do your homework
20. my fathers friend mr davis bought this new house

 ACCEPTABLE HANDWRITING

We write for *others* to read. Writing must be *readable*. Simply stated, that's all! It's a matter of communication of ideas by means of symbols, and it's based on consideration for others. Experience shows that handwriting reveals more than the words themselves say. It is rooted in the habits and attitudes of human personality. Therefore, be careful lest a little note, hastily and carelessly scribbled, may serve to damage your reputation. Handwriting is a factor in judging you as well as your message. You know by this time that your handwriting has identified you to your friends; that your teachers include it in rating your work; and that in the world outside the classroom it has even greater importance. Employers ask applicants to fill in blanks or write a letter for a job in their own personal handwriting because it offers many clues to habits of work, attitudes, and other factors. Don't you realize, then, how necessary it is for you to develop a clear, legible script?

In a pamphlet published by the Board of Education of the City of New York, *A Brief Guide to the Teaching of Handwriting in the Elementary Schools,* the following suggestion is made. Study it carefully.

JOINING LETTERS

Sometimes the difficulty does not lie in the formation of the letter itself but rather in the way the letter is joined to another letter. An individual may write letters well in one combination but may need help when the letters are combined in different ways.

Some examples of letter combinations follow. When practice is needed in writing any of these combinations, it should take the form of writing words containing such combinations, and should not be practiced in writing isolated letter combinations.

Joining Small Letters

a	man	sale	n	name	nest
b	bat	bite	o	oats	toe
c	cat	city	p	pad	pen
d	does	desk	q	queen	quit
e	sea	set	r	rate	read
f	far	flat	s	sat	seat
g	egg	age	t	tall	ten
h	have	hill	u	sun	sent
i	big	begin	v	value	very
j	jam	jet	w	write	went
k	know	kind	x	exact	next
l	last	let	y	yard	year
m	man	same	z	zone	zero

Joining Capital Letters to Small Letters

A	Act	Ail	N	Nancy	Ned
B	Ball	Bell	O	Oct. or	Oct.
C	Call	Cell	P	Paris	Price
D	Dec. or	Dec.	Q	Queen	Quart
E	Each	Ellis	R	Rose	Rita
F	Far	Fear	S	Same	Sir
G	Gone	Give	T	Tom	Test
H	Has	His	U	United	Upon
I	Iowa	Into	V	Vera	Very
J	John	Jet	W	Will	Wall
K	Kansas	Kent	X	X Ray	X Ray
L	Let	Live	Y	Yard	Yes
M	Mary	Miss	Z	Zone	Zero

288

DEVELOPING READING COMPREHENSION SKILLS

HOW CAN YOU BECOME A BETTER READER?

Reading is the ability to get the meaning from written or printed words.

Doesn't that definition sound simple? Yet, reading means more than understanding words. It is the art of grasping thought, sharing emotion, and responding to both. It is a basic tool in all study and learning. It is a doorway to new experience through the world of books. Thus, for general purposes, *reading may be classified as two types of skills:* work-study and recreational.

WORK-STUDY READING

This type of reading requires skill in understanding facts, information, and instruction in textbooks in history, science, mathematics; magazines like *Popular Science, Time, Flying, Better Homes and Gardens;* newspapers, almanacs, etc. This is basic intensive reading for *meaning.*

RECREATIONAL READING

This type of reading requires skill in understanding, enjoying, and appreciating literature in various forms, such as short-stories, novels, plays, poems, biographies, essays, travel books, etc. This is usually "free choice" or extensive reading for *pleasure* or pastime.

SPECIAL SKILLS IN READING

1. Finding the central thought in a selection.
2. Finding supporting ideas for a statement.
3. Following printed directions accurately.
4. Reading to fill out forms and blanks correctly.
5. Reading rapidly to locate quickly some bit of information.
6. Reading carefully to summarize a paragraph in one sentence.
7. Reading imaginatively to predict the outcome of a story.
8. Learning how to use the various parts of a textbook.
9. Learning how to use the dictionary and other reference tools.
10. Learning how to use the alphabetical order of arrangement of material.

CORRECTION OF FAULTY READING HABITS

The best way to correct is to prevent. Form the right reading habits from the start. Ask your teacher to diagnose your reading to see whether you have any faults. Then get to work to remove them.

1. Lip movement or whispering

Read silently with "still lips" for greater speed. You can read five times as fast silently as you can speak.

2. Mental pronouncing

Avoid this kind of reading. Train yourself to read more rapidly and omit that echoing of the sound of words in your mind.

3. Mental attitude

Build up confidence in yourself and approach the task of reading with pleasurable emotions. If you are indifferent or worried about it, you will not read as well as when you say to yourself, "I *can* do it!"

4. Too many pauses and backward eye movements

Your eyes should swing from left to right in rhythmical sweeps with no more than two pauses per line. If you find that practice does not overcome this fault, see an oculist.

5. Visual confusion

If you find that letters are blurred or you substitute words for the actual ones printed in the book, have your vision examined.

6. Lack of power of attention

Get a grip on yourself when you are reading and concentrate on the passage. A good device is to have questions listed which will direct your attention to specific items in the passage you are reading.

7. Poor word-recognition

Do not guess at words by pouncing upon the first few letters and skipping the rest. Use the sentence or context as a clue and notice the whole pattern of the word. Build up your vocabulary!

8. Disregard of proper word-grouping

Watch the punctuation marks and the structure of the sentence instead of concentrating on individual words. Train your eyespan to take in phrases and clauses as units of meaning.

9. Slow rate in reading

Comprehension is always more important than speed. A normal reading rate is 240 words a minute for narrative material. More difficult selections will naturally require more time for grasping the thought.

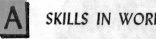

A SKILLS IN WORK-STUDY READING

Since the chief purpose of work-study reading is to get the meaning, the two most important elements are word-recognition and paragraph-meaning. Let's consider each one separately.

◗ SKILL IN WORD-RECOGNITION

To build *word-recognition,* use these techniques:

1. Firsthand experience

Try to widen your direct knowledge of things by personal contact; trips to museums, farms, factories, offices; classroom activities; camping experience; work experience; traveling; making field trips. Take notes!

2. Pictorial aids

Collect photographs and clippings; make drawings; see movies, slides, filmstrips, exhibits; study maps, diagrams, graphs. Label each correctly!

3. Clues in the context

Learn to watch the sentence idea or paragraph for suggestions as to the meaning of a strange word. Note especially whether a synonym or antonym has already been used, in order to guess the meaning of the new word in relation to words you already know.

4. Dictionary definitions

Make sure you select the right meaning to fit the passage according to the way the word is being used. Develop the habit of looking up words and keeping a notebook record of new words.

Skill in building word-recognition often depends on clues in the context which suggest meaning.

Every morning you salute the flag and recite the pledge of allegiance. Do you realize what you are saying? Read it carefully, noticing the meaning of the words as given between the lines.

I pledge allegiance to the flag of the United States of America
    promise loyalty

and to the Republic for which it stands: one nation under God,
         government   country

indivisible, with liberty and justice for all.
not to be   freedom   fairness
separated

These words have a special effect on us because they stir us with the emotion of patriotism as we recite the pledge. They also have an ordinary meaning when used in everyday sentences, as the following:

1. I *pledge* to deposit ten cents in the school bank every week.
2. Buck proved his *allegiance* by saving his master's life.
3. Our General Organization is a student *republic*.
4. Many *nations* in the world today are fighting for human rights.
5. The number 7 is *indivisible* by any other number except 1.
6. You are at *liberty* to leave the room now.
7. The policeman demanded *justice* for the teenager.

The first step in reading, then, is to understand the meaning of words. A good reader is also aware of the emotional effect of words by their association with ideas or experiences.

EXERCISE

WORD-RECOGNITION

Explain the meaning of each italicized expression as *used* in the sentence.

1. As the plane approached the *runway*, the landing gear dropped.
2. Johnny is still tied to his mother's *apron strings*.
3. Highway speed is checked by *radar* in roving patrol cars.
4. On a spring day, we *stroll* through the park.
5. The laundry door opened by means of an *electronic eye*.
6. Children take polio *shots* for protection against disease.
7. Some of the *gags* on television come from Miller's Joke Book.
8. The *pitch* of the roof leads the rainwater to the drain.
9. She sang alto while he harmonized with his *bass*.
10. An eleven-year-old boy smiles at the *tantrums* of a four-year-old girl.
11. Smart parents *put their foot down* in such situations.
12. If you *mend* your manners, you will make more friends.
13. Please ship the material now and *bill* me later.
14. Bringing an apple to the teacher shows you have an *ax to grind*.
15. Children loved her because she had a *honeyed* voice.
16. Riding in a taxi may be *old hat* to you, but new to me.
17. The *topnotch* player in the game was my brother.
18. A good reporter is said to have a *nose* for news.
19. Service to others brings the reward of *satisfaction*, not riches.
20. School tries to discover each pupil's *talent* or ability.

STEPS IN GETTING PARAGRAPH-MEANING

Reading is a thinking process. You need not only eyes for silent reading, or eyes and lips for oral reading, but the brain as the chief instrument in getting the meaning. Therefore, you must think actively while reading. This does not mean skimming along idly, or daydreaming, or fixing upon whatever ideas you happen to like. Your job is to try to find out exactly what the passage says. You must be alert and concentrate on the message. As you read, ask mental questions, make comparisons, apply the ideas. Reading is a sort of silent conversation between you and the print. Get the habit of seeing a group of words as the expression of an idea rather than as a group of individual letters or unrelated words.

The reading comprehension test, which is part of every examination in English, usually consists of a series of passages dealing with such subjects as history, geography, aviation, housing, zoology, nature study, current affairs, etc. You are expected to size up the meaning of the paragraph as a whole, to discover implications or "read between the lines," to find supporting evidence for certain statements, to locate the topic or "title" that fits the paragraph, to figure out the meaning of unusual words as used in the paragraph, to see the relation between cause and effect. Since most paragraphs are factual in type, you must select details intelligently. If the paragraph argues for a certain point of view, you must be able to follow the logical presentation of ideas. In brief, you must read thoughtfully and carefully, rereading as many times as necessary to find the right answers.

After you have finished reading the passage carefully, look over the questions printed at the right and figure out the correct choice of answer by rereading the passage as many times as necessary. Avoid guesswork by following these steps in getting the meaning:

GETTING THE MEANING

1. What is the *central idea* of the passage?

The main theme or subject of the selection is a general overall topic which underlies the entire material. It is the main thought which is put across.

2. Which is the *topic sentence?*

This sentence is usually near the beginning and serves to introduce the main idea of the passage. It points to what the author is trying to say.

3. What *supporting evidence* helps to develop the central idea?

This includes reasons, illustrations, examples, etc., to build up the message.

4. What *conclusion* or application is made at the end of the passage?

Watch the closing sentences for a summary statement which interprets the facts or data presented and offers a new or different point of view.

5. What is the *author's attitude* or reaction to the material?

Notice the general tone of the passage to find whether you are being asked to agree or to disagree with the views presented.

EXERCISE

GETTING THE MAIN IDEA

Try this short paragraph to see whether you get the main idea in a single reading, as you should.

The great French naturalist, Fabre, observed that certain caterpillars travel in a procession, each with its head pressed snugly against the rear extremity of the caterpillar in front of it. He lured a group of them to the rim of a large flower pot and succeeded in connecting the first with the last. They formed a complete ring which went around and around without stopping. Fabre expected that after a while they would catch on to the joke—get tired of their useless march, and start off in a new direction. But, they kept going on and on for seven days and nights. Doubtlessly, they would have continued longer except for starvation and tiredness. By the way, there was plenty of food close at hand and plain to be seen. They followed the leader blindly because of instinct or habit. They mistook activity for accomplishment. I sometimes wonder whether we, too, occasionally behave as if we based our conduct on that of caterpillars like these.

The main idea of this paragraph is:

1. Caterpillars are really stupid creatures.
2. People are funny if you watch them.
3. Scientists are very patient in their experiments.
4. Don't act blindly; plan ahead.
5. Follow your instinct; habit cannot be broken.

Answer: The main idea is *suggested* by the last sentence of the paragraph; 4 is correct.

READING TESTS AND EXPLANATION OF ANSWERS

Let's examine some sample reading tests. Try to figure out the three following selections (*A, B,* and *C*) yourself and then compare your answers with the models given. Study the explanations to find out why you may have missed some of the points.

Directions: At the right of each of the following selections, you will find several incomplete statements about the selection. Each statement is followed by five words or expressions numbered 1 to 5. After reading each selection, read the statements at the right. Then choose the word or expression that most satisfactorily completes *each* statement and write its *number* in the parentheses after the statement.

Model Reading Selection A

Many people know that Ben Franklin's kite experiment helped to prove that lightning is electricity. Kites have been used for scientific purposes since the middle 1700's— for testing weather conditions, taking aerial photographs, etc. They have also been employed in many interesting ways during wartime. Centuries ago, a Korean general sent a kite, with line attached, to the opposite bank of a river. A cable followed the line, forming the nucleus from which a bridge was built. The Japanese developed a man-carrying kite, invaluable in scouting the enemy's position. Many armies used to employ kites for signaling purposes. Now some airplane lifeboats are equipped with kites carrying radio antennas which automatically signal S.O.S.

a. The title below that best expresses the main theme or subject of this selection is:
1. Kite making as a hobby
2. Methods of signaling
3. Uses of kites through the years
4. Our debt to Ben Franklin
5. Wartime use of kites ( )

b. The author tells us that the Japanese used kites for (1) photography (2) scouting (3) radio signaling (4) scientific studies (5) weather predicting ( )

c. The most recent use of kites mentioned is carrying (1) bridge cables (2) soldiers (3) photographers (4) electricity (5) radio antennas .... ( )

296

Model Answers:

a.(3) *b*.(2) *c*.(5)

Explanation of Answers:

a. The title that best expresses the main theme or subject of the selection is . . . .

    RIGHT: (3) Uses of kites through the years
               This includes *all* the illustrations given.

    WRONG: (1) (2) (4) (5)
               These contain only *one* illustration apiece of the many uses of kites mentioned in the selection.

---

b. The author tells us that the Japanese used kites for . . . .

    RIGHT: (2) scouting
               Sentence #6 supplies this information directly.

    WRONG: (1) (3) (4) (5)
               None of these statements refers to the *Japanese*.

---

c. The most recent use of kites mentioned is carrying . . . .

    RIGHT: (5) radio antennas
               The last sentence begins with the word "Now" which is, of course, the most *recent*.

    WRONG: (1) (2) (3) (4)
               These all refer to *past* years, not the most recent.

Model Reading Selection B

On the whole the Eskimos are a coastal people. Their total number is not more than 35,000. Of these about 14,500 live along the coast of Greenland. Eskimo settlements are scattered along the northern coast of North America from Labrador to Alaska's panhandle. On Baffin Island and on other large islands there are

a. The title below that best expresses the main theme or subject of this selection is:
1. The Caribou Eskimos
2. The Eskimos
3. Eskimo fishing
4. Eskimo homes
5. The Copper Eskimos ( )

Eskimo villages. The Eskimos spend most of their time near the sea and get much of their living from the sea. However, one tribe, the Caribou Eskimos, live inland west of Hudson Bay. Some of them have never seen the sea.

Although life in one village is in many ways very much like life in another, there are some differences. The reason is that the Eskimos must use what they find in the particular district where they live. The Copper Eskimos who live beside Coronation Gulf build thick-walled winter houses of snow blocks. Alaskan Eskimos do not use such houses and most of them have never even seen one. Their winter homes are made of turf and mud. The Eskimos of southern Greenland are expert in handling a kayak, or Eskimo canoe. They fish in the open water of the sea. The Eskimos of northern Greenland have little chance to use kayaks because the water along the coast is frozen almost all the year. All tribes, however, have one thing in common. They are primarily fishermen and hunters.

b. Most Eskimos live (1) near the water (2) on the plains (3) in the forests (4) inland (5) on islands ....( )

c. The Caribou Eskimos are (1) from the coast of Greenland (2) not hunters and fishermen (3) scattered along the coast of North America (4) not coastal people (5) skilled at gaining their living from the sea ....( )

d. A comparison of different Eskimo villages shows that the way of life in each (1) is quite similar to that in the others (2) is very unlike that in the others (3) has nothing to do with the location (4) is very civilized (5) is much like our own way of life ( )

e. Alaskan Eskimos make their winter homes of (1) snow blocks (2) skins and furs (3) wood (4) turf and mud (5) stones ....( )

f. A kayak is a kind of (1) sled (2) house (3) boat (4) animal (5) spear ....( )

g. All Eskimo tribes (1) are skilled in the use of the kayak (2) hunt and fish for a living (3) make homes of snow blocks (4) live in Greenland (5) depend on the ocean for a living ....( )

Model Answers:

a.(2) *b.*(1) *c.*(4) *d.*(1) *e.*(4) *f.*(3) *g.*(2)

Explanation of Answers:

a. The title that best expresses the main theme or subject of the selection is ....

RIGHT: (2) The Eskimos
This includes *all* the tribes, homes, and occupations.

WRONG: (1) (5) These describe certain tribes: Caribou, Copper.
(3) (4) These tell only about their fishing and homes.

---

b. Most Eskimos live ....

RIGHT: (1) near the water
Numerous references make this clear: "coastal people," "near the sea," "open water," etc.

WRONG: (2) (3) (4) (5)
These all refer to land: "plains," "forests," etc.

---

c. The Caribou Eskimos are ....

RIGHT: (4) not coastal people
The passage tells us they "live inland," meaning that they are not coastal people.

WRONG: (1) (2) (3) (5)
These may be checked against the passage and eliminated as untrue, one by one.

---

d. A comparison of different Eskimo villages shows that the way of life in each ....

RIGHT: (1) is quite similar to that in the others
Sentence #9 tells us, "Life in one village is in many ways very much like life in another." (similar = like)

299

WRONG: (2) (3) (4) (5)
Since the correct choice is so apparent, these may be easily eliminated as untrue.

e. Alaskan Eskimos make their winter homes of . . . .

RIGHT: (4) turf and mud
This is the exact phrase used in sentence #13.

WRONG: (1) (2) (3) (5)
Once you locate the right information, you can readily omit these inaccurate statements.

---

f. A kayak is a kind of . . . .

RIGHT: (3) boat
It is described in sentence #14: "a kayak, or Eskimo canoe."

WRONG: (1) (2) (4) (5)
These all are obvious decoys or misstatements.

---

g. All Eskimo tribes . . . .

RIGHT: (2) hunt and fish for a living
This is clearly stated in the last two sentences.

WRONG: (1) (3) (4) (5)
These statements are true for *some* Eskimos, but not true for *all* Eskimos (as required by the question).

Model Reading Selection C

Education was free. That subject my father had written about repeatedly, as comprising his chief hope for us children, the essence of American opportunity, the treasure that no thief could touch, not even misfortune or poverty. It was the one thing he was able to promise us when he sent for us, surer, safer than bread or shelter. On our sec-

a. The title below that best expresses the main theme or subject of this selection is:
1. My first day in America
2. The schools of Boston
3. My father's education
4. Our greatest opportunity in America
5. The little girl next door
( )

ond day I was thrilled with the realization of what this freedom of education meant. A little girl from across the alley came and offered to conduct us to school. My father was out, but we five between us had a few words of English by this time. We knew the word *school*. We understood. This child, who had never seen us till yesterday, who could not pronounce our names, who was not much better dressed than we, was able to offer us the freedom of the schools of Boston! The doors stood open for every one of us. The smallest child could show us the way. This incident impressed me more than anything I had heard in advance about the freedom of education in America. It was a concrete proof—almost the thing itself. One had to experience it to understand it.

b. When the father sent for his children, the only thing he could surely promise them was (1) bread (2) friends (3) shelter (4) schooling (5) wealth . . . . ( )

c. The father believed that (1) he should have stayed in Europe (2) education was not worth while (3) the children could not learn English (4) he would always live in poverty (5) education was one possession that could not be stolen . . . . ( )

d. The word *school* (1) was unknown to the children (2) frightened the children (3) was one of the first English words the children had learned (4) reminded the children of unhappy days in Europe (5) was difficult for the children to understand . . . . ( )

e. The children fully realized the meaning of their father's words when they discovered that (1) the little girl across the way had better clothes than they did (2) they could not understand the little girl (3) the Boston schools didn't want them (4) in America even a little girl could take them to school (5) the little girl could not pronounce their names . . . . ( )

Model Answers:

a.(4)   *b.*(4)   *c.*(5)   *d.*(3)   *e.*(4)

Explanation of Answers:

a. The title that best expresses the main theme or subject of the selection is ....

RIGHT: (4) Our greatest opportunity in America
Sentence #2 describes education as "the essence of American opportunity." (essence = chief quality)

WRONG: (1) (2) (3) (5)
These items are all mentioned in the passage, but they do not summarize the *main theme.*

---

b. When the father sent for his children, the only thing he could surely promise them was ....

RIGHT: (4) schooling
Sentence #3 states: "It (education) was the one thing he was able to promise us."

WRONG: (1) (2) (3) (5)
Obviously, these are not the *one thing,* though mentioned in passing as desirable additions.

---

c. The father believed that ....

RIGHT: (5) education was one possession that could not be stolen (See sentence #2.)

WRONG: (1) (2) (3) (4) Excluded as false.

---

d. The word *school* ....

RIGHT: (3) was one of the first English words the children had learned (See sentences #6 and #7.)

WRONG: (1) (2) (4) (5) Excluded as false.

---

e. The children fully realized the meaning of their father's words when they discovered that ....

RIGHT: (4) in America even a little girl could take them to school (See sentences #11 and #12.)

WRONG: (1) (2) (3) (5) Excluded as false.

EXERCISES

READING COMPREHENSION

Directions: At the right of each of the following selections, you will find several incomplete statements about the selection. Each statement is followed by five words or expressions numbered 1 to 5. After reading each selection, read the statements at the right. Then choose the word or expression that most satisfactorily completes *each* statement and write its *number* in the parentheses after the statement.

READING EXERCISE 1

A. The regular unit of European life in the Middle Ages was not the city or the open farmstead. It was the feudal castle—a fortification situated if possible upon a lofty hill, and often with a little village of the crude huts of the lord's peasants clustered close beside it. During the earlier feudal period the castle in most cases would be simply a single huge tower, round or square, with merely a crude palisade and a ditch for outworks. The height would baffle any scaling-ladder. There would be no opening in its blank masonry until a considerable distance from the ground. Then the narrow door would be entered only by a flimsy wooden bridge, easy to demolish, or by a frail ladder, drawn up every night. Inside the tower there would be a series of dark, cavernous rooms, one above another, communicating by means of ladders. The sole purpose of such a comfortless castle was defense, and that defense by mere height and mass, not by any special skill in arranging the various parts.

Little by little this simple donjon became more complicated. The original tower was kept, but inclosed by other lines of defense. To force the outer barriers meant simply that you had a far

a. European life in medieval times centered around the (1) king's army (2) farm (3) city (4) castle (5) peasant village ....( )

b. The most important part of the fortifications was the (1) palisade (2) ditch (3) tower (4) drawbridge (5) hill ....( )

c. The chief value of the castle was (1) strategy in attack (2) a good view (3) simple defense (4) warmth (5) comfortable living ....( )

d. To defend a well-built castle the lord needed a (1) small group of soldiers (2) kingly army (3) peasant family (4) great deal of skill (5) more complicated system ( )

e. A true statement about the medieval castle is that (1) a hill was its ideal situation (2) the peasants lived in the tower (3) its innermost fortifications were its weakest parts (4) it was entered through a wide door (5) it was made completely of wood ....( )

stronger inner bulwark before you. The best kind of medieval castle needed only a very small number of soldiers. From behind its walls even an inferior baron could protect himself from a kingly army.

B. Money has now become so important that we often lose sight of what lies behind it. The usual way to regain our focus is to ask a question like this: "If you were without food on a desert island with no chance of rescue for a long time and had to choose between a million dollars in gold or a fifty-pound Wisconsin cheese, which would you take?" I think it is extremely necessary to see clearly and simply what lies behind the dollars. I doubt if we can solve our financial problems unless we see the people, the land, the machines, the houses, the freight cars, the loaves of bread which alone give dollars any meaning. In the long run it is human labor, capital investment, raw materials, mechanical energy and scientific knowledge which form the chief parts of the economic machine.

a. The title that best expresses the main theme or subject of this selection is:
1. Solving our financial problems
2. The real meaning of dollars
3. Wisconsin cheese
4. Money and the machine
5. Living on a desert island . ( )

b. The author suggests that if one were away from civilization (1) money would be his most important possession (2) he would miss the economic machine (3) food would be of greater value than money (4) it would be necessary to solve financial problems (5) human labor would be unnecessary ( )

C. The Tuaregs, wanderers of the Sahara Desert, are born fighters. Tall, muscular, capable of almost superhuman resistance and patience when stalking a human prey, the Tuareg prince hides his light complexion and fine, intelligent features under the litham. This dark cloth, which entirely covers his face except for the eyes, he is supposed to wear even during sleep and barely to raise while eating. Like the Bedouin of Central Arabia, he firmly believes that a man is surrounded by malignant spirits constantly endeavoring to penetrate into him by way of his lips and nostrils, in order to take possession of his soul—a superstition that is probably only a poetic way of describing the whirling, all-pervading sands of the desert.

a. The complexion of the Tuaregs is (1) light (2) brown (3) black (4) yellow (5) red . . . . ( )

b. The litham worn by the Tuareg man is a (1) turban (2) sash (3) veil (4) robe (5) neck scarf . ( )

c. The litham is supposedly worn for protection from (1) the glare of the sun (2) sandstorms (3) evil spirits (4) cold (5) tribal enemies . . ( )

D. Liberia, the tiny republic on the west coast of Africa, has long been of interest to the United States. This is

a. The title that best expresses the main theme or subject of this selection is:

partly because it was founded as a sovereign state by little bands of freed slaves from the United States and the West Indies who settled there a little over a century ago, and partly because of its fast-developing rubber plantations.

Only slightly larger than Ohio, Liberia is unique in that it is the only part of the African continent remaining in Negro hands and under Negro control. Its name refers to the new-found liberation of the former slaves who colonized its shores, and whose descendants today rule the little nation. Besides some 2,000,000 primitive natives who live in the tropical inland areas, there are about 70,000 civilized inhabitants with a standard of living patterned after that of the United States or Europe. Only Negroes may be citizens of Liberia.

Although tiny, Liberia is of some military importance. It has no good ports, but its capital, Monrovia (named for President Monroe), is practically next door to the great British naval base at Freetown. Liberia exports some $3,000,000 worth of crude rubber annually.

1. Rubber from Liberia
2. The west coast of Africa
3. Descendants of the slaves
4. A Negro republic
5. A colony of the U. S. .....( )

b. Liberia was settled (1) before the United States (2) twenty-five years ago (3) more than one hundred years ago (4) about eighty years ago (5) two hundred years ago ....( )

c. The name "Liberia" was chosen because (1) it described the small size of the country (2) the founders had recently been freed from slavery (3) the United States was interested in it (4) rubber was an important crop (5) President Monroe suggested it ....( )

d. The citizens of Liberia are (1) of many races (2) American slaves (3) all Negroes (4) British subjects (5) mostly civilized inhabitants ....( )

READING EXERCISE 2

A. Hatting was one of the first domestic industries to develop in the colonies. As early as 1640, American hats were one of the homemade articles used for barter and exchange. By the beginning of the eighteenth century, hatting had become one of New England's important industries; in the 1730's hats were being exported from the colonies in sufficient numbers to arouse uneasiness among hatters in the mother country and to cause them to exert successful pressure on Parliament for a law prohibiting the export of hats from one colony to another, and from any colony to Great Britain or any other country.

Wool was the principal raw material, but a considerable proportion of the hats

a. The title that best expresses the main theme or subject of this selection is:
1. Raw materials for hats
2. Colonial exports
3. How hats were made
4. Kinds of hats in America
5. An early American industry ( )

b. A law regarding the hat trade was enacted by Parliament in response to a complaint by (1) colonists (2) Indians (3) English noblemen (4) citizens of foreign countries (5) English hatmakers ......( )

c. This law made it illegal for (1) Great Britain to export hats (2)

were made of fur felt, using beaver fur as the base. The average price of wool hats during the eighteenth century ranged from 40 to 80 cents, and beaver hats ranged from $2.50 to $3.50.

the colonies to import hats (3) the hatters to use beaver fur (4) the colonies to export hats (5) the colonies to change the price of hats
( )

d. American hats (1) were made principally of wool (2) did not suit the customers in Great Britain (3) were an unimportant part of New England industry (4) were sent only to Great Britain (5) were not made until 1730 ....( )

e. Beaver hats (1) were unpopular (2) were much cheaper than those of wool (3) were made mainly for barter with the Indians (4) cost more than wool hats (5) were not exported ....( )

B. Compared with the world's larger nations, Italy is very small. The whole land area could be tucked into the borders of California, with plenty of room to spare. And yet Italy has a population of 45,000,000. Shaped like a boot, the country is 760 miles long and, at most points, only 100 to 150 miles wide.

Italy is practically cut off from the rest of Europe. In the north, she is separated from her neighbors—France, Switzerland, Germany, and Yugoslavia —by a towering arc of mountain chains. On the south, east, and west, she is surrounded by water.

Most of Italy—two thirds to be exact —is mountainous. In addition to the Alps in the north, there are the Apennines running almost the entire length of the peninsula. This chain is cut across by highly fertile river valleys.

Italy has only one region of plains, in the north, hemmed in between the Alps and the Apennines and watered by the Po and Adige rivers. This "Plain of Lombardy" is the richest farm region and is equal in size to Vermont and New Hampshire combined.

The climate of Italy is similar to that of Florida and California, except that the

a. The title that best expresses the main theme or subject of this selection is:
1. The climate of Italy
2. Italy and the rest of Europe
3. Good farmers
4. Agriculture and geography of Italy
5. Tourists in Italy ....( )

b. In shape Italy is (1) longer than she is wide (2) 760 miles across and 150 miles long (3) wider than she is long (4) wider and longer than California (5) almost square
( )

c. A fact stated by the writer about Italy is that (1) there is no region of plains (2) natural boundaries separate her almost completely from her neighbors (3) very few of her citizens cultivate the soil (4) she is underpopulated (5) she is one of the larger nations ....( )

d. The Apennines are (1) river valleys (2) peninsulas (3) mountains (4) tourists (5) plains ......( )

winter is likely to be colder in northern Italy than in the northern part of either of these states.

The tourist to Italy is surprised at the full use to which the Italians put their soil. Crowded as they are in a small area, they cannot afford to let any land go to waste. They are good farmers. Along the silt-enriched banks of rivers, in the valleys and northern plains region, they have cultivated every inch of ground they can. They have cut terraces into the mountainsides. Nearly half the population lives on the soil.

e. **Winter in northern Italy is (1) warmer than that of California (2) colder than that of Florida (3) similar to that of New Hampshire (4) comparable to that of Switzerland (5) longer than that of Vermont** .... ( )

f. **The Italians show that they are good farmers by (1) surprising tourists (2) being isolated from Europe (3) cultivating the valleys only (4) living on mountains (5) making full use of their soil** . ( )

C. One hundred and fifty years ago, nine American families out of ten lived on farms. They raised their own corn in their own fields, built their houses from the trees in the wood lot and wove their own clothes with wool from sheep in the pasture. Nine tenths of the things consumed in a typical New England village were grown and made right in the village. Less than one tenth came in from other villages or towns. Only a tiny fraction came from other countries. The harder the family worked—and that meant the children too—the more they produced and the better they lived. The standard of living was a direct result of the energy exerted by the father, mother, sons and daughters.

Today, like my great-great-great-grandfather, I live on a New England farm. But I produce on my own place less than ten per cent of what I consume. I raise vegetables and apples, I cut firewood, and I bang my thumb with a hammer making a few rough benches and bookshelves. That is all. My wife spins no thread and weaves no cloth. Not ten per cent of our supplies originate in our town.

My great-great-great-grandfather was ninety per cent self-sufficient; that is, he was able to produce ninety per cent of the goods he needed. I am, you are, nearly every American is, at most, ten per cent self-sufficient. We cannot live unless millions of people we have never seen keep sending us goods.

a. **The title that best expresses the main theme or subject of this selection is:**
1. **Supplies from all over the world**
2. **An old-fashioned New England farm**
3. **Changes in self-sufficiency**
4. **My great-great-great-grandfather**
5. **Family labor** .... ( )

b. **In the 1790's most American families (1) imported many articles (2) lived in cities (3) produced their own supplies (4) carried on a large trade (5) worked for someone else** .... ( )

c. **The standard of living in former times depended directly on (1) the amount of money in circulation (2) the work of all members of the family (3) factory production (4) weaving cloth (5) the neighboring towns** .... ( )

d. **Today the average American is (1) not more than 10 per cent self-sufficient (2) entirely independent of others (3) 90 per cent self-sufficient (4) wholly dependent on others (5) opposed to importing goods** ( )

A. It has been said that the Eskimos, until their contact with Europeans, had trouble with counting. That idea, however, cannot have come from any close knowledge of the Alaskan Eskimos. They count by twenties, using both fingers and toes where we use only the fingers, so that what corresponds to our 100, ten times ten, is 400, twenty times twenty. Occasionally some Eskimo might tell you that it was not possible to count higher than 400, but if you pressed him, he could usually devise an extension. An idea or at least a word that they did not have was *year.* They spoke of spring, summer, autumn and winter, and they reckoned years either in winters or in summers. They had months in the sense of moons and usually knew that there were thirteen in the complete cycle. One of the strangest ideas to an Eskimo, though, is that of our cardinal points (north, east, south, west). Their thinking in this respect is not governed by the sun; it is governed by the shore line, for most of them are coastal people. Their directional words, therefore, are "up the coast," "down the coast," "inland" and "out to sea."

The title that best expresses the main theme or subject of this selection is:
1. The Eskimo year
2. Eskimo method of counting
3. Eskimo ideas of time, place and number
4. Geography among the Eskimos
5. Eskimo colonies in Alaska ...( )

The Eskimos in Alaska (1) cannot count (2) count by tens (3) count by twenties (4) can count only to 20 (5) can count only to 100 ....( )

Long periods of time are reckoned by the Eskimos in (1) days (2) weeks (3) months (4) seasons (5) years ( )

Most Eskimos live (1) inland (2) along rivers (3) on the seashore (4) on lakes (5) in boats ....( )

Eskimos indicate direction in relation to the (1) North Pole (2) sun (3) moon (4) coast line (5) cardinal points ....( )

B. In every town in China one will find in operation the smallest and most modest retail establishments on earth. The stock is sometimes displayed on a makeshift trestle-board counter but as frequently on a square yard of bamboo matting spread on the ground. The pitiful stock invariably consists of the most useless collection of articles it is possible to imagine—crooked nails, rusty screws, defective buttons, broken doorknobs, cracked saucers, a couple of empty cigarette tins. It is just the sort of nondescript collection that a child might make to "play shop" with, but the players are old men instead of children. Every fine morning you can see these ancient merchants trudging to their favorite corners, carrying their cargo with them. There they sit all day in the sun. If it is a rainy day,

The title that best expresses the main theme or subject of this selection is:
1. Useless merchandise
2. How Chinese old people are treated
3. Keeping shop for pleasure in China
4. Chinese children
5. The way Chinese business is conducted ....( )

The old Chinese street merchants (1) make much money (2) enjoy life (3) find their existence unpleasant (4) worry a great deal (5) suffer hardship ( )

According to the selection, people in China try to please (1) foreigners (2) loafers (3) young men (4) shopkeepers (5) old men ....( )

the shops do not open. It is a pleasant life. They see the moving picture of the crowds on the street, chatter with acquaintances and once in a long time they may actually make a sale for a few coppers. But these old merchants do not have to worry about their customers or sales. A son or a grandson provides them with bed and board and they keep shop for the fun of the thing. If that is the way they want to spend their time, their children see that they are allowed to do so, for in China the whims of babies and of old men are always gratified.

C. Since the invention of papermaking in the second century after Christ, workers in this craft have had to contend with mechanical imperfections due to the construction of the hand mold and the limitations of human skill. Most pronounced among these imperfections were the deckle edges caused by the moist fibrous pulp running against the boundary frame, or wooden deckle, of the mold. The Oriental papermakers cut away these rough edges, leaving a clear-cut edge on each of the four sides of the sheet. In Europe also, during the early centuries of book printing, the deckle edges were eliminated in many cases. The rough edges were regarded as blemishes in the making of the paper and therefore were discarded. It was not until the beginning of the machine age with its mechanical perfection that deckle edges on paper began to be considered artistic and desirable as evidence of handwork.

Deckle edges are (1) smoothly cut (2) scalloped (3) irregular (4) bordered with color (5) edged with gold ( )

Centuries ago deckle edges were regarded as (1) imperfections (2) indications of good taste (3) evidence of careful work (4) marks of beauty (5) expensive finishes ....( )

The term *deckle edge* is derived from (1) an Oriental papermaker (2) the frame of a paper mold (3) the cover of a book (4) a printing machine (5) paper pulp ....( )

D. Paricutín is Mexico's newest volcano, a huge baby christened from the hamlet where it was born. One Dionisio Pulido and his son were plowing their field for the spring planting of corn, when their crude ox-drawn plow turned up a wisp of white smoke. The startling vision was accompanied by odd rumbling sounds in the earth. The place was two miles outside the Michoacán village called Paricutín and the date was February 20, 1943. The

The title that best expresses the main theme or subject of this selection is:
1. Mexico's largest volcano
2. How a volcano grows
3. The story of Paricutín
4. A sight to remember
5. Destruction brought about by Paricutín ....( )

frightened Pulido hastened to tell the priest of his village and then the head man of Parangaricutiro, another village slightly more important and slightly farther away. Everyone thought the man crazy but he had only to lead them to the spot and let them see for themselves. Within a few hours the wisp was a column of ash-dust and within a day there was a true volcanic cone thirty or forty feet high. Now it is a mass of lava half a mile high, erupting from a crater in the midst of a desolate area of ash thirty-five miles in diameter. Despite the size and activity of Paricutín, however, its life expectancy is indeterminable. Other volcanic cones in the neighborhood have been shortlived.

Mexico's newest volcano was named for the (1) man who owned the field (2) parish priest (3) head man (4) nearest village (5) district .... ( )

This volcano is now a (1) wisp of smoke (2) column of ash-dust (3) cone thirty feet high (4) huge erupting crater (5) dead heap of ash ( )

The life period of Paricutín (1) will last only a few years (2) will cover many centuries (3) will continue forever (4) cannot be calculated (5) is over .... ( )

READING EXERCISE 4

A. Whales today are sought for food and fat substitutes, and to make glycerin, high explosives and soap. In early days the average whaling ship was of three hundred tons' burden; the average catch, three thousand barrels of oil. To get this amount of oil took from three to four years. The so-called mother ships of today are in reality great factories. Their average tonnage is thirty thousand, their season averages no more than four months, and they catch five hundred thousand tons a year. These mother ships have every improvement. The crew consists of two hundred and forty men, who receive a salary and a percentage. The mother ships have a number of killer boats which use guns firing a one-hundred-fifty-pound bomb or explosive harpoon. The whale is towed back to the mother ship and is hoisted to the vessel, which opens a vast door in its side to admit the entire whale. Eighty per cent of the whales are taken in the Antarctic. Today's whalers cannot capture the sperm, right and bowhead whales, which were the standby of the old whalers, for these mammals can hear a powerboat twelve miles away.

The title that best expresses the main theme or subject of this selection is:
1. The dangers of whale fishing
2. Whale fishing today
3. The importance of whale fishing
4. Whaling boats
5. Whale fishing as an occupation .... ( )

The season for whaling in modern times is about (1) 120 days (2) 240 days (3) 300 days (4) 3 years (5) 4 years .... ( )

The average tonnage of whaling ships at the present time is about (1) 150 (2) 300 (3) 3000 (4) 30,000 (5) 500,000 .... ( )

Sperm whales are no longer captured, because they (1) have become extinct (2) have changed the place where they live (3) are warned by the noise of the boats (4) are too small to be profitable (5) are dangerous fighters .... ( )

B. The continent of South America is one of the richest, most varied, most dramatically beautiful land masses on the face of the globe. Everything is huge; everything is extreme. South America has every variety of climate, from the tropics to the Antarctic cold of Cape Horn. Among the many nations of South America, most of which are republics, those hampered by the hot, damp climate of the tropics in the North have advanced more slowly in civilization than those in the southern part where the climate is temperate. South American nations also have been faced with the problem of how to utilize the treasures of their lands for national prosperity. Their mountains contained vast stores of valuable minerals; their jungle forests were rich in useful woods; their plains were capable of supporting animal life and of producing immense food crops. In every nation, however, it was necessary to replace trails with roads and railways, to span mountain rivers with bridges and set steamers to navigating streams. But the republics had neither the capital nor the skilled men for such difficult undertakings. They possessed the raw materials greatly needed by the industrial nations, particularly the United States, Germany and England. These nations had money, machinery and experts to help the South Americans develop their resources. So it came about that foreign capital and experts built railways, telegraph lines and power plants; they developed mines and plantations. South American nations based their economic life on the export of raw materials and the import of manufactured goods.

The title that best expresses the main theme or subject of this selection is:
1. How South America solved her economic problems
2. The richest continent in the world
3. South American people
4. The backwardness of South America
5. Why South Americans dislike foreigners ....( )

The climate of South America is (1) hot (2) cold (3) moderate (4) dry (5) varied ....( )

Civilization in South America has progressed most slowly in the (1) North (2) South (3) East (4) West (5) central part ....( )

Progress in South America has been hampered by (1) scarcity of wood (2) lack of mineral products (3) barrenness of soil (4) difficulty of transportation (5) scanty rainfall ( )

South Americans have been dependent on other countries for (1) raw materials (2) expert engineers (3) laborers (4) food products (5) farmers ....( )

Most of the South American countries are (1) colonies of other nations (2) monarchies (3) republics (4) empires (5) federations ....( )

C. The use of wood as a material from which to make paper was first suggested in the Western world in a treatise dated November 15, 1719, by René de Réaumur (1683-1757), a celebrated naturalist residing in France. Réaumur had observed the habits of certain wasps and concluded that the wood filaments used

The title that best expresses the main theme or subject of this selection is:
1. What a French naturalist decided
2. The habits of wasps
3. Wasp nests
4. The papermaking industry
5. The contribution of the wasp to papermaking ....( )

by these insects to construct their paper-like nests could also be used in the actual process of papermaking. Human invention in the making of paper had been anticipated by the wasp, which may be considered as a professional papermaker, devoting most of her time and energies to the making of this material which she uses in the construction of nests. For this purpose the wasp seeks dry wood, which she saws or rasps by mastication. She mixes the material with a gluey substance exuded for the purpose, and, working the whole into a paste, spreads the paper substance in a manner truly remarkable. The nest is usually a prolonged irregular spheroid, exceptionally light in weight, of a dark color, and bound with repeated bands of paper to the bough from which it is suspended. The nest is water resistant to a high degree, partly because of the rounded top but more because of the fact that the paper strips overlap like the shingles of a house.

The man who first suggested the making of paper from wood was a specialist in (1) farming (2) papermaking (3) printing (4) trade (5) nature study ....( )

The primary source of the material used in the nests of papermaking wasps is (1) dirt (2) water (3) paste (4) wood (5) glue ....( )

The shape of the nest of the papermaking wasp is usually (1) oblong (2) regular (3) flat (4) spherical (5) square ....( )

The papermaking wasp makes its nest highly waterproof by (1) constructing it of heavy material (2) putting bands around it (3) overlapping the strips of material (4) hanging it on a bough (5) turning it upside down ....( )

READING EXERCISE 5

A. The Samoans are pure Polynesians and are unequaled in appearance by most of the other Pacific islanders. Samoans are light brown in color, of splendid physique, and are regular in feature. The men are tall, and, as a group, they are honorable, generous and hospitable. Simple and ordinarily friendly, they nevertheless are brave fighters. Fine dress appeals to the Samoans, and they are very fond of singing. Dancing, fishing, swimming and oratory are all popular. Prior to the coming of the white men, they believed in many gods, but indulged in no human sacrifices, and thought that their dead reached a hereafter by way of a pool at the western end of the island of Savaii. Women and children were well treated. Tattooing was so important to them that a youth was regarded as ineligible for marriage until he had been tattooed from the hips

The title that best expresses the main theme or subject of this selection is:
1. The Pacific islanders
2. Popular sports in Samoa
3. Appearance of Samoan people
4. Religion in Samoa
5. Samoan characteristics and customs ....( )

The people of Samoa are (1) small (2) inactive (3) fond of dress (4) unfriendly (5) cruel .... ( )

According to the paragraph, the primitive Samoans used to (1) believe their dead went on to a hereafter (2) burn their dead (3) offer human sacrifices (4) think death ended everything (5) drown their old people ....( )

In early times a Samoan youth (1)

to the knees. Originally, courtship was carried on by proxy. Property was vested in the family, not in the individual.

B. Milk is a suspension of nourishing materials in water, which constitutes about 86 per cent of the total weight. The 14 per cent of nutrient solids consist of milk sugar five per cent, fat about four per cent, protein just a fraction less than that, and finally minerals and vitamins. It can readily be seen that milk is a kind of natural combination containing most of the body's requirements for growth and health. What is unique about milk is its richness in minerals and vitamins. Fat, sugar and protein can come from other sources, but the vitamin A and the minerals of milk cannot be easily obtained elsewhere. It is also rich in the vitamin B group so urgently needed for health. Calcium and phosphorus are two minerals contained in milk that are of primary importance. These minerals are essential for normal development and maintenance of bones and teeth. Not only is milk rich in bone-forming calcium and phosphorus but it carries them in a form that is much more readily assimilated than the same minerals found in vegetables. Yet it is fortunate for us that we do not have to subsist on milk alone. Milk does not supply the body with the iron needed to prevent anemia. Milk also lacks vitamin D, although sunshine easily compensates for that shortage. Under our conditions of preparing milk, it also lacks vitamin C, which is the antiscurvy vitamin of many fruits and vegetables. Cream and butter contain the fat of the milk, while cheese contains its solidified protein plus some fat, its vitamin A and some minerals. We also have, of course, the concentrated forms of milk, such as evaporated, condensed and powdered. These are whole milk equivalents minus some or all of the water.

did not marry until he had reached a certain age (2) never saw his bride before marriage (3) secured someone else to do his courting for him (4) was expected to carry off his bride by force (5) had to win his bride by combat ....( )

The title that best expresses the main theme or subject of this selection is:
1. A history of milk
2. The sources of milk
3. Milk, a perfect food
4. Food values in milk
5. Popular milk products ......( )

The largest part of milk is composed of (1) fat (2) sugar (3) water (4) minerals (5) vitamins ....( )

Milk is an especially important food because (1) it is cheap (2) it is easily available (3) it contains so much protein (4) its fat content is so large (5) its minerals cannot be readily obtained otherwise ....( )

Milk is deficient in (1) phosphorus (2) iron (3) fat (4) protein (5) vitamin A ....( )

In order to have good teeth, a person should have plenty of (1) calcium (2) iron (3) protein (4) sugar (5) cheese ....( )

Sunshine is a good source of (1) vitamin A (2) vitamin C (3) vitamin D (4) phosphorus (5) calcium ....( )

C. Military pigeons have been trained to meet the needs of our soldiers, sailors and airmen for night flyers. It takes months to teach a pigeon that naturally flies in the daytime to wing through the darkness at night. Training begins as soon as the baby birds or squeakers are hatched—even before, since they are selected from parents choosing to fly at early dawn or at dusk. They are kept all day in dark lofts and allowed out only at night. When hungry, they are tossed first near home, then farther and farther away until they become perfect messengers for night flights of fifty miles. Just before World War II, a frequent sound at Fort Monmouth was the tinkle of a bell announcing the arrival of a night flyer, while a pigeoneer with a flashlight stood ready to pull out the message brought.

The need of generals at the front has always been a two-way flyer that, on a short flight, could not only deliver a message but make a quick turnabout and bring back an answer. Our Signal Corps filled this need with a great company of two-way pigeons. Of these Mr. Corrigan was the fastest; and well he might be, for he was a great-great-grandson of Always Faithful that once snatched the prize from a thousand birds in a 750-mile race, covering the airline from Chattanooga to Fort Monmouth at almost a mile a minute. How these birds were trained is a military secret but it is no secret that Italy's and later Germany's two-way flyers were fed at one place and watered at the second.

The title that best expresses the main theme or subject of this selection is:
1. Noted carrier pigeons
2. Habits of pigeons
3. Night flying
4. Pigeon racing
5. Specialized training of military pigeons ....( )

Night flyers (1) learn to ring a bell (2) are specially fed (3) are kept in streamlined lofts (4) are bred from birds that like to fly at dawn or dusk (5) carry tiny flashlights ......( )

Two-way pigeons are those that (1) fly at night as well as in the daytime (2) fly to their destination and return without stopping (3) make only long flights (4) carry two messages at once (5) can carry a message and return with the answer ....( )

Mr. Corrigan was (1) a night flyer (2) the commander of the Signal Corps (3) a general (4) a trainer (5) a two-way flyer ....( )

One way of training two-way pigeons is to (1) race them often (2) feed them at the starting place and water them at the other end of the route (3) keep them always hungry (4) keep them in the dark (5) fly them in pairs ....( )

READING EXERCISE 6

A. An advertising agency in Shanghai placed the first lipstick and vanishing cream advertising in Chinese papers about 35 years ago, and since that time the advertising and sale of cosmetics have been important businesses there. It must not be assumed, however, that such advertisements started Chinese girls

The title that best expresses the main theme or subject of this selection is:
1. Advertising cosmetics
2. Why Chinese girls always find husbands
3. The oldest retail shop in the world
4. The use of cosmetics in China
5. A beauty kit for every woman ( )

on the cosmetic road to beauty. Five thousand years ago, according to authentic Chinese history, Chinese girls were plucking useless hairs from their eyebrows and putting rouge on their cheeks. The oldest retail shop in China is an establishment in Hangchow, which was the Chinese equivalent of a beauty shop centuries ago and still does a thriving business in rouge, talcum and other aids to daintiness and beauty. The best Chinese customers for cosmetics, though, are the married women and not the debutantes. Chinese women discovered many centuries ago that, if they would make themselves attractive enough, their husbands would willingly employ servants to do the cooking and scrubbing. The result is that Chinese women are the most perfectly groomed in the world and, everything considered, enjoy the greatest measure of luxury. Every woman, rich or poor, has a beauty kit. Only aged widows deny themselves such vanities, because the use of cosmetics might imply a desire to remarry, which would be looked upon as wantonness.

Chinese women (1) never use any cosmetics (2) have just begun to use cosmetics (3) have used cosmetics only during the past 35 years (4) have used some form of cosmetics for 5000 years past (5) have used cosmetics for five centuries only ( )

The best customers for cosmetics in China are (1) young girls (2) wives (3) servants (4) middle-aged spinsters (5) old widows ....( )

Chinese women as a whole (1) are unattractive (2) are overworked (3) are careless about their appearance (4) are better groomed than most women (5) do not like to have servants ....( )

B. Haraldr Harfagri (Harold the Fairhaired) succeeded his father as a petty king in Norway about the year 863 and soon set out to make himself ruler of all Norway. Some of the other rulers, however, rather than submit to the domination of Haraldr, left their homeland to settle in Iceland and other islands. Thus it happened that in 874 Ingolfr Arnarson came to Iceland with 400 followers to seek a new home. On arriving off Iceland, Ingolfr threw into the sea his high seat pillars, which had stood in front of the high seat in the hall in his home, and vowed that he would settle at the spot where they floated ashore. After a long search his messengers found them on the beach in an ideal spot at the head of a bay near some steaming craters. Here he settled, calling the place Reykjavik—Smoky Bay. But the Irish had known of the existence of Iceland long before this. Indeed, they had been the first settlers there.

The title that best expresses the main theme or subject of this selection is:
1. The reason for migration to Iceland
2. Settlement of Iceland
3. First republic in the world
4. Norwegian colonists
5. An interesting bit of history .( )

The first settlers in Iceland were (1) Norwegians (2) Swedes (3) Irishmen (4) Englishmen (5) Scotchmen ( )

The location of the first Norwegian settlement in Iceland was determined by (1) the advice of men already there (2) the coast line (3) the variations in climate (4) a vow made by the leader (5) the nearness to the sea ....( )

The name of the main settlement in Iceland was derived from (1) the king of Norway (2) its founder (3)

When Ingolfr reached Iceland, he heard that "some Christian men had already been there but later had gone away because they did not wish to live together with pagans." According to the Landnamabok or book of the settlements, however, the majority of the settlers came from Norway, some from Sweden and a few from the British Isles and Ireland. At the beginning of the 10th century there were said to be about 25,000 people in Iceland. Lawlessness increased and some sort of centralized control became necessary. A member of a distinguished family named Ulfljot assumed the task of framing a general code of laws. This he submitted in 927. After three years' consideration, the first general assembly or Althing was held near Reykjavik, and the code was adopted. By this act the Icelandic republic was founded, and the island became a free and independent state, to remain so until joined to Norway in 1262.

C. The rebirth of politics in Europe has brought two political terms prominently into the news—"Left" and "Right." Readers might be interested in knowing the source of those terms. At one time during the French Revolution, when the revolutionary assembly moved into new quarters, it happened quite by chance that those who thought the revolution had gone far enough occupied the seats which were at the right as they faced the chairman. Those who wanted to go further with the revolution sat over on the left, while moderates sat in the center. Since that time, it has been the custom in all of the parliaments on the continent of Europe for the more conservative forces to sit on the right, while the liberals or radicals or socialists, who want to modify the older forms of government, have occupied the seats on the left. This custom has given rise to the practice of calling conservative political parties "the Right" or "Rightist," and liberal or radical political parties "the Left," or "Leftist."

the shape of the coast line (4) the smoke from the craters near it (5) the color of the water in its harbor ( )

The earliest Irish inhabitants of Iceland left the island because (1) they could not make a living (2) they did not wish to live among people who were not Christians (3) the Norwegians threatened to kill them (4) they found the climate too cold (5) they wanted to be alone ......( )

Iceland became a republic in (1) 863 (2) 874 (3) 900 (4) 927 (5) 930 ....( )

The Althing was the name of (1) a volcano (2) the first settlement in Iceland (3) the record of the settlements (4) the general assembly (5) the head of the government ...( )

The title that best expresses the main theme or subject of this selection is:
1. Effect of the French Revolution
2. Modern politics
3. Origin of "Rightist" and "Leftist"
4. Parliamentary procedure
5. The type of government in Europe ....( )

The writer indicates that in Europe there is increased interest in (1) higher birth rates (2) revolution (3) politics (4) conservation (5) socialism ....( )

The present-day European representatives who occupy seats on the left are usually (1) wrong in their views (2) satisfied with conditions as they are (3) supporters of the head of the government (4) slow to change (5) in favor of change ....( )

A. As much as is possible, all scenes in motion pictures are shot on the lot. Forests, ships, country lanes, mountains, canals—all are built up and tricked. The best standard by which to judge a setting is, of course, the feeling of reality that it gives. However, this does not mean that the setting will be exactly as it would be in real life. To the facts of life must be added the imagination of the scenic artist who develops the set. It is true that the modern settings are usually realistic, but sometimes impressionistic or symbolic effects are also used. Settings should, therefore, be judged by their appropriateness, that is, by the way in which they fit the characters in the play. Another standard of judgment is the historical accuracy of the settings. The customs and traditions of the period concerned must be followed. Still another standard for settings is variety. It is possible, of course, that the settings might be accurate and appropriate but that they might be too few or too much the same throughout the entire picture. There might also be too much sameness in the settings from picture to picture. Good directors, however, do not make such mistakes.

The title that best expresses the main theme or subject of this selection is:
1. Where motion pictures are made
2. Why some motion pictures fail
3. Settings for motion pictures
4. Variety in motion pictures
5. Realistic motion pictures ....( )

Settings of motion pictures should always be (1) modernistic (2) symbolic (3) beautiful (4) expensive (5) appropriate ....( )

A factor to be avoided in developing the scenes in a motion picture is (1) reality (2) sameness (3) variety (4) imagination (5) historical detail ( )

B. Many of the upper-class families of Chile came from the Basque provinces of Spain where the character of the people was more energetic and practical than in other parts of Spain. When these Spaniards intermarried with the English, Scotch and Irish who settled in Chile, they founded a nation very different in character from the Indian-dominated nations of Peru and Bolivia. Chile, through the port of Valparaiso, had more contact with foreign nations than other West Coast countries in the colonial period. Chileans also went into maritime commerce and developed an ambition to control the sea on the Pacific coast.

From Arica to the fertile valleys a

The title that best expresses the main theme or subject of this selection is:
1. The home of the nitrate industry
2. The people and products of Chile
3. Chile, a wealthy country
4. Various races in Chile
5. Exports of Chile ....( )

The people of Chile are (1) lazy (2) impractical (3) energetic (4) dominated by the Indians (5) backward ....( )

The desert valley of Chile proved to be (1) valuable for dry farming (2) a hindrance to development (3) useful for grape growing (4) a source of wealth (5) a great danger ....( )

rampart of seamed reddish cliffs lines the coast. Behind the cliffs, for 450 miles, stretches a narrow desert valley, containing the only commercially exploitable nitrate deposits in the world. For many years the rulers of Chile ran the government on royalties collected from these mines, but after World War I, other nations began to manufacture synthetic nitrates instead of buying nitrates from Chile, so at present Chile furnishes only about 10% of the world supply. The loss of nitrate profits, however, has been offset by the development of immensely rich copper mines. Although copper and nitrates make Chile important to industrial nations, it is fundamentally an agricultural country. Its great central valley feeds its people with beef, mutton, grain, vegetables and luscious fruits. Many landowners have great vineyards, producing grapes for the excellent wines of Chile.

Chile supplies about one tenth of the world's (1) grain (2) beef (3) wine (4) copper (5) nitrates ....( )

Chile lost a great part of her nitrate trade because (1) labor was scarce (2) other countries began to manufacture nitrates (3) the men went to work in the new copper mines (4) the mines stopped producing (5) the government could not control the mines ....( )

The government of Chile has been largely supported by (1) payments from wine makers (2) income taxes (3) taxes on land (4) levies on sea trade (5) royalties from mines ( )

C. From earliest times eggs have been an important human food. The Eskimos gather the eggs of ducks that visit the Arctic in the spring. African Bushmen and Hottentots eat ostrich eggs. The eggs of sea birds are the chief and favorite native food of the Easter Islanders. Turtle eggs are eaten in South America. Eggs of fishes are considered a great delicacy. The eggs or roe of the sturgeon of the Caspian Sea are salted and appear on our tables as caviar.

Since eggs must give rise to full-fledged organisms, it is not surprising that their yolks are extremely rich in minerals, such as phosphorus and particularly iron. Milk, perhaps the most valuable of protective foods, has a weak spot in its shortage of iron. Eggs have a far richer supply of iron, but they have less calcium proportionately than milk. Young chicks get their calcium from the eggshells. Eggs also have a good supply of phosphorus, which is as badly needed in the formation of bones and teeth as is calcium. So far as vitamins are concerned, eggs are about as

The title that best expresses the main theme or subject of this selection is:
1. A comparison of milk with eggs
2. The formation of an egg
3. Various kinds of eggs
4. Eggs as a food
5. Vitamins in eggs ....( )

Ostrich eggs form an article of diet among the (1) South Americans (2) Eskimos (3) Easter Islanders (4) Europeans (5) Hottentots ....( )

Milk as a food is deficient in (1) water (2) fat (3) iron (4) calcium (5) vitamins ....( )

The part of the egg that provides the young chicken with the needed calcium is the (1) white (2) yolk (3) shell (4) watery content (5) membrane lining the shell ....( )

Most of the food substance of the egg is composed of (1) proteins (2) fats (3) carbohydrates (4) calcium (5) phosphorus ....( )

318

rich and varied a source as can be found. They contain all the vitamins but C. There is an abundance of vitamin A in them and they also form an excellent source of the several components of the vitamin B group. Besides, eggs also contain the precious sunshine vitamin known as vitamin D. Their principal nutrient is protein. All of these nutrients—minerals, vitamins and proteins—make eggs an excellent protective food.

Eggs lack vitamin (1) A (2) B_1 (3) B_2 (4) C (5) D ....( )

READING EXERCISE 8

A. Pearls are found in many seas but the best and the greatest number come from the Persian Gulf. There are many fine points about a pearl that contribute to determining its value. First, though not most important, is color. Then there is shape, which may be round, pear-shaped, pendant, oval or flat. Further, there is size, which does not determine value except as found in combination with color and shape. But the determining factor is luster, and the luster of a really valuable pearl is unmistakable.

Just what makes a pearl? Arab poets say that as the oyster comes to the surface of the sea on a summer evening, a dewdrop falls into its heart and eventually becomes a gem. As a matter of fact, to an oyster a pearl is a foreign article made tolerable, but one it would gladly be rid of. A grain of sand or a parasite gets into the shell, and to rid itself of the irritation the oyster moves and squirms, and in doing so covers the irritating object with a secretion. As the secretion hardens, it becomes round and forms a pearl. The more effort the oyster makes to expel the nuisance, the more abundant is the secretion and the larger the pearl becomes.

B. Schenectady is a very old community. Arendt Van Corlaer, steward of the huge estate of the patroon Van Rensselaer, obtained, in company with fourteen others, permission from the Dutch authorities to establish a new settlement. They bought from the Indians a strip of

The title that best expresses the main theme or subject of this selection is:
1. Persian jewels
2. Where pearls are found
3. Why pearls are valuable
4. Uses of the oyster
5. The qualities and formation of pearls ....( )

The value of a pearl depends chiefly on its (1) size (2) age (3) color (4) shape (5) luster ....( )

The making of a pearl is started by (1) a hard place in the shell (2) a drop of dew (3) a severe wound (4) an irritating object (5) an oyster disease ....( )

The size of a pearl is chiefly affected by the (1) length of time in forming (2) amount of secretion produced (3) depth of the water (4) rapidity of motion (5) size of the oyster ( )

The title that best expresses the main theme or subject of this selection is:
1. Indians on the Mohawk River
2. Origin of Schenectady
3. Why Schenectady is noteworthy
4. How the settlers of Schenectady protected themselves

319

land 8 miles wide and 16 miles long on the Mohawk River a few miles to the west of Albany. The Indians called this tract *Schonowe* and the Dutch *Groote Vlacte* or Great Flat.

On this tract the owners built a town in the year 1661. For the sake of security they constructed their homes in a compact plot and surrounded them with a stockade 10 feet high, made of logs squared on two sides to form a continuous wall and sharpened at the top to keep marauders from crawling over. These settlers did not, at least at first, go out and build houses on their individual farms as many other pioneers did. During the day they went out and cultivated their land but they returned to the inclosure within the stockade at night. Then and for many years thereafter, they were on the edge of a vast and unmapped wilderness filled with Indians and dangerous wild animals.

The name of this town, Schenectady, has caused untold trouble to strangers when they first try to pronounce and spell it. It is an Indian name and it is unique. There is not another Schenectady anywhere else in the world. Pages have been written about its meaning but the one most commonly accepted is "beyond the pine plains," indicating that it was first applied from a distance by people in the neighborhood of Albany.

C. Niuafoo, which has been nicknamed "Tin Can Island," lies about 190 miles northeast of Suva, Fiji. It is five miles in diameter and is controlled by the British from Suva. The odd part of it is that, though Niuafoo is purely volcano and has no reef, it is an almost perfect circle of land surrounding an almost equally circular lake in its center. The land rises from the sea in cliffs 60 to 70 feet high. From this elevation the land slopes upward for three fourths of a mile and then rises abruptly to a ridge of about 400-foot elevation. From this narrow ridge rise eight volcanic cones to elevations of 500 to 700 feet, but the

5. Dangers of pioneer life .....( )

The age of the town of Schenectady is approximately (1) 60 years (2) 100 years (3) 200 years (4) 300 years (5) 1600 years ....( )

The origin of the name of *Schenectady* is (1) Indian (2) English (3) French (4) Dutch (5) German ....( )

The pioneers who settled Schenectady lived (1) inside a central fortification (2) in widely separated cabins (3) on the pine plains (4) on farms (5) in Albany ....( )

A stockade is (1) a cattle pen (2) a fortification made of earth (3) a wall of sharpened timbers (4) a frontier town (5) an Indian village .( )

The town of Schenectady is particularly unusual because of its (1) size (2) location (3) early settlement (4) having no duplicate in name (5) Dutch origin ....( )

The title that best expresses the main theme or subject of this selection is:
1. How Tin Can Island got its name
2. Life in the Pacific islands
3. The water supply of Niuafoo
4. The geography of Niuafoo
5. Volcanic islands ....( )

Niuafoo has several (1) lakes (2) volcanoes (3) plains (4) rivers (5) reefs ....( )

Niuafoo received its nickname of "Tin Can Island" because (1) water is stored in tin cans (2) one of its volcanoes looks like a tin can (3) the inner side of the ridge drops precipitously to the lake shore. The waters of the lake are alkaline and are said to rise and fall with the tide. There is no pure water on the island and the rain water is insufficient for the needs of the 1229 people. They do not suffer, however, because they are able to obtain liquid from coconuts. Mangoes, breadfruit, bananas, oranges, yams, tars, arrowroot, tapioca, melons, pineapples and other products are also raised. Landing on Niuafoo is difficult. The island got its nickname because the natives swim or canoe out to passing mail ships and carry the mail from and to the island in a tin can lashed to a pole.

mail is carried in a tin can (4) it is circular in shape (5) the British rulers live on canned foods .... (   )

The inhabitants of the island get drinking water from (1) the ocean (2) the lake (3) rain (4) springs (5) wells .... (   )

The fact that the lake rises and falls with the tide would seem to show that (1) there is an underground connection between the lake and the ocean (2) the rain water all runs into the lake (3) the lake is below sea level (4) the lake has no bottom (5) the tide is very high .... (   )

READING EXERCISE 9

A. It is none too soon that a national forest should bear the name of Gifford Pinchot, and it is appropriate that the forest selected for this honor should be the Columbia National Forest on the slopes of the Cascade Range in Washington. This national forest was originally established and named when Gifford Pinchot was Chief of the United States Forest Service, and its administration was begun under his direction. In June of 1949, President Truman signed a proclamation officially changing the name to Gifford Pinchot National Forest, and in October the million and one-quarter acres were officially dedicated when the Society of American Foresters held its annual meeting in Seattle. Mr. Pinchot was born in the greatest era of waste of national resources in our country's history. And he chose a profession then almost unknown in America—forestry. As the country's first "consulting forester" he discovered, however, that there were many who felt some concern for the future of our forest resources. In 1898 Mr. Pinchot became Chief of the Division of Forestry in the Department of Agriculture; in 1900 he helped or-

a. The title that best expresses the main theme or subject of this selection is:
1. The boyhood of Gifford Pinchot
2. A memorial to a great conservationist
3. The United States Forest Service
4. The importance of our national forests
5. The waste of natural resources
( )

b. It is appropriate to name this forest after Mr. Pinchot because (1) it is more beautiful than any other forest in the country (2) it is the only national forest (3) it is the one Mr. Pinchot wanted (4) it is one of those forests he supervised when they first became national forests (5) it is in the state of Washington .... (   )

c. Mr. Pinchot devoted his life to (1) satisfying his own selfish desires (2) serving the public in the field of forestry (3) withdrawing from public contact (4) choosing a suitable memorial (5) encouraging lumbermen .... (   )

321

ganize the Society of American Foresters; in 1905 he became Chief of the new United States Forest Service and took over the administration of the forest reserves of the public domain. The rest of his life was devoted to public service, with conservation ever foremost in his mind. No memorial to his contribution could be more appropriate than a great forest of green and growing trees.

B. The Gulf Stream, which runs like a friendly blue river across the cold green Atlantic Ocean, is one of the mightiest powers in the world. By comparison, the Mississippi and the mighty Amazon are but small rivers. Two million tons of coal burned every minute would not equal the heat that the Stream gives forth in its Atlantic crossing. Without the Stream's warmth, England's pleasant green countryside would be as cold as Labrador, which is no farther north than England. If this "river of blue" were cooled as much as 15 degrees, England, Scandinavia, northern France and Germany would probably become a region for the Eskimos.

The general course of the blue river has never been known to change. From Florida north the Stream follows the curve of the coast but stays well away from the shore. When the warm waters meet the icy Labrador currents, the Stream loses some speed and heat, but even with icebergs at its margin it stays warm enough for tropical sea life.

As the Stream nears Europe it divides north and south. The northern drift mixes with the Arctic Ocean. The southern drift comes again into the path of Africa's hot trade winds, and the waters hurry back to the Gulf of Mexico, gathering again their store of heat. The complete course of the Stream, therefore, is like a tremendous 12,000-mile whirlpool.

Scientists think that it takes three years for the Stream to make a complete round trip. Their belief is based on the courses of bottles that have been thrown into

d. The author of the selection shows clearly that he (1) admires the work that Mr. Pinchot did (2) does not approve of changing the name of forests (3) thinks the need for conservation is overrated (4) is himself a "consulting forester" (5) was a close friend of Gifford Pinchot ....( )

a. The title that best expresses the main theme or subject of this selection is:
1. Interesting facts about the Gulf Stream
2. Current similar to the Gulf Stream
3. What Florida owes to the Gulf Stream
4. Scientific experiments on the Gulf Stream
5. Tropical sea life in the Gulf Stream ....( )

b. The water in the Gulf Stream is (1) cold and green (2) coal-colored (3) icy and blue (4) warm and blue (5) pleasantly green ...( )

c. The effect of the Gulf Stream on England is to (1) cool the air pleasantly (2) make possible the green countryside (3) make necessary the burning of two million tons of coal (4) cool England's rivers 15 degrees (5) make England a region for Eskimos ...( )

d. The number of miles covered by the waters of the Gulf Stream is (1) considerably different each year (2) about 100 billion (3) about 12 thousand (4) undetermined (5) about 2 million ..( )

e. Scientists have used papers in bottles to determine the number of (1) languages spoken along the course of the Gulf Stream (2)

the Stream to drift. These bottles contain papers, printed in many languages, requesting the finders to note the places and dates of finding and mail them back. Government experts on ocean currents have records of thousands of these "bottle papers."

Other oceans have such currents. In the North Pacific, for example, the Japanese Current makes the climate of coastal Alaska and our west coast moderate. Science is still not satisfied with what it knows about these currents. But for most of us it is enough to know that the Gulf Stream and similar currents give warmth to countries that would otherwise be very cold indeed.

people who are alert to such things (3) government experts on ocean currents (4) beliefs about the course of the bottles (5) years needed for the Gulf Stream to make a complete round trip . ( )

f. The author says that a person who finds one of the bottles is asked to tell (1) his name and birth date (2) when and where the bottle was found (3) how many languages he speaks (4) how many other bottles he has found (5) how far he was from home at the time ...... ( )

g. Many countries should be thankful to the Gulf Stream and similar currents for (1) cool summers (2) moderate climates (3) thousands of scientific records (4) scientific progress (5) trade winds .. ( )

C. Tom Sawyer said to himself that it was not such a hollow world after all. He had discovered a great law of human action without knowing it—namely, that in order to make a man or boy desire a thing it is only necessary to make the thing difficult to attain. If he had been a great and wise philosopher, he would now have understood that work consists of whatever a body is obliged to do, and that play consists of whatever a body is not obliged to do. And this would help him to understand why constructing artificial flowers or performing on a treadmill is work, while rolling tenpins or climbing Mont Blanc is only amusement. There are wealthy men in England who drive four-horse passenger coaches 20 or 30 miles on a daily line in the summer, because the privilege costs them considerable money; but if they were offered wages for the service, that would turn it into work, and then they would resign.

a. The "law of human action" discovered by Tom could be stated as follows: A man wants most that which (1) he already has (2) he is obliged to do (3) he cannot easily attain (4) no one else likes (5) he can get for nothing .. ( )

b. According to the author, play consists of (1) the things a person does of his own free will (2) the things a person has to do (3) jobs such as working a treadmill (4) the things that make this a hollow world (5) tasks done for wages ( )

c. A man who does such a thing as drive a coach for amusement would resign if offered wages for the activity because (1) he doesn't want to earn money (2) it is a dangerous activity (3) he would lose money (4) he doesn't have time (5) the activity would then become work .... ( )

READING EXERCISE 10

READING EXERCISE 10

A. High in the Swiss Alps long years ago, there lived a lonely shepherd boy who longed for a friend to share his vigils. One night, he beheld three wrinkled old men, each holding a glass. The first said: "Drink this liquid and you shall be victorious in battle."

The second said: "Drink this liquid and you shall have countless riches."

The last man said: "I offer you the happiness of music—the alphorn."

The boy chose the third glass. Next day, he came upon a great horn, ten feet in length. When he put his lips to it, a beautiful melody floated across the valley. He had found a friend. . . .

So goes the legend of the alphorn's origin. Known in the ninth century, the alphorn was used by herdsmen to call cattle, for the deep tones echoed across the mountainsides. And even today, on a quiet summer evening, its music can be heard floating among the peaks.

B. On the population map of the world the tropical deserts are shown as great blank spaces; yet they have contributed many things to our lives. When you step into a store to buy a box of dates, you are buying the sunshine and the dryness of the oases of the Sahara, Arabia, Mesopotamia or the Coachella Valley. A lettuce salad or fresh peas for dinner in winter represent the work of an irrigation farmer in the Salt River Valley or the Imperial Valley. The fine broadcloth shirt or balloon-cloth dress which you received on your birthday was made of silky, long-fibered cotton either from the Imperial Valley or from Egypt. Your half-wool and half-cotton sweater may contain Australian wool and Peruvian cotton—both steppe and desert products.

These are only a few of the physical contributions which the tropical deserts make to our daily lives. In addition they have made important cultural contributions. Our number system is from Arabia. The desert people developed irri-

a. The story tells us that of the three old men, the one whose glass the boy chose was the (1) smallest in size (2) most wrinkled (3) first to speak (4) oldest (5) last to speak ( )

b. One liquid offered to the boy would have brought him (1) defeat in battle (2) great wealth (3) lonely vigils (4) another boy to help him (5) three wishes ...( )

c. To the boy, the alphorn (1) seemed too heavy to play (2) seemed like a real friend (3) brought unhappiness (4) sounded unpleasant (5) brought great riches ( )

a. The population of the deserts of the world is (1) scant (2) dense (3) starving (4) large (5) unfriendly ....( )

b. Some products of the Imperial Valley mentioned in the paragraph are (1) dates (2) wool and cotton (3) borax and wool (4) cotton and lettuce (5) nitrates ....( )

c. Balloon cloth is made (1) of silk (2) of cotton (3) of wool (4) partly of cotton (5) partly of wool ( )

d. Surveying was developed because people needed to (1) determine land boundaries after floods (2) find their way across the desert at night (3) have some means of irrigation (4) learn a number system (5) study the stars ....( )

e. Culturally, the deserts have (1) been of no value (2) contributed

324

gation. The necessity of measuring water and noting land boundaries after the Nile floods led to surveying and the development of mathematics and engineering. The desert people studied the stars so that they could find their way at night across the limitless expanses of the desert; in this way they became our early astronomers.

C. The word *atom* has captured man's imagination. In addition to atomic bombs and atomic energy, we see signs advertising products with names such as "atomic-energized gasoline." Who invented the word *atom* and what does it mean?

The inventor was a Greek philosopher named Democritus, who lived about 400 B.C. Even then Greek physicists were wondering about the structure of matter. Democritus suggested that matter is not what it seems—a continuous mass of material. He thought that matter could be broken up into finer and finer parts until finally it could be broken no further. These basic particles he called atoms, something which could not be cut or divided.

We can see for ourselves that Democritus did have a good idea. When a teaspoonful of sugar is put into a cup of coffee, the sugar dissolves and disappears. If coffee—or water—were solid and continuous, there would be no room for the sugar. But since the sugar does disappear, we must conclude that the water and sugar are both made up of tiny particles with spaces between them. The sugar particles slip into the spaces between the water particles.

In one way, however, we have come to disagree with Democritus. Following his lead, for hundreds of years, men thought of atoms as solid little bits of matter. Newton spoke of them as being "so very hard as never to wear or break into pieces." John Dalton, an English chemist, in 1807 called atoms "indivisible, eternal and indestructible."

several important sciences and processes (3) not influenced our lives (4) been retarded by the Nile floods (5) been blank spaces ( )

f. The early astronomers used stars to guide them across (1) seas (2) rivers (3) forests (4) deserts (5) mountains ....( )

a. The word *atom* was first used by (1) an English chemist (2) a Greek philosopher (3) an American scientist (4) an advertising writer (5) a Greek physician ( )

b. The author indicates that Democritus' theory of the atom was (1) partly right (2) completely wrong (3) never accepted by others (4) too imaginative (5) contradicted by Dalton's theory ....( )

c. Sugar is believed to dissolve in water because (1) the water is solid and continuous (2) the sugar is solid and continuous (3) they are both solid and continuous (4) only a teaspoonful is used (5) there is room for sugar particles between the water particles ....( )

d. For centuries men believed that atoms (1) were destructive (2) had revolving parts (3) were really unimportant (4) could not be divided (5) were like sugar particles ( )

e. An atom can be compared to a solar system because an atom (1) is round (2) is unbreakable (3) has particles revolving around a center (4) is "indivisible, eternal and indestructible" (5) is a continuous mass of material ......( )

Today we know that atoms are not solid and not indestructible. We now think of an atom as a miniature solar system, with a central nucleus or "sun" around which tiny particles revolve.

THE DIFFERENCES BETWEEN PROSE AND POETRY, AND BETWEEN PROSE FICTION AND NONFICTION

All forms of writing may be divided into two main classes: prose and poetry. "Prose" is ordinary spoken or written language without the meter or rhythm which marks poetry. (See page 340 for a fuller discussion of poetry.) This sentence which you are now reading is called "prose." Of course, in good literature "prose" means more than just one word following the other. Prose has *style,* the individual expression of the personality of the author. Prose has *form,* the clear organization of ideas and opinions and emotions. Prose has *substance,* the human experience which is the stuff out of which all literature is made.

Prose works are of two kinds: fiction and nonfiction.

Fiction

Fiction comes from a Latin word *fictio* meaning "something invented"; therefore, fiction is that type of literature which tells imaginary events and describes imaginary characters. In other words, the author has "invented" these persons and made up their story. Librarians include novels, romances, and short-stories under the heading FICTION. Some examples of fiction are the following prose works:

Will James: *Smoky, the Cowhorse*
Rudyard Kipling: *Captains Courageous*
Louisa May Alcott: *Little Women*

Nonfiction

Nonfiction includes all prose works except fiction; notice the prefix *non* = not (fiction). Librarians include biography, history, science, travel, play, essay, and other miscellaneous prose works under the heading NONFICTION. Do not make the mistake of believing that all nonfiction must be true or real. It is simply a useful division of writing and a convenient way of classifying prose works. Fiction emphasizes *narrative,* or the story element. Nonfiction lends itself more to the *interpretation* of actual happenings. Some examples of nonfiction are the following prose works:

Carl Sandburg: *Abe Lincoln Grows Up*
Theodore Roosevelt: *Daniel Boone*
E. B. Frost: *Let's Look at the Stars*

Worth Remembering!

PROSE—straightforward expression of either real or imagined experiences.

POETRY—imaginative and emotional language marked by meter or rhythm.

FICTION—story-telling based on incidents, characters, suspense, setting, climax, and atmosphere.

NONFICTION—skillful presentation of factual material and interpretation of events or ideas.

KINDS OF PROSE WORKS

Fiction	1. NOVEL—Twain: *Huckleberry Finn* 2. ROMANCE—Pyle: *Men of Iron* 3. SHORT-STORY—Kipling: "Wee Willie Winkie"
Nonfiction	4. BIOGRAPHY—White: *Daniel Boone, Wilderness Scout* 5. HISTORY—Van Loon: *The Story of Mankind* 6. TRAVEL—Meader: *Trap-lines North* 7. SCIENCE—Morgan: *A First Electrical Book for Boys* 8. PLAY—Saunders: *The Knave of Hearts* 9. ESSAY—Page: *The American's Creed* 10. MISCELLANEOUS—Seton: *Biography of a Grizzly*

DEFINITIONS OF PROSE WORKS

A few definitions of the kinds of prose works listed in the chart above may help you to tell them apart more readily.

1. Novel

A prose work of fiction about 200 pages or more in length presenting a picture supposedly of real life by means of a story.

2. Romance

A prose work of fiction about 200 pages or more in length stressing adventure and unusual incidents rather than reality or insight into character as in the novel.

3. Short-story

A prose work of fiction, anywhere from a few to a hundred pages in length, presenting either real or imaginary characters in a narrative; the emphasis is chiefly on a single incident or a single character.

4. Biography

A prose work of nonfiction giving an account of a person's life. It often gives an interesting view of the times in which he lived and inspires the reader by showing how he met and solved certain hardships or problems.

5. History

A prose work of nonfiction giving an organized account of past facts, events, and outstanding persons. It is usually grouped around large centers of interest, such as social conditions, political factors, economic backgrounds, etc.

6. Travel

A prose work of nonfiction dealing with the voyages, discoveries, and explorations of certain individuals. It is interesting chiefly for its accurate description of faraway lands, peoples, and customs different from our own.

7. Science

A prose work of nonfiction discussing the various discoveries and inventions made in a particular field, such as astronomy, electronics, aeronautics, etc. It appeals mainly to readers who like to make or do things or have hobbies relating to scientific progress.

8. Play

A prose work of nonfiction telling a story by means of dialog or conversation between characters. It differs from the novel and the short-story in that it does not contain long descriptive passages or interpretations by the author; the persons in the play tell their own story in their own words. It is interesting when acted out upon a stage or in the classroom because it reveals the clash between personalities and ideas.

9. Essay

A prose work of nonfiction, usually short, in which the author attempts to give his personal experiences or individual reactions to a subject. Because the essay is a personal bit of writing, the author may choose to be gay or serious and to select a subject either trivial or important.

10. Miscellaneous

Any other prose work of nonfiction not specified above may be included here, such as editorials, animal books, art books, music stories, hobbies, current events, etc.

A good story gives delight. While reading fiction, you live another secret life and return to this world refreshed.

UNDERSTANDING PROSE WORKS

Fiction is the art of story-telling. From the days of the cavemen huddled around a fire listening to someone telling how he had killed a bear to the present day when youngsters gather around a television set to watch the adventures of Robin Hood, all the world enjoys a good story. What qualities make a story good? Usually the listener or reader wants to know: (1) What happens next? (2) Where does it take place? (3) Who are the persons in the story? (4) How does it end? (5) Could that really happen?

The art of fiction includes *incidents, suspense, setting, character, climax,* and a *general atmosphere* of either realism or romantic adventure. If you really enjoy prose fiction, you identify yourself with the hero or heroine of the story so that while you read you share their experiences imaginatively. To understand the secret of the story-teller's art, you should be aware of a few elements of the author's technique mentioned above. Let us apply them to Stevenson's *Treasure Island.*

1. Incidents	*These are the happenings or events that take place in the story.*
	Some of the important incidents in *Treasure Island* are the coming of Billy Bones to the Admiral Benbow Inn, the finding of the map by Jim Hawkins, the sailing of the *Hispaniola*, the fight with the pirates at the stockade, the meeting between Jim Hawkins and the man of the island, Ben Gunn, and the escape of Long John Silver.
2. Suspense	*This is the arrangement of incidents in such a way as to keep you guessing about the outcome, or what happens next.*
	A fine example of suspense in *Treasure Island* occurs when Jim Hawkins is hiding in the apple barrel on the deck of the *Hispaniola*. As he overhears the pirates planning mutiny and murder, we wonder whether one of them will reach for an apple and discover the eavesdropper inside the barrel.
3. Setting	*This includes the time and place of the story, the occupations and customs of the people.*
	Treasure Island is set in the days of sailing vessels and the story moves from Bristol, England, to a little island in the South Seas. The piratical flavor and seagoing talk are also part of the setting.
4. Characters	*The chief persons in the story whether heroes, heroines, or villains hold the reader's interest.*
	Some characters whom we admire in *Treasure Island* are Jim Hawkins, Captain Smollett, and Squire Trelawney; among the pirates, the outstanding ones are Long John Silver, Ben Gunn, Blind Pew, and Israel Hands.

Six Elements That Make a Story (Continued)

5. Climax	*The incidents in a story build up to a definite turning point after which the outcome is fairly evident.*
	The climax in *Treasure Island* occurs when Jim Hawkins finds Ben Gunn and the cave of treasure because we feel sure that the pirates will never succeed in wresting the gold from the ship's party now.
6. Atmosphere	*Is the story true to life? Is it purely imaginary and fanciful?*
	A story like *The Revolt of Mother* by Mary Freeman rings true because the mother's determination to have a new house instead of a new barn is realistically described. On the other hand, Stevenson's story about a map, pirates, buried treasure, and murder is a romantic adventure aiming purely at excitement. For no boy of fourteen could get into as many impossible situations as Jim Hawkins does and manage to escape almost every time! Life is not like that. We enjoy the story but do not believe it.

JUDGING TRUE-TO-LIFE STORIES (FICTION)

Fiction or story-telling may be classified as either (1) true to life (or *realistic*), or else (2) escape from life (or *romantic*). As a growing-up boy or girl, you should be able to recognize that *The Man Without a Country* is true to life because it describes an experience that could have happened to a person, whereas *Treasure Island* is an escape from life because it deals with an imaginary adventure. How can you tell whether a story is true to life?

Ask yourself these questions in judging a story:

> Are the *events* possible?
> Are the *characters* like real people?
> Are the *motives* true to experience?
> Is the *ending* a natural outcome?

1. Are the events possible?

In a true-to-life story, the plot contains events that could really happen, nothing contrary to the laws of nature. For example, a man can actually climb the highest mountain, but only "superman" can spread his hands before him and fly off into space! *Gulliver's Travels* is romantic, but Hamlin Garland's *The Camping Trip* is realistic fiction.

2. Are the characters like real people?

In real life we find people are a mixture of good and bad, and gradually their personalities change with new surroundings, friends, or experiences. In romantic fiction, the characters appear as exaggerated models of goodness or evil and the hero usually triumphs over the villain. For example, Philip Nolan regretted the fact that he had cursed the United States and said he never wanted to see it again. Change is true to life. But, the cruel master Fagin in *Oliver Twist* remained evil to the end, without ever showing a single trace of kindness.

3. Does each character do the things that his kind of person would do in a similar situation in real life?

We behave like human beings because, basically, we all have the same desires, such as these motives:

own things	have friends
gain power	improve ourselves
be admired	help others
have fun	be loyal to a cause
be free from pain or fear	enjoy the beautiful

In other words, we try to satisfy these desires in our pursuit of happiness. Therefore, we can judge whether a story is true to life if the characters do the things we normally expect them to do in certain situations. For example, a man swinging from a high branch of a tree would cling to it for dear life. But, in a fantastic story, he would recklessly jump unhurt to the ground! Barbour's *The Crimson Sweater* is realistic, but Sabatini's *Captain Blood* is romantic.

4. Is the ending a natural outcome of what has gone before?

In real life we know that every act has its consequences. A criminal as smart as Willie Sutton was finally caught by the police. But, in romantic fiction a weird character like Dr. Jekyll-Mr. Hyde kept his dual personality secret till death. Defoe's *Robinson Crusoe* is realistic, but Melville's *Moby Dick* is romantic.

EXERCISE

JUDGING TRUE-TO-LIFE STORIES

In a paragraph of about 100 words tell how one of the following short-stories or novels meets the test of realism or truth to human nature. (SS = short-story; N = novel)

Bret Harte: THE LUCK OF ROARING CAMP (SS)
Jack London: THE CALL OF THE WILD (N)
John Galsworthy: THE APPLE TREE (SS)
Anton Chekhov: THE BET (SS)
Joseph Conrad: YOUTH (N)
Stephen Crane: THE OPEN BOAT (SS)
Rudyard Kipling: THE MAN WHO WOULD BE KING (SS)
Dorothy Canfield Fisher: THE BENT TWIG (SS)
Nathaniel Hawthorne: THE SCARLET LETTER (N)
Robert Nathan: THE PORTRAIT OF JENNIE (N)
Booth Tarkington: ALICE ADAMS (N)
Guy de Maupassant: THE NECKLACE (SS)
Willa Cather: MY ANTONÍA (N)
Mark Twain: THE ADVENTURES OF TOM SAWYER (N)
O. Henry: THE COP AND THE ANTHEM (SS)
Howard Pyle: MEN OF IRON (N)

JUDGING THE GENUINENESS OF A NONFICTION BOOK

It is harder to tell whether a nonfiction book has solid genuineness or real value because a good writer can "lie like the truth." It requires some research or "digging" into the reputation of the author, as well as the ability to tell the difference between fact supported by evidence or backed by mere opinion. This does not mean that nonfiction books are written to deceive the reader. Rather, we question the authenticity of some who make claims in their writings. For example, the famous explorers of the polar regions have all written accounts of their discoveries: Peary, Scott, Byrd, Amundsen. For many years, Peary was considered a "hero," yet recently some of his claims have been challenged and disputed by researchers. A fair way of evaluating nonfiction books is to arrange them in a kind of scale of varying degrees of reliability. This is a job for the experts. Yet, the ordinary reader can ask himself certain guiding questions while reading nonfiction to help judge the genuineness of a book.

1. What is genuineness?

Nonfiction means "not imagined," "not made up"; it refers to actual happenings and existing facts or conditions. In other words, genuineness means a truthful and honest account. A science book or a history book must be true and accurate in order to be reliable and worthy of being believed. We place our confidence in William Beebe's *Descent in the Bathysphere,* but merely enjoy without believing Jules Verne's *Twenty Thousand Leagues Under the Sea.*

2. What is the author's reputation?

Some writers are recognized as authorities or specialists in certain fields. They may be qualified by training or personal experience to deal with such topics as animals, sports, war, medicine, politics, and so on. Carl Sandburg spent many years of research in preparation for writing a biography of Lincoln. Paul de Kruif, the scientist, had the necessary background for describing *Microbe Hunters.* You can discover such facts about authors by reading their life story, or by consulting *Who's Who,* or by reading what other specialists in the same field say about them.

3. Where did the author get his information?

Some nonfiction books are based on firsthand experience, travel, personal knowledge, and so on. Others are based on research into letters, diaries, journals, experiments, magazine articles, and other sources. A reliable author of a nonfiction book usually lets his readers know where he got his information. He may do this in several ways: (*a*) a preface or foreword in the book, (*b*) footnotes naming references at the bottom of certain pages, (*c*) direct quotation from sources in the text itself, (*d*) a bibliography or list of reference works at the end of the book showing what books the author consulted. Learn to look for these in judging the genuineness of a nonfiction book. See Charles Lindbergh's *We* as a good example of this.

4. Is there any evidence of tampering with the truth?

Some writers have a personal slant or "bias" in favor of an idea or against a theory, and this may be quite apparent in their work. Others may try to make their books more interesting by using their imagination to supply vivid details. This leads to "fictionizing," such as in the essays about nature and outdoor living by Thoreau in *Walden,* or in the accounts of hunting in Africa by Osa and Martin Johnson. You can notice this when the author tells you what emotions the animal felt or what the animal probably thought, even though you know that it is "imagined." Sometimes, whole "conversations" are invented by the author, as for example, Eve Curie in her biography of *Madame Curie,* her mother. This does not necessarily mean that the book is unreliable, but surely the love of the author may have blinded her to some of the faults or wrongs in the character she described.

Caution: The purpose of this series of questions to test the genuineness of a nonfiction book is to help you develop the inquiring mind. If you learn to challenge what you read rather than swallow it whole, you will become a more intelligent reader. On the other hand, you should not lose faith in reading as a means of enlarging your experience and increasing your knowledge. Fiction is a re-creation of life, just the way a portrait *creates* an image of a person more selective than a camera snapshot. The general outline and spirit are similar, but the details may differ. The effect is true to life, but the lights and shadows make a distinct impression.

EXERCISE

JUDGING THE GENUINENESS OF A NONFICTION BOOK

In a paragraph of about 100 words tell how one of the following nonfiction books measures up to the tests of genuineness or reliability. Explain why you rate it high or low in the scale of accuracy as a truthful account.

David Livingston: AN ADVENTURE WITH A LION (essay)
Richard Halliburton: THE ROYAL ROAD TO ROMANCE (travel)
Carl Sandburg: ABE LINCOLN GROWS UP (biography)
Wilfred T. Grenfell: ADRIFT ON AN ICE-PAN (travel)
Mark Twain: PERSONAL RECOLLECTIONS OF JOAN OF ARC (essay)
Frank R. Stockton: BUCCANEERS AND PIRATES OF OUR COASTS (essays)
Harry la Tourette Foster: BEACHCOMBER IN THE ORIENT (travel)
William H. Davies: AUTOBIOGRAPHY OF A SUPER-TRAMP (biography)
Hendrik Van Loon: STORY OF MANKIND (essay)
Will James: LONE COWBOY (biography)
Alpheus H. Verrill: GASOLINE ENGINE FOR BOYS (essay)
Benjamin Franklin: AUTOBIOGRAPHY (biography)
William Beebe: ARCTURUS ADVENTURE (travel)
John Buchan: BOOK OF ESCAPES AND HURRIED JOURNEYS (essays)

HOW TO DISCUSS PROSE SELECTIONS ON EXAMINATIONS

The type of question dealing with prose selections usually poses a problem or points to a center of interest and then asks you to show how the book you read answers the problem or illustrates the center of interest. For example, you may be asked to show how your book "helped you to learn about different people or places and their customs." Your answer should tell how the background or setting of the book differed from your own and, in addition, include one or two references to unusual customs. Your choice of book would deal with life somewhere else in the world: Jack London's *Cruise of the Snark,* an amateur expedition to cannibal islands; Francis Smith's *White Umbrella in Mexico,* an account of our neighbors to the south; etc.

You are expected to give specific names of places and show first-hand acquaintance with the book. You are *not* allowed to give a mere summary of the story. You should select material from the book directly related to the problem for discussion. If the question calls for a special type of book (travel, history, biography, etc.) and you discuss a different type, you will receive only half credit. Avoid penalties by noticing what kind of book the question actually calls for and by supplying the information required by the problem.

SUGGESTIONS FOR WRITING YOUR ANSWER

1. Begin by stating the *author and title* of the book as an example of the problem presented in the question.

    In the book called *Lure of the Labrador Wild* by Dillon Wallace, I learned about the hardships that men go through in the cold regions of the north.

2. Tell one or two incidents to support your opening sentence and to show *actual acquaintance* with the book.

    One incident that I remember describes how the men buried the empty wooden containers of lard, and later during their return journey they were so hungry they had to dig them up and try to make soup by boiling the pieces of wood in melted snow. They even cut up their leather belts and shoes in order to get something into the soup to stop the pangs of hunger in their stomach.

3. Tie up the story with the *problem stated* in the question.

    The grueling experiences of these explorers helped me to realize that their life is not just travel and adventure but full of unexpected obstacles and serious difficulties in order to obtain information useful to the rest of the world.

MODEL ANSWERS DISCUSSING PROSE WORKS

Question 1

By reading books we may increase our knowledge of people and customs in different countries and consequently broaden our understanding of their way of life and of their problems. Select a prose work which you have read and in about 150 words show how it has developed your understanding of people of a nationality different from yours.

Student's Answer:

When I read Van Loon's *Geography* I learned many things about people all over the world. For example, Switzerland is a country full of high mountains and the people have become wonderful engineers in building roads for travelers and tourists and bridges for railroads. I found out that the Swiss people love mountain climbing and act as guides for visitors on vacations. They make world-famous watches and other fine articles which show they are skilled craftsmen. Because of their rugged country they have become rugged people and have managed to keep out of many wars with their neighbors. They used to hurl giant boulders down on the heads of their enemies who dared to attack them. There are many beautiful lakes and interesting tunnels built right out of the rocks in the Alps which I hope to see some day. The peasants wear colorful costumes, especially on festivals. I admire the Swiss people because they are able to get along so well in a very difficult place to live.

Question 2

While reading books you often imagine that you are one of the characters and are experiencing his or her adventures. In about 150 words describe some adventure your reading has enabled you to enjoy. Give the author and title of the story and the name of the character.

Student's Answer:

I am going to tell you about Jack Thornton and his faithful dog Buck. One day when Thornton and some other men were drinking and talking at a bar in Alaska they started to brag about the dogs they owned. Thornton made a bet that his dog Buck could pull more dead weight than any other husky in the country. He said that Buck could start a sled with its runners frozen in the snow and ice and loaded with 1,000 pounds of flour. As I read this, I just couldn't believe it myself. But Buck was put into the traces and heaved with all his might. Maybe he was more than just a dog for he seemed to understand what was expected of him. He strained and heaved and dug his paws into the snow to keep from slipping, but he could not budge the sled. Just as I started to feel sorry for him, the ice started to crack around the runners of the sled and the sled slowly began to move. I felt just as thrilled as Thornton when Buck won the bet. Jack London, the author of *The Call of the Wild,* really makes you see and hear the whole exciting adventure.

EXERCISE

PROSE WORKS

1. In about 150 words, tell why young people should read good books and illustrate your statements by referring to at least one prose work that you have read.
2. Some books are magic carpets to faraway lands or days of long ago. Choose a prose work which carries you to another land or into the past and explain what you learned of a life different from your own.
3. Select a prose work that you have recently read and in about 100 words show why it is a good book for young people to read. Tell enough of the content to make your answer clear.
4. Name your favorite hero (or heroine) from prose literature and tell why he or she is a good example for young people.
5. Write a useful or interesting bit of information that you have learned from a prose work (other than a textbook) that you have read in the last year or two.
6. Give an account of a magazine article (not a story) that you have recently read.

7. What makes a story worth reading? Illustrate by a prose story that you consider worth-while.

8. Relate, from a prose work that you have read, an incident that made you laugh (or cry).

9. What prose work or story should you like to read next? Why?

10. From your reading, select a prose work that could be read purely for enjoyment and in about 150 words tell enough of the story to make your reader wish to read the book.

11. Before we can read good books, we must know how to select good books. Suppose you are on a book committee to select an outstanding book of value and interest. Recommend a book and in about 100 words tell why you would select it as being of value and interest to pupils.

12. Suppose that for an assembly program your class is to dramatize an incident from some book. From your prose reading, select an incident that you think would make an interesting dramatization and in about 100 words tell it as if you were speaking to your classmates.

 GETTING THE MEANING IN POETRY

APPRECIATING A POEM

What is *poetry* according to the poets themselves? Wordsworth said that poetry is "the spontaneous overflow of powerful emotions." Arnold defined poetry as "a criticism of life." Poe stated that poetry is "the rhythmical creation of beauty." Hundreds of other definitions have been given. In general, all agree that poetry contains certain definite qualities: *thought, imagination, emotion,* and *rhythm.* Good poetry contains not only these four elements, but that original touch of genius called *inspiration.* Your enjoyment of a poem depends largely upon your ability to share the poet's mood or feeling as suggested by the subject of the poem. In order to feel as the poet, you must understand the thought, see the picture or image described, share the emotion, and catch the rhythm of the lines. To appreciate these, you must read the poem aloud and listen to it with the sensitive ear of the mind and the heart. The language of poetry is more exact and vivid than ordinary writing because the poet makes every word count in creating an impression. You can refine your taste for poetry by reading good poems aloud and by listening to poetry readings on the radio and in numerous excellent recordings.

Let's take a typical poem for an illustration of the points we have mentioned in appreciation of poetry.

TREES

I think that I shall never see
A poem lovely as a tree.

A tree whose hungry mouth is prest
Against the earth's sweet flowing breast;

A tree that looks at God all day,
And lifts her leafy arms to pray;

A tree that may in summer wear
A nest of robins in her hair,

Upon whose bosom snow has lain;
Who intimately lives with rain.

Poems are made by fools like me,
But only God can make a tree.

—"Trees," from *Trees and Other Poems,* by Joyce Kilmer, copyright 1914, by Doubleday and Company, Inc.

1. What is Joyce Kilmer *trying to say?*

He says that the beauty of a tree far surpasses the loveliness of a bit of poetry because whatever God creates is infinitely better than anything that man can make. This is the thought or message of the poem.

2. What *picture-making* details of nature does the poet use to stimulate your imagination?

He describes the tree in terms of a beautiful lady who "lifts her leafy arms to pray" and who "may in summer wear a nest of robins in her hair." Other lines may also be quoted to show other seasons of the year.

3. What is the poet's *feeling* or emotion as aroused by this vision of a tree?

He shows a series of moods in the gradual unfolding of the poem: first, there is a sense of wonder and admiration for nature; then, a feeling of reverence for God; and, finally, a mood of humility.

4. How does the *rhythm* or swing of the lines fit the subject of the poem and help to express the poet's emotion?

The first 10 lines sweep along with the rush of the poet's passion for beauty as symbolized by the tree. Then the closing pair of lines shows

341

a pause, a change of pace and tone, as he stops to consider the power of God and the smallness of man.

5. Why is this an *inspired* poem?

Although we have all seen a tree, it remained for Joyce Kilmer to notice it with the sensitive, inner eye of a poet who finds untold loveliness in things we accept as commonplace. He has opened our eyes to the mystery of creation which has shaped not only the tree but the whole world around us.

EXERCISE

THE THOUGHT IN POETRY

A. After reading carefully each poem, read the three statements at the right of it and then select the statement that most nearly expresses the thought in the poem.

1. Truth, be more precious to me than
    the eyes
    Of happy love; burn hotter in my
    throat
    Than passion, and possess me like
    my pride;
    More sweet than freedom, more de-
    sired than joy,
    More sacred than the pleasing of a
    friend.

    ....Friendship is the most precious thing in the world.

    ....Everyone should seek happiness.

    ....Truth is of the greatest value.

2. Flower in the crannied wall,
    I pluck you out of the crannies,
    I hold you here, root and all, in my
    hand,
    Little flower—but *if* I could under-
    stand
    What you are, root and all, and all in
    all,
    I should know what God and man
    is.

    ....Flowers should be picked to be enjoyed.

    ....Understanding of nature would bring understanding of God.

    ....Flowers are beautiful.

3. He is gone from us! Yet shall we
   march on victorious,
      Hearts burning like Beacons—eyes
      fixt on the Goal!
   And if we fall fighting, we fall like
      the Glorious;
      With face to the Stars, and all
      heaven in the soul!
   And aye for the brave stir of battle
      we'll barter
      The sword of life sheathed in the
      peace of the grave:
   And better the fieriest fate of the
      Martyr,
      Than live like the Coward, and
      die like the Slave!

....Death is better than cowardice.

....The man who fights hard always
wins.

....Fighting never decides anything.

4. We shape ourselves the joy or fear
      Of which the coming life is made,
   And fill our Future's atmosphere
      With sunshine or with shade.
   The tissue of the Life to be
      We weave with colors all our own,
   And in the field of Destiny
      We reap as we have sown.

....By our present actions we determine what our future will be.

....Our future will be happy.

....We should never feel sad.

5. They set the slave free, striking off
      his chains . . .
   Then he was as much of a slave as
      ever.
   He was still chained to servility,
   He was still manacled to indolence
      and sloth,
   He was still bound by fear and su-
      perstition,
   By ignorance, suspicion, and sav-
      agery . . .
   His slavery was not in the chains,
   But in himself . . .

   They can only set free men free . . .
   And there is no need of that:
   Free men set themselves free.

....Unless we work hard, we shall be
slaves.

....We can be really free only if we
free ourselves.

....Chains will always keep a man in
slavery.

6. Stars over snow
      And in the west a planet
   Swinging below a star—
      Look for a lovely thing and you
      will find it,
   It is not far—
      It never will be far.

....Beauty is always near us.

....Beauty is hard to find.

....Everyone should enjoy beautiful
things.

343

7. Riches I hold in light esteem,
   And love I laugh to scorn;
   And lust of fame was but a dream,
   That vanished with the morn:

   And if I pray, the only prayer
   That moves my lips for me
   Is, "Leave the heart that now I bear
   And give me liberty!"

   Yes, as my swift days near their
       goal,
   'Tis all that I implore;
   In life and death, a chainless soul,
   With courage to endure.

. . . . The author considers wealth the
        most important thing in the world.

. . . . If the author can have fame, she
        will be content.

. . . . Freedom is the gift the author
        desires most.

EXERCISE

IMAGINATION IN POETRY

B. How does the picture in the following lines intensify the idea or mood which the poet is trying to express?

1. I hear them grinding, grinding through the night,
   The gaunt machines with arteries of fire,
   Muscled with iron, bowelled with smouldering light.
   —"Machines," from *Bright Harbor,* by Daniel Whitehead Hicky, by permission of Henry Holt and Co., Inc., copyright 1932 by Daniel Whitehead Hicky.

2. The high, white shoulders of the gables
   Slouch together for a consultation.
   —"The Old Houses of Flanders," by Ford Madox Hueffer, by permission of Dodd, Mead and Company, Inc.

3. Joy lights the candles in my heart
   When you come in.
   —"Candles," from *Banners,* by Babette Deutsch, copyright 1919 by Doubleday and Company, Inc.

4. **Frail as a gossamer, a thing of air,**
   A bow of shadow o'er the river flung.

   —"Brooklyn Bridge at Dawn," by Richard Le Gallienne, by permission of Dodd, Mead and Company, Inc.

5. They say that life is a highway and its milestones are the years,
   And now and then there's a toll-gate where you buy your way with tears.

   —"Roofs," from *Main Street and Other Poems*, by Joyce Kilmer, copyright 1917, by Doubleday and Company, Inc.

EXERCISE

EMOTION IN POETRY

C. Poets as well as artists and musicians express feelings and ideas. For each selection below, tell in one or two sentences what the author is trying to get the reader to feel and think.

1. They are all gone away,
   The House is shut and still,
   There is nothing more to say.

   Through broken walls and gray
   The winds blow bleak and shrill:
   They are all gone away.

   —*E. A. Robinson*

2. Fair is the land from sea to sea,
   Strong are its folk and bravely free;
   Deaf if they are to a distant drum,
   All will be true when the need shall come.

   Tame though it seem when your war cries cease,
   Calm as the cote of the dove of peace,
   Tyranny learn, if you can or will,
   This is the eagle's aerie still!

   —*Arthur Guiterman*

3. There was a young lady of Niger
   Who smiled as she rode on a tiger;
   They returned from the ride
   With the lady inside,
   And the smile on the face of the tiger.

   —*Cosmo Monkhouse*

4. Look out how you use proud words.
   When you let proud words go, it is not easy to call them back.
   They wear long boots, hard boots; they walk off proud; they can't hear you
        calling—
   Look out how you use proud words.

                                        —*Carl Sandburg*

5. Beyond the East the sunrise, beyond the West the sea,
   And East and West the wander-thirst that will not let me be;
   It works in me like madness, dear, to bid me say good-bye;
   For the seas call and the stars call, and O, the call of the sky!

                                        —*Gerald Gould*

EXERCISE

RHYTHM IN POETRY

D. How does the rhythm or swing of the lines help to express the idea or feeling? Read them aloud.

1. I must down to the seas again, for the call of the running tide
   Is a wild call and a clear call that may not be denied.

   —"Sea-Fever," from *Salt-Water Poems and Ballads*, by John Masefield, by permission of The Macmillan Company.

2. This is the forest primeval. The murmuring pines and the hemlocks
   Bearded with moss, and in garments green, indistinct in the twilight,
   Stand like Druids of eld, with voices sad and prophetic.

   —"Evangeline," from *Longfellow's Complete Works,* by Henry Wadsworth Longfellow, by permission of Houghton Mifflin Company.

3. I am the master of my fate:
   I am the captain of my soul.

   —"Invictus," by William Ernest Henley, by permission of Charles Scribner's Sons.

4. These be
Three silent things:
The falling snow . . . the hour
Before the dawn . . . the mouth of one
Just dead.

—"Triad," from *Verse*, by Adelaide Crapsey, by permission of Alfred A. Knopf, Inc., copyright 1915, 1934 by Algernon S. Crapsey, Adelaide T. Crapsey.

HOW TO DISCUSS POETRY ON EXAMINATIONS

Since the purpose of poetry is to give delight, no question can really measure the reader's enjoyment. However, there are some definite things that are often asked for and you can prepare yourself in advance along these three general areas:

1. The nature of poetry

Questions refer to poetry as "a revelation of beauty in the commonplace," or as "the expression of sincere feeling," or as "a story told in musical language." Be ready to explain how certain poems and authors illustrate such kinds of verse. Keep a list in your notebook for review before the test. Be frank in stating whether you agree or disagree with the statement. Don't let your immaturity lead you to condemn something without first trying to understand it.

2. The themes of poetry

Questions refer to poetry which "delivers a message" or makes a point through a particular story. Such themes as the following occur frequently in poetry: *nature* (the seasons, the ocean, the sky, etc.), *patriotism* (love of country), *courage* (adventure), *faith* (belief in God), *loss* (death, separation), *love* (romance, friendship). Mention authors and works which carry these meanings or ideals. Your notebook will help you remember suitable poems you have read.

3. The elements of appreciation

Questions refer to poetry as a "source of enjoyment" because of *imagination* (figures of speech), *rhythm* (the dance of words), *rhyme* (musical sound effects), *emotion* (mood or feeling), *inspiration* (the theme or message). Keep these five elements of appreciation clearly in mind and be ready to apply them to definite poems you have read. It is not enough to say, "I like it because it is interesting or different." It is better to say, "I like it because it gives a picture of a storm at sea in such a way that you can feel the terror of wind and waves." Once again, it is necessary to recall actual titles and authors. Refer to Coleridge's "The Vision of Sir Launfal" for inspiration and imagination; refer to Poe's "The Bells" for rhyme and rhythm; refer to Wordsworth's "The Daffodils" for emotion.

In other words, your discussion should show that you understand what the poet is trying to say and also that you appreciate the poet's skill in conveying his message or mood to the reader. Notice whether the question places its main emphasis on the nature of poetry, the themes of poetry, or the elements of appreciation. Write your answer in terms of the question and use appropriate poems to support your point of view.

SUGGESTIONS FOR WRITING YOUR ANSWER

Question:

Poetry gives enjoyment. Describe at least one example of *humorous* verse that you have enjoyed reading. In your answer refer to specific elements in the poem which help to create the mood of laughter.

1. Begin by stating the title of the poem and the name of the author as an illustration of the point called for in the question.

   "The Ballad of the Oysterman" by Oliver Wendell Holmes is a sample of humorous verse that I have enjoyed reading.

2. Refer to the poem to support your opening sentence. Mention some unusual images or the use of rhythm or rhyme to convey the message or mood. Better still, quote one or two lines.

   I liked the description of the "tall young oysterman" as he "leaped into the waves" in order to swim across the river to see his girl friend. She must have been a pretty sight when "her hair drooped round her pallid cheeks, like seaweed on a clam." Even their drowning for love becomes funny rather than sad because the poem ends: "And now they keep an oyster-shop for mermaids down below."

3. Conclude by comparing the poem with some other poem dealing with a similar situation or a contrasting ending.

   This poem reminds me of the story in the old myths about Narcissus, the young man who fell in love with his own reflection in a pool. When he drowned, he was changed into a flower near the river-bank.

348

MODEL ANSWERS DISCUSSING POETRY

Question 1

Name two poems that have some relation to our country's history, people, ideals, or activities. In about 100 words, tell what each of the poems named means to you.

Student's Answer:

"O, Captain, My Captain" tells how the whole nation mourned the death of Lincoln. He was the president of our country and in command, just as a captain is in charge of a ship. The Civil War had ended in victory and the nation was rejoicing. Suddenly, the news of the killing of the beloved leader changed all the gladness into sorrow. It was a very sad ending for a man who had gone through the storms of the war years.

"In Flanders Fields" was written by an American soldier who died in the trenches in World War I. He says that he will feel that he did not die in vain so long as we do our best to keep peace. He and others like him paid with their lives. They will not sleep unless we make the world safe against war. The poem means that we must keep faith with our fighting men even after the shooting is over.

Question 2

A friend of yours says that he "just hates poetry." You feel that he may dislike it because he has never read poems that would interest him. From your reading, select a poem that you think he would enjoy and in about 100 words tell enough about it to prove that not all poetry is dull. Give author and title.

Student's Answer:

The kind of poetry that I like is the kind that tells an exciting story in rhyme. If it's a good story like "The Highwayman" by Alfred Noyes, the poetry doesn't get into the way of the reading. In fact, the sound of the words and the swing of the lines help you to hear and feel the things as they happen. This poem tells how a robber fell in love with

Bess, the landlord's daughter, and made a date to see her at midnight. Meanwhile, Tim the ostler reported the robber to King George's men. When the highwayman came riding back to the inn, his sweetheart shot herself in order to warn him. Later, he heard how she had died for his sake, so he came galloping back like a madman. The soldiers shot him down like a dog on the highway, but at the end of the poem the ghosts of the lovers keep their secret meeting. I think you will enjoy the suspense when Bess hears the sound of the horse's hoofs bringing the highwayman back into the trap, and you will feel sorry when they both have to die.

EXERCISE

POETRY APPRECIATION

1. Suppose that you have have been asked to write an article called "The Poetry Corner" for the final issue of your grade magazine. Choose two poems that you believe your class enjoyed reading. Give the titles and authors of the poems and tell in some detail why each of these two poems was greatly enjoyed.

2. At the right of each of the five poems given below you will find three statements. After reading each poem carefully, read the three statements at the right and then select the statement that most nearly expresses the thought in the poem.

NOBILITY

True worth is in *being*, not *seeming*,——
  In doing, each day that goes by,
Some little good——not in the dreaming
  Of great things to do by and by.
For whatever men say in their blindness,
  And spite of the fancies of youth,
There's nothing so kingly as kindness,
  And nothing so royal as truth.

            —Alice Cary

....We should plan to do great things.

....We should work hard each day.

....We should do small deeds of kindness.

A SMILE

Let others cheer the winning man,
There's one I hold worth while;
'Tis he who does the best he can,
Then loses with a smile,
Beaten he is, but not to stay
Down with the rank and file;
That man will win some other day,
Who loses with a smile.

—*Unknown*

....The man who wins deserves great praise.

....The man who loses cheerfully will some time conquer.

....The man who loses will stay defeated.

THE WINDS OF FATE

One ship drives east and another drives west,
With the self-same winds that blow,
   'Tis the set of the sails
   And not the gales
That tells them the way to go.

Like the winds of the sea are the winds of
   fate,
As we voyage along through life,
   'Tis the set of the soul
   That decides its goal
And not the calm or the strife.

—*Ella Wheeler Wilcox*

....A man's character determines what he strives for.

....Life is largely a matter of chance.

....Everyone should work hard to attain his goal.

THE HAPPIEST HEART

Who drives the horses of the sun
Shall lord it but a day;
Better the lowly deed were done,
And kept the humble way.

The rust will find the sword of fame,
The dust will hide the crown;
Ay, none shall nail so high his name
Time will not tear it down.

The happiest heart that ever beat
Was in some quiet breast
That found the common daylight sweet,
And left to Heaven the rest.

—*John Vance Cheney*

....Fame and honor are lasting.

....True happiness is to be found in simple things.

....Everyone should try to find happiness.

351

Work Done Squarely

The longer on this earth we live
And weigh the various qualities of men,
The more we feel the high stern-featured
    beauty
Of plain devotedness to duty,
Steadfast and still, nor paid with mortal
    praise,
But finding amplest recompense
For life's ungarlanded expense
In work done squarely and unwasted days.

—*James Russell Lowell*

.... Work well done is in itself a reward.

.... We should receive praise for work we do well.

.... It is foolish to waste time.

3. In our reading of poetry we often find a poem that we especially like. From your reading select three poems that you really enjoyed and, in not more than 40 words for each, tell what you particularly liked about each one.

4. Read the following poem and then answer the questions below:

At evening when I go to bed
I see the stars shine overhead;
They are the little daisies white
That dot the meadow of the night.

And often while I'm dreaming so,
Across the sky the moon will go;
It is a lady, sweet and fair,
Who comes to gather daisies there.

For, when at morning I arise,
There's not a star left in the skies;
She's picked them all and dropped them down
Into the meadows of the town.

—*Frank Dempster Sherman*

  a. Suggest a suitable title for the poem.
  b. To what are the stars compared?
  c. What is meant by "the meadow of the night"?
  d. What is called "a lady, sweet and fair"?
  e. What is meant by the last two lines of the poem?
  f. Do you like the poem? Explain why you do or do not like it.

5. A poet often describes familiar things in such a vivid and unusual way that we feel we never really appreciated them before. Choose a poem you have read and show how it has increased your appreciation of the world about you. Write from memory one or more passages that are particularly well expressed in the poem selected.

USING THE DICTIONARY AND OTHER REFERENCE BOOKS

An educated person is not one who knows everything. Rather, he is a person who has an alert curiosity about everything and knows how to find out for himself. The chief sources of information are reference books, encyclopedias, and dictionaries. The famous Van Doren family at Columbia University consists of experts in literature, philosophy, current affairs, and other fields. Yet, it is reported that their table talk never becomes heated discussions about when the next train will leave for a certain city, or who is the ruler of a certain country. The father just says, "If it is a *fact* that you are arguing about, stop arguing and *look it up!* The timetable or the almanac will give the right answers."

How true this is of some of us! How often we hear boys or girls arguing about which team won the world series five years ago, or who is the present middleweight champion, when all they really have to do is look it up in the *World Almanac!*

Be educated. Learn to use reference books to improve your background and increase your knowledge.

USES OF A DICTIONARY

The dictionary is the reference aid most frequently used in school and in adult life. Whenever you write, speak, or read, you find the dictionary the one book you cannot do without. It is indispensable because the information contained within the covers of this single volume ranges over practically the whole field of knowledge. Its alphabetical system of word-entry makes finding things a quick and simple task. The *guide words,* printed at the top of each page, help you to locate a word without having to run your eye up and down the whole page. For example, if the guide words are LADLE—LAMB at the top of the page, and you are looking for the word LAIR, then you know you have the right section. The *pronunciation key,* printed at the bottom of every two adjoining pages, tells you how to say a particular word by comparing the sounds with similar sounds in short, everyday words. For example, the first *a* in *data* is pronounced like the long ā in āle; the second *a* in *data* is pronounced like the unaccented à in sofà; therefore, *data* = dā′tà, with the accent on the first syllable.

Most often we consult the dictionary to find the correct spelling, pronunciation, or meaning of a word. But, the dictionary offers much more information. Here is a mnemonic device (memory-helper) to help you remember the chief uses of the dictionary: P-E-S-T-G-U-M-S (the first letter of each use listed below).

CHIEF USES OF THE DICTIONARY

USE	SAMPLE WORD	WHAT THE DICTIONARY SAYS
Pronunciation	chic	shêk (as in the word êvent)
Etymology	telephone	[tele + phone] (from Greek *tele,* far off + *phone,* sound)
Spelling	committee	com mit tee (notice the double *m, t, e*)
Technical terms	calorie	*Physics.* The amount of heat required to raise the temperature of one gram of water one degree centigrade.
Grammar	produce	May be used as v.t. (transitive verb), v.i. (intransitive verb) when pronounced pro-duce′; as n. (noun) when pronounced prod′-uce.
Usage	good deal of	Colloquial phrase meaning *considerable.*
Meaning	surplus	That which remains when use or need is satisfied; excess.
Synonyms	process	progress; course; a series of actions, motions, or operations.

Get acquainted with the special purpose of each type of information given.

Etymology means the derivation or origin of a word. Most English words have been borrowed during the centuries from all the languages of the world.

Technical terms means words having special uses in such fields as science, law, music, medicine, printing, banking, architecture, etc.

Grammar means the indication of the part of speech. Some words may be used as a noun and as a verb, etc.

Usage means the accepted level or rank of an expression in current usage. It may be literary (bookish), colloquial (conversational), slang or vulgar, archaic (old-fashioned), or obsolete (no longer in use).

OTHER USES OF THE DICTIONARY

USE	SAMPLE WORD	WHAT THE DICTIONARY SAYS
Antonyms	join	*Ant.:* separate, sever, disconnect, part
Abbreviations	i.e.	[Latin] *id est* = that is
Biographical data	Socrates	Athenian philosopher (469-399 B.C.)
Foreign words and phrases	faux pas	[French] = a false step; esp., an offense against social convention
Illustrations	lynx	see picture of this animal in the text
Location of a place	Nashville	capital of Tennessee (in western part of state)
Mythological characters	Cyclops	one-eyed monster in Greek legend
Names in fiction	Scrooge	miser in Dickens' *A Christmas Carol*
Tables of measurement	mile	5,280 feet, unit of linear measure
Proofreader's symbols	l.c.	lower case (use small letters)

EXERCISE

THE DICTIONARY

1. Find the *meaning:*

biography	camouflage	endorse	fragile	invest
abolition	decoy	experiment	generate	leisure

2. Find the *pronunciation:*

athlete	blackguard	champion	exquisite	luxury
alias	bronchial	deity	frivolous	mania

3. Find the *etymology* or *origin:*

benevolent	automobile	escalator	galaxy	lucid
cantaloupe	delirium	fraternal	intaglio	monocle

4. Find *synonyms:*

affection	cargo	entire	grim	narrate
brevity	debate	function	liberal	obstacle

5. Find some *general information:*
   - a. Location of Pearl Harbor.
   - b. Book in which Long John Silver appears.
   - c. Names of the Great Lakes.
   - d. Population of London.
   - e. Biographical data about Leonardo da Vinci.
   - f. Meaning of foreign phrase, "Laborare est orare."
   - g. Number of square feet in one acre of land.
   - h. Meaning of proofreader's symbol "stet."
   - i. Meaning of English phrase, "to pay the piper."
   - j. Height of Mt. Everest.

6. Below is the word *journey* as it appears in a student dictionary.

   journey (jûr′ nĭ), n.; pl. journeys (-niz). [OF. *journée* a day, a day's work or travel, fr. L. *diurnum* day, fr. *diurnus* daily.] Travel or passage from one place to another. Syn. tour, trip.

   Tell what information about the word each of the following items gives you:
   - a. (jûr′ nĭ)
   - b. n.
   - c. pl. journeys
   - d. Travel or passage from one place to another
   - e. Syn. tour, trip

7. Read carefully the following entry taken from a standard dictionary. Then answer the questions below, using only the information given in the entry.

beau′ ti·ful (bū′ tĭ·fŏŏl; -f'l), *adj.* Full of beauty; having the qualities that constitute beauty. ——Syn. Lovely, fair, handsome, pretty. ——Ant. Ugly, plain, homely. ——beau′ ti·ful·ly, *adv.*

a. How many syllables are there in the word *beautiful?*
b. Which syllable of the word *beautiful* is accented?
c. Which part of speech is the word *beautiful?*
d. What is a word that means the same or nearly the same as *beautiful?*
e. What is a word that means the opposite of *beautiful?*

8. When you say the following words, you do not pronounce every letter. Select a silent letter from each word below and write the letter.

rate	gnat	knot	debt	came
honor	sign	hymn	ghost	island

9. When we say *knife,* the first sound we hear is that of the letter *n.* For each word below, write the letter whose sound is pronounced first in that word.

wreck	knowledge	gnaw	pneumonia	Europe
honesty	aisle	whole	ptomaine	psychology

10. The dictionary is consulted most often to find out the correct spelling, meaning, and pronunciation of words we meet in reading. Look up these words and complete this chart in your notebook.

SPELLING	PRONUNCIATION	MEANING
1. penicillin		
2. rhythm		
3. bouquet		
4. luxurious		
5. fidelity		
6. delinquency		
7. penance		
8. restitution		
9. exhibition		
10. acclaim		

② ALPHABETICAL FILING

One of the greatest contributions to civilization was the invention of the alphabet. These twenty-six letters, arranged in various groups, have made communication possible for millions of people all over the world. If you consult Webster's (Unabridged) *New International Dictionary,* you will find 600,000 separate entries based entirely on these twenty-six letters. What a wealth of ideas and information can be expressed by means of the alphabet! It has made possible the free flow of knowledge to all the ends of the earth. It provides a link between ourselves and the many generations which preceded us. The alphabet and the printing press have liberated our minds forever from the darkness of ignorance. Therefore you, as the heir of all the ages, should know and use these letters as the steppingstones to learning.

To turn now to a more practical level, a knowledge of A—B—C is as important as knowing how to walk or breathe. You use this alphabetical order in your everyday experiences: names in a telephone book, articles in an order catalog, words in a dictionary, tellers' windows in a bank, foods in a recipe book, seats in a classroom, topics in a book index, etc. Granted that you already know the alphabet, do you have skill in judging the relative position of letters? For example, do you know whether *o* comes before *j*? Which letter follows *r*? Must you mumble through the whole alphabet to figure these out? Do you know that *m* is the *middle* or thirteenth letter? To become adept in filing, you must practice putting words into alphabetical order. Whether you are using a dictionary, an encyclopedia, a telephone directory, or a road map, you will save time and succeed in finding the desired information if you have skill in alphabetical filing.

In order to visualize the approximate position of any letter in the alphabet, study the letters in groups as follows:

GROUP I	GROUP III
a b c d	n o p q
e f g	r s t

GROUP II	GROUP IV
h i j k	u v w x
l m	y z

Your study should help you—

a. to visualize the four groups of letters.

b. to think accurately of the approximate position in the alphabet of each of the four groups.

c. to think rapidly of any given letter as belonging to the first, second, third, or fourth group.

d. to associate easily any given letter with its neighbor.

For example, *j* should call instantly to mind the series *h, i, j, k* or the series *k, j, i, h*. When you want to find a word beginning with *s* in an alphabetical list, there should flash into your mind something like the following: "*s* is in the last line of the third group; hence, it is probably about three-quarters of the way down the list (in the dictionary, or other material)." You turn approximately to that place and hit a *q* or *r* or *t*. By quickly visualizing the third group, you *see* whether to turn the pages backward or forward to find *s*.

EXERCISE

ALPHABETICAL ORDER

1. Arrange these words according to the alphabetical order of their *initial letter:*

goodness	arrest	lettuce	remark	model
blanket	cousin	youth	duty	foreign

2. Arrange these words according to the alphabetical order of *all the letters:*

coconut	cubic	civil	charcoal	cloud
commerce	center	calm	current	cross

3. List the names of ten members of your class in correct alphabetical order.
4. List the names of ten cities in correct alphabetical order.
5. List the titles of ten books or movies in correct alphabetical order.
6. Arrange the following names in strictly alphabetical order (last name first):

Albert Jones	Julia Johnson	Mary Kinney	Carol King
Henry King	Alfred Jones	Jane Crandall	Harold Downs

7. List the following names in alphabetical order (last name first):

Brown, Marjorie	Jones, Harry	Yachim, Joseph	Downs, Arlie
Adams, John	Case, Carol	Johnson, Sarah	Castro, Mary
Smith, Carlton	Brown, Martin	Smithers, William	Opelt, John

8. Arrange the following words in strictly alphabetical order:

   ache, afford, aboard, attic, advertise, awful, account, afraid, attitude, activity

9. Arrange the following names of islands in the order in which they would be found in the index of an atlas:

   Asuncion, Azores, Awo, Ata, Avon, Atafu, Aurh, Atka, Attu, Atiu

10. On one page of a certain dictionary the first word is *order* and the last word is *oriental*. Which of the following words could be found on that page?

organdie	orient	ordinal	ordinary	orderly
orchard	ore	ornate	orphan	oral

The library and the classroom should contain certain sources of information about all sorts of subjects ready to be consulted whenever a question arises. Reference tools are up-to-date arrangements of articles on all subjects written by experts in the various fields. The most often used reference books—books that all boys and girls need to know and to use—are the following: a dictionary, a children's encyclopedia, an almanac, and an atlas. Become acquainted with the kind of material these tools contain and the order in which the material is arranged. You will soon find yourself turning to reference books to help you with your assignments and to satisfy your natural curiosity about the things in the world about you.

Other reference tools that you will enjoy using are: (1) *Rue's Subject Index to Readers*, (2) the *Children's Catalog*, (3) the *Junior Book of Authors*, (4) quotation books, (5) indexes to tales, poetry and plays, (6) science reference books and identification guides, (7) direction books used for games and hobbies, (8) the *Boy Scouts' Handbook* and similar books, and (9) the *Abridged Readers' Guide to Periodical Literature* for recent magazine articles or pictures to illustrate topics.

CHILDREN'S ENCYCLOPEDIAS

The two most widely used encyclopedias published for children and young people are the following:

World Book Encyclopedia. Contains a tremendous number of interesting articles, pictures, maps, diagrams; the arrangement is alphabetical by subject, so that it can be used as easily as a dictionary to locate any topic; 19 volumes, published by Quarrie.

Compton's Pictured Encyclopedia. Contains factual articles and excerpts from literature; profusely illustrated; the arrangement requires the use of a fact-index at the end of each volume to locate a particular topic; 15 volumes, published by Compton.

ALMANACS AND YEARBOOKS

Some useful almanacs are the *World Almanac, Information Please Almanac,* and the *Statistical Abstract of the United States.* Some yearbooks of interest are *Sports Annual* and *Statesman's Yearbook.*

As its name implies, the *World Almanac* is published annually and is a useful handbook of miscellaneous information. It contains statistics on social, industrial, political, financial, religious, and educational subjects; and information regarding sports, government, law, public affairs, historical events, scientific progress, organizations, and institutions. It is a concise storehouse of information, sold at a very moderate price. A copy at home will answer many questions for you!

ATLASES

You have probably had some experience in map using and map making in connection with your study of history and geography. An atlas is a fine reference tool because it is a collection of maps. Whenever you use an atlas, carefully notice the title page, copyright date, table of contents, and index. Some atlases refer to maps by page; other atlases refer to maps by number. The indexes of some atlases help the user locate the particular place on the particular map by indicating the small section marked by letters and numbers; other atlases give latitude and longitude.

Some popular atlases are *J. P. Goode's School Atlas, The Times Survey Atlas of the World, Rand McNally's Commercial Atlas of America, Hammond's World Atlas.*

GAZETTEERS

Whenever you want geographical information, a gazetteer, or geographical dictionary, will give you the quickest service because it is alphabetically arranged and condensed. You may use a separately published gazetteer or the gazetteer section of an unabridged dictionary. Usually, a gazetteer is an alphabetically arranged list of geographic names (countries, cities, rivers, mountains, etc.) with information regarding their pronunciation, location, and other brief facts.

The following are well-known gazetteers: *Lippincott's Gazetteer of the World;* A Pronouncing Gazetteer—found in *Webster's New International Dictionary;* Gazetteer—Index of the World—found in *Hammond's World Atlas.*

REFERENCE BOOKS AND QUIZ SHOWS

Librarians have noted a greater interest in all kinds of reference books in recent years because of the quiz shows which give away fortunes to those who can answer questions.

Some contestants have become famous because of their ability to supply information not related to their own daily lives and occupations. For example, a shoemaker knew all about opera, a marine correctly identified foreign foods, a jockey recognized masterpieces of painting and art, a policeman knew Shakespeare and his plays. Knowledge indeed is power—and cash! Learn to locate information and someday *you* may be a winner. At any rate, it is a useful skill in school, on the job, and in life.

EXERCISE

REFERENCE BOOKS

Write the name of the reference book you would use to locate the information.

1. Author of short story entitled, "The Lady or the Tiger."
2. Title of poem with this opening line:
   "I must down to the seas again."
3. Name of vice-president during 1914-1918 in U.S.A.
4. Chief exports of Egypt during 1940-1950.
5. An article about fluoridating the water supply.
6. A description of the jet stratoliner for passenger flying.
7. Some biographical material for a talk about a living writer, either American or British.
8. Winners of Nobel Prize Awards for outstanding work in science during the past five years.
9. A recent magazine article dealing with the UN.
10. A map showing the main currents in the Pacific Ocean.
11. The winners of the World Series in baseball for the past five years.
12. Name of Italian opera in which a clown dies brokenhearted.
13. A description of the game of tennis or soccer.
14. Book used by Dickens for historical background of the French Revolution in writing his novel, *A Tale of Two Cities.*
15. The source of the quotation, "A penny saved is a penny earned."

 ## USING LIBRARY SKILLS

DEWEY DECIMAL SYSTEM

Your school library, your neighborhood public library, and most of the libraries throughout the country have adopted the *Dewey Decimal System* because it is a very useful and convenient method of classifying books. It gets its name from the man who devised the plan in 1876— Melvil Dewey. It is called a "decimal" system because *decimal* comes from a Latin word *decem* meaning *ten,* and there are ten large groupings or classes in the system. These ten classes of books correspond to the main divisions of human knowledge. The mnemonic device (memory-helper) in the chart may help you to remember the plan.

TEN CLASSES OF BOOKS		MNEMONIC
000—099	General works	Good
100—199	Philosophy	Pupils
200—299	Religion	Require
300—399	Social Sciences	Speedy
400—499	Language	Learning
500—599	Science	So
600—699	Useful Arts	Use
700—799	Fine Arts	Fine
800—899	Literature	Library
900—999	History	Helps

Each of the ten large classes is further subdivided to include ten smaller subjects or topics. For example, LITERATURE **(800)** books are grouped on library shelves as follows:

800 LITERATURE
810 American
820 English
830 German
840 French
850 Italian
860 Spanish
870 Latin
880 Greek
890 Minor languages

WHAT THE CARD CATALOG IS

The *card catalog* is a series of small cards alphabetically filed in a cabinet of drawers. These library cards are a guide to the books in the library. Each book is listed on three cards, arranged for convenience in three ways: (1) by author, (2) by title, (3) by subject. In the top left-hand corner of each card for nonfiction, the call number appears; this is the Dewey Decimal System of numbering books. Fiction is always listed without call numbers.

Books Are Silent Servants

Books stand ready to serve you in many ways, to increase your knowledge, and to satisfy your leisure time. Learn the *Dewey Decimal System* and the *card catalog* so that you will be able to locate any book in the library.

THE CALL NUMBER

The *call number* is the class number of a particular book together with a capital letter showing the initial of the author's last name. Call numbers are found on the back binding of books on the library shelves, and they also appear on the cards filed in the library card catalog. Examples:

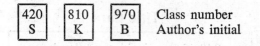

| 420 | 810 | 970 | Class number |
| S | K | B | Author's initial |

Thus, if you are looking for a volume of poetry by Keats, you will first look in the card catalog and find the call number **821K;** then you look on the library shelves for the main class LITERATURE **800;** then for the class number ENGLISH LITERATURE **821;** and, finally, for the call number **821K,** which identifies the volume of poetry you want.

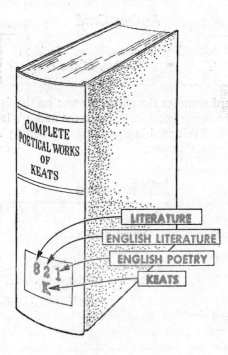

USING THE CARD CATALOG FOR A NONFICTION BOOK

Suppose your teacher has told you about an interesting book dealing with submarine warfare during the European War, 1914-1918. She may have mentioned the title, *Raiders of the Deep,* but you do not recall the author. If you wish to find the book in the library, go to the card catalog and look in the drawer containing **R**. You will find this:

Title Card

940.45	Raiders of the deep.
T	Thomas, Lowell Jackson

The title card contains the call number in the upper left corner. The title appears on the first line, and the card is filed by the first letter of the title. The author appears below the title.

Author Card

940.45	Thomas, Lowell Jackson
T	Raiders of the deep.

The author card contains the author's name on the first line and the call number in the upper left corner. Since the author's last name begins with **T**, you will find this card in the drawer containing **T**. The title appears below the author's name.

Subject Card

940.45	European War, 1914-1918
T	Naval operations
	Submarine
	Thomas, Lowell Jackson
	Raiders of the deep.

The subject card contains the subject on the first line; the call number in the upper left corner; the author below the subject; the title below the author. You would find this card in the drawer containing **E**, since the first word of the subject is European.

Cross-reference Card

> World War
> To be found in this catalog under
> European War, 1914-1918

The cross-reference card helps you to find the information listed under another heading. For example, the **European War** is also referred to as the **World War,** so the card catalog provides a cross-reference.

HOW TO FIND FICTION BOOKS

The only exception to the Dewey Decimal System of numbering is *fiction,* which includes novels and short-stories. The field of fiction contains such a wide collection of books that it often fills half the space in a library. Since these fiction books cover life in general, they cannot be classified according to any of the 10 Dewey Decimal groups. Author and title provide the usual guide to novels and short-stories. Therefore, all works of fiction are arranged on the shelves *alphabetically* according to the initial of the last name of the *author.*

Alcott, Louisa May—*Little Men*
Barrie, James Matthew—*Peter and Wendy*
Carroll, Lewis—*Alice's Adventures in Wonderland*
Dickens, Charles—*A Christmas Carol*

and so on, down through the alphabet, by authors.

HOW TO FIND BIOGRAPHIES

For convenience, the entire section dealing with biography is usually separated from the shelves containing fiction and nonfiction.

1. Individual biography

The life story of one person is marked **B.** These books are arranged alphabetically by the last name of the person *written about.* Example: *Daniel Boone, Wilderness Scout* by Stewart Edward White has this call number:

B	Biography
Boone	Boone
W	White

2. Collections of biographies

Books containing the lives of several persons are marked **920** and are arranged alphabetically by *author*. Example: *Heroes of Progress* by E. M. Tappan has this call number:

920	Biography
T	Tappan

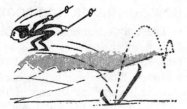

THE CARD CATALOG

Correctly match the items in column *A* with those in column *B*.

Column A	*Column B*
1. arranged on shelves under call number B	*a.* card catalog
2. arranged on shelves under call number 920	*b.* Dewey Decimal classification
3. arranged on shelves alphabetically by author's last name	*c.* call number
4. a set of drawers with a system of cards serving as a complete guide to the books in the library	*d.* author card
5. the first line of this card contains the title of the book	*e.* title card
6. the first line of this card contains the author's name	*f.* subject card
7. this system of arranging books was introduced by Melvil Dewey in 1876	*g.* cross-reference card
8. the Dewey Decimal classification together with the initial of the subject or author or both	*h.* individual biography
9. the first line of this card contains the subject of the book	*i.* fiction
10. this card refers you to another word or heading under which you may locate information regarding a particular book or subject	*j.* collective biographies

PARTS OF A BOOK

A good book is a key to information. Have you ever explored the books which you are studying in school in order to discover the principal parts? Textbooks are tools for learning, and you should make it your business to know how to use these tools to your best advantage. Take your history or geography book in hand and see whether you can identify the following principal parts and their use:

1. Title Page

This is usually the first printed page facing you as you open the book. From the title page you learn (*a*) the full title, (*b*) the author's name, (*c*) the publisher's name. Sometimes included are (*d*) the place of publication, (*e*) the date of publication, (*f*) editor.

2. Copyright Page

This is usually the reverse side of the title page. From the copyright page you learn (*a*) the copyright date, (*b*) the copyright owner's name, (*c*) whether permission is granted to reproduce any part of the book. The copyright date indicates how up-to-date or out-of-date the book's information or material is. In which types of books is newness or recency of copyright date important? (Example: Science books usually need to be brought up-to-date.) In what kind of book does age of the material make no difference to its interest value? (Example: Good literature is timeless in its appeal to the reader.) Revisions bring a book up-to-date.

3. Table of Contents

This is a topical outline showing the organization of material into chapters and giving the specific page reference for the beginning of each chapter. It tells you at a glance the main subjects discussed in the book.

4. Index

This is a detailed list of all the subjects, titles, and materials in the book arranged in alphabetical order with specific page references. It is located at the end of the book and is the most practical and time-saving way of locating any particular information in the book.

5. Preface or Foreword

This is usually about a page or two long, near the front of the book. In it the author states the aims and purposes of the book.

6. Introduction

This is a brief statement near the front of the book telling how the book may be profitably used and suggesting various exercises and other materials to be consulted.

7. List of Illustrations

This is a handy guide to the drawings, photographs, diagrams, and sketches. It is near the front of the book.

8. The Vocabulary

Sometimes this is called a "Glossary" or "List of Technical Terms" and is placed at the end of the book. It is a series of definitions for unusual words in the text.

9. Appendix

The appendix includes any supplementary or explanatory material placed at the end of the book.

10. Bibliography

This is a list of books, usually reference texts, placed at the end of a chapter or a book as a guide for the reader who wishes further material on a particular subject.

11. Notes

Sometimes there are "cross-references" or "footnotes" at the bottom of a page in the regular text. These draw the attention of the reader to the source of certain information or advise him to consult other sections of the book.

12. Dedication

Usually the author honors a particular person by dedicating the text in his (or her) name. The dedication follows the copyright page.

13. Acknowledgments

Near the copyright page, you may find a list of publishers who have granted permission to the author (or publisher) to use certain copyrighted materials which are specified by title and author.

EXERCISES

PARTS OF A BOOK

Correctly match the items in column *A* with those in column *B*.

<table>
<tr><td colspan="2">Column A</td><td>Column B</td></tr>
</table>

Column A

1. pictures, maps, etc., in order of appearance
2. alphabetical list of topics with references to pages
3. explanatory material at bottom of page
4. statement of author's purpose in writing the book
5. list of books or other materials used as sources for the text, or suggested as references for further reading
6. supplementary notes, material, or bibliography
7. list of special terms or unusual words used in the book and the definitions for them
8. gives titles or subjects of chapters in order of appearance in the book
9. date of registry of copyright in the U. S. Copyright Office; appears on back of title page
10. full title, author, publisher, place

Column B

a. title page
b. copyright date
c. preface
d. glossary
e. table of contents
f. list of illustrations
g. bibliography
h. footnote
i. appendix
j. index

LIBRARY SKILLS

1. Name the 10 main classes of books according to the Dewey Decimal System.
2. What is meant by the *call number* of a book?
3. How are books of fiction (novels and stories) arranged on library shelves?
4. What is the *card catalog* and how is it used?
5. Name three ways in which a nonfiction book may be listed in the card catalog.
6. Name the five most useful parts of a book and tell what kind of information each part gives.
7. List 10 uses of the dictionary as a source of information regarding words.
8. Name two well-known children's encyclopedias.
9. Which annual book of facts offers the most complete gathering of information at very low cost?
10. Name the reference book you would use to find:

    a. The legend about Orpheus and Eurydice.
    b. How to identify wild flowers in your neighborhood.
    c. A play suitable for a Christmas assembly program.

UNDERSTANDING AND ENJOYING LITERATURE

WHAT IS LITERATURE?

Literature is an artistic record of the human race, containing its hopes, dreams, problems, failures, and successes. It differs from purely informational reading in that it seeks to present a re-creation of persons and places, rather than a straightforward account of facts and figures.

What Is Literature?

Literature is a work of art in writing which combines thought and emotion and imagination to give a picture of life. It is an author's interpretation of experience, either real or imagined.

A good geography or history book will tell you the facts about the Revolutionary days in Boston, but the story of the Sons of Liberty dumping the tea in Boston harbor comes alive in Esther Forbes' novel, *Johnny Tremain.*

Literature requires on the part of the reader more than just getting the thought. It requires imagination and insight, a surrender to the magic of mood, a sharing of the literary experience. In other words, a good reader identifies himself with the story, and he not only understands it but enjoys it. For example, a newspaper account of a crime involves your understanding; but Stevenson's story of Markheim, a murderer—or Poe's tale, *A Cask of Amontillado,* stirs deeper feelings and responsiveness.

EXERCISE

IDENTIFYING LITERATURE

Write *L* next to each reference you believe is *literature.* Justify your choices.

1. Edwin A. Grozier: *100 Best Novels Condensed*
2. Milton Cross: *Complete Stories of the Great Operas*
3. William Shakespeare: *Julius Caesar*
4. Charles Dickens: *A Christmas Carol*
5. C. S. Hammond & Co.: *New Supreme World Atlas*
6. Arthur Conan Doyle: *The Adventures and Memoirs of Sherlock Holmes*
7. Mark Twain: *A Connecticut Yankee in King Arthur's Court*
8. Stephen Vincent Benét: *The Devil and Daniel Webster*
9. Herman Melville: *Moby Dick*
10. *Who's Who in America*
11. Paul Henry deKruif: *Microbe Hunters*
12. Donn Byrne: *Messer Marco Polo*
13. Thor Heyerdahl: *Kon-Tiki*
14. *Readers' Guide to Periodical Literature*
15. Kathryn Forbes: *Mama's Bank Account*
16. John Kieran: *The Story of the Olympic Games*
17. Robert Louis Stevenson: *Kidnapped*
18. Nathaniel Hawthorne: *The Scarlet Letter*
19. E. C. Brewer: *Dictionary of Phrase and Fable*
20. William J. Pelo: *The Secretary's Desk Book*

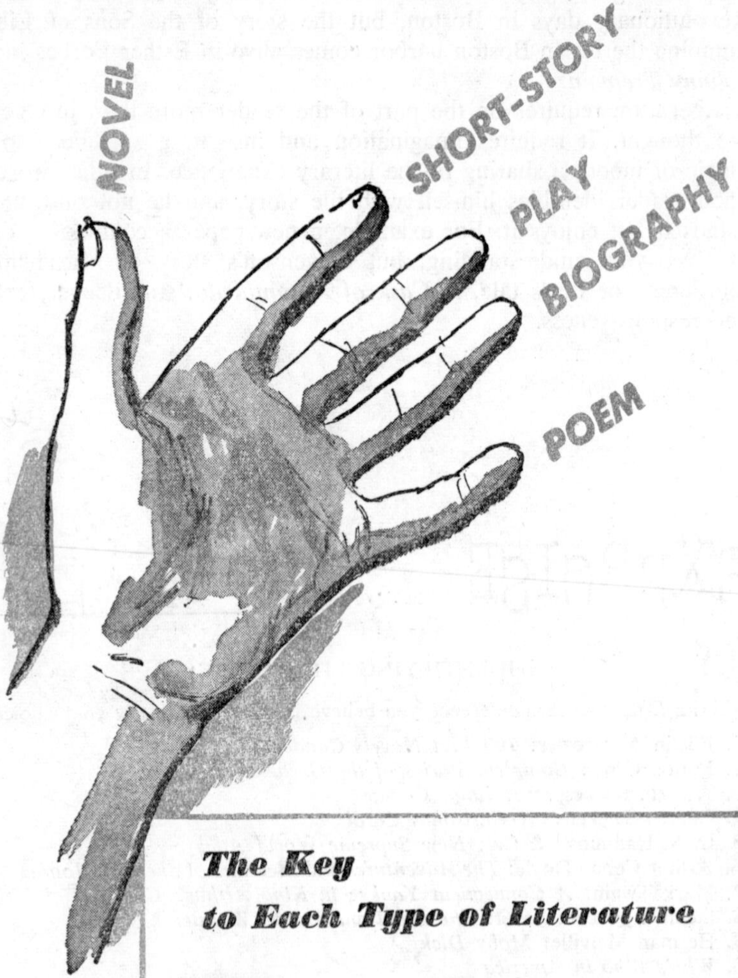

NOVEL

SHORT-STORY

PLAY

BIOGRAPHY

POEM

The Key to Each Type of Literature

NOVEL	unfolding plot
SHORT-STORY	single character
PLAY	struggle or conflict
BIOGRAPHY	personality growth
POEM	imagination and rhythm

APPRECIATING THE VARIOUS TYPES OF LITERATURE

To some children all books in the library are "stories." In one sense, they are right because most books tell a story. Yet, each book tells its story in a different way or in a special form. These various ways are called "types of literature," and include the *novel,* the *short-story,* the *play,* the *biography,* and the *poem.*

The **novel** uses characters and setting in a *plot* which unfolds the story. The heart of a **short-story** is the single *character* involved in an incident or setting. The main factor in a **play** is the *conflict* leading to a climax for the leading person in the story. A **biography** details the obstacles and events that helped shape the subject's *personality.* In a **poem,** the *emotion* and *rhythm* convey the thought through the use of imaginative language.

TECHNIQUE OF THE NOVEL

A novel is an extended narrative, anywhere from 100 to 1,000 pages long, telling a story in which main and minor characters are involved in plots and subplots. It contains a picture true to life, presented with details of setting and background to create the atmosphere of an age or particular country. It offers sufficient action and dialog, situations and events, persons and places, to make clear a cross section of social living. The main interest concerns the hero and/or heroine engaged in a series of complications that lead to a definite outcome. The reader's attention follows the line of action because of suspense regarding such problems as these:

What is the true identity of the hero? (*Ivanhoe*)
Will they find the pirate gold? (*Treasure Island*)
How can he obtain his inheritance? (*Kidnapped*)
Will he ever be allowed to return to his native land? (*Man Without a Country*)

The author gives the reader insight into the minds of his characters by explaining their motives and feelings. Pupils who skip these passages and read only the "conversation" often miss the story. Notice the time and place of the story because they influence the setting and customs of the novel's background.

Novel — Dickens: *David Copperfield*

1. The **plot** of *David Copperfield* was based on the author's own life. It told how the boy David spent an unhappy childhood after his widowed mother married a cruel man named Mr. Murdstone. David ran away from home and traveled from London to Dover in order to be with his aunt, Betsey Trotwood. Since David's mother died shortly, the aunt adopted David and sent him to school at Canterbury. There he boarded with his aunt's lawyer, Mr. Wickfield, and fell in love with his daughter Agnes. After graduation, David went to work for Mr. Spenlow and married his daughter Dora.

Meanwhile, by means of deceit, Mr. Wickfield's clerk, a mean and unattractive person named Uriah Heep, gained control of the business and wanted to wed lovely Agnes. A friend of David's, a kind but penniless father of a large family, Mr. Micawber, revealed the evil work of Uriah Heep in a public exposure. Dora died, the Micawbers went to Australia, and David traveled abroad for several years. On his return to England, he found his true love, Agnes, and was finally happily married.

This plot is rather long and complicated. The hero meets many persons, visits many places, gets involved in numerous situations. Yet, all these are tied together as a means of developing the story of David Copperfield from boyhood to manhood.

2. The **setting** was England about 1800. The scene changed from London to Dover and included the seaside at Yarmouth, the school at Canterbury, the old warehouse of Murdstone and Grimby, the brutal school of Master Creakle, Micawber in prison, the lawyer's office, and the happy home at last. The setting created the flavor of old England with its pictures of the countryside as well as the city and the seashore. It was the age of horse and carriage, of long sentimental letters, of pretty ladies swooning, of dashing heroes and black-hearted villains.

3. The **characters** filled the book with living persons: David Copperfield and his mother Clara; Peggotty and Barkis who was "willin' "; Murdstone and his cruel sister; Betsey Trotwood, the kindly aunt; Little Emily and Ham and the handsome but unreliable Steerforth; Micawber and his wife who "would never desert him"; Wickfield and his charming daughter Agnes and "the snake in the grass" called Uriah Heep; Dora Spenlow, the child bride who faded and died; school and work

companions like Mick Walker and Meally Potatoes. These characters gave the story of *David Copperfield* the dimensions of life, including the good and the bad.

Do you understand why Dickens said, "Of all my books, I like this the best"?

 ## TECHNIQUE OF THE SHORT-STORY

The short-story differs from the novel not only in length but in effect. Since it may have only ten or twenty pages instead of five hundred, it focuses attention on a single character, in a single situation, and a single setting. Furthermore, since it is read at a single sitting, it strives for brevity in reaching a unity of effect. Thus, it is much easier to follow the plot and to keep track of the main character. No wonder that the short-story is the most popular form of literature today.

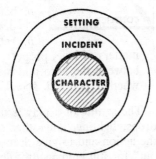

Short-Story—O. Henry: "The Ransom of Red Chief"

1. The **plot** of "The Ransom of Red Chief" is a simple situation. Two would-be bandits plan to kidnap a small boy and hope to collect $1500 in ransom money. Unfamiliar with the town, they happen to select as their victim a terrible youngster who makes their life miserable. The surprise ending shows these "desperate men" paying the father $250 to take the brat off their hands!

2. The **setting** is a sleepy town down South in Alabama, described as "flat as a flannel cake, and called Summit, of course." The story takes place in a hideout or cave in a mountain about two miles away from town. There Red Chief prepares to scalp the kidnapers.

3. The **characters** are four: Bill and Sam, the pair of kidnapers; Red Chief and his father, Ebenezer Dorset. The spotlight falls on the boy, Red Chief, a fearless rowdy, hated by the whole town. He enjoys tormenting his captors with his wild antics.

You will remember this short-story not only for its surprise ending, which is O. Henry's trademark, but also for its humor.

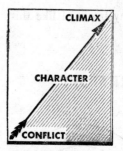

A play presents a story in the form of live conversation and action between persons on a stage. It differs from a novel or short-story in that the author does not speak directly to the reader (or listener) as he does in prose fiction. The plot unfolds itself in the form of a conflict which leads to a climax. The conflict may exist—

a. between the hero and himself, his wishes or desires struggling against his conscience; or

b. between the hero and some other person, over matters of love, property, business, social position, etc.; or

c. between the hero and his environment, the forces in his community whether political, social, economic, or religious.

The setting of a play is usually represented by painted scenes, backdrops, lighting, and other stage effects. The setting serves to localize the action and to give dramatic effect. The play really should be "acted out" for full enjoyment. Silent reading requires imagination to visualize all the entrances and exits, gestures and movements, tone and look of the actors.

Play — Constance Mackay: *The Three Wishes*

1. The **plot** of *The Three Wishes* concerns the foolishness of two persons who think they would be happier if they could get anything they wanted just by wishing. André and Lizette are husband and wife living in a simple cottage and dreaming of a palace. Into their ordinary home comes a Stranger with a piece of the Fairy Tree which will grant them three wishes. Instead of winning their hearts' desire, the couple get into mischief. First, the husband accidentally wishes "there was a fine brown pudding in that pot." Then, the wife angrily wishes the pot would stick to his nose. Finally, the wife repents and wishes "that the pudding would go." Thus, at the end of the play they are left just as poor as at the start, but they have learned the lesson that they can be happy together just as they are.

The conflict is between the couple's wild hopes and their simple, real-life existence. The climax occurs as the last wish returns them to normal conditions.

2. The **setting** is the inside of a country cottage showing a kitchen, a fireplace, a plain table and wooden chairs. Since it takes place in Breton (France), the two main characters are dressed as peasants with wooden shoes and colorful costumes. A few details suggest their workaday living: a spinning wheel, a cupboard, black bread and cheese, etc.

3. The **characters** are homey folks. The husband and wife are superstitious dreamers who long for the nicer things which they do not possess. The Stranger represents the spirit of discontent who tempts them with his magic branch of the Fairy Tree. At first, husband and wife are unbelieving, then delighted, then dismayed by their foolish wishes, angry with each other, and finally happy together. André and Lizette sit down at the table as the curtain falls and say, "Let's eat our black bread and be thankful!"

 ## TECHNIQUE OF BIOGRAPHY

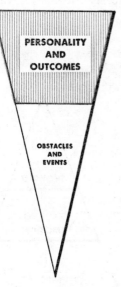

Biography means life-story. It is a record of a person's experience as he overcomes the obstacles and hardships of living to reach his goal or outcome. The reader watches events as they help to develop the subject's personality. The interest in the person is greater than the interest in action or setting. There is no real "plot" in the sense that a novel or a short-story arranges situations and complications. Here we have only the actual entanglements of life. If the subject of the biography has popular appeal, it is easy for teenagers to identify their own problems with those of the hero or heroine and gain insight into solutions.

Biography — Bob Feller: Strikeout Story

1. The **obstacles** and **events** that Bob Feller had to face were the typical ones of the average schoolboy who is "crazy" about baseball and hungry for fame. He was born in 1918 in a small town in Iowa and was

raised on a farm. Luckily, his parents were also baseball fans and encouraged the boy. His father bought Bob a complete baseball outfit when Bob was ten years old and trained him to pitch potatoes into the side of a barn. Bob developed a strong pitching arm and played on local teams. At seventeen, he pitched in the major league. At twenty-eight, he struck out 348 men in one season; that was the year (1946) when he pitched a no-hit, no-run game against the Yankees. Two years later, with the Cleveland Indians he helped win the World Series Championship.

2. Bob Feller's **personality** showed an honest ambition, love of hard work, and respect for his parents and elders. He admired his fourth-grade teacher, Miss Wycoff, because she encouraged him to keep playing and be happy as long as he also kept up with his studies. He was always faithful to his fans and courteous with news reporters. Souvenir hunters amused him, even when they tried to steal his cap. He remembered with gratitude the efforts of his parents and honored them with his success. He was an all-around good sport!

5 TECHNIQUE OF POETRY

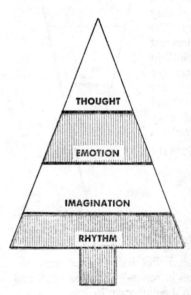

A poem tells a story through the use of emotion and imagination expressed in rhythm and form. The poem moves along with a pace that corresponds to the ideas and moods and happenings in the story. A gay mood stirs a quick lively rhythm; a sad one moves along with a slow, measured tread. The poet uses word-pictures to convey emotion and to describe persons. Having a lively imagination, the poet is always comparing things at hand with other things he has seen or remembered. For example, a lovely girl reminds him of a rose; the moon slipping through a cloud bank suggests a ghost ship sailing across a dark moor; the tang of October stirs the gypsy blood of a vagabond. These are called "figures of speech" because they lend vividness and force to language. Sometimes the word-order is reversed intentionally to get a rhyming word at the end of a line or to put stress on an idea; for example, the subject comes *last* in this line: "Strode, with a martial air, Miles Standish the Puritan Captain." Learn also "to read right over the capital letters" in poetry because they do not begin new sentences as in ordinary prose writing. Practice reading poetry *aloud* in order to get the rhythm, share the emotion, and stimulate the imagination.

Poem — Longfellow: "The Courtship of Miles Standish"

1. **Thought.** The story of "The Courtship of Miles Standish" is based on a proposal of marriage. The bold Puritan Captain wants to win the lovely Priscilla as his wife. He sends a handsome younger man, John Alden, to state his offer. Priscilla makes the famous reply to the young suitor, "Speak for yourself!" Out of loyalty to his friend, John keeps silent for himself. After a battle with the Indians, Standish is reported dead. John feels free to declare his love and prepares to wed Priscilla. Surprisingly, at the wedding, Standish reappears, safe and sound, and willing to forgive the lovers. The poem closes with a happy bridal procession.

2. **Emotion.** This story portrays many human feelings: love of man for woman; loyalty of man for his friend; sincerity of a woman; hatred of the Indians for the settlers; bravery of the colonists; sorrow over death; forgiveness and reunion of friends; joy and gladness in marriage.

3. **Imagination.** Many figures of speech and word pictures convey the emotions of the persons in the story. Some examples are these quotations as explained below:

a. The cannon is compared to a preacher—

"My brazen howitzer planted high on the roof of the church, a preacher who speaks to the purpose."

b. The hot temper of the Captain is compared to a chimney—

"He is a little chimney, and heated hot in a moment!"

c. The flight of arrows is compared to a snowstorm—

"Like a flurry of snow on the whistling wind of December, Swift and sudden and keen came a flight of feathery arrows."

d. The final uniting of the lovers is compared to two streams meeting in the forest—

"So these lives that had run thus far in separate channels Rushed together at last, and one was lost in the other."

4. **Rhythm.** The music of the verse matches the military mood of
the Captain in certain lines and then the tenderness of the lovers in
other passages. The lines do not rhyme at the end. They are rather
long and sweeping, often echoing lines from the Bible, which was familiar to the Puritans in the story. Most of the lines are called *hexam-
eters* because they contain six stressed syllables. A quotation to illustrate these qualities of rhythm follows: (Stressed and unstressed
syllables are indicated.)

| "So they re | turned to their | homes; but | Alden | lingered a | little, |

| Musing a | lone on the | shore, and | watching the | wash of the |
   billows |

| Round the | base of the | rock, and the | sparkle and | flash of the |
   sunshine, |

| Like the spi | rit of God, | moving | visibly | over the | waters." |

EXERCISES

LITERATURE

A. Correctly identify each of the following works of literature by writing next
to each title *novel, short-story, play, biography,* or *poem* as the case may be:

1. Oliver Wendell Holmes: OLD IRONSIDES
2. Arthur Conan Doyle: THE SPECKLED BAND
3. Thomas Hughes: TOM BROWN'S SCHOOL DAYS
4. Eugene Pillot: TWO CROOKS AND A LADY
5. William F. Cody: ADVENTURES OF BUFFALO BILL
6. Howard Pyle: MEN OF IRON
7. Stewart Edward White: DANIEL BOONE, WILDERNESS SCOUT
8. Washington Irving: THE LEGEND OF SLEEPY HOLLOW
9. Katharine Lee Bates: AMERICA THE BEAUTIFUL
10. Lady Gregory: THE WORKHOUSE WARD
11. Booth Tarkington: PENROD'S BUSY DAY
12. Edward Everett Hale: THE MAN WITHOUT A COUNTRY

13. Henry Wadsworth Longfellow: KING ROBERT OF SICILY
14. Mark Twain: HUCKLEBERRY FINN
15. Herbert E. Bates: THE KING'S ENGLISH
16. Carl Sandburg: ABE LINCOLN GROWS UP
17. James Russell Lowell: THE FIRST SNOWFALL
18. Rudyard Kipling: WEE WILLIE WINKIE
19. Charles E. Lindbergh: WE
20. Thomas Augustine Daly: MIA CARLOTTA

B. Correctly match the descriptions in column *A* with the items in column *B*.

Column A

1. marked by strong emotion, word-pictures, and rhythm
2. singleness of purpose and single main character
3. intensive reading, "digging in" for facts and meaning
4. conflict expressed in dialog and leading to a climax
5. story of a subject's life and effect of events on personality
6. long series of incidents in a plot unfolding gradually
7. free choice of literary selections for enjoyment and relaxation
8. surprise ending in a humorous account of a kidnaping
9. a love-triangle in which youth wins against age
10. a poor orphan grows up to be a successful businessman

Column B

a. Ransom of Red Chief
b. play
c. recreational reading
d. David Copperfield
e. poetry
f. Christmas Carol
g. novel
h. Courtship of Miles Standish
i. work-study reading
j. biography
k. Man Without a Country
l. essay
m. short-story

C. Write an analysis for five different types of literature following the outline for each as illustrated in this section. Choose at least one from each of these groups, or any other that is recommended by your teacher.

NOVELS

1. Frances Hodgson Burnett: *The Secret Garden*
2. Mark Twain: *The Prince and the Pauper*
3. Louisa May Alcott: *Little Women*
4. Mary O'Hara: *My Friend Flicka*
5. Marjorie Kinnan Rawlings: *The Yearling*

SHORT-STORIES

1. Mary Raymond Shipman Andrews: "The Perfect Tribute"
2. Victor Hugo: "Fight with an Octopus"
3. Washington Irving: "Rip Van Winkle"
4. Richard Harding Davis: "Gallegher"
5. Charles Tenny Jackson: "The Sea Horse of Grand Terre"

PLAYS

1. François Coppée: *The Violin Maker of Cremona*
2. Allan Monkhouse: *The Grand Cham's Diamond*
3. Percival Wilde: *Confessional*

4. James Barrie: *The Old Lady Shows Her Medals*
5. Rachel Lyman Field: *The Fifteenth Candle*

BIOGRAPHIES

1. Eve Curie: *Madame Curie*
2. Mildred Pace: *Clara Barton*
3. Will James: *Lone Cowboy*
4. Frank Graham: *Lou Gehrig, a Quiet Hero*
5. Anne Frank: *The Diary of Anne Frank*

POEMS

1. John Greenleaf Whittier: "Barbara Frietchie"
2. Alfred Tennyson: "The Lady of Shalott"
3. Robert W. Service: "The Cremation of Sam McGee"
4. Edna St. Vincent Millay: "The Ballad of the Harp-Weaver"
5. Robert Browning: "The Pied Piper of Hamelin"

 # RECOMMENDED READING LISTS FOR GUIDANCE

Reading books for enjoyment leads to the development of literary taste. Often, the choice of books depends on your interests or hobbies. Sometimes, the selection is based on a problem, such as finding a career, understanding other people, historical backgrounds, sports and games, etc. Various printed book lists offer valuable suggestions to help the reader locate the kind of book he likes. Here are some useful guides to reading that you can consult in your school or public library.

BOOK LISTS

Granger, Edith: *Index to Poetry and Recitations* (verse)
Firkins, I. T. E.: *Index to Short Stories* (fiction)
Logasa and Ver Nooy: *Index to One-Act Plays* (drama)
Readers' Guide to Periodical Literature (magazines)
Becker, May: *Adventures in Reading* (miscellaneous)
Bennett, J. O.: *Much Loved Books* (miscellaneous)
Taba, Hilda: *Reading Ladders for Human Relations* (miscellaneous)
Williams, Mabel: *Books for Young People* (N. Y. Public Library) (miscellaneous)
Wilson, H. W.: *Essay and General Literature Index* (miscellaneous)
Arbuthnot, May Hill: *Too Good to Miss*
Neville, Mark: National Council of Teachers of English—*Books for You* (miscellaneous) (recommended for purchase by pupils; inexpensive and excellent)

What should you read?

Here is God's plenty! These books have been enjoyed by other boys and girls. Try them. Have fun.

GUIDE TO 100 SELECTED BOOKS

Adventure and Mystery

AUTHOR	TITLE	DESCRIPTION
Atwater, Montgomery	*Avalanche Patrol*	Exciting experiences of a snow-ranger in the mountains.
Corbett, James	*Man-eaters of Kumaon*	Tiger-hunting expeditions by fearless big-game hunters.
Cousteau and Dumas	*The Silent World*	Marvelous view of strange creatures and life underseas.
Floherty, John	*Our F.B.I.*	Inside story of crime and criminals tracked by government agents.
Grace, Dick	*Visibility Unlimited*	Daredevil test pilot gives true account of stunt flying experiences.
Kyne, Peter B.	*Cappy Ricks*	Shrewd owner of large shipping business matches wits with his son-in-law.
Rinehart, Mary Roberts	*Circular Staircase*	Topnotch writer of murder-mysteries shows clever detective work.
Stevenson, Robert Louis	*Dr. Jekyll and Mr. Hyde*	Thrilling portrait of a person who can split himself into either a good doctor or an evil monster.

Twain, Mark	*Pudd'nhead Wilson*	The mistaken identity of two young men involved in a murder solved by a set of fingerprints.
Van Dine, S. S.	*Bishop Murder Case*	Detective story of an unusual case solved by a slick sleuth.
White, Stewart Edward	*Daniel Boone, Wilderness Scout*	Real life story and true adventures of a famous scout blazing a trail through the Indian country to Kentucky.
Wibberley, Leonard	*Deadmen's Cave*	Pirate treasure in the kind of thriller that keeps you full of suspense.

Sports, Games, Hobbies

AUTHOR	TITLE	SPECIALTY
Bufano, Remo	*Be a Puppet Showman*	Puppet making
Eadie, Thomas	*I Like Diving*	Diving adventures
Frankel and Frankel	*101 Best Games for Teenagers*	Assorted pastimes
Henie, Sonja	*Wings on My Feet*	Ice skating
Jacobs, Helen	*Judy, Tennis Ace*	Tennis playing
Lowell, Frederick	*Jiu-jitsu*	Oriental wrestling
Meany, Tom	*The Artful Dodgers*	Professional baseball
Miers, Earl S.	*Touchdown Trouble*	Football playing
Pelus, Marie J.	*Yankee Ballerina*	Stage dancing
Sheridan, Martin	*Comics and Their Creators*	Cartoon illustrating
Stiles, Kent	*Stamps*	Stamp collecting
Thurston, Howard	*400 Tricks You Can Do*	Variety of magic tricks
Young, Dick	*Roy Campanella*	Baseball playing

Humorous Stories

AUTHOR	TITLE	KIND OF FUN
Bowman, J. C.	*Pecos Bill, the Greatest Cowboy of All Time*	Tall tales about a cowboy who was lost as a baby and raised by a coyote till found by his brother.
Day, Clarence S.	*Life with Father*	Crotchety but lovable father raises a tempest over family incidents, such as opening mail, making telephone calls, going to church, etc.
Forbes, Kathryn	*Mama's Bank Account*	Shrewd Norwegian mother manages to conceal her poverty and encourages her children to grow up confident and resourceful.
Gilbreth and Carey	*Cheaper by the Dozen*	Twelve children in one family make life full of unexpected crises and funny happenings.
Irving, Washington	*Legend of Sleepy Hollow*	Hilarious love affair of Ichabod Crane who loses Katrina Van Tassel to the headless horseman on a moonlit night in the Catskill Mountains.
Lawson, Robert	*Ben and Me*	Amazing life of Benjamin Franklin as written by a mouse, Amos, who lived in Ben's fur cap.
MacGregor, Ellen	*Miss Pickerell Goes to Mars*	Amusing science fiction tells how it feels to ride a rocket ship and what you may find on a strange planet.

Scoggin, M. C.	*Chucklebait*	A fine collection of funny stories of all kinds used to catch the reader with "chuckle bait."
Skinner and Kimbrough	*Our Hearts Were Young and Gay*	Two young American girls tell their exciting experiences traveling abroad to gay "Paree" for a holiday.
Smith, E. S.	*Just for Fun*	Another collection of humorous tales and poems just to make you laugh at doughnuts, new cars, bears, etc.
Tarkington, Booth	*Penrod*	Taking medicine, borrowing his sister's love letter, getting into trouble always made Penrod's life busier than any other boy's.
Travers, P. L.	*Mary Poppins Comes Back*	Magical fairy tales telling how Mary appears on a kite string and later disappears on a merry-go-round horse.
Twain, Mark	*Adventures of Huckleberry Finn*	Boys enjoy sailing on a raft along the muddy Mississippi, visiting caves, and fishing, better than going to school.

Animals and Pets

AUTHOR	TITLE	KIND OF ANIMAL
Cothren, Marion	*Pigeon Heroes*	Carrier pigeons
Eardley-Wilmot, S.	*Life of a Tiger*	Wild and tame beasts

Henderson, J. Y. and Taplinger, R.	*Circus Doctor*	All kinds of trained circus animals
James, Will	*Smoky, the Cow-horse*	Western cow-pony
Kipling, Rudyard	*All the Mowgli Stories*	Jungle animals
Knight, Eric	*Lassie Come Home*	Yorkshire collie
McCracken, Harold	*Lions 'n Tigers 'n Everything*	Various jungle beasts, "big game"
Mayer, Charles	*Jungle Beasts I Have Captured*	Elephants, pythons, rhinoceroses
O'Hara, Mary	*My Friend Flicka*	Ranch horse
Ollivant, Alfred	*Bob, Son of Battle*	Sheep dog
Seton, Ernest T.	*Wild Animals I Have Known*	Rabbit, fox, mustang
Terhune, Albert P.	*Lad: A Dog*	Sunnybank collie
Wright, William H.	*Ben the Black Bear*	Bear cub

Travel and Discovery

AUTHOR	TITLE	REGIONS OF THE WORLD
Coffman, Ramon P.	*Famous Explorers for Young People*	Sea, land, and air explorers from Columbus and Marco Polo to Livingstone and others in brief accounts.
Cottler, Joseph and Jaffe, Haym	*Heroes of Civilization*	Describes the achievements of explorers, inventors, and scientists, such as Magellan, Fulton, Curie, Amundsen.
Duvoisin, Roger A.	*They Put Out to Sea*	Early traders, explorers, mapmakers, including Phoenicians, Carthaginians, Alexander, Genghis Khan.

Gallant, Roy A.	*Exploring the Moon*	An imaginary trip to the moon to explore its craters, mountains, and other strange features.
Halliburton, Richard	*Royal Road to Romance*	Exciting personal travels by plane to the mysterious lands and peoples of the East by a gay playboy.
Hartman, Gertrude	*Builders of the Old World*	Egypt, Greece, Rome and even prehistoric man are included in this account showing how geography influences history.
Hewes, Agnes	*Spice Ho!*	Venice, Portugal, England, Holland, and America each played a part in the spice trade in history.
Johnson, Martin	*Lion*	Lion hunting in Africa with a camera is more exciting than with a gun.
Lucas, Mary S.	*Vast Horizons*	India, Africa, Mongolia, and other unknown areas were explored by Vasco da Gama, Marco Polo, etc., seeking trade routes.
Owen, Russell	*Conquest of the North and South Poles*	Peary's attempts to reach the North Pole and Byrd's trips to the Antarctic reveal hardships and scientific results.
Reed, William M. and Bronson, Wilfrid S.	*Sea for Sam*	Discoveries of the origins of continents and oceans and strange sea life provide excellent science reading.

AUTHOR	TITLE	PEOPLE AND PLACES
Van Loon, Hendrik, W.	*Story of Mankind*	Egypt, France, Britain, Russia, the United States, Rome, and the history of the human race from prehistoric times are traced up to the present.
Verne, Jules	*Mysterious Island*	Story of travel by balloon with five prisoners of war and a dog stranded on an island in the Pacific; sequel to *Twenty Thousand Leagues Under the Sea.*

Other Lands and Other People

AUTHOR	TITLE	PEOPLE AND PLACES
Bothwell, Jean and Sowers, P. A.	*Golden Letter to Siam*	Manners and customs of the Siamese, now famous because of *The King and I* in movie and stage play.
Bragdon, Lillian	*The Land of Joan of Arc*	Short history of France with maps and photographs showing the country, cities, customs, and activities.
De Angeli, Marguerite	*The Door in the Wall*	Story of a boy in London during medieval days and how he helped save a castle attacked by enemies of the king.
Fuller, H. K.	*Manuel Goes to Sea*	Nova Scotia fishing stories about the brave men who dare the deeps to make a "catch."
Gollomb, Joseph	*Albert Schweitzer, Genius in the Jungle*	African village where a dedicated doctor with reverence for life works among the poor natives.

Guareschi, Giovanni	*The Little World of Don Camillo*	A small town in Italy since World War II, under a Communist mayor who is outwitted by a parish priest, Don Camillo.
Kelly, Eric	*The Trumpeter of Krakow*	The ancient city of Poland during the fifteenth century in an adventure and mystery story showing bravery and self-sacrifice.
Lindbergh, Anne	*North to the Orient*	China and other countries were visited by Anne and her famous husband, Charles Lindbergh, on a goodwill tour by plane.
Nevins, Albert J.	*Adventures of Duc of Indochina*	Vietnam and Vietminh clashes between peasants and Communists provide a village boy with a chance to help his own people.
Pyle, Howard	*Otto of the Silver Hand*	Germany in the days of chivalry when stories clanked with armor and damsels were rescued by brave knights on horseback.
Tarshis, Elizabeth	*The Village That Learned To Read*	Mexican village in which the setting up of a school creates a problem for Pedro, who would rather be a bullfighter than a schoolboy.
Wong, Jade Snow	*Fifth Chinese Daughter*	Delightful account of ancient and modern customs in Chinese family life with reverence for ancestors and traditions.

Occupations and Careers

AUTHOR	TITLE	KIND OF JOB
Caudill, Rebecca	*Susan Cornish*	Teaching in a one-room country schoolhouse in a poor area offers chance for social service work.
Floherty, John J.	*Troopers All*	State Police in the U. S. patrol the highways to maintain safety and protect life and property.
Hill, Margaret	*Hostess in the Sky*	Airline hostess needs poise, health, coolness to perform her duties well.
Kjelgaard, James A.	*Forest Patrol*	Forest rangers protect our forests and wildlife against poachers and fires in rugged regions.
Lewellen, John	*Boy Scientist*	Famous scientists from Galileo to Einstein offer inspiration through brief biographical sketches about their work and times.
Lingenfelter, Mary R.	*Vocations for Girls*	Many occupations for women today in various fields of work are based upon personal ability, interest, and training.
MacDonald, Zillah K.	*Rosemary Wins Her Cap*	Nursing combines hard work, service to others, and sometimes romance and excitement.
Morgan, Alfred P.	*First Chemistry Book for Boys and Girls*	Chemistry experiments may be safely tried in the home if you carefully follow the directions.

Nash, Eleanor A.	*Kit Corelli: TV Stylist*	Selecting dress designs and outfits for television actresses helps put across dramatic productions.
Paradis, Adrian A.	*For Immediate Release*	Public relations is a growing field, very important in business, labor, government, etc.
Poole, Lynn	*Diving for Science*	Divers equipped with the latest devices risk their lives for science and for fun to discover new knowledge.
Winchell, Prentice	*Danger! Detectives Working*	Detectives in real life must investigate their sources of information and follow up clues by hard, patient work.

Boys and Girls Worth Knowing

AUTHOR	TITLE	PERSONAL EXPERIENCES
Angelo, Valenti	*Big Little Island*	Lorenzo, an Italian boy, learns our ways of living and playing in the streets of Manhattan (New York City).
Bolton, Sarah K.	*Lives of Girls Who Became Famous*	Short sketches of such noted women as Florence Nightingale, Jenny Lind, Rosa Bonheur, Helen Keller, etc.
Boylston, Helen	*Sue Barton, Student Nurse*	Popular book on the experiences of a beginning nurse; also try *Sue Barton, Head Nurse*.

Daly, Maureen	*Seventeenth Summer*	Angela, not too popular a teenager, blossoms during her seventeenth summer: mixes in with the crowd, meets a boy with a boat, etc.
Forbes, Esther	*Johnny Tremain*	Colonial days in Boston find Johnny an apprentice to a silversmith, and later with the Sons of Liberty he dumps tea in the harbor.
Hémon, Louis	*Maria Chapdelaine*	Love story of a Canadian girl, Maria, for a fur trapper in the lonely North woods during pioneer days.
Meader, Stephen	*Bulldozer*	Ambitious boy in Maine enjoys the struggle when he starts a contracting business with a rebuilt old bulldozer.
Paine, Albert B.	*Girl in White Armor*	Joan of Arc was a simple peasant girl of France, yet she became the general of the armies of France when inspired by "her voices."
Pyle, Howard	*Men of Iron*	Myles Falworth was a brave, young English squire in the days of chivalry and he won his knighthood the hard way.
Rawlings, Marjorie K.	*The Yearling*	Jody was a young, sensitive boy who loved the spotted fawn "yearling" that destroyed his father's crops.

Rourke, Constance	*Davy Crockett*	This is a popular biography about an exciting figure in American history and it combines facts with legends for fine reading.
Runbeck, Margaret L.	*Miss Boo Is Sixteen*	Miss Boo is even more engaging as a teenager than as an unpredictable little girl in the famous series about "Miss Boo."

EXERCISE

LITERATURE APPRECIATION

Appreciation of literature consists of understanding the thought, sharing the emotion, and responding to both. We do this quite naturally when we talk about books to our friends. Here you are asked to give your *personal reaction* to literature in another way, namely, by writing short paragraphs. Be frank in stating your preferences and be able to support your opinions by referring to actual books, etc.

1. Sometimes in our reading we meet characters who are not the kind of people we would like for our friends. Choose a character that you have met in your reading and tell in about 100 words why you would not like him or her as a friend or companion.
2. Most boys and girls like animals. Reading offers them an opportunity to enjoy animal friends. Mention two animals you have read about and in about 100 words tell why you enjoyed reading about them.
3. Many of the stories we read would be very interesting if presented on television. Give the name of a story that contains humorous or exciting incidents and in about 100 words describe one incident that you would like to see on television.

4. Choose two poems you have read. Give the titles and authors of the poems, and in about 50 words each tell why you did or did not enjoy reading them.

5. Each year, awards are given for the best books and literature for young people. Suppose you were asked to give your opinion about one book or selection to be considered for an award. From the reading you have done, state your choice and in about 100 words give the reasons for your choice.

6. The ending of a book pleases us when we feel that the characters get what they deserve. Name one character that has impressed you, and in about 100 words tell what he (or she) did to deserve the reward or punishment he (or she) received.

7. Some characters in our reading show in their actions fairness and consideration for others; other characters show that they place their own welfare or desires above those of others. Select a character from your reading and show in about 100 words how this character is fair and considerate of others or how he (or she) looks out for his (or her) own welfare and desires.

8. In these times it is more important than ever for us as world citizens to increase our knowledge of people whose lives are very much different from our own. In about 100 words show how a selection you have read has increased your knowledge of people from other lands or from backgrounds different from yours. Mention the title and the author.

9. Suppose that you have been selected by your literature class to write for your school paper a short review of a poem, a humorous story, or an adventure story. In about 100 words write a review that will make your schoolmates want to read the original poem or story. Mention the title and the author.

10. Some stories or poems are enjoyed best by boys and others by girls. Select a poem or a story that you think would appeal especially to a boy (or a girl) and explain why in about 100 words.

11. Write a paragraph of at least five sentences in answer to each of the following:
    a. Why should a boy or girl read modern biographies about popular heroes?
    b. Name a book or story (other than a textbook) that helped you to learn more about the world around you and tell how your understanding was helped.
    c. What kind of poetry do you like best? Mention at least one poem of this kind.
    d. How can you judge whether a book that you have read was really worth reading?
    e. Name a story or poem that you have read more than once and tell why you were interested enough to read it again.

12. No doubt you have a favorite center of interest in reading. Perhaps you like to read about animals or inventions or adventure or some other subject. State your favorite center of interest and recommend a story in that field. In about 100 words tell why that story is a good choice for anyone having the same center of interest.

13. In your reading experience you have read nonfiction (true stories) and fiction (not true stories). Tell which kind of reading you prefer and in about 100 words explain why.

14. During your school life you read many books. Occasionally you read a passage, a poem, or a story that you remember because you liked it so much. From your reading, select something that you remember because of the good

impression it made on you. In about 100 words show why you made such a choice.

15. Sir William Osler, a great English physician, once said, "We are here, not to get all we can get out of life for ourselves but to try to make the lives of others happier." From your reading, select a story (either prose or poetry) and in at least 100 words show how someone's unselfishness, devotion, companionship, or helpfulness brought happiness or light to another's life.

16. Some people say that they do not like poetry because they cannot get the meaning or story that the poet is trying to tell. Select a poem that you have read and in about 100 words give the meaning or tell the story of the poem selected.

17. Choose a story from your reading that you would like to see in a motion picture. In about 100 words explain why you think it would make a good motion picture, telling enough of the story to enable your readers to judge its worth.

18. During your school life you have either read or have had read to you many books, magazines or current publications. In about 100 words show how such reading has helped you. Give examples if you wish.

19. In at least 100 words write an account of an imaginary trip that you have taken by reading a story. Name some of the characters that you met in the story and tell where you went on this trip.

20. Choose a story that you have enjoyed that you think might be translated for the children of European countries to read. In at least 100 words tell why you have selected this particular story for this purpose.

21. By reading we are able to have experiences and gain information from which we develop opinions and judgment about life. In about 100 words, describe the type of reading you should do in order to be better prepared for life as a wholesome and worthwhile citizen.

22. Occasionally in your reading you find a character who seems to be just the kind of person you would like to have for a friend in real life. From your reading select such a character and in about 100 words tell why he or she would make you a good friend.

23. Choose a story from your reading that you think could be well adapted for use on the radio. In about 100 words explain why you think it could be adapted for radio use, telling enough of the story to enable your readers to judge its worth.

24. In at least 100 words describe a place that you have visited in your imagination while reading a story. Name two or three of the characters that you met in this place and tell how they were connected with the place.

25. Reading helps us in various ways. Sometimes it gives us useful information. Sometimes it provides pleasure by showing us the humor in life. Sometimes it brings inspiration through a beautiful or noble character or again it warns us through the unhappy experiences of those who do wrong. From your reading select and name a work that has helped you in one or more of these ways. In at least 100 words make clear what you have gained from the work selected.

RADIO
TELEVISION
MOVIES

Mass Media of Communication

Remember that every hour you give to these activities is a portion of
your life. Life is worth living by itself, not by substitutes for the real
thing. Use these in moderation; never let them abuse you.

NEWSPAPERS
MAGAZINES
COMICS

VI ENRICHMENT THROUGH OTHER CHANNELS OF COMMUNICATION

One of the aims of the English language arts is to develop the habitual and intelligent use of the mass media of communication—radio, television, movies, newspapers, magazines, comics—and to become aware of propaganda. These are called *mass media* because they reach large audiences of readers, viewers, and listeners.

The chief problem in the widespread use of these various sources of information and entertainment is mainly one of standards of good taste in selecting a balanced diet for fun and instruction. The temptation for youngsters is to choose the sensational, the cheap, the exciting, the fantastic; and to omit or ignore the worthwhile, the cultural, the approved types offering genuine enrichment rather than mere time-killing pastime. Feeding the mind and emotions with trash can only result in low-level personal values and distorted notions of reality.

Study the following sections carefully with a view to formulating sensible standards and good habits in enjoying the various media of mass communication.

A GUIDE TO TELEVISION PROGRAMS

The latest giant in the field of home entertainment and the one having the most powerful influence on family life in America is unquestionably—television! The vast networks with their supporting advertisers as sponsors reach into millions of homes, night and day. The opportunities for entertainment and relaxation are endless on TV, and youngsters as well as grownups enjoy watching some of the numerous plays, sports, comedies, telecasts, and quiz shows. Recently, the public has learned to tune in to more of the educational programs for balanced viewing: panel discussions, film documentaries, personal interviews, modern dramas, music festivals, and scientific experiments.

HARMFUL INFLUENCE OF TV	SUGGESTED REMEDIES
A *specialist in the study of mass media* recently wrote that a youngster spends an average of 15 to 25 hours a week with his eyes glued to a TV screen. This has a greater force than the home and the school in shaping the child. A *judge* in a Children's Court said that many cases of juvenile delinquency could be traced to the bad effect of horror stories, murders, and robberies on TV. A *psychiatrist* reported some mental cases had been the result of disturbance stimulated by TV programs.	All these responsible persons conclude that there are two steps necessary to stop this harmful influence: *First,* children should cut down the amount of time spent watching TV and instead engage in other wholesome activities. *Second,* parents and teachers should help youngsters develop the ability to judge program offerings so that they will become more intelligent in selecting shows.

In order to help the pupils in the class to work out a set of acceptable *standards for judging* television programs, various committees or individuals may prepare oral or written reports on such questions as these:

1. How many hours a week should be spent viewing TV?
   (Consider the time left for meeting friends, engaging in hobbies, reading books, playing ball, helping with house chores, etc.)
2. What are the types of programs offered on TV?
   (Consider entertainment, information, instruction, etc.)
3. What are the educational uses of TV?
   (Consider school subject areas, world affairs, family problems, etc.)
4. How has TV influenced our thinking and habits?
   (Consider music, arts, sports, politics, leisure-time activities, etc.)

Pupils may discover other ways of measuring the good and the bad features of TV programs by reading about the standards established by such critics or agencies as the following:

1. The newspaper critics who review TV programs for the daily press: Harriet van Horne, John Crosby, etc.
2. The show business magazines (*Variety* and *TV Guide*) which indicate preferences for shows.

Television

Don't be glued to the set! Budget your time to allow for viewing, reading books, playing outdoors, meeting friends, going places, helping at home, etc.

The lure of TV is based chiefly on its visual as well as auditory appeal. This attraction of eye and ear leads to simple "watching" or passive condition. It requires no imagination and promotes no participation or responsiveness. Therefore, the youngster becomes a kind of sponge just soaking in everything, good or bad. Since crime, sex, and violence dominate most of the action stories, the influence on character weakens the solid virtues needed for moral growth. To balance this, a TV Log or schedule supervised by parents and limited in number of hours seems a practical solution.

CLASS PROJECT IN TV

An excellent way of getting students to develop better standards and habits of televiewing is to organize a class project with the purpose of preparing a TV guide. Here is a brief description, together with samples, of the manner in which a class of average boys and girls worked it out under the guidance of the teacher. The youngsters were assigned or selected to do the following:

JOBS	ASSIGNMENTS
Editors (2)	Prepare all material for publication.
Cover designers (3)	Sketch an original cover for the booklet.
Typists (8)	Neatly typewrite the material on stencils.
Mimeographers (2)	Run off and staple together all material.
Program critics (28)	Write original reviews of TV shows.

They spent three weeks in discussing, preparing, and assembling materials. The class approved all final selections. At the end, the results appeared in the form of a mimeographed booklet which was distributed to all members of the class. It contained critical reviews of 25 programs written in paragraph style and a weekly TV guide listing the name of each program, day, time, channel, and type.

STUDENT TV REVIEWS

CONFIDENTIAL FILE

Confidential File is on every Wednesday from 9:00 to 9:30 P.M. on Channel 11. *Confidential File* is a program that portrays authentic cases. Every week they show a short film on one particular topic. Paul Coates, the interviewer, interviews people who are concerned with the problem on the show, such as blindness, narcotics, comics, and old age. They had a film that showed how blind children live and work. A blind person can live normally like any other person even though he lives in a dark world. A program everybody remembered was the one about horror and mystery comics and how they affect children who read them. A group of boys were reading horror comics and it showed how a man killed someone with a rock. After reading the comic, one boy picked up a rock and held it over his friend's head.

TV STAMP ALBUM

TV Stamp Album is on Sundays at 5:45 on Channel 13. It is a short program but during this short period of time you learn many interesting facts about stamps. Each week they have a guest who tells about his stamps. One week, host Jack Taub's guest was Civil War historian, Van Dyk MacBride. We saw his collection of stamps and among the stamps was a rare letter from the infamous Andersonville prison. Even if you do not have a stamp album, you will enjoy this program and, who knows, you may become a stamp enthusiast.

DU PONT CAVALCADE THEATER

Du Pont Cavalcade Theater is on every Tuesday at 9:30 on Channel 7. The stories of famous men and women are dramatized. One interesting story was about the test pilot who had tested the first plane to stand upright called, by the United States Navy, the *Pogo Stick*. The commercials are also educational. The sponsor is the Du Pont Company, makers of synthetic fibers, and they often show how some products are made today and how they used to be made.

YOU ARE THERE

This program takes you back in history to many important events. It is a very educational program. Many people are unaware of some of the great events that happened in our history. The events are shown to us exactly the way it was then, except "You Are There."

They bring you back to such events as, "Eli Whitney Invents the Cotton Gin," "The First Texas Oil Strike," "Washington Crosses the Delaware," "The Discovery of Radium," "The Chicago Fire," and "Benedict Arnold's Plot Against West Point."

The last was particularly interesting. Arnold, hero of the battle of Saratoga and commander of the West Point fort, met secretly at Belmont, on the Hudson River, with a courier from the British warship *Vulture*. Walter Cronkite and his news staff reported the results of the traitorous act.

On this program, you not only learn history, but you also enjoy it.

EXERCISES

TELEVISION

A. Match the programs in column *A* with their descriptions in column *B*.

Column *A*

1. *Hallmark Hall of Fame*
2. *Youth Forum*
3. *Playhouse 90*
4. *Omnibus*
5. *Life Is Worth Living*
6. *Adventures of Robin Hood*
7. *Famous All-Star Movie*
8. *Ted Steele's Band Stand*
9. *$64,000 Question*
10. *Meet the Press*

Column *B*

a. exciting episodes in Merry England
b. Bishop Sheen talks on democracy, Communism, faith, and family living
c. quiz contest on art, sports, and other fields
d. re-showings of former hit films by Metro-Goldwyn-Mayer
e. daily dance sessions for teenagers
f. informative and entertaining variety of scenes from plays and books
g. live dramatic show, staged and planned in good taste
h. alert youngsters discuss current problems
i. interviews with outstanding persons and reporters
j. live show in color on Sunday night

B. Here are some suggestions for TV activities:

1. In your notebook or at the blackboard, list programs viewed by members of the class, and discuss favorite or disliked shows.
2. Compare a radio and a television broadcast of the same program; e.g., a sports event.
3. Write letters to studios commenting on programs, either in favor of or against sponsored or sustaining programs.
4. Discuss television advertising as to the number of interruptions, quality of ads, value to viewers, etc.
5. Visit a local television station and write a brief report on the transmission of a program from the studio to the viewers.
6. Compare pupils' own reactions to television broadcasts (such as the "spectaculars") with professional reviews in newspapers or magazines.
7. Hold a teenage forum discussion of school problems in the style of a TV broadcast.
8. Keep a class bulletin board of recommended TV programs.
9. Write to favorite TV performers telling them how you enjoyed a particular program.

C. After class discussion, take a vote on your favorite people and programs that give you the most enjoyment on television. If possible, mimeograph or copy the following ballot so that each pupil will have a chance to vote. Then, enter the final count or class tally below. As a follow up, send the results to one or two television studios, as from a "fan club."

TV FAVORITES OF OUR CLASS

☆ MALE VOCALIST _____

☆ FEMALE VOCALIST _____

☆ COMEDIAN _____

☆ COMEDIENNE _____

☆ MALE PERSONALITY _____

☆ FEMALE PERSONALITY _____

☆ SPORTSCASTER _____

☆ VARIETY PROGRAM _____

☆ DRAMATIC PROGRAM _____

☆ SITUATION COMEDY _____

☆ NEWS PROGRAM _____

☆ CHILDREN'S PROGRAM _____

☆ FORUM PROGRAM _____

☆ DAYTIME PROGRAM _____

☆ QUIZ SHOW _____

☆ EDUCATIONAL SERIES _____

☆ PANEL SHOW _____

Class _____

Teacher _____

School _____

This ballot speaks for _____ members of our class.

HOW TO READ THE NEWSPAPER INTELLIGENTLY

Newspapers bring the latest happenings here and abroad into the hands of the public. Besides gathering news, the daily papers sell advertising and mold opinion. So important are newspapers as a means of communication that "freedom of the press" has become a tradition in American history. Here in the United States there are about 1760 daily newspapers published in English. The total circulation is about 57 million daily. Thus, you can see that practically every family in America has the habit of getting at least one paper a day. Which is your favorite newspaper?

What's the latest news? Our daily newspapers are a kind of living history. Keep up-to-date with what is going on in the world. Read the paper intelligently.

EXERCISES

NEWSPAPERS

A. An interesting classroom exercise is to have the members of the class bring in various newspapers and compare them as follows:

1. Which newspapers are sensational tabloids? Why?
2. Which newspapers are very conservative? Why?
3. Which newspapers are liberal or progressive? Why?
4. Find out the owners or "chain" for each paper. How does this influence the news presented?
5. Figure out the proportion of space devoted to news and to advertising; a rough calculation of the number of pages or columns will serve the purpose. Why are some papers 90% advertising? Can an "adless" newspaper remain in business? Why?
6. Why do the tabloids play up stories dealing with crime, sex, murder, etc., with pages of pictures?
7. Why do certain full-length newspapers use such slogans as "All the news that's fit to print?"
8. How do you account for a daily circulation of over 2 million for a tabloid?
9. Since all these newspapers receive most of the foreign news from "syndicates," figure out which of these news services supplies most of the items: Associated Press, United Press, International News Service.
10. Compare the index or table of contents in two full-length papers to discover the wide variety of human activities which are reported every day.

Advertising	Obituaries	Music
Editorials	Comics	Gardens
Columnists	Sports news	Finance
City news	Stock market reports	Business
Washington reports	Human interest stories	Weather
National affairs	Art	Book reviews
Foreign news	Screen reviews	Crossword puzzles
Science	Radio programs	Television programs

11. Take a particular event or news item and see whether the headlines and substance of the matter are reported differently in other newspapers.
12. Select a debatable issue of the day and read the editorial comment in at least two papers to see why there is a difference in point of view.
13. Compare the headlines in a tabloid with the headlines for the same story as reported in a full-length newspaper. Why the difference in size and wording?
14. Which newspaper would you recommend for daily reading if a person wanted to be well-informed about current events? Why?

B. Newspapers give us much of our reading material. Select a good newspaper with which you are acquainted and in about 100 words tell what it usually contains and why it is of value to young people.

C. Through our reading experiences in newspapers, we can gain information that may be useful in helping us to choose the occupation or profession for which we should like to prepare ourselves. In about 100 words write about some story or article, telling how it may be helpful to you in deciding on your life work.

D. Divide your notebook into separate sections headed as follows:

FIELDS OF INTEREST	SAMPLE TOPICS
1. National events	Presidential campaign
2. World affairs	Atomic power
3. Scientific progress	Cancer research
4. Inventions and discoveries	Uranium mines
5. Government problems	National budget

For two or three weeks clip items related to these five fields of interest and paste them neatly into your notebook. At the end of the study, write a brief summary in one or two sentences at the bottom of each section telling what you consider the most important trend or event.

E. Make a study of headline English by copying the words most often used in daily newspapers and finding out their meaning. Here are some sample words and phrases:

WORDS	PHRASES
curb (verb)	holds suspects
ban (verb)	drops suit
irk (verb)	end walkout
clue (noun)	probes charges
oust (verb)	gambler testifies
parley (noun)	hails decision
rally (noun)	seek motive
pact (noun)	raps court
laud (verb)	outlook improves
drive (noun)	falls short

F. Write a letter to the editor of your favorite newspaper to state your opinion regarding some community problem, such as recreation facilities, road repairs, garbage disposal, etc. Notice the difference in style and content between such letters as published in the *New York Times* and "The Voice of the People" in other daily newspapers.

What's playing tonight? Shall we go to see a murder mystery, a western romance, or a social comedy? Maybe there will be a double-feature program with an animated cartoon and news of the week. Recreation and information, even social and moral conduct, can be found on the silver screen. Some movies have such distinction of story or acting or both that patrons will stand in line for hours in order to see the show. Unfortunately, there are many third-rate and tenth-rate productions which serve only to "kill an evening." Guidance is necessary.

MOVIES

Choose your entertainment according to the quality of the story, the ability of the actors, the truth to experience. Life does not follow the Hollywood formula of "boy meets girl."

SODA

Some useful sources of information on current films are (1) *periodicals* that list outstanding movies, (2) *guides* that are published for teachers and pupils, (3) *books* that explain the appreciation of photoplays.

EXERCISES

MOVIES

A. Some activities in connection with the movies include the following:

1. Choose the "best films of the year."
2. Visit the projection room of the local theater.
3. Select from a novel or short-story scenes deemed suitable for the screen.
4. Formulate a set of standards by which to judge motion pictures.
5. Attend good pictures in a class group.
6. Compare the treatment of story and character of the screen version of a well-known book with the original version.
7. Prepare a scrapbook on motion pictures.
8. Organize a motion picture club.
9. Prepare a library or classroom exhibit.
10. Keep a clipping file.
11. Write letters to favorite stars.
12. Evaluate the historical truth and the accuracy of pictures.
13. Post motion picture clippings on the bulletin board.
14. Obtain "stills" from local theaters or producers.
15. Vote for the best film presented in local theaters.

B. By seeing motion pictures, it is possible to increase our knowledge of places we have never seen. In about 150 words describe some place from a motion picture you have seen. Make your account so vivid that your readers will wish to visit the place. Give the title of the picture.

C. Compare the book or play as originally written with the film version as to characters, plot, and setting. Do you agree with any of the changes made by Hollywood producers and directors? Tell why or why not. Sample films based on books are:

Treasure Island	*David Copperfield*
Moby Dick	*The King and I*
War and Peace	*Around the World in 80 Days*
The Barretts of Wimpole Street	*The Spirit of St. Louis*
The Caine Mutiny	*Giant*

GUIDE TO POPULAR TEENAGE MAGAZINES

Magazines provide materials of great value in leisure time activities and in supplementary classwork in English, science, and the social studies. As in the study of the other forms of media of mass communication, you should make a wide acquaintance with the numerous possibilities offered and develop standards of good taste in selection. Most pupils early form the habit of reading certain magazines. Unfortunately, some pupils never make the acquaintance of the better periodicals but devour comics until they get mental indigestion. Avoid the sensational stories of impossible exploits by fantastic creatures and enlarge your experience by reading fiction based on real life adventures. There are magazines suited to every taste and appealing to every interest. Why not browse through a half-dozen good magazines in your school library or public library to discover one you like and subscribe for it? A group plan whereby each member of the class makes a small contribution will enable you to form a Magazine Club and read several magazines regularly at a very low cost.

Here is a list of magazines which boys and girls have recommended as the most popular reading:

American Boy	*Good Housekeeping*	*Popular Science*
American Girl	*Junior Red Cross*	*Saturday Evening Post*
American Red Cross	*Junior Scholastic*	*Science Digest*
Boy's Life	*My Weekly Reader*	*Sports Afield*
Child Life	*National Geographic*	*Story Parade*
Children's Digest	*Nature*	*World Horizon*
Current Events	*Outdoor Life*	*Young America*
Field and Stream	*Popular Mechanics*	*Youth's Companion*

You will find much interesting material in the current issues of these and many other magazines. Whether you like to make things at home in your own workshop, or wish to get acquainted with the latest fashions and designs, or want to read about recent scientific discoveries, you will find informative articles on a host of topics in these publications. On the other hand, if you simply wish to relax and read some stirring stories of action and adventure, you will enjoy fresh and absorbing narratives. Sports-lovers and nature-lovers and hobbyists of all kinds will discover a wide variety of articles. So, don't miss these lively periodicals.

Magazines

Flashy covers are bait to catch the unwary. Learn to select according to your genuine interests, hobbies, tastes — and occasionally try something different!

EXERCISE

MAGAZINES

1. Magazines give us much of our reading material. Select a good magazine with which you are acquainted and in about 100 words tell what it usually contains and why it is of value to young people.

2. During these times it is very important for us to be informed about world affairs, especially our part in them, as a nation and as individuals. Give the name of a magazine or current-events publication with which you are familiar and in about 150 words tell how it helps you to keep informed.

3. Suppose that your teacher has asked each member of your class to recommend a magazine for the school library. What magazine would you select? In about 150 words explain why the magazine you are recommending is worthwhile and would interest other students. Refer to specific features of the magazine that you like.

4. Using the *Readers' Guide to Periodical Literature,* locate a series of articles dealing with a topic in your science or social studies classwork. Include the title of publication, date of issue, and page references.

5. Compare the original article in a magazine as written by its author with the digest version of it as it appears in a digest magazine.

6. Have the class prepare and mimeograph a Class Magazine (for example, a Graduation Issue) containing original contributions by members of the class in the form of interviews, letters, poems, quizzes, pictures, stories, articles, etc.

 EVALUATING COMIC BOOKS — PRO AND CON

Boys and girls, do you still read *Donald Duck, Mickey Mouse, Superman, Batman,* and *Death Valley Days?* When you wait in the dentist's office or the barbershop, do you skim through the latest western? Do you hide *Mad Comics* inside your notebook when you are supposed to be doing your homework? Maybe someday you will realize you are growing up and drop these "pulps" just as you dropped the building blocks of your childhood days.

Why Read Comics?

No one really *reads* the comics. The comic story is followed easily and quickly by the eyes. No brainwork or imagination is required. What a waste of time! Be a grownup and *read* a magazine or a book instead.

WHY DO COMICS APPEAL TO YOUTH?	WHAT'S WRONG WITH THE COMICS?
1. full of pictures 2. easy to read in a few minutes 3. slim in size 4. colorful 5. show action 6. inexpensive to obtain	1. They destroy reading habits because you just look at pictures. 2. The words appear in "balloons" scattered over the page. 3. The language is often crude. 4. The persons in the story are not true to life but sharply divided into heroes and villains, beauties and monsters. 5. The things they do are not according to law and order, but full of crime and violence. 6. They fill your imagination with horrible happenings that make ordinary, everyday living seem very tame. 7. In general, their influence is bad.

What's the Cure for Comic Craze?

Ever try reading a good book? Your teacher can suggest many worthwhile stories you will enjoy—recommended by other boys and girls.

EXERCISE

COMIC BOOKS

1. Compare a comic book with the original story book using these points:
   a. Are the persons in the story true to life or exaggerated?
   b. Are the happenings real or fantastic?
   c. Is the background accurate or distorted?
   d. Is the language acceptable English or tending toward slang?
   e. Are the pictures in color as stimulating as the word-pictures?

2. **Write** a letter to a publisher of comic books, suggesting ways for improving the choice of stories, pictures, language, etc.
3. **Prepare** with your classmates a set of standards to judge good and bad qualities found in comics.
4. **Appoint** class committees to make your own comic book for a work of literature you are studying. Use the actual persons, incidents, and language as far as possible.

TO THE TEACHER

Comics of certain kinds serve a good purpose. There are the Classic Comics which present in pictures a short version of famous books: *Treasure Island, Tale of Two Cities, Ivanhoe,* etc. They may help to introduce pupils to good stories and lead them to read the full-length original books. Then, there are educational comics published by large industries as guides to learning; General Electric and Westinghouse offer excellent ones free in science. Catholic schools distribute comic books with lives of the saints and Bible stories to counteract the sensational types sold on newsstands. Children's comics dealing with juvenile literature and fairy tales, like *Bugs Bunny* and *Cinderella,* fascinate even older youngsters. All of these have some merit as forms of reading for escape or information. But, even these have drawbacks because they use "balloons" for the message, rather than straightline print, and cause eyestrain. The art is a crude combination of exaggerated drawings and overuse of primary colors. The main disadvantage is the fact that some comic readers never read anything else but comics!

Other comics have been condemned as bad, vicious, and harmful because of their immoral appeal. They may be described as shocking, vulgar, obscene, sensational. They portray crime, violence, sex, brutality, and all sorts of evil. They have lurid pictures of persons indecently exposed and describe murder, robbery, beatings, and other unlawful acts. Various organizations have tried—and often successfully—to stop the sale of these to the general public, especially to minors.

Rather than list the forbidden comics, teachers and parents responsible for the moral growth of children have sought to promote the reading of worthwhile books. If boys and girls develop a taste for exciting stories and clean fun, they will not seek satisfaction in the comics. As an aid for pupil selection of books based on live interests as recommended by boys and girls, the New York State Education Department has prepared a useful list of books arranged according to types. It will prove a convenient guide for individual or class reading.

Do you wake up in the morning to a clock-radio? Do you hear the news headlines and weather report while eating breakfast? Do you go to dance sessions at your friend's house to the music of popular bands? Sports events, plays, comedies, forums, symphonies, mysteries, and many other varieties of programs make radio a companion to daily living.

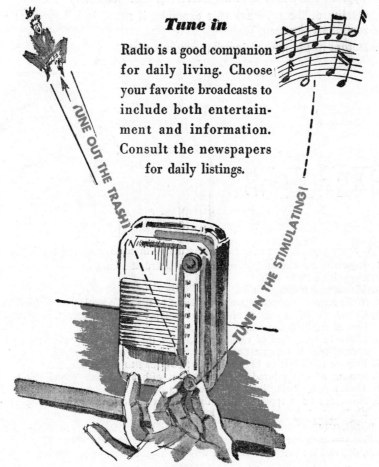

Tune in

Radio is a good companion for daily living. Choose your favorite broadcasts to include both entertainment and information. Consult the newspapers for daily listings.

TUNE OUT THE TRASH!

TUNE IN THE STIMULATING!

Radio, therefore, may serve as an important gateway to learning and experience. It brings fine music, well-known speakers, most recent events in history and science; but, alas, it also brings trash!

Here are some of the things you can talk over with your classmates in judging whether certain broadcasts are worth-while:

1. The authority or ability of the speaker or performer
2. Skill in presentation (voice, diction, microphone technic)
3. Nature of the program, if commercially sponsored
4. Nature of sustaining program (no sponsor)
5. Type of emotional appeal (sincere, sentimental, etc.)
6. Quality of the program (for example, if news, is it important and accurately reported?)
7. Nature of the advertising that accompanies the program

EXERCISES

RADIO

A. Some suggested activities in connection with radio work are the following:
1. Report to the class regarding programs heard at home.
2. Organize a radio club.
3. Visit a broadcasting studio.
4. Write letters of appreciation or criticism to the radio station or performers.
5. Choose the best program of a particular type: dramatic, literary, news, discussion of public questions.
6. Listen to a number of radio speakers for the purpose of determining standards of speech, organization of material, method of presentation.
7. Prepare a booklet or keep a notebook relating to the radio.
8. Present an original radio script in class with appropriate sound effects, etc.
9. Hold a radio forum in class to discuss a controversial topic.
10. Announce book reports in the form of an author-critic interview "over the air."

B. Select two radio programs that you consider outstanding, one for the information you gain and one for the enjoyment you receive. In about 75 words for each, describe the programs and tell why you regard them as outstanding.

C. Prepare a "Radio Log" as a guide to listening. Tune in to at least one program for each type listed below. Write about 50 words describing it and telling why you consider it worthwhile listening to (or not).

TYPES OF RADIO PROGRAMS	SAMPLES OF EACH TYPE
1. News reports	*Washington; World Affairs* *Newsreel Theater* *News* (Kenneth Banghart) *The World Tonight* *At the U.N.* (Leon Pearson)
2. Sports events	*Sports* (Stan Lomax) *Sports* (Jimmy Powers) *Sports Highlights* *New York Sports* *Sports Focus*
3. Comedies and fun	*People Are Funny* (Art Linkletter) *Jack Benny Show* *Our Miss Brooks* (Eve Arden) *Bob Hope Show* *Amos 'n Andy*
4. Dramas and plays	*Indictment* *Gunsmoke* *Dragnet* *X Minus One, Science Fiction* *Counterspy*
5. Music and opera	*Masterwork Hour* *Symphony Hall* *Make Believe Ballroom* (Martin Block) *Metropolitan Opera* (Milton Cross) *The Nation's Hits* (Peter Tripp)
6. Discussions of problems	*The American Forum* *Meet the Press* *Citizens Union* *Invitation to Learning* *Edward R. Murrow*
7. Other varieties	*Breakfast Club* (Don McNeill) *The McCanns at Home* *Fred Waring Show* *Arthur Godfrey* *Catholic Hour*

D. Compare a radio broadcast with a TV broadcast of the same program as to its interest and effectiveness. Which do you prefer?

E. Much interest has been shown in FM broadcast and Hi-Fi sets. If you are a music fan, tell the class about your favorite programs.

EXERCISE

VARIOUS TYPES OF MASS MEDIA

1. A modern *newspaper* presents such different kinds of news and services as the following:

current events	weather reports
editorials	homemaking suggestions
radio and television	science
sports	stories
advertisements	special features

   Choose two items from the above list and, in about 50 words for each, tell why you think it is interesting for boys and girls of your age.

2. Suppose that your aunt or uncle wishes to give you a *magazine* subscription as a birthday or graduation gift and has asked you to select the magazine you would like. Name the one you would select and in at least 100 words make clear what special features or contents led you to select that magazine.

3. Suppose a friend who wishes to subscribe to a *magazine* for vacation reading has asked you to recommend one. What magazine would you suggest? In about 100 words tell why you think it would be interesting or enjoyable.

4. Much has been written about the effect of *comic books* on young people. In about 100 words express your ideas about this type of reading material.

5. *Television* presents daily news highlights. Why is it still necessary to read newspapers?

6. *Movies* present fiction stories in color and action. Why do the original books on which these films are based offer greater opportunities for growth?

7. *Radio* listening is part of our daily lives. How can we make this habit a more intelligent means of improving ourselves?

8. Write the answer in 100 words to this problem: "Since mass media must reach millions of people, they often appeal to the lowest level of intelligence. How can you wisely use mass media for the greatest benefit?"

ENGLISH (Preliminary)—JANUARY 1956 (1)

Part I

Answer all questions.

1. Dictation (to be given by the examiner) [10]

The examiner should dictate the following paragraph to the pupils, without emphasizing or otherwise indicating the italicized words. The pupils should write the entire paragraph. Only spelling of the italicized words should be considered in rating papers.

The *national* park *idea* was *born* around a campfire. A party of *explorers* had found it *necessary* to spend the night in a *section* of our Northwest now *known* as Yellowstone National Park. The men were *discussing* how this new-found *territory* could be *divided* so that each new *owner* might have *equal advantage.* Then one of the campers said that there *ought* to be no *private* ownership of any portion of such a *scenic region,* but that all of it should be set apart as a national park to be enjoyed by *everyone.* About two years *later* Congress created Yellowstone National Park for the "*benefit* and enjoyment of the people forever."

2. Spelling words (to be given by the examiner) [20]

The following words are to be dictated to the pupils and each should be used in a sentence to make the meaning clear:

1. title	11. naturally	21. academy	31. amendment
2. liberty	12. central	22. decide	32. disease
3. comic	13. comfortable	23. annually	33. desert (noun)
4. hurriedly	14. arrangement	24. privilege	34. license (or licence)
5. original	15. diamond	25. companies	35. accept
6. authority	16. practical	26. professional	36. illustrate
7. exist	17. label	27. woman	37. disappoint
8. bulletin	18. doubtless	28. height	38. prefer
9. assistant	19. librarian	29. possibility	39. statue
10. brief	20. decrease	30. garage	40. especially

3. Dictation (to be given by the examiner) [5]

The examiner should dictate the following paragraph without emphasizing or otherwise indicating the italicized words. The pupils should write the entire paragraph. Only spelling of the italicized words should be considered in rating papers.

Our *whole* class of *course* wanted to see the graduation exercises, but the *principal sent* word that the crowd *would* be *too great* and

ENGLISH (PRELIMINARY)—JANUARY 1956 (2)

that if we were to stand in the *aisles,* the graduates could not be *seen* by *their* parents.

4. In the spaces provided, copy the following conversation, capitalizing and punctuating wherever necessary to make correct sentences.   [10]

betty youre good at solving riddles said susan can you tell me what has four eyes and runs two thousand miles

thats the mississippi was the other girls prompt reply

5. Cloth is usually sold by the yard, abbreviated *yd.* In the first column at the right of *each* item below, write the *word* that tells how the item is usually sold, and in the last column write the *abbreviation* for that word.   [5]

ITEM	SOLD BY THE	ABBREVIATION
[Example: cloth	yard	yd.]
a. eggs	....	....
b. milk	....	....
c. butter	....	....
d. gasoline	....	....
e. shoes	....	....

6. In the space at the *left* of each sentence write the part of speech of the *first* word of that sentence; and in the space at the *right* of each sentence, write the part of speech of the *last* word of that sentence.   [10]

FIRST WORD OF SENTENCE   LAST WORD OF SENTENCE

[Example: noun   Boys like to hike.   verb]

.... a. Oh! look out at the garden!   ....

.... b. You will soon see the first flowers of spring.   ....

.... c. Take the hoe when we go to plant the seeds. ....

.... d. In a short while the flowers will blossom gaily. ....

.... e. Then the garden will look truly beautiful.   ....

7. Classify *each* group of words below by writing one of the following in the space provided.   [10]

I for an incomplete sentence
S for a simple sentence
Cd for a compound sentence

a. What are you talking about?
b. Do watch your step.
c. Not realizing that the time was short.

d. Everyone had agreed to come, but later Jane changed her mind.

e. During the parade the children cheered and waved their banners.

f. After dinner before clearing the table and doing the dishes.

g. I lent the book to Jack, and he read it in one night.

h. We were late for school; our alarm clock had failed us again.

i. Pleased with the way his marks were improving in every subject.

j. I could find neither a pencil nor a pen on the desk.

8. In the following passage there are 10 errors in the use of words. Underline *each* error and write your correction above it.   [10]

In order to travel on horseback it were necessary for the early settlers to cut wider and better trails than those used by the Indians. Some of the Indian trails had been used so frequent that they had became wore down. These trails was soon made passable for horses and then for wagons. Now many a concrete road lies over an old Indian trail.

North America was a wonderful country in them day's. It has been said that the forest was so dense a squirrel could have went from the Atlantic Ocean to the Great Lakes by jumping from tree to tree and wouldn't never have been obliged to touch the ground. It would be interesting to estimate how long it would have took a squirrel to make that trip.

9. On the line at the right of each of *ten* of the following statements, write the *number* of the word or phrase that correctly completes the statement.   [5]

[Example: To find the correct spelling of a word, a person should first consult   (1) an encyclopedia   (2) a dictionary   (3) a spelling textbook   ..2..]

a. The *o* in the word *hold* has the same sound as the *o* in the word   (1) dog   (2) most   (3) move

b. In the word *walked*, the ending *ed* is pronounced   (1) *d*   (2) *k*   (3) *t*

c. In the dictionary, the word *commerce* appears before the word   (1) commence   (2) comedy   (3) commute

d. The word *examine* would appear in a dictionary on the page with the following guide words: (1) evaporation — exaggerate   (2) exaggerated — excrescence   (3) **excrete** — exodus

e. In the word *bicycle* the accent falls on the   (1) first syllable   (2) second syllable   (3) third syllable

f. A synonym for the word *here* is the word   (1) absent   (2) present   (3) hear

g. To find an article about the history of glassmaking, a person should consult   (1) a desk dictionary   (2) an encyclopedia   (3) *The World Almanac*

h. The topics covered in a textbook are listed alphabetically in the   (1) table of contents   (2) footnotes   (3) index

i. The topics in an encyclopedia are arranged in   (1) alphabetical order   (2) the order of their importance   (3) numerical order

j. The name of the publisher of a book is most likely to be found   (1) on the book's front cover   (2) on the title page   (3) in the introduction

k. The copyright date of a book is most likely to be found   (1) on the back of the title page   (2) on the book jacket   (3) in the appendix

l. The surest way to discover whether a library owns a particular book is to   (1) look for the book on the shelves   (2) ask a schoolmate who reads widely   (3) look in the **card catalog**

10. In each sentence below one word is italicized. Underneath the sentence is a group of five words or expressions. From these select the word or expression that has most nearly the same meaning as the italicized word and write its *number* on the line at the right.   [15]

a. Grandfather *acquired* ten acres of pasture land.
   (1) obtained   (2) plowed   (3) sold   (4) leased   (5) desired

b. A feeling of *exhaustion* came over the players during the game.
   (1) fear   (2) extreme tiredness   (3) overconfidence   (4) unsteadiness   (5) complete happiness

c. We pitied the child in the *grimy* clothes.
   (1) ill-fitting   (2) secondhand   (3) poorly **made**   (4) dirty   (5) ragged

d. The mechanic's calculations were *approximate.*
   (1) nearly exact   (2) remarkable   (3) hastily made   (4) worthless   (5) mathematically correct

e. A *competent* young woman was given the position.
   (1) busy   (2) pretty   (3) capable   (4) friendly
   (5) good-natured
f. We had *barely* finished by six o'clock.
   (1) easily   (2) only just   (3) partly   (4) more or less
   (5) unexpectedly
g. His second offense was more *grievous* than his first.
   (1) serious   (2) stupid   (3) deliberate   (4) excus-
   able   (5) peculiar
h. All air traffic was *suspended* during the emergency.
   (1) turned back   (2) speeded up   (3) stopped tempo-
   rarily   (4) checked carefully   (5) regulated strictly
i. The antics of the monkeys *diverted* the children.
   (1) upset   (2) amused   (3) surprised   (4) disgusted
   (5) frightened
j. The man *survived* his three sisters.
   (1) loved   (2) envied   (3) outlived   (4) destroyed
   (5) excelled
k. Franklin was a man of *exceptional* ability.
   (1) well-trained   (2) active   (3) mechanical   (4) self-
   educated   (5) unusual ˴
l. Their aim seems to be to *thwart* our plans.
   (1) simplify   (2) direct   (3) rely on   (4) block
   (5) keep up with
m. He heard the warning cry of another *pedestrian*.
   (1) agent   (2) walker   (3) passenger   (4) workingman
   (5) traffic officer
n. They boasted about the *superiority* of their product.
   (1) beauty   (2) abundance   (3) excellence   (4) popularity   (5) permanence
o. We considered their point of view *absurd*.
   (1) disgusting   (2) old-fashioned   (3) insincere   (4) reasonable   (5) foolish

Part II

Answer all questions.

The answers to question 2 (*A, B* and *C*) should be written on the question paper. The answers to questions *3, 4* and *5* should be written on paper distributed by the examiner. The question paper should be handed in with your other answer paper.

ENGLISH (PRELIMINARY)—JANUARY 1956 (6)

1. Credit will be given on handwriting (0 to 10 points), based on the average quality of the handwriting on the paper as a whole.   [10]

2. *Directions:* At the right of each of the following selections you will find several incomplete statements about the selection. Each statement is followed by five words or expressions numbered 1 to 5. After reading each selection, read the statements at the right. Then choose the word or expression that most satisfactorily completes *each* statement in accordance with the meaning of the selection and write its *number* in the parentheses after the statement. [2 credits each.]   [30]

A. The Caribbean Sea is to the Americas what the Mediterranean is to Europe — a central sea. The American body of water is not entirely landbound. Double strings of islands — the Cuba group and the Bahamas — form an arc at the Atlantic entrance. This arc is now firmly fortified. This Mediterranean of the West is the water passage between the Americas, and consequently it must be controlled by them if trade is carried on. The sea is as necessary to the Caribbean countries as the Mediterranean is to Italy.

The surrounding lands produce more oil than any other region of the same size in the world. They are rich in minerals, and the fertile soil produces great quantities of tropical fruits and vegetables. They are capable of supplying much of the goods formerly imported into the United States from Asia and Africa. In exchange, they need manufactured goods. Living standards, particularly in the beautiful but undeveloped islands, are low, and tropical diseases still exact a deadly toll.

a. The Caribbean Sea and the Mediterranean are alike in their   (1) variety of exports (2) epidemics of serious diseases   (3) undeveloped islands   (4) geographical importance to surrounding areas (5) living standards ......( )

b. The Americas must control the Caribbean Sea in order to (1) carry on trade   (2) prevent disease   (3) compete with Italy   (4) supply goods to Asia   (5) form a landbound arc ....( )

c. Lands bordering on the Caribbean are outstanding for their (1)   manufacturing   centers (2) production of oil   (3) healthful living conditions   (4) exports to Africa   (5) lack of mineral supplies ....( )

B. From Gettysburg to the Battle of the Bulge, carrier pigeons have winged their way through skies fair and foul to deliver the vital messages of battle. Today, in spite of electronics and atomic weapons, these feathered heroes are still an important comunications link in any army.

No one could be surer of this than the men at Fort Monmouth, N. J., sole Army pigeon breeding and training center in this country. On the roosts at Fort Monmouth, perch many genuine battle heroes, among them veteran G.I. Joe.

In 1943, 1,000 British troops moved speedily ahead of the Allied advance in Italy to take the small town of Colvi Vecchia, north of Cassino. Since communications could not be established in time to relay the victory to headquarters, the troops were due for a previously planned Allied bombing raid. Then, one of the men released carrier pigeon G.I. Joe. With a warning message on his back, he flew 20 miles in 20 minutes, arriving just as the bombers were warming up their motors. For saving the day for the British, the Lord Mayor of London later awarded G.I. Joe the Dickin Medal, England's highest award to an animal.

Even when regular message channels are set up, equipment can break or be overloaded or radio silence must be observed. Then, the carrier pigeon comes into his own. And 99 times out

a. The writer of this passage evidently believes that carrier pigeons (1) have no usefulness in modern warfare (2) should be forced to fly only in emergencies (3) are remarkably reliable as message carriers (4) should receive regular promotions (5) can travel only short distances at high speed ....( )

b. G.I. Joe was rewarded for (1) preventing an unnecessary loss of life (2) guiding a bomber's flight (3) returning in spite of an injured wing (4) completing 99 out of 100 missions (5) bringing the news of an Allied defeat ..( )

c. G.I. Joe's reward was (1) a promotion (2) a reception given by the Lord Mayor (3) a chance to retire to Fort Monmouth (4) a medal (5) a veteran's pension ....( )

d. Pigeons serve as important links in communications when (1) the weather is fair (2) radio silence is necessary (3) bombing missions start out (4) victories have been won (5) electronic devices are in use ....( )

of 100 he completes his mission. Recently in Korea, Homer the homing pigeon was flying from the front to a rear command post when he developed wing trouble. Undaunted, Homer made a forced landing, hopped the last two miles and delivered his message. For initiative and loyalty, Homer has been promoted to Pfc. — Pigeon First Class!

C. Stovewood is what is used on the farm for heat and in the city for fun. But if our farmers keep on buying oil burners, the time may soon be here when wood will no longer be used for fuel except in the suburban fireplace. As foresters we would like to see more fuel wood consumption on the farm, because that's the best way to "clean up the woodlot" and get rid of inferior and defective trees. It will be too bad if we give up burning wood altogether, for it is a home-grown product and, when properly handled, an efficient fuel. At the present time, more than a million cords of fuel wood are cut every year in New York.

What is a cord? Some people say it's the most elastic unit of measure ever devised by the mind of man. A "standard" cord is a pile of stacked wood 4 x 4 x 8 feet; that's 128 cubic feet. But wait a minute: How much of this is wood? That depends on what kind of wood, the size and straightness of the sticks, and who does

a. The title below that most nearly expresses the main theme or subject of this selection is:
(1) Fuel
(2) Stovewood
(3) Kinds of trees
(4) Standard measures
(5) Modern heating

b. Foresters would like to have more fuel wood used on farms because   (1) too many farmers have oil burners   (2) they fear forest fires   (3) it is the best fuel   (4) city dwellers do not have wood stoves   (5) it is the best way to clear woodlots of poor trees ....( )

c. The author predicts that (1) farmers will give up planting inferior trees   (2) someone will find a less elastic standard for measuring wood (3) firewood will soon be used only as fireplace fuel   (4) woodlots will become neater   (5) foresters will see more wood consumed ....( )

the piling. Small crooked sticks, cut from hardwood limbs and piled by one of those cordwood artists who know how to make air spaces, may contain less than 30 cubic feet of solid wood per cord. Smooth, round wood such as birch or spruce, in sizes eight inches and better, will average 100 cubic feet or more per cord. (That's with the bark on. Peeled wood will make 10 to 12 per cent more cubic volume in the same sized stack.)

The heating value of wood varies enormously with the kind of tree. Black locust, white oak, hickory, black birch, and ironwood are the best. A cord of any of these woods, when seasoned, is worth approximately a ton of coal. Beech, yellow birch, sugar maple, ash, and red oak are next. White birch, cherry, soft maple, sycamore, and elm are comparatively poor fuel woods, with basswood, butternut, popple, and the softwoods at the bottom of the scale.

d. The article states that (1) millions of trees are cut for fuel wood yearly in New York (2) more than a million cords of fuel wood are cut every year in New York (3) cutting wood for fuel has become a suburban occupation (4) oil burners have practically eliminated the use of fuel wood (5) millions of dollars were spent for fuel wood in New York last year ....( )

e. A standard cord of wood (1) always contains 128 cubic feet of wood (2) will average 100 cubic feet of smooth wood (3) contains less than 30 cubic feet of solid wood (4) is stacked wood in a pile 4 feet high, 4 feet wide, and 8 feet long (5) is measured by weight of the wood per foot ....( )

f. Removal of the bark from wood before stacking (1) increases the cubic volume of wood in a cord (2) makes the stacking easier (3) allows more air spaces in a cord of wood (4) prevents seasoning of wood (5) decreases the measurements of the pile ( )

g. The amount of heat supplied by wood depends upon (1) the person who has piled the wood (2) the type of tree from which the wood came (3) the way the wood was cut

(4) the straightness of the sticks   (5) the amount of bark left on the wood ....( )

h. The most valuable fuel woods come from   (1) all kinds of birches and oaks   (2) any kind of wood that is well-seasoned   (3) home-grown beech, maple, cherry, and elm trees   (4) hickory, ironwood, black birch, black locust, and white oak   (5) sycamore, ash, butternut, and popple that have been sprayed ....( )

3. Answer either *a* or *b:*

   a. (1) Chief of Police John E. Doe of Ourtown, New York, visited your class recently and spoke on winter safety. As class secretary, write Chief Doe a letter thanking him for addressing your group. Mention also the benefits the class received from his talk.   [15]

   (2) Draw a rectangle to represent the envelope in which the above letter will be sent and prepare this envelope for mailing.   [5]

   b. (1) Suppose that one of your classmates has been a patient for some weeks in a hospital in a distant city. Write him (or her) a letter about activities in your school and community which you think would serve to cheer him (or her).   [15]

   (2) Draw a rectangle to represent the envelope in which the above letter will be sent and prepare this envelope for mailing.   [5]

4. Choose *one* of the following topics and write a well-planned composition of about 100 words: [20]

   a. A story my family tells about me
   b. Why I prefer to live in the country (or the city)
   c. My first day at................School
   d. The most important member of our family
   e. A room of my own
   f. Fun in the kitchen
   g. My favorite sport

h. When our car wouldn't run
i. Why I enjoy science
j. A man who fought for freedom

5. Answer *a* or *b* or *c:*   [20]

   a. Man has long believed that many animals are helpful, loyal, and dependable. In about 100 words, describe how an animal in a book you have read proved to be a friend to a human being. Give the title and author of the book.

   b. Often we do our best when we are not thinking of ourselves. Name a character that you have read about in a story or poem, and in about 100 words show how this character's love for God, for his country, or for another person inspired him to do a good deed. Give the title and author.

   c. Suppose that you are to be given a gift subscription for one year to a magazine of your choice. Mention a magazine that you would like to receive under these circumstances, and tell in a paragraph of about 100 words some of the features of this magazine that make it seem valuable to you.

ENGLISH (Preliminary)—JUNE 1956 (1)

Part I

Answer all questions.

1. Dictation (to be given by the examiner)   [10]

The examiner should dictate the following paragraph to the pupils, without emphasizing or otherwise indicating the italicized words. The pupils should write the entire paragraph. Only spelling of the italicized words should be considered in rating papers.

One of the real joys of my *recent* trip *across* the Atlantic Ocean was the thrill of *sailing* back into the *great* harbor of New York. On deck with the other *passengers,* I scanned the horizon for the first *sight* of the Ambrose Lightship, that *welcome* signal that told us that we were *finally* nearing home. A *pilot* came aboard and *guided* the *vessel* through the channel, past the Statue of Liberty into full *view* of the *beautiful* skyline. As the vessel moved slowly *forward,* I *again* had an *opportunity* to see the *activities* of a busy *harbor,* and I enjoyed *watching* the *tiny* tugboats pushing the big ship into the dock.

2. Spelling words (to be given by the examiner)   [20]

The following words are to be dictated to the pupils and each should be used in a sentence to make the meaning clear:

1. vacation	11. imagine	21. numerous	31. speech
2. teacher	12. tired	22. beginning	32. truly
3. busy	13. character	23. volume	33. belief
4. suppose	14. waste	24. exercise	34. ninety
5. ought	15. arithmetic	25. odor	35. appearance
6. quite	16. political	26. customer	36. independence
7. already	17. lose	27. valuable	37. qualities
8. statement	18. planned	28. completely	38. certificate
9. answer	19. safely	29. meant	39. usually
10. latter	20. straight	30. government	40. agreement

3. In the spaces provided, write the contraction for *each* of the italicized expressions: [No credit for misspelled words.]   [5]

      (1)   (2)   (1) **He's**

[Example: *He is* sure that he *cannot* swim across the pond.   (2) **can't**]

        (1)   (2)

a. Be sure that *you are* ready when *it is* time to go.

      (3)   (4)

b. I am pleased that *they have* been invited.

      (5)   (6)

c. Joe *does not* know whether *he will* be able to play tomorrow.

(7) (8)
d. *She would* be happier if she *were not* required to do the shopping.

(9) (10)
e. *Who is* going to the picnic? Mary *will not* tell us.

4. On the line at the right of *each* sentence, write the part of speech of the italicized word. [10]

    a. (1) Almost every pupil attended the *dance.*
       (2) We usually *dance* at our class parties.
    b. (1) *This* book has been very popular.
       (2) *This* is another interesting book.
    c. (1) The broom was left on the *back* porch.
       (2) Please *back* the car out of the garage.
       (3) The *back* of the coat was badly torn.
    d. (1) He walked slowly *past* her house.
       (2) Events seemed to move more slowly in the *past.*
       (3) The cars went *past* at a great rate of speed.

5. In the spaces provided, copy the following, capitalizing and punctuating wherever necessary to make correct sentences: [10]

    a. jack can you recommend a shop which sells mens and boys clothing
    b. we have learned that doctor davis our neighbor for several years will retire soon
    c. the prince and the pauper is one of my favorite books it is about a poor english boy and a kings son

6. Below are three main topics and seven subtopics. Arrange these topics and subtopics in correct topical outline form, using the title "Reviewing for Examinations." Write the outline in the spaces provided. [5]

Topics and subtopics

English	Growth of industry
Punctuation	Decimals
Fractions	Citizenship Education
Literature	Vocabulary
Mathematics	Problems of immigration

REVIEWING FOR EXAMINATIONS

I. ....
  A. ....
  B. ....
  C. ....

II. ....

   A. ....

   B. ....

III. ....

   A. ....

   B. ....

7. In the spaces provided, combine the short sentences in *each* group below into *one* smooth, well-constructed sentence.   [10]

    a. Mary is giving a party. It is to be a graduation party. I have been invited. Mother has given me her consent.

    b. The farmer's family did not have a comfortable home. He built a house. His wife moved the family into the new house.

8. Some of the following sentences contain errors. If a sentence contains an error, underline the incorrect expression and write your correction on the line at the right. If a sentence is correct as it stands, write *C* on the line at the right.   [15]

    a. Oral English helps us to speak distinct.

    b. Usually she don't get up in time for school.

    c. Dad allowed Maureen and me to take violin lessons.

    d. How many trees were blowed down during the hurricane?

    e. How surprised I am to know who the winner is!

    f. Mack hardly never says anything in class.

    g. The prize is there's if they win today's game.

    h. We seen only the last part of the game.

    i. You have came at just the wrong time.

    j. Why are we three girls always on the clean-up committee?

    k. Jack run as hard as he could, but Larry arrived ahead of him.

    l. If a person likes word games, he will enjoy this contest.

    m. How many pieces of candy have you ate?

    n. Only the most talented musicians was chosen to play in the orchestra.

    o. Each girl was given a flower to pin on their dress.

9. In each sentence below one word is italicized. Underneath the sentence is a group of five words or expressions. From these select the word or expression that has most nearly the same meaning as the italicized word and write its *number* on the line at the right.   [15]

    a. Our neighbor *purchased* his home last year.

      (1) bought   (2) rented   (3) painted   (4) remodeled   (5) built

b. The only sound was the *steady* ticking of the clock.
   (1) noisy   (2) rapid   (3) regular   (4) cheerful
   (5) tiresome

c. The desks in our room are *stationary*.
   (1) heavy   (2) not movable   (3) metal   (4) easily
   adjustable   (5) standard

d. Before signing the papers, Mr. Edmond consulted his *attorney*.
   (1) banker   (2) clerk   (3) lawyer   (4) secretary
   (5) employer

e. We *imitate* those whom we admire.
   (1) protect   (2) attract   (3) study   (4) copy   (5)
   appreciate

f. They reached the *summit* of the mountain by noon.
   (1) base   (2) wooded area   (3) side   (4) face
   (5) top

g. The motorist *heeded* the signals.
   (1) worried about   (2) passed by   (3) took notice of
   (4) laughed at   (5) disagreed with

h. The *severity* of their criticism upset us.
   (1) purpose   (2) harshness   (3) method   (4) suddenness   (5) unfairness

i. We made a very *leisurely* trip to California.
   (1) roundabout   (2) unhurried   (3) unforgettable
   (4) tiresome   (5) speedy

j. The little girl shook her head *vigorously*.
   (1) sadly   (2) hopefully   (3) sleepily   (4) thoughtfully   (5) energetically

k. Before long this machine will be *obsolete*.
   (1) out-of-date   (2) broken down   (3) as good as new
   (4) replaced   (5) remodeled

l. In her lifetime she *surmounted* many difficulties.
   (1) overlooked   (2) escaped   (3) stirred up   (4)
   overcame   (5) complained about

m. The police were *lax* in enforcing parking regulations.
   (1) cross   (2) faithful   (3) not fair   (4) too late
   (5) not strict

n. The door was *cunningly* concealed.
(1) partly   (2) cleverly   (3) amusingly   (4) completely   (5) easily

o. The letter *emphasized* two important ideas.
(1) introduced   (2) overlooked   (3) contrasted   (4) questioned   (5) stressed

Part II

Answer all questions.

The answers to question 2 (A, B and C) should be written on the question paper. The answers to questions 3, 4, and 5 should be written on paper distributed by the examiner. The question paper should be handed in with your other answer paper.

1. Credit will be given on handwriting (0 to 10 points), based on the average quality of the handwriting on the paper as a whole. [10]

2. *Directions:* At the right of each of the following selections, you will find several incomplete statements about the selection. Each statement is followed by five words or expressions numbered 1 to 5. After reading each selection, read the statements at the right. Then choose the word or expression that most satisfactorily completes *each* statement in accordance with the meaning of the selection and write its *number* in the parentheses after the statement. [2 credits each.] [30]

A. If you are asked the color of the sky on a fair day in summer, your answer will most probably be, "Blue." This answer is only partially correct. Blue sky near the horizon is not the same kind of blue as it is straight overhead. Look at the sky some fine day and you will find that the blue sky near the horizon is slightly greenish. As your eye moves upward toward the zenith, you will find that the blue changes into pure blue, and finally shades into a violet-blue overhead.

Have you heard the story of

a. The title below that best expresses the ideas of this passage is:
1. The summer sky
2. Artists vs. farmers
3. Recognizing colors
4. Blue hills
5. Appreciating art ..... ( )

b. At the zenith, the sky is usually (1) violet-blue   (2) violet-red   (3) greenish-blue   (4) yellow-orange   (5) green
.... ( )

c. The author suggests that (1) farmers are color-blind   (2)

a farmer who objected to the color of the distant hills in the artist's picture? He said to the artist, "Why do you make those hills blue? They are green. I've been over there and I know!"

The artist asked him to do a little experiment. "Bend over and look at the hills between your legs." As the farmer did this, the artist asked, "Now what color are the hills?"

The farmer looked again, then he stood up and looked. "By gosh, they turned blue!" he said.

It is quite possible that you have looked at many colors which you did not really recognize. Sky is not just blue; it is many kinds of blue. Grass is not plain green; it may be one of several varieties of green. A red brick wall frequently is not pure red. It may vary from yellow-orange to violet-red in color, but to the unseeing eye it is just red brick.

ability to see colors varies (3) brick walls should be painted pure red (4) some artists use poor color combinations (5) the sky is always blue .... ( )

B. In the year 1799, an officer of the French army was stationed in a little fortress near Alexandria on the Rosetta River, one of the mouths of the Nile in Egypt. He was interested in the ruins of the ancient civilization of Egypt; he had seen the Sphinx and the Pyramids, those mysterious structures erected by men of another age. One day, when a trench was being dug, he found to his surprise a stone of black slate on which were cut letters he could read. He had

a. The title below that best expresses the main ideas of this passage is:
1. A French officer's courage
2. The work of Champollion
3. Values in the study of Greek
4. The story of the Rosetta Stone
5. Ancient Egyptian writings .... ( )

b. The Rosetta Stone derived its name from (1) the man who found it (2) its size and shape (3) the place

studied Greek in school and knew that this was an inscription written in that language. Along with the Greek letters there ran an inscription in the same kind of Egyptian letters which he had seen carved on other ruins. There were three kinds of writing on the stone: one set of lines in Greek, and the other two sets in characters which, while both unknown, were plainly unlike each other.

The young officer had his wits about him. As soon as he saw the lines of Greek letters below the other two inscriptions, he said to himself, "If each line should be telling the same fact in a different language, the Greek letters would give the key to what the other letters meant." So he took good care of the stone and turned it over to scholars who were puzzling over Egyptian carvings.

In 1802 a French professor by the name of Champollion began to work on the inscriptions, trying to study out by the Greek key how the Egyptian characters told the same story. Champollion worked for twenty years on that stone. Other scholars began, worked a year or two, found out one or two letters, and gave it up. But Champollion kept right on until finally he made out the stone's secret. In 1823 he announced to the world of scholars that he had found out what fourteen of the signs meant. Twenty years to find out what the four-

near which it was found   (4) the person who translated the inscriptions   (5)   its color .... ( )

c. The discoverer of the stone apparently   (1) spent more than twenty years in Egypt   (2) liked to dig trenches   (3) was fond of puzzles   (4) was familiar with more than one language   (5) could speak Egyptian .... ( )

d. The author suggests that Champollion discovered the meaning of the inscriptions because he   (1) knew more Greek than the other scholars   (2) used the work of other students of language to gain fame for himself   (3) was more interested in ancient civilization than the other scholars   (4) did not give up as easily as the other scholars   (5) had more time to spare than anyone else .. ( )

e. The carvings on the stone were considered very important because they   (1) explained the reasons for building the Sphinx and the Pyramids   (2) provided work for Champollion for twenty years   (3) proved the value of learning Greek   (4) gave a clue to the meaning of ancient inscriptions   (5) proved that, even in digging trenches, there is glory .... ( )

teen signs meant! But in finding out those fourteen puzzle signs, he had discovered the secret of Egyptian writing. He had unlocked the secret of the Rosetta Stone; this let all the written records of Egypt be known to the world some five thousand years after an unknown person had inscribed the same information in three different tongues!

C. People have always been fond of ornaments. Among some of the oldest remains of human settlement, there were ornaments that these early people valued. It was quite natural, therefore, that ornaments should be used as money. Whales' teeth are one example; rare and bright-colored feathers woven into rings are another. But strings of shells have been the most common.

Along the shores of the Indian Ocean, from Africa around to the large islands southeast of Asia, is found a pretty little shellfish which is noted for furnishing what may have been the first money in all the world. Its shell, called a *cowrie,* is white or light yellow, and is about one inch long. Millions of people around that ocean were using these cowries, separate or on strings, for money long before furs or cattle or other kinds of money were so used anywhere, as far as is known. In Assyria, many miles inland, cowries have been found, and in China, on another ocean, they

f. The inscriptions on the stone were (1) all in the same language (2) all in unknown languages (3) in Greek, French, and an unknown language (4) in French and two unknown languages (5) in Greek and two unknown languages .. ( )

a. It is natural that early man used ornaments as money because (1) he valued ornaments highly (2) he lived on the shores of a great ocean (3) he liked rings made of feathers (4) he had no furs or cattle (5) he found ornaments in the remains of human settlements ...... ( )

b. The author believes that the earliest money may have been in the form of (1) cattle (2) furs (3) shells (4) feathers (5) string ... ( )

c. It is surprising to learn that cowries were used in Assyria because (1) cowries are only one inch long (2) cattle were plentiful in Assyria (3) the inhabitants were not fond of ornaments (4) Assyria is away from the seacoast (5) tortoise shells took the place of dollars .... ( )

were used along with several other kinds of shells. Tortoise shells had the highest values there, so that it might be said that the tortoise shells were the dollars while the cowries were the cents. And now, after thousands of years, there are still some tribes in Africa, India, and the South Seas that use cowries.

D. Track and field events are the oldest sports in the world today which have retained anything like their original form. They go back more than twenty-five hundred years to the ancient civilization of Greece and have continued ever since. The Greeks felt very much as we do about athletics. They held their athletes in high esteem, and champions were looked upon as national heroes.

Thinking along these lines, the Greeks developed the Olympic games to assemble all the greatest athletes of their country. The games were religious pageants as well as peerless athletic events, and they were held every four years for more than eight centuries. They were discontinued only when the Romans conquered Greece and spoiled the spirit of the games by entering professional athletes.

A great Frenchman, Baron Pierre de Coubertin, established the modern Olympics in 1896 with the hope that they would help the nations to understand

a. The title below that best expresses the main ideas of this passage is:
1. Early Greek games
2. Olympic game sites
3. Good sportsmanship
4. Track and field events
5. History of the Olympic games .... ( )

b. In ancient Greece, athletes were
(1) trained as professionals (2) forced to participate in games (3) usually defeated by Roman athletes (4) regarded very highly by the public (5) more concerned about religion than other people .... ( )

c. The present-day Olympic games were established to (1) win wars (2) honor national heroes (3) develop great athletes (4) observe religious holidays (5) promote good feeling among nations .... ( )

one another, and promote international friendship. They were to be held in a different country every four years, although the United States has been host twice —in St. Louis years ago and in Los Angeles in 1932. Other Olympiads have been held in Paris, London, Berlin, Stockholm, Antwerp, and Amsterdam.

3. Answer either *a* or *b:*

   a. (1) Your class is planning a day's outing at the close of school, and each pupil may invite a friend to attend. Write a letter of invitation to a friend, pointing out why you think he or she will enjoy the day.   [15]

      (2) Draw a rectangle to represent the envelope in which the above letter will be sent and prepare this envelope for mailing.   [5]

   b. (1) You have been chosen to be chairman of a book exhibit in your school. Write a letter to the American Library Association, 50 East Huron Street, Chicago 11, Illinois, requesting book lists, posters, and any other materials which may be used in connection with the exhibit.   [15]

      (2) Draw a rectangle to represent the envelope in which the above letter will be sent and prepare this envelope for mailing.   [5]

4. Choose *one* of the following topics and write a well-planned composition of about 100 words: [20]

    a. It's baseball time.
    b. Conquering the fire (*or* the flood)
    c. Advice for a gardener
    d. What I value most
    e. A place of historical interest
    f. The paintbrush and I
    g. My closest friend
    h. An example of fair play
    i. A nickname that I like
    j. Insects are interesting.

5. Answer *a* or *b* or *c*.   [20]

 a. In our reading we sometimes meet a character whose life is greatly benefited or greatly harmed by another person. Name such a character from a short story, play, or book that you have read, and in about 100 words show how the character was influenced for good or evil by another person. Give title and author.

 b. Poems frequently present a thought or an idea that a reader can apply to his own everyday life. In about 100 words summarize such a poem that you have read, and show how the idea it presents can be applied to a person's own life. Give title and author.

 c. Many television and radio programs have an educational value for pupils in junior high school. Name a television or radio program of this kind, and in about 100 words tell why you believe that pupils might profit by watching it or listening to it.

ENGLISH (Preliminary)—JANUARY 1957 (1)

Part I

Answer all questions.

1. Dictation (to be given by the examiner)   [10]

The examiner should dictate the following paragraph to the pupils, without emphasizing or otherwise indicating the italicized words. The pupils should write the entire paragraph. Only spelling of the italicized words should be considered in rating papers.

I have recently read a book filled with *strange* and *exciting happenings*. This book, *written* by a *doctor*, tells how he left a comfortable home in a large city and went to *practice medicine* in the jungle. Carrying his *supplies* on his back, he blazed his own trail, made a strenuous *march* through the jungle, *appeared* before the *chief* of a savage *tribe*, and asked for a guide into the *heart* of unknown *territory*. All the *events* of the story make the reader *realize* that *adventure* is often accompanied by danger. *However*, many *people* would be willing to risk the danger in order to *experience* such thrills.

2. Spelling words (to be given by the examiner)   [20]

The following words are to be dictated to the pupils and each should be used in a sentence to make the meaning clear:

1. later	11. tales	21. governor	31. convenience
2. giant	12. production	22. science	32. probable
3. expect	13. constantly	23. heroes	33. imagination
4. pleasure	14. enjoyable	24. committee	34. peaceful
5. laid	15. stations	25. patience	35. sources
6. past	16. nineteen	26. connection	36. entrance
7. certainly	17. musical	27. earliest	37. twelfth
8. social	18. excellent	28. session	38. proceed
9. difference	19. strength	29. liquid	39. officials
10. organized	20. argument	30. accurate	40. courteous

3. Fill in the blanks in *each* sentence below with the correct form of the word in parentheses. [No credit for misspelled words.]   [5]

[Example: We watched the two (boy) .... boys painting (they) .... their boat.]

    a. One of the (calf) .... had lost (it) .... way.

    b. Two (box) .... of (tomato) .... fell from (Thomas) .... truck.

    c. A sale of (child) .... coats attracted many (woman) .... to the store.

d. Many (city) .... in the state are located in river (valley) ....

e. I wonder (who) .... books these are.

4. In the spaces provided, copy the following, capitalizing and punctuating wherever necessary to make correct sentences.   [10]

as she strolled along the corridor with joan a new girl in her class the teacher asked are you going to the party friday afternoon

well I am not sure that I should go she replied I havent met many of the students yet

5. In the spaces provided, give the part of speech of *each* of the italicized words: [5]

Gracefully, the *youthful* skater *glided across* the *rink* toward her instructor.

Gracefully	glided	rink
youthful	across	

6. In the following passage, there are 10 errors in the use of words. Underline *each* error and write your correction above it.   [10]

Don't it seem good to get back to school? Last Saturday was a busy time to our house. Because our mother was away, my sister and me had to do the housework. You should of seen how hard we worked. We couldn't hardly take time to sit down all day. During the afternoon, one of our friends come over and brought us some fresh doughnuts that was delicious. After we had ate the doughnuts, he helped us with our work. They're not to many friends who would do that.

7. The following paragraph is faulty because the sentences, numbered (1) to (6), are *not* arranged in the proper order and because one sentence does *not* belong in the paragraph. Read the paragraph, and answer the questions below by writing the *number* of the proper sentence in the space provided.   [5]

(1) The sale of the lumber paid for the expense of the enterprise. (2) A method was devised to save the pine forest from the ravages of the pine bark beetle. (3) The next spring, foresters cut down all the marked trees. (4) The wood was sold for lumber. (5) Oak trees and maple trees are also used for lumber. (6) In the fall, tree surgeons marked all the infected trees.

a. Which sentence in the above paragraph should be left out?
b. Which sentence should be the first one of the paragraph?
c. Which sentence should be second?
d. Which sentence should be the last one of the paragraph?
e. Which sentence should be next to the last?

8. Print a capital S on the line after each of the following that is a complete sentence, a capital N after each that is *not* a complete sentence, and a capital T after each that consists of more than one sentence.   [10]

a. A jet plane can fly at unbelievably high speeds.
b. We skated until nearly dark and then raced home to supper.
c. Running across the street and ringing the doctor's doorbell.
d. He is an excellent dentist he has a large office downtown.
e. Such homes as that little one over there with vines almost covering it.
f. Down the slope came first a single skier, and later came a toboggan carrying several children.
g. Much depends upon your help you won't fail us, will you?
h. I plan to go to the party, but I may arrive late.
i. Although he had followed the coach's advice about getting enough rest before the game.
j. Planning the design and carrying it out on the leather took real skill.

9. Read carefully the following entry taken from a standard dictionary. Then answer the questions below, using only the information given in the entry. Write your answers in the spaces provided at the right.   [5]

gen u ine (jĕn′ u ĭn), *adj.* **1.** Actually being what it seems or is claimed to be; real; true. **2.** without pretense; sincere; frank. [< L *genuinus*, native, natural] **—gen′ u ine ly,** *adv.* **—gen′ u ine ness,** *n.* **—Syn.** **1.** authentic **2.** unaffected. **—Ant. 1.** false, sham.

a. How many syllables are there in the word *genuine?*
b. Which syllable of the word *genuine* is accented?
c. What foreign language does the word *genuine* come from?
d. What noun is formed from the word *genuine?*
e. What is a word that means the same or nearly the same as *genuine?*

10. In column *B* below there are five incomplete statements dealing with library study. Read these statements, and after *each,* write the *number* of the expression from column *A* that makes the statement correct.   [5]

Column A	Column B
(1) card catalog	*a.* presents detailed articles about per-
(2) Dewey Decimal System	sons, places, and things
(3) index	*b.* lists the books in a library by title,
(4) encyclopedia	author, and subject
(5) table of contents	*c.* is the name given to a method of
(6) call number	numbering books in a library
(7) dictionary	*d.* lists the topics in a book in alphabeti-
(8) copyright date	cal order
	e. appears on the upper left-hand corner
	of a title card

11. In each sentence below one word is italicized. Underneath the sentence is a group of five words or expressions. From these select the word or expression that has most nearly the same meaning as the italicized word, and write its *number* on the line at the right.   [15]

a. The hunters explored the *marshy* land.
  (1) rocky   (2) sandy   (3) flat   (4) swampy   (5) wooded

b. The document proved to be *counterfeit.*
  (1) false   (2) priceless   (3) unreadable   (4) mysterious   (5) harmful

c. Helen never *neglects* her homework.
  (1) finishes   (2) fails to do   (3) wants to do   (4) understands   (5) looks over

d. They pledged their *allegiance* to the grand duke.
  (1) fortune   (2) homeland   (3) loyalty   (4) freedom   (5) future

e. In his speech to the voters he expressed his *gratitude.*
  (1) thankfulness   (2) sympathy   (3) disappointment   (4) happiness   (5) excitement

f. We thought that the traveler's story was *incredible.*
  (1) comical   (2) thrilling   (3) unbelievable   (4) uninteresting   (5) convincing

g. She *yearned* for a vacation.
  (1) begged   (2) made application   (3) saved   (4) gave up hope   (5) longed

h. This liquid, which is *inflammable,* should be stored in a tight container.
  (1) poisonous   (2) of great value   (3) easily set on fire   (4) secret in nature   (5) likely to give off fumes

i. He was *conscious* that his friend's attitude had changed.
    (1) surprised   (2) afraid   (3) angry   (4) aware
    (5) disappointed

j. I *assumed* that he had been elected president.
    (1) knew   (2) wished   (3) decided   (4) indicated
    (5) supposed

k. The old *mariner* had many strange tales to tell.
    (1) soldier   (2) hermit   (3) storekeeper   (4) miner
    (5) seaman

l. Let's *assemble* the reference books for our project.
    (1) read   (2) gather   (3) separate   (4) report on
    (5) inquire about

m. The *humid* weather made us all uncomfortable.
    (1) damp   (2) stormy   (3) chilly   (4) changeable
    (5) disagreeable

n. He follows that schedule *invariably.*
    (1) now and then   (2) unwillingly   (3) of necessity
    (4) constantly   (5) thoughtlessly

o. The stock market report showed a *substantial* gain during the
week.
    (1) slow   (2) slim   (3) sudden   (4) deceiving   (5)
considerable

Part II

Answer all questions.

1. Credit will be given on handwriting (0 to 10 points), based on the average quality of the handwriting on the paper as a whole.   [10]

2. *Directions:* After reading each selection below, read the statements and questions at the right. Then choose the word or expression that most satisfactorily completes *each* in accordance with the *meaning of the selection,* and write its *number* in the parentheses. [2 credits each.]   [30]

A. The moon is the nearest of all our celestial neighbors, at a distance from the earth of about a quarter of a million miles. It is a globe 2,000 miles in diameter with mountains, plains, cliffs, deserts— a very rugged landscape indeed, but decidedly distasteful to a sailor because there is no ocean there at all! There is not a river, lake, or pond, for that matter. It never

a. The title that best expresses the main idea of this selection is:
    (1) Meteorites
    (2) Life on the moon
    (3) A sailor on the moon
    (4) The moon's atmosphere
    (5) Conditions on the moon
    ....( )

b. Which would most likely be found on the moon?   (1)

rains there either, because there is no water and no atmosphere. It is a hard doctrine to teach and believe, but all the evidence points to the fact that the beautiful silvery moon, sublime and serene as it appears, is only a barren desert utterly devoid of any life as we know it, suffering from great extremes of temperature and exposed to a constant barrage of meteorites and debris which easily reaches the surface without hindrance because there is no atmosphere to slow it down or consume it in friction-generated fire.

B. In the British Museum a little glass case contains the mummies of two Egyptian kings who lived beside the Nile. With them are a few farm utensils used in the days when the two kings walked the earth—a broken plow, a rusted sickle, two sticks tied together with a leather strap. Those were the "bread tools" used in the Egyptian civilization 4,000 years ago. In the 1700's in America the same kinds of crude instruments were still the "bread tools" of most American farmers. In George Washington's Virginia home, Mount Vernon, some early American sickles are still preserved. They are very much like the reaping tools of farmers 4,000 years ago when the Egyptian kings were buried.

shrubs   (2) insects   (3) rocks   (4) tides   (5) snowstorms..................( )

c. Which statement is *true* according to this selection?   (1) The moon is drawing closer to us. (2) The appearance of the moon is deceiving.   (3) Sailors say that they dislike the moon.   (4) The moon sends off frequent showers of meteorites.   (5) The temperature on the moon is always extremely hot....................( )

a. From this selection we may conclude that ancient Egyptians (1) kept their tools in glass cases (2) expected their rulers to walk long distances   (3) engaged in farming   (4) had only two wise kings   (5) neglected their equipment.........( )

b. The "bread tools" mentioned in this selection were used in (1) preserving food   (2) baking bread   (3) constructing tombs   (4) growing grain (5) helping walkers.......( )

c. A visitor to Mount Vernon may see on exhibition farm utensils that   (1) were found in Egyptian tombs   (2) are tied together with leather straps (3) have been lent by the British Museum   (4) were invented by George Washington   (5) are similar to ones used long ago in Egypt................( )

C. Some of you still enjoy reading fairy tales, but you are not so deeply absorbed in them as you were a few years ago. It is an interesting part of growing up to keep adding to our enthusiasms, never wholly discarding what we outgrow, but tying on new pieces of muslin to the tail of our kite. The age of fairy tales belongs to a period when we are interested chiefly in a world of unreality. Goblins, wizards, dwarfs—all those creatures of the imagination—seem to children so much more engaging than water lilies or tadpoles or bread and butter.

Grown people find pleasure in remembering their childish imaginings. But other interests have displaced those early flights of fancy. In fairy tales, you know, all one needs for success or happiness is a fairy godmother. Then everything always turns out all right for the hero or heroine. But as we grow older, these imaginary victories which once satisfied us lose their power of enchantment. We want real success and real happiness. It is this growing interest in a real world, in contrast to the fanciful world of fairy lore, that marks the first great advance made in reading taste. An interest in *The Adventures of Alice in Wonderland* gives way to an interest in deep-sea diving. The fascination of "Jack the Giant Killer" is lost to a keen interest in Commander Byrd on his Antarctic exploration. The world of real people, real problems, real victories, real facts

a. The title that best expresses the main idea of this selection is:
(1) Fairy tales
(2) Growing up in reading taste
(3) Real happiness
(4) Our interest in goblins
(5) Winning imaginary victories....................( )

b. "Tying new pieces of muslin to the tail of our kite" means
(1) adding new interests to our lives   (2) finding new excuses
(3) forgetting the past   (4) making up stories   (5) flying a kite rather than reading..( )

c. According to the selection, grown people remember their childish imaginings with   (1) difficulty   (2) enchantment
(3) enthusiasm   (4) pleasure
(5) regret...............( )

d. In a fairy tale all one needs for success or happiness is a   (1) wizard   (2) hero   (3) fairy godmother   (4) heroine
(5) goblin...............( )

e. According to the author, realistic stories appeal chiefly to a person who is   (1) childish
(2) undeveloped   (3) successful and happy   (4) becoming mature   (5) reading fairy tales...............( )

—these are the reading interests of a mind growing up.

D. Like the United States today, Athens had courts where a wrong might be righted. Since any citizen might accuse another of a crime, the Athenian courts of law were very busy. In fact, unless a citizen was unusually peaceful or very unimportant, he would be sure to find himself in the courts at least once in every few years.

At a trial both the accuser and the person accused were allowed a certain time to speak. The length of time was marked by a water clock. Free men testified under oath as they do today, but the oath of a slave was counted as worthless.

To judge a trial, a jury was chosen from the members of the assembly who had reached 30 years of age. The Athenian juries were very large, often consisting of 201, 401, 501, 1,001, or more men, depending upon the importance of the case being tried. The juryman swore by the gods to listen carefully to both sides of the question and to give his honest opinion of the case. Each juryman gave his decision by depositing a white or black stone in a box. To keep citizens from being too careless in accusing each other, there was a rule that if the person accused did not receive a certain number of votes, the accuser was condemned instead.

a. The title that best expresses the main idea of this selection is:
(1) Athens and the United States
(2) Justice in ancient Athens
(3) Testifying under oath
(4) Accusing the accused
(5) The duties of juries....( )

b. People in Athens were frequently on trial in a law court because (1) they liked to serve on juries (2) a juryman agreed to listen to both sides of a question (3) the people of Athens were unusually peaceloving (4) the slaves were troublesome (5) any person might accuse another of a crime..................( )

c. An Athenian was likely to avoid accusing another without a good reason because (1) the jury might condemn the accuser instead of the accused man (2) the jury might be very large (3) cases were judged by men over 30 years old (4) there was a limit on the time a trial could take (5) a juryman gave his decision by putting a stone in a box............( )

d. Which statement is true according to this selection? (1) An accused person was denied the privilege of telling his side of the case. (2) The importance of the case determined the number of jurors. (3) A jury's decision was handed down in writing. (4) A citizen had to appear in court every few years. (5) Older jurors were used for the most important cases...( )

3. Answer either *a* or *b*:   [20]

   a. You ordered a pair of ski boots, catalog number 2S326, from the Outdoor Sporting Goods Company, 41 Hamilton Street, Townville, New York. When the boots arrived, they were not the size you had ordered. Write a letter explaining why you are returning the boots. Make clear what size you need.

   b. Suppose that your aunt or uncle has invited you to take an automobile trip during your spring vacation and has asked you to suggest points of interest you would like to visit. Write a letter accepting the invitation and mentioning two or three places that you both might enjoy visiting.

4. Choose *one* of the following topics and write a well-planned composition of at least 100 words: [20]

   a. A worthwhile organization
   b. A favorite daydream
   c. Why I like to draw
   d. Hunting in the fall
   e. When I reach sixteen
   f. A problem facing my community
   g. Fun with a chemistry set
   h. The common cold
   i. What school means to me
   j. Learning to play a musical instrument

5. Answer either *a* or *b*:   [20]

   a. Some people make life pleasant for others; some people make it unpleasant. From the stories and poems you have read, select a character, and in about 100 words show how this person made life pleasant *or* unpleasant for other people. Give the title and author.

   b. The experiences that people have as children often prepare them for their work in later life. From the stories and books you have read, select a man *or* a woman, and in about 100 words show how this person's experiences as a child helped him in his life work. Give the title and author.

ENGLISH (8TH Grade)—JUNE 1957 (1)

Part I—*Answer all questions.*

1. Dictation (to be given by the examiner) [10]

The examiner should dictate the following paragraph to the pupils, without emphasizing or otherwise indicating the italicized words. The pupils should write the entire paragraph. Only spelling of the italicized words should be considered in rating papers.

Early in *February* our student council planned and organized a *recreation program which* included a *series* of dances and musical shows held in the *gymnasium here* at school. *Almost* every *eighth* grader who participated in these *activities* made new *friends* and enjoyed some valuable *learning* experiences. *Since* the great *majority* of our students attended these *affairs, there can't* be any doubt about the *success* of the *whole* project.

2. Spelling words (to be given by the examiner) [20]

The following words are to be dictated to the pupils and each should be used in a sentence to make the meaning clear:

1. women	11. younger	21. approach	31. grateful
2. choose	12. pioneers	22. memories	32. discussion
3. sincerely	13. area	23. silence	33. signature
4. cupboard	14. victory	24. conclusion	34. possession
5. separate	15. postage	25. citizenship	35. lightning
6. weight	16. machine	26. tongue	36. heavier
7. studying	17. attack	27. recognize	37. automatic
8. weather	18. hidden	28. mystery	38. privilege
9. sensible	19. prisoner	29. electrical	39. trial
10. experiment	20. theory	30. chairman	40. executive

3. In the spaces provided, copy the following, capitalizing and punctuating wherever necessary to make correct sentences: [10]

    a. yes mary was in texas during the month of july

    b. have you read heidi my favorite book

    c. if were going to win this game said the coach you boys must play better than you did last week

4. In the spaces provided, combine the short sentences in *each* group below into *one* smooth, well-constructed sentence. [10]

    a. Our parents went to New York. They went to visit relatives. They traveled to New York by plane.

    b. Peter had been ill during the term. He studied very hard. He was able to pass his examination.

    c. I have an album. My brother gave me the album. It is brown. I keep all my photographs in it.

    d. The beaver is a water animal. The beaver drags trees into the stream. The beaver builds a dam.

5. Print a capital *S* on the line after each of the following that is a complete sentence, a capital *N* after each that is *not* a complete sentence, and a capital *T* after each that consists of more than one sentence.   [10]

   a. All materials are similar in certain ways they may not look or feel alike.

   b. An empty glass containing gases.

   c. Every material occupies space.

   d. Because all matter has weight.

   e. Electric current is not a material it does not take up space.

   f. Neither hard nor firm, yet is a solid.

   g. A liquid, which has a definite volume, has no definite shape, for it assumes the shape of any container it fills.

   h. Air, a mixture of colorless gases, some of which are nitrogen, oxygen, and carbon dioxide.

   i. When heated, dissolved in water, mixed with other materials, or frozen.

   j. There are three states of matter material is another name for matter.

6. Below is a dictionary entry that gives the parts of speech and some meanings of the word *well*. Study this entry.

   well (wĕl), *n.* 1. A pit or hole sunk in the earth to reach a supply of water, gas, oil, etc. 2. A source of supply; wellspring; as, a *well* of knowledge. 3. Something like a well in shape or use; as, the *well* of a fountain pen.

   — *v.* 1. Flow; rise; gush. 2. To send welling forth.

   — *adv.* 1. In such a manner as is desirable, pleasing, or satisfactory. 2. Thoroughly; in detail; as, mix ingredients *well* before using. 3. Fairly, reasonably; as, I can't *well* criticize him. 4. Closely; intimately.

   — *adj.* 1. In good health; not diseased. 2. Satisfactory; suitable; good; right; as, all is *well*.

Using the entry above, write in the spaces provided at the right of *each* sentence below the part of speech and the *number* of the meaning for *well* as it is used *in that sentence*.   [10]

	Part of Speech	Number of Meaning
[*Example:* Shake *well* before opening.	...adv...	......2]....

(1) Have you been *well* this spring?

(2) The abandoned *well* on the farm has been covered over.

(3) It was *well* that he had enough money with him.

(4) Bill sings very *well*.

(5) Tears began to *well* up in the child's eyes.

7. In the following passage there are 15 errors in the use of words. Underline *each* error and write your correction in the space at the right.   [15]

When our mother seen her good rugs being wore out, she would not leave Bob and I keep our puppy indoors. We couldn't hardly blame her, but we felt that she might change her mind if we learned him to play more careful.

We soon found out that it is not to easy to train a dog. Many a hour passed before we was satisfied. Finally we begun to make progress. The dog would lay down or set up whenever we ordered him to do so. In fact, he has became so obedient that our mother don't object to having him in the house.

8. In each sentence below one word is italicized. Underneath the sentence is a group of five words or expressions. From these select the word or expression that has most nearly the same meaning as the italicized word and write its *number* on the line at the right.   [15]

a. The barking of dogs is a *familiar* sound in my neighborhood.

   (1) disagreeable (2) dreaded (3) well-known (4) rare (5) welcome

b. Jack planned to *exhibit* his collection of arrowheads.

   (1) trade (2) destroy (3) sell (4) label (5) display

c. The center fielder caught the ball *expertly*.

   (1) awkwardly (2) quickly (3) angrily (4) skillfully (5) unexpectedly

d. We sought a *responsible* person to sell the tickets.

   (1) hard-working (2) reliable (3) prompt (4) courteous (5) self-confident

e. A pleasant *aroma* drew us to the campfire.

   (1) welcome (2) sound (3) warmth (4) breeze (5) fragrance

f. Did you enjoy the *conclusion* of the story?

   (1) plot (2) suspense (3) end (4) theme (5) background

g. The parade *detained* us.

   (1) delayed (2) upset (3) inspired (4) entertained (5) tired

h. She knew that she was foolish to buy *nonessential* articles.

   (1) expensive (2) damaged (3) poorly made (4) unnecessary (5) foreign-made

i. My brother's announcement *bewildered* me.

(1) worried (2) puzzled (3) offended (4) delighted (5) hindered

j. The pain in his back was *acute.*

(1) alarming (2) new (3) sharp (4) dull (5) slight

k. The soldier received a medal for *valor.*

(1) good conduct (2) honesty (3) cooperation (4) courage (5) long service

l. Only the first line of the address was *legible.*

(1) present (2) correct (3) blotted (4) printed (5) readable

m. The players felt *dejected* after the game.

(1) discouraged (2) angry (3) cheerful (4) proud (5) relieved

n. The mechanic failed to *detect* the trouble.

(1) report (2) remove (3) discover (4) stop (5) overcome

o. We worried about the *origin* of the rumor.

(1) truth (2) source (3) seriousness (4) meaning (5) unpleasantness

Part II—*Answer all questions.*

1. Credit will be given on handwriting (0 to 10 points), based on the average quality of the handwriting on the paper as a whole. [10]

2. *Directions:* After reading each selection below, read the statements and questions at the right. Then choose the word or expression that most satisfactorily completes *each* in accordance with the *meaning of the selection* and write its *number* in the parentheses. [2 credits each.] [30]

A. Early in the 19th century American youth in the Eastern states was playing a game, somewhat akin to the English game of rounders, which contained all the elements of modern baseball. It was neither scientifically planned nor skillfully played, but it furnished considerable excitement. The playing field was a square, sixty feet on a side, with four goals or bases at its four corners. In the center of the square was stationed a pitcher. A catcher and

a. The title below that best expresses the main theme or subject of this selection is:
1. Baseball rules
2. A player's skill
3. An English game
4. An early form of baseball
5. The layout of a baseball field .... ( )

b. The game described in this selection required (1) eight fielders (2) twenty fielders (3) one fielder near each base (4) an an indefinite number of fielders completed the team supporting the pitcher. Usually there were from eight to twenty players on a side, none of them stationed at the bases, for the batter was out on balls caught on the fly or on the first bound, and the base runner was out if he was hit by a thrown ball while off a base. The bat was generally nothing more than a stout paddle with a blade two inches thick, while the ball was apt to be an impromptu affair composed of a bullet, a piece of cork, or a metal slug, wound around tightly with wool yarn and string. Under the name of town ball, this game with simple equipment and a few rules steadily increased in popularity during the first half of the century.

B. How can we know that the birds we see in the South in the winter are the same ones that come north in the spring? One time John J. Audubon, a bird lover, wondered about this. Every year he watched a pair of little phoebes nesting in the same place. He wondered if they were the same birds. He decided to put tiny silver bands on their legs. The next spring back came the birds with the bands to the very same place. Back came the young birds to build their nests on the walls of farm buildings in the neighborhood. The phoebe, it was learned, wintered wherever it was warm enough to find flies. In summer, phoebes could be seen

even number of fielders (5)
no set number of fielders..( )

c. The author suggests that the game he is describing (1) required expensive equipment (2) required trained, skilled players (3) was more scientific than modern baseball (4) was less complicated than modern baseball (5) was popular for only eight or ten years....( )

a. The title below that best expresses the main theme or subject of this selection is:
1. The migration of birds
2. The work of John Audubon
3. The habits and needs of birds
4. The Fish and Wildlife Service
5. Studying birdlife through birdbanding .... ( )

b. According to the selection, Audubon proved his theory that (1) birds prefer a diet of flies (2) birds return to the same nesting place each spring (3) silver is the best material for birdbands (4) phoebes are the most interesting birds to study (5) the government

from Georgia to Canada; in winter, anywhere from Georgia to Florida and Mexico. The phoebe was the first kind of bird to be banded, and Mr. Audubon was the first birdbander. Today there are hundreds of birdbanders all over America. These people band all kinds of birds.

The government of the United States has a special birdbanding department which makes all the birdbands. The bands do not hurt the birds, as they are made of aluminum and are very light. They come in different sizes for different size birds. Each band has a special number. On each band are these words: "Notify Fish and Wildlife Service, Washington, D. C." Anyone who finds a dead bird with a band on its leg is asked to send the band to Washington with a note telling where and when the bird was found. In this way naturalists add to their knowledge of the habits and needs of birds.

C. Between 1780 and 1790, in piecemeal fashion, a trail was established between Catskill on the Hudson and the frontier outpost, Ithaca, in the Finger Lakes country. This path, by grace of following the valleys, managed to

should make a scientific study of birds .... ( )

c. Audubon's purpose in banding the phoebes was to (1) satisfy his curiosity (2) notify the government (3) start a birdbanding department (4) gain fame as the first birdbander (5) prevent the birds from flying too far south .... ( )

d. The migration habits of phoebes depend upon (1) nesting places (2) the help of bird lovers (3) the available food supply (4) the number of young birds (5) protection by the Fish and Wildlife Service .... ( )

e. Which statement is *true* according to the selection?
1. Residents of Georgia may expect to see phoebes all year long.
2. The weight of a band causes a bird considerable discomfort.
3. The government offers a reward for information about dead birds.
4. All young birds build their nests on the walls of farm buildings.
5. Phoebes are more plentiful in the East than any other kind of bird. .... ( )

a. The title below that best expresses the main theme or subject of this selection is:
1. New York State roads
2. An early turnpike
3. Finger Lakes country
4. Over the Catskills

thread its way through the mountains by what are on the whole surprisingly easy grades. Ultimately this route became the Susquehanna Turnpike, but in popular speech it was just the Ithaca Road. It was, along with the Mohawk Turnpike and the Great Western Turnpike, one of the three great east-west highways of the State. Eventually it was the route taken by thousands of Yankee farmers, more especially Connecticut Yankees, seeking new fortunes in southwestern New York. Along it the tide of pioneer immigration flowed at flood crest for a full generation.

As the road left Catskill, there was no stream that might not be either forded or crossed on a crude bridge until the traveler reached the Susquehanna, which was a considerable river and a real obstacle to his progress. The road came down out of the Catskills via the valley of the Ouleout Creek and struck the Susquehanna just above the present village of Unadilla. Hither about the year 1784 came a Connecticut man, Nathaniel Wattles. He provided both a skiff and a large flat-bottomed scow so that the home-seeker, his family, team, and household baggage, and oftentimes a little caravan of livestock, might be set across the river dry-shod and in safety. Wattles here established an inn where one might find lodging and entertainment, and a general store where

5. A frontier outpost ....( )

b. The author indicates that the Susquehanna Turnpike (1) began as a narrow trail (2) was the most important north-south highway in the State (3) furnished travelers with surprising obstacles (4) went out of use after a generation (5) ceased to be important after 1890 ....( )

c. The western end of the Susquehanna Turnpike was located at (1) the Hudson River (2) the Connecticut border (3) the outlet of Ouleout Creek (4) Catskill (5) Ithaca. ( )

d. The Susquehanna Turnpike was also known as (1) Wattles' Ferry (2) the Catskill Trail (3) the Mohawk Turnpike (4) the Ithaca Road (5) the Great Western Turnpike ....( )

e. The chief difficulty that the traveler met on the Susquehanna Turnpike was (1) the steep grades (2) a wide, deep river (3) the great volume of traffic (4) a lack of places to rest (5) unfriendly Indians ....( )

f. The best known landmark on the Susquehanna Turnpike was (1) a wayside inn (2) the village of Unadilla (3) Wattles' Ferry (4) Ouleout Creek (5) a general store.( )

g. According to this selection, Nathaniel Wattles was prepared

might be purchased such staples as were essential for the journey. So it was that Wattles' Ferry became the best known landmark of the Ithaca Road.

to offer travelers all of the following *except* (1) entertainment (2) a place to sleep (3) guides (4) groceries (5) the use of a boat........( )

3. Answer either *a* or *b*:   [20]

a. Suppose that you have left an article of considerable value on a seat of a theater in a nearby city. Write a letter to the manager of the theater, asking whether the article has been turned in to his office. Indicate what you would like to have done with the article in case it has been found.

b. Suppose that the principal of your school has received from a teacher-friend in West Germany a list of names of teen-agers who want to correspond with American young people. You have decided to write a letter to either Wilhelm Mueller or his sister, Lisa. In the letter, introduce yourself and describe some of your activities. In addition, show your interest in knowing more about the life of boys and girls of other lands.

4. Choose *one* of the following topics and write a well-planned composition of at least 100 words: [20]

a. A first aid kit for summer
b. A ship that became famous
c. Television (*or* radio) in the classroom
d. A great American
e. The state (*or* county) fair
f. My worst fright
g. School clothes
h. When I get a car
i. Earning my first money
j. How science helps us

5. Answer *a* or *b* or *c*:   [20]

a. Suppose that a pupil in your class is moving to California. As class treasurer, you have been asked to buy a book for him (*or* her) to read on the long trip. In about 100 words tell what book you would purchase, giving reasons for your selection. Give title and author.

b. An old saying goes: "A friend in need is a friend indeed." We often see the truth of this statement in our reading. In about 100 words describe a difficult situation faced by a character in a play or story, and show how another person gave him (*or* her) the help that was needed. Give title and author.

c. One of the most popular types of fiction is the mystery story. Name the title and author of one such story or book you have read, and in about 100 words tell why you think it might appeal to anyone who enjoys a good mystery.

Part I

Answer all questions.

1. Dictation (to be given by the examiner)   [10]

The examiner should dictate the following paragraph to the pupils, without emphasizing or otherwise indicating the italicized words. The pupils should write the entire paragraph. Only spelling of the italicized words should be considered in rating papers.

During the *winter months* the game of basketball is *enjoyed* by *hundreds* of boys who find it an *exciting* sport. Playing basketball, *however, does* more for a *player than* just *provide* excitement. It helps him to keep his body *strong* and *active.* As a *member* of a *team,* he *learns* to think of the *honor* of the *group* as well as his own *personal* glory. It is little wonder that basketball has become such a *popular* sport.

2. Spelling words (to be given by the examiner)   [20]

The following words are to be dictated to the pupils and each should be used in a sentence to make the meaning clear:

1. until	11. legislature	21. preparing	31. farewell
2. studies	12. ease	22. register	32. ornament
3. surely	13. occurred	23. presence	33. struggle
4. fuel	14. supplied	24. tariff	34. career
5. circle	15. icy	25. equally	35. supreme
6. science	16. attempt	26. admitted	36. document
7. agent	17. thoroughly	27. mathematics	37. artificial
8. receipt	18. losing	28. Wednesday	38. candidate
9. degrees	19. benefit	29. vitamin(e)	39. exclusive
10. winning	20. restaurant	30. atmosphere	40. insurance

3. Many words can be given an opposite meaning by the addition of a prefix. Choose *five* of the following sentences, and from the *italicized* word in each sentence chosen, form a new word of opposite meaning by adding a prefix. Select the prefix from the list below and write the new word in the space provided. [No credit for a misspelled word. A prefix may be used more than once.]   [5]

Prefixes

dis-	im-	ir-
il-	in-	mis-

[Examples: 1 I *like* oranges.   1 dislike
. . . .

2 We hired an *experienced* guide.   2 inexperienced]
. . . .

a. His answer to the question was quite *definite.*
b. There is wide *agreement* as to the meaning of the sentence.
c. He sold the *perfect* diamond to the customer.
d. His conduct was *proper* for the occasion.
e. They *understood* the directions for getting to my house.
f. We noted his *regular* breathing.
g. His excuse for absence from school was *legal.*

4. In the spaces provided, copy the following, capitalizing and punctuating wherever necessary to make correct sentences. [10]

The wright brothers two bicycle repairmen from dayton ohio made their first successful flight on a december day in 1903

As their frail craft rose awkwardly into the air wilbur shouted excitedly orville youve done it

There were only five witnesses to the historic flight but they were thrilled by the brothers achievement

5. From *each* of the following sentences select an example of the part of speech indicated in the parentheses, and write the word in the space provided. [5]

[Example: (Noun) My car stalled. . . . . .car]. . . . .

(Adjective)   *a.* Fortunately, it had stalled near a new garage.
(Pronoun)   *b.* A mechanic came out to see why it wouldn't run.
(Verb)   *c.* He tested the motor several times.
(Adverb)   *d.* He smiled broadly and wiped his hands.
(Preposition)   *e.* Winking at me, he said, "You need gasoline!"

6. Below is an entry from a dictionary. After you have studied this entry, on the line at the right of *each* statement or question below write the *number* of the word or expression that best completes the statement or answers the question. [5]

man i fest (măn' ĭ fĕst), *adj.* apparent to the eye or mind; plain. — *v.* 1. show plainly. 2. prove. — *n.* list of a ship's cargo. — **man' i fest ly,** *adv.* — **Syn.** *adj.* obvious, evident, unmistakable.

a. The number of syllables in the word *manifest* is (1) one (2) two (3) three (4) four

b. Which syllable is accented? (1) first (2) second (3) third (4) fourth

c. The letter *a* in the word *manifest* is pronounced like the *a* in the word (1) ate (2) hat (3) arm (4) jaw

d. The word *manifestly* most nearly means (1) mentally (2) secretly (3) completely (4) plainly

e. The abbreviations **Syn.** *adj.* mean that the words which follow (1) have a meaning similar to that of *manifest* (2) are from the same language as *manifest* (3) have an opposite meaning from *manifest* (4) are less commonly used than *manifest*

7. Suppose that the following index appeared in a daily newspaper:

	Page		Page
Books in Review	5	Obituaries	13
Classified Ads	14	Radio and Television	6
Editorial Page	4	Society	8
Financial Page	11	Sports	10
Home and Garden	9	Theater	7
National and World News	1	Weather Map	2

On the line at the right of *each* of the following, write the *number* of the page of the above newspaper on which you would most likely find the desired information. [5]

a. The score of your school basketball game
b. The latest international news
c. A report of dealings on the New York Stock Exchange
d. A review of a forthcoming motion picture
e. A new recipe for making pie
f. Letters from readers concerning possible solutions for local problems
g. A list of job openings for delivery boys
h. An account of a local wedding
i. The time at which the news is broadcasted
j. A discussion of a best-selling novel

8. Below are *three* main topics and *seven* subtopics. Arrange these topics and subtopics in correct topical outline form, using the title "Being a Good School Citizen." Write the outline in the spaces provided.   [10]

Topics and subtopics

Keeping the school grounds clean   Taking pride in the school's appearance
Taking part in sports   Completing daily assignments
Serving on the student council   Doing good work in studies
Reviewing for examinations   Participating in extracurricular activities
Singing in the chorus   Keeping the corridors clean

Being a Good School Citizen

I. ....

  A. ....

  B. ....

II. ....

  A. ....

  B. ....

III. ....

  A. ....

  B. ....

  C. ....

9. Some of the following sentences contain errors; others are correct. If a sentence contains an error, underline the incorrect expression and then show your correction on the line at the right. If a sentence is correct as it stands, write *C* on the line at the right.   [15]

a. There is tall tales in every nation of the world.
b. These exaggerated stories are a part of a nation's heritage.
c. There great fun to read.
d. Mother gave my brother and I some books of tall tales.
e. She could not of given me a better gift.
f. My favorite among the storybook heroes is Paul Bunyan.

g. Will you leave me tell you a little about him?

h. Hardly any other logger could compare with Paul.

i. He was one of those mighty men whose strength was fabulous.

j. This rugged fellow could lift tremendous weights off of the ground.

k. He cut down forests easy.

l. One winter, a blue ox appeared at the camp and became Paul's pet.

m. Babe, the blue ox, use to haul huge loads.

n. In one day, Babe he ate all the food that a crew of men could bring into the camp in a year.

o. I hope my comments have interested you in Paul Bunyan, which is probably the most remarkable person in folklore.

10. In each sentence below one word is italicized. Underneath the sentence is a group of five words or expressions. From these select the word or expression that has most nearly the same meaning as the italicized word and write its *number* on the line at the right.   [15]

a. New *regulations* are needed for the playgrounds.

(1) supervisors (2) rules (3) organized games (4) pieces of equipment (5) penalties

b. He is trying to *accumulate* a great variety of stamps.

(1) discover (2) buy (3) trade (4) collect (5) identify

c. Sounds were *curiously* muffled in the fog.

(1) entirely (2) strangely (3) partially (4) actually (5) unquestionably

d. He began his new job with a great deal of *uncertainty*.

(1) pleasure (2) confidence (3) doubt (4) assistance (5) complaining

e. The carnival later became *an annual* affair.

(1) a daily (2) a weekly (3) a monthly (4) a twice-a-year (5) a yearly

f. It is difficult not to be *impatient* at times.

(1) uneasy (2) rude (3) careless (4) gloomy (5) jealous

g. It is easy to work with an able *assistant*.

(1) helper (2) friend (3) adviser (4) teacher (5) guide

h. She was told to *respond* at once.

(1) vote (2) write (3) answer (4) return (5) step forward

i. Rubber will *contract* in cold weather.

(1) snap (2) rot (3) soften (4) expand (5) shrink

j. A drinking glass was *inverted* by the teacher during the experiment.

(1) rolled back and forth (2) placed to one side (3) turned upside down (4) set down hard (5) filled to the brim

k. He undertook the *arduous* task with a smile.

(1) assigned (2) difficult (3) unpopular (4) unfinished (5) pleasant

l. Many colonists *bartered* with the Indians.

(1) traded (2) fought (3) hunted (4) feasted (5) smoked

m. The king ignored the *petition* of the colonists.

(1) gift (2) meeting (3) representative (4) formal request (5) unfortunate condition

n. I picked up the vase *clumsily*.

(1) slowly (2) suspiciously (3) carelessly (4) awkwardly (5) unexpectedly

o. He found himself in the middle of a *controversy*.

(1) celebration (2) friendly talk (3) large meeting (4) fit of laughter (5) dispute

Part II

Answer all questions.

1. Credit will be given on handwriting (0 to 10 points), based on the average quality of the handwriting on the paper as a whole.   [10]

2. *Directions:* After reading each selection below, read the statements and questions at the right. Then choose the word or expression that most satisfactorily completes *each* in accordance with the *meaning of the selection,* and write its *number* in the parentheses.   [2 credits each.]   [30]

A. Thorns are a nuisance in anybody's garden today. But to the paleolithic man they meant more than an unexpected jab in the foot or a prick in a finger. For when safety pins, buttons, snaps, and zippers were still undreamed of, he used the simple thorn to fasten his tunic and clasp his animal-skin cape. Thus he discovered the first pin, and the principle hasn't changed at all in 150,000 years. Even the history of the word *pin* itself is a striking clue to its background. It comes from the Latin *spina,* which means a thorn.

It took a New England Yankee, however, to make a pin-making machine. The first pin factory was set up in Derby, Connecticut, in 1835. To this day the Nutmeg State has continued its lead in the field. Of the eight companies which make almost all the pins in the United States, five are located in Connecticut. The others are in Chicago, New York, and Philadelphia.

Unlike hundreds of other items, pin sales just don't respond to a fast-talking, glittering advertising campaign. The housewife, it seems, goes out to buy pins only when she needs them. But even this has its consolations. Come what may, the market sells a steady 2,500,000 to 3,000,000 pounds of pins every year.

a. The title below that best expresses the main theme or subject of this selection is:
1. Selling pins
2. The Nutmeg State
3. The earliest fasteners
4. How pins were named
5. The history of pins ....( )

b. From this selection, a reader may conclude that a paleolithic man is one who (1) lived thousands of years ago (2) invented the metal safety pin (3) developed pin-making machinery (4) was jabbed continuously by pins (5) first used the Latin word for pin ....( )

c. Which statement is *true* according to the selection? (1) Early users of pins considered them a nuisance. (2) Plants supplied the material first used as pins. (3) Sales of pins are seriously affected by yearly business trends. (4) High-pressure advertising influences women to buy more pins than they can use. (5) Connecticut has lost its position as the state leading in the manufacture of pins. ....( )

B. For generations, historians and boat lovers have been trying to learn more about the brave ship which brought the Pilgrims to America. The task was a difficult one because the *Mayflower* was such a common name for ships back in

a. The title that best expresses the main theme or subject of this selection is:
1. The fate of the *Mayflower*
2. A symbol of good will
3. The scrapping of the *Mayflower*
4. The *Mayflower*—old and new

early seventeenth century England that there were at least twenty of them when the Pilgrims left for the new world.

An exact duplicate of the *Mayflower* has been built in England and given to the people of the United States as a symbol of the good will and common ancestry linking Britons and Americans. The Pilgrims' *Mayflower* apparently was built originally as a fishing vessel. It seems to have been 90 feet long by 22 feet wide, displacing 180 tons of water. The duplicate measures 90 feet by 26 feet, displaces 183 tons, and has a crew of 21, as did the original vessel. The new *Mayflower* has no motor but travels faster than the old boat.

What happened to the historic boat? So far as can be told, the *Mayflower* went back to less colorful jobs and, not too many years later, was scrapped. What happened to the beams, masts, and planking is questionable. In the English city of Abingdon, there is a Congregational church which contains two heavy wooden pillars. Some say these pillars are masts from the *Mayflower*. A barn in the English town of Jordans seemed to be built of old ship timbers. Marine experts said these timbers were impregnated with salt and, if put together, would form a vessel 90 feet by 22 feet. The man who owned the farm when the peculiar barn was built was a relative of the man who appraised the *Mayflower* when it was scrapped.

So the original *Mayflower* may still be doing service ashore while her duplicate sails the seas again.

C. About the year 1812 two steam ferryboats were built under the direction of Robert Fulton for crossing the Hudson River, and one of the same description was built for service on the East

5. The search for the Pilgrims' boat ....( )

b. A long search was made for the Pilgrims' boat because it (1) contained valuable materials (2) might still do sea service (3) has historical importance (4) would link Great Britain and America (5) could serve as a model for other boats ....( )

c. It has been difficult to discover what happened to the original *Mayflower* because (1) it has become impregnated with salt (2) it was such a small vessel (3) the search was begun too late (4) records of fishing boats were not carefully kept (5) many ships bore the same name. .( )

d. The British recently had a duplicate of the *Mayflower* built because (1) the original could not be located (2) they wanted to make a gesture of friendship (3) parts of the original could be used (4) historians recommended such a step (5) England is a nation of boat lovers ....( )

e. Compared with the original *Mayflower*, the modern duplicate (1) is longer (2) displaces less water (3) carries a larger crew (4) is somewhat wider (5) is less speedy ....( )

f. When the author says that the original boat may still be doing service ashore, he means that (1) it may be whole and entire somewhere (2) present-day buildings may include parts of it (3) it may be in a boat lover's private collection (4) its memory creates good will (5) historians still discuss it ....( )

a. The title below that best expresses the main theme or subject of this selection is:
1. Crossing the Hudson River by boat
2. Transportation of passengers

River. These boats were what are known as twin boats, each of them having two complete hulls united by a deck or bridge. Because these boats were pointed at both ends and moved equally well with either end foremost, they crossed and recrossed the river without losing any time in turning about. Fulton also contrived, with great ingenuity, floating docks for the reception of the ferryboats, and a means by which they were brought to the docks without a shock. These boats were the first of a fleet which has since carried hundreds of millions of passengers to and from New York.

3. The invention of floating docks
4. The beginning of steam ferryboat service
5. Twin boats on the East River ( )

b. The steam ferryboats were known as twin boats because (1) they had two distinct hulls (2) they could move as easily forward as backward (3) each ferryboat had two captains (4) two boats were put into service at the same time (5) two sides of the river could be served at once ....( )

c. Which statement is *true* according to the selection? (1) Boats built under Fulton's direction are still in use. (2) Fulton planned a reception to celebrate the first ferryboat trip. (3) Fulton piloted the first steam ferryboat across the Hudson. (4) Fulton developed a satisfactory way of docking the ferryboats (5) Because of their design, the steam ferryboats had to be turned around in midstream ....( )

D. Each year, in May, the shade of Mark Twain hovers over Angel's Camp, California, when this colorful old mining town has all eyes on tailless, leaping amphibians of the genus Rana in the sort of contest Twain made famous in his early humorous story "The Celebrated Jumping Frog of Calaveras County."

Here, thousands of spectators gather each year to watch the country's finest jumpers leap their way to fame—and compete for a $500 first prize. And just to keep tradition straight, every frog must undergo a rigid inspection before the main event to make sure there is no foul play like loading the other fellow's frog with buckshot, as happened in Twain's merry tale.

As for record leaps, back in 1944, Alfred Jermy, of Calaveras County, was proud owner of Flash, a frog which held the world's championship with a leap of fifteen feet ten inches. In 1950, a seven-year-old boy's pet, X-100, stole top

a. The amphibians mentioned in the first paragraph are (1) storytellers (2) frogs (3) miners (4) race officials (5) people of Angel's Camp ....( )

b. Nowadays rigid inspection is made of the frogs before the contest because (1) there is a desire to carry on a tradition (2) there is a state law requiring such an inspection (3) so many spectators attend the contests (4) the finest jumping frogs are present (5) the stories of the prospectors need to be checked ....( )

c. The author suggests that (1) a first prize of $500 is too high (2) a small boy cannot properly train a champion (3) Mark Twain would disapprove of the modern contests (4) a frog cannot jump more than fifteen feet ten inches (5) old timers' stories of earlier contests stretch the truth ( )

honors with three leaps averaging fourteen feet nine inches. But, as amazing
as these records might seem to the
novice, be assured they are mere "pud-
dle-jumps."

Half the fun in visiting this famous
Calaveras County jubilee is to hear the
old prospectors talk about jumping contests in their day: a leap of 600 feet in a
favorable wind—well, why not?

3. Answer either *a* or *b*:   [20]

   a. Suppose that your uncle has sent you some maps and newspaper clippings to
   help you with a project for citizenship education class. Write a letter thanking him for his thoughtfulness and telling him how the materials which he
   sent have helped you.

   b. Suppose that your class is giving its annual party. As chairman of the
   decorating committee, you have been asked to order crepe paper for decora-
   tions. Write to the Royal Stationery Company, 24 Grant Street, Hilltop 3,
   New York, ordering four dozen packages of yellow crepe paper and two
   dozen packages of green crepe paper. In your letter indicate when you will
   need the paper, where it is to be sent, and how payment will be made.

4. Answer either *a* or *b*:   [20]

   a. Choose *one* of the following topics and write a well-planned composition of
   at least 100 words:

(1) In the days of the pioneers	(6) A wonderful machine
(2) It pays to advertise.	(7) Teen-age hobbies
(3) A gift I made	(8) I learn to skate.
(4) Never again!	(9) The pleasures of winter
(5) Fun for every season	(10) Planning for high school

   b. An eighth grade in another section of New York State is planning a class
   trip to your section of the state. To help these pupils, your class is preparing
   a booklet of information about your area. As your part of the project, write
   an article of at least 100 words about *one* place in your area which you think
   the visitors will enjoy seeing.

5. Answer *a* or *b* or *c*:   [20]

   a. Some poems may have a special appeal for readers because of the ideas expressed; other poems may be appealing because of the beautiful language
   used. Give the title and author of a poem that you have read, and in a
   paragraph of about 100 words show why it appealed to you in one or both of
   the ways mentioned.

   b. There are some stories which are told so vividly that the reader feels he
   actually knows a character about whom he has read. Give the title and
   author of a book containing a character that has impressed you in this way,
   and in a paragraph of about 100 words tell why the character has become
   real to you.

   c. Today there are many ways by which a person may learn about other lands
   or peoples. In a paragraph of about 100 words show how a book, a radio
   program, a television program, or a motion picture has helped to make another land or people more familiar to you.

Part I

Answer all questions.

1. Dictation (to be given by the examiner)   [10]

The examiner should dictate the following paragraph to the pupils, without emphasizing or otherwise indicating the italicized words. The pupils should write the entire paragraph. Only spelling of the italicized words should be considered in rating papers.   [10]

Life in the *frontier* days of our country, when *thousands* of people pushed westward, was *quite* *different* from life today. As these *pioneers* crossed the vast *plains* and rugged *mountains*, they had few *comforts* of any kind. Life was full of *dangers* from unfriendly *Indians* and wild *animals*. There was *often* little or no *shelter* from the heat of *summer* and the cold of winter. In many new *settlements* no agencies existed to *enforce* laws for the *protection* of life and *property*. Yet, people *continued* to move westward and helped build the *America* of today.

2. Spelling words (to be given by the examiner)   [20]

The following words are to be dictated to the pupils and each should be used in a sentence to make the meaning clear: [20]

1. children	11. probably	21. resources	31. representative
2. tomorrow	12. absence	22. scheme	32. disappointment
3. suppose	13. advise	23. vicinity	33. historical
4. among	14. height	24. width	34. scene
5. all right	15. necessary	25. brilliant	35. audience
6. instead	16. physical	26. democracy	36. intention
7. surprised	17. neither	27. escape	37. prosperous
8. appreciate	18. communicate	28. humorous	38. athletic
9. closing	19. decision	29. twelfth	39. welfare
10. cough	20. odor	30. unusual	40. refrigerator

3. Choose 10 of the following, and by adding a suffix, or an ending, change the verb chosen to a noun that represents a person. Use the spaces provided. [No credit for a misspelled word.]   [5]

[Example: play   . . . . player . . . .
           serve   . . . . servant . . . .]

a. begin	*d.* guard	*g.* operate	*j.* plan
b. act	*e.* study	*h.* write	*k.* superintend
c. assist	*f.* govern	*i.* type	

4. In the spaces provided, copy the following, capitalizing and punctuating wherever necessary to make correct sentences: [10]

bills mother was surprised that her son a typical teen-aged boy wanted an automatic dishwasher as a christmas gift she jokingly remarked youve never helped do the dishes well I wont have to feel guilty about it any more he replied

5. The first and last words on page 378 in a certain dictionary are *illustration* and *immediate*. The first and last words on page 379 are *immediately* and *impartial*. Place the number 378 beside *each* word below that would be found on page 378, and the number 379 beside *each* word that would be found on page 379. Place an *N* beside any word that would *not* appear on either page.   [5]

immortal	impassable	illustrate	illusion	imitate
immaterial	imaginary	immaculate	impart	immune

6. In the spaces provided, give the part of speech of *each* of the italicized words in the following sentence: [5]

> Although *we* have *very little space*, we *always plant some* vegetables *and* flowers *in* our garden *plot*.

we	little	always	some	in
very	space	plant	and	plot

7. Print *S* on the line after each of the following that is a complete sentence; *N* after each that is *not* a complete sentence, and *T* after each that consists of more than one sentence.   [10]

- *a.* Draw a circle around the silent letters in each word.
- *b.* Hoping that you are enjoying your vacation at the seashore.
- *c.* The Indians' canoe, plunging through the dangerous rapids, with water splashing the occupants.
- *d.* He rested for two weeks he felt better.
- *e.* A person who has never left his hometown since his childhood.
- *f.* Around the corner, with the siren shrieking, came the new hook-and-ladder truck.
- *g.* The committee finally decided to hold a dance, for which there would be an admission charge of fifty cents.
- *h.* The children ran into the street heedlessly they never stopped to look either way.
- *i.* Where I lost the money I shall never know.
- *j.* The town that we live in, the town that we should like to live in.

8. Each group below, *a* through *e*, contains one main topic for a simple outline; three subtopics related to the main topic, and one topic *not* related to the main topic. In the spaces provided, write the main topic and the unrelated topic in each group.   [5]

	Main Topic	*Unrelated Topic*
[Example: Hat, Suit, Clothing; Basketballs, Shoes	Clothing	Basketballs]

- *a.* Cupcakes, Dessert, Ice Cream, Pie, Soup
- *b.* Spring, Summer, November, Winter, Seasons
- *c.* Transportation, Airplane, Boat, Train, Telephone
- *d.* North America, New York, Europe, Asia, Continents
- *e.* Honesty, Laughter, Patience, Obedience, Qualities

9. Some of the following sentences contain errors. If a sentence contains an error, underline the incorrect expression and write your correction on the line at the right. If a sentence is correct as it stands, write *C* on the line at the right. [15]

a. We arrived at the park to late to see the parade.

b. Although their my best friends, I seldom see them.

c. With more practice, John would of become a good fullback.

d. He lay the plans on the table and left the room.

e. Mother divided the doughnuts between John and me.

f. She realized that us boys needed more encouragement.

g. Not one of the girls were willing to admit feeling tired.

h. The lecture was given by a novelist who's books are very widely read.

i. Dad's car has certainly run well ever since it was overhauled.

j. We were surprised that the next word began with a capitol letter.

k. The actors were all ready to begin as the curtain rose.

l. Haven't you never taken a boat ride on Lake Erie?

m. John was asked to list the principal products of our country.

n. Your objection don't make any sense to me.

o. Even though I had seen the movie before, I set and watched it once more.

10. In each sentence below one word is italicized. Underneath the sentence is a group of five words or expressions. From these select the word or expression that has most nearly the same meaning as the italicized word and write its *number* on the line at the right. [15]

a. Jack thanked the champion for his *autograph*.
(1) picture   (2) signature   (3) card   (4) program   (5) ticket

b. Stories about our *ancestors* have always interested us.
(1) forefathers   (2) associates   (3) enemies   (4) cousins   (5) offspring

c. They tried to help the child overcome his *timidity*.
(1) slowness   (2) boastfulness   (3) thoughtlessness   (4) shyness
(5) helplessness

d. The property owner finally *withdrew* the complaint.
(1) drew up   (2) acted on   (3) laughed at   (4) objected to   (5) took back

e. This poem was written by a *celebrated* author.
(1) foreign-born   (2) young   (3) famous   (4) clever   (5) gay

f. *Heretofore*, he had been cooperative.
(1) Up to this time   (2) Occasionally   (3) To be sure   (4) For the time being   (5) Without fail

g. The musician played a *sprightly* tune on his flute.
(1) popular   (2) simple   (3) lively   (4) shrill   (5) clear

h. Her *previous* actions showed her to be selfish.
(1) cruel   (2) former   (3) first   (4) reckless   (5) sly

i. He felt as though he were *groping* in the dark.
(1) lying   (2) running   (3) feeling his way   (4) screaming   (5) digging a tunnel

j. Rheumatism *plagued* him during his childhood.
(1) retarded   (2) tormented   (3) left   (4) disgusted   (5) interested

k. The writer did not concern himself with *trivial* details.
(1) unsuitable   (2) disagreeable   (3) embarrassing   (4) unimportant
(5) weighty

l. An investigation was made of the *wretched* slum areas.
(1) miserable   (2) out-of-the-way   (3) industrial   (4) old-fashioned
(5) crowded

m. Her *attire* was not suitable for the occasion.
(1) attitude   (2) behavior   (3) question   (4) clothing   (5) language

n. The man acted *impulsively.*
(1) with calmness   (2) with good judgment   (3) with care   (4) in a
childish manner   (5) without thinking

o. The book has *inflexible* covers.
(1) rigid   (2) ill-fitting   (3) crooked   (4) spotless   (5) ugly

Part II

Answer all questions.

1. Credit will be given on handwriting (0 to 10 points), based on the average quality of the handwriting on the paper as a whole.   [10]

2. *Directions:* After reading each selection below, read the statements and questions at the right. Then choose the word or expression that most satisfactorily completes *each* in accordance with the *meaning of the selection* and write its *number* in the parentheses. [2 credits each.]   [30]

A. When we say a snake "glides," we have already persuaded ourselves to shiver a little. If we say that it "slithers," we are as good as undone. Suppose we try saying, for our reassurance, what is the simple fact: a snake walks.

A snake doesn't have any breastbone. The tips of its ribs are free-moving and amount, so to speak, to feet. A snake walks along on its rib tips, pushing forward its ventral scutes at each "step," and it speeds up this mode of progress by undulating from side to side and by taking advantage of every rough "toehold" it can find in the terrain. Let's look at it this way: A man or other animal going forward on all fours is using a sort of locomotion that's familiar enough to all of us and isn't at all dismaying. Now: Suppose this walker is enclosed inside some sort of pliable encasement, like a sacking. The front "feet" will still step forward, the "hind legs" still hitch along afterward. It will still be a standard enough sort of animal walking, only all

a. The title below that best expresses the main theme or subject of this selection is:
1. Snakes' "legs"
2. Don't be afraid
3. How a snake moves
4. Snakes are like people
5. People and snakes move alike
.........................(   )

b. A snake's "feet" are its (1) toes (2) ribs (3) side (4) sacking (5) breastbone.......................(   )

c. According to the selection we may conclude that the author (1) raises reptiles (2) dislikes snakes (3) is well informed about snakes (4) likes snakes better than people (5) thinks a snake "walks" better than man........(   )

we'll see now is a sort of wiggling of the sacking without visible feet. That's the snake-way. A snake has its covering outside its feet, as an insect has its skeleton on its outside, with no bones on the interior. There's nothing "horrid" about the one arrangement any more than about the other.

B. As you step through the door, the first thing you notice is the smell of Stockholm boltrope. Then you pick out the fresh smell of new sailcloth. The broad, pillarless floor looks clean enough to eat from.

It's quiet here, too. All you hear is the hum of sewing machines. As you look around, you see the old-time craftsmen working alongside these modern machines. These handcraftsmen sit at their unique benches and sew by hand with palm and needle. There must be at least an acre of cloth around each sailmaker.

No two ways about it, mister. You're in a sail loft.

In spite of the businesslike whir of the sewing machines, those fellows sewing by hand still make the finest sails. Their craft is an ancient one. Their tools, the sailmaker's bench, and their methods— all have been handed down from generation to generation.

The sailmaker's bench is a model of efficiency. All his tools are in easy reach, and the bench provides him with a third "hand." There's a hook on that bench that holds the canvas while the sailmaker pulls each stitch taut.

Working by hand, the sailmaker uses that leather palm he wears on his right hand to push the needle through the canvas. He makes about three or four stitches to the inch. Sewing this way, even an experienced sailmaker sews only 12 to 15 feet an hour.

We watched these sailmakers practice their ancient art just a few miles from the heart of the nation's largest city. They turn out their product in a City Island sail loft.

a. The title below that best expresses the main theme or subject of this selection is:
1. Sails for boats
2. A visit to a sail loft
3. The sailmaker's bench
4. Interesting sounds and smells
5. A clean place to work........( )

b. The sentence, "There must be at least an acre of cloth around each sailmaker," is most probably (1) an exaggerated statement (2) a deliberately misleading statement (3) a statement based on accurate measurement (4) a proof of the writer's poor eyesight (5) the report of a man too lazy to measure the cloth...........( )

c. The selection makes it clear that (1) a sail loft is a noisy place (2) sailmaking is a comparatively new art (3) the finest sails are made by hand (4) an experienced sailmaker works very rapidly (5) new methods have improved the quality of sails....( )

d. The sailmaker's third "hand" is (1) the sewing machine (2) the needle (3) an errand boy (4) a leather palm (5) a hook....................( )

e. The author's chief purpose appears to be to (1) make the reader laugh (2) show how slowly some craftsmen work (3) teach the reader how to make sails (4) encourage the reader to visit a loft (5) praise the owners of the sail loft
..........................( )

Pictures may give you a pretty good idea what a real sail loft looks like. But for the sounds and smells you'll have to visit a sail loft yourself. There's no substitute.

C. So natural does it seem to us to have exact standards of weights and other measures that it takes a strong effort of the imagination to picture conditions when men weighed gold, silver, and precious stones against dried grains of wheat "taken from the middle of the ear"; and when they measured short lengths by grains of barley (barleycorns) or the first joint of the index finger, and longer distances by the length of the human foot, by the distance from the elbow to the tip of the middle finger (cubit), by the pacing stride, or by the day's journey.

With the growth of commerce and progress in civilization such rough-and-ready measures were replaced by more accurate and uniform standards. In the days of the Roman Empire, standard weights and measures were preserved in a Roman temple and served as standards for the whole civilized world. After the fall of the Empire these standards were lost, and there ceased to be any uniformity of weights and measures. In the Middle Ages almost every town had its own standards of weights and measures, and there were even variations between those of one trade or guild and another. As late as the 18th century, in Italy alone there were more than 200 units of length called the "foot." Conditions in England were about as bad until John Bird made standard yardsticks in 1758.

f. The person who wrote this selection is most likely (1) a reporter (2) a shipbuilder (3) a mechanic (4) an official of City Island (5) a manufacturer of sailcloth....................(

a. The title that best expresses the main theme or subject of this selection is:
1. The beginning of the yardstick
2. The growth of civilization
3. Why we measure by the foot
4. Exact standards of measurement
5. Early methods of measurement
.........................( )

b. In the past, one standard for measuring *weight* was (1) a piece of jewelry (2) the joint of a finger (3) John Bird's yardstick (4) a quantity of wheat grains (5) the human foot......( )

c. A cubit is a measure roughly equal to (1) a day's journey (2) the first section of the index finger (3) a man's foot (4) the distance between elbow and fingertip (5) a single barleycorn
...........................( )

d. The author indicates that some of the more exact measuring standards of the ancient world (1) required a strong effort of the imagination (2) existed at the time of the Roman Empire (3) were discovered after the fall of Rome (4) were used only in the city of Rome (5) helped to make nations more civilized........................ ( )

e. During the Middle Ages, standards of measurement were (1) ignored by most city dwellers (2) used chiefly in places of worship (3) different in different areas (4) uniform in Italy (5) exact in England.............( )

f. Which statement is *true* according to this selection? (1) Lack of imagination kept men from making accurate measurements. (2) Nowadays people have become used to exact standards of measurement. (3) Romans preferred rough-and-ready standards of measurement. (4) Exact standards of measurement came later to Italy than to other civilized nations. (5) The English were less careful in making measurements than the Italians......( )

3. Answer either *a* or *b*:   [20]
   a. Recently Mr. John Traveler visited your class and described his experiences in Europe last year. As part of the program he showed many colored pictures of the places that he had visited. As a representative of your class, write a letter of thanks to Mr. Traveler, mentioning details of his talk which your class particularly enjoyed.
   b. Write a letter to the program director of a radio or television station, praising a program which you felt was very worthwhile and telling why you think that the program should be presented again.

4. Answer either *a* or *b*:   [20]
   a. Choose *one* of the following topics and write a well-planned composition of at least 100 words:

   A great day in history
   A good news commentator
   Entering the space age
   Fun with a camera
   Summer in the country
   A good neighbor
   A secret I tried to keep
   Breakfast at our house
   Our school cafeteria
   My first experience away from home

   b. There has been a great deal of discussion recently about appropriate clothing for school wear. In an article of at least 100 words that might appear in the school newspaper or a local newspaper, discuss what you think suitable dress for school should be.

5. Answer either *a* or *b*:   [20]
   a. In stories, as in life, young people often meet with serious disappointments. Choose a young person from a story you have read, and in a paragraph of about 100 words, describe a disappointment which this person had to meet and tell how he or she overcame it. Give title and author.
   b. Many books tell of the achievements of real men and women who have led active lives. Choose such a man or woman from a biography or an autobiography that you have read, and in a paragraph of about 100 words describe what you consider to be one of his or her most important achievements. Give title and author.

Part I

Answer all questions.

1. Dictation (to be given by the examiner)   [10]

The examiner should dictate the following paragraph to the pupils, without emphasizing or otherwise indicating the italicized words. The pupils should write the entire paragraph. Only spelling of the italicized words should be considered in rating papers.

One of the *strongest* substances *known* to man is glass. A two-inch glass block can withstand the *weight* of a loaded *freight* car. A glass *window* one inch thick can stop a machine gun bullet.

Glass has many *unusual* uses. Scientists have *discovered* that *curtains* and even stockings can be *manufactured* from glass. Such *material* is more practical than woolen, *cotton,* or silk, *since* it will not run, rot, nor attract moths. Some architects have designed *buildings* made *almost entirely* of glass. Who knows what the *future* may bring? All of us may sometime be *wearing* glass *clothing,* living in glass *houses,* and riding in glass *automobiles* or airplanes.

2. Spelling words (to be given by the examiner)   [20]

The following words are to be dictated to the pupils and each should be used in a sentence to make the meaning clear: [20]

1. piece	11. civilized	21. battery	31. mayor
2. loose	12. inviting	22. available	32. provisions
3. Tuesday	13. oxygen	23. correctly	33. stopping
4. fourth	14. funniest	24. wealth	34. diameter
5. ache	15. ambition	25. loveliest	35. genuine
6. chocolate	16. investigate	26. peculiar	36. bargain
7. terrible	17. pressure	27. aboard	37. reference
8. elevator	18. medal	28. veto	38. apologize
9. poison	19. limited	29. merely	39. straighten
10. scarce	20. enormous	30. planet	40. permanent

3. In the spaces provided, copy the following, capitalizing and punctuating wherever necessary to make correct sentences.   [10]

The river of wolves an exciting tale of adventure tells of the capture of dave foster by indians that attacked his uncles farm in maine

Would you like to read it Dan inquired its a very well-written and dramatic story

4. On the line at the right of *each* sentence, write the part of speech of the italicized word.   [10]

a. (1) *That* girl is my sister.

(2) *That* is a puzzling situation.

b. (1) He painted an attractive *sign.*

(2) Father must *sign* your report card.

c. (1) Put the book *down,* Mary.

(2) He ran *down* the street.

d. (1) *Good!* He won the race!

(2) What *good* marks he received!

e. (1) A motion-picture actor may employ a *double* for dangerous scenes.

(2) We had a *double* purpose in asking for his help.

5. Read carefully the following entry taken from a standard dictionary. Then answer the questions below, using *only* the information given in the entry. Write your answers in the spaces provided at the right.   [5]

> **in ter fere** (ĭn' tẽr fẽr'), *v.*, **-fered, -fer ing.** **1.** come into opposition; clash **2.** enter into, or take part in, the affairs of others; meddle **3.** *Football, etc.* obstruct the action of an opposing player in a way barred by the rules. **4.** *Physics.* of waves, act one upon another. [< L *inter-* between + *ferire* to strike] — in' ter fer' er, *n.* — in' ter fer' ing ly, *adv.* — **Syn.** 1. conflict. 2. meddle.

a. How many syllables are there in the word *interfere?*

b. Which syllable of the word *interfere* receives the principal accent?

c. What does the prefix *inter-* mean in the word *interfere?*

d. What noun is formed from the word *interfere?*

e. What is the correct spelling of the past tense form of *interfere?*

6. Print a capital *S* on the line after each of the following that is a complete sentence, a capital *N* after each that is *not* a complete sentence; then, in the spaces provided, rewrite the incomplete sentences to form complete sentences, making any necessary changes or additions.   [10]

a. When the wounded soldier returned home last spring.

b. The girls hastened to report the accident to the proper authorities.

c. Under the porch, in a dark corner near the tin container.

d. A map which portrays the surface features of the United States.

e. Return immediately.

f. Sometimes, entering a contest just for fun.

7. The following paragraph is faulty because the sentences numbered (1) to (6) are *not* arranged in the proper order and because one sentence does *not* belong in the paragraph. Read the paragraph, and answer the questions below by writing the *number* of the proper sentence in the space provided.   [5]

(1) The starter raised his arm, fired the pistol, and the race was on! (2) Over the loud-speaker came the order for all the contestants to line up at the starting point. (3) Not until he heard the cheers of the crowd and the congratulations of his friends did he realize that he had won the race for Central High. (4) Central High has won a football and a basketball championship this year. (5) In the final lap, John, finding his rival close beside him, hurled himself at the tape with a fresh burst of speed. (6) The cheering section of Central High shouted loudly as John, their star runner, took his place on the starting line.

a. Which sentence in the above paragraph should be left out?

b. Which sentence should be the first one of the paragraph?

    c. Which sentence should be second?

    d. Which sentence should be third?

    e. Which sentence should be the last one of the paragraph?

8. Some of the following sentences contain errors; others are correct. If the sentence contains an error, underline the incorrect expression and then write your correction on the line at the right. If the sentence is correct, write *C* on the line at the right. [15]

    a. All the members of our family are keenly interested in all kinds of winter sports.

    b. Although I can't ski very good yet, I am practicing to become more expert.

    c. In spite of the many times I have fell, I keep on trying.

    d. Every Saturday, Dad teaches my brother and I more about this delightful activity.

    e. Even when we have no snow, we hardly never miss a practice session.

    f. Our attic is surely a perfect place for learning to handle skis.

    g. Also, we are fortunate that a county park and a state park is nearby.

    h. Both of them offers excellent opportunities for this active recreation.

    i. We think, however, that the state park is the better of the two.

    j. The ski trails there are very carefully laid out.

    k. In addition, there is more chances to practice jumping.

    l. At the present time, my brother he has advanced to the intermediate jumping level.

    m. I am afraid to jump off of such a high place.

    n. By next year, though, I should of gained more confidence and skill.

    o. Anyone whose an expert skier realizes that I must work hard.

9. In each sentence below one word is italicized. Underneath the sentence is a group of five words or expressions. From these select the word or expression that has most nearly the same meaning as the italicized word and write its *number* on the line at the right. [15]

    a. The boys have hobbies that are *similar.*

      (1) much alike (2) odd (3) inexpensive (4) easy to perform (5) useful

    b. The committee *rejected* her proposal.

      (1) changed (2) agreed to (3) refused to accept (4) criticized (5) respected

    c. The choir sang the *ancient* melody.

      (1) sweet (2) sacred (3) difficult (4) old (5) tuneful

    d. Her brother will *restore* the missing necklace.

      (1) damage (2) hide (3) sell (4) return (5) lose

    e. She *seized* the trembling puppy.

      (1) pushed aside (2) frightened (3) grasped (4) petted (5) begged for

    f. I could plainly hear the *clamor* of the crowd.

      (1) murmur (2) arrival (3) questions (4) singing (5) noise

    g. After hours of practice came the day of *triumph.*

      (1) effort (2) strife (3) victory (4) enjoyment (5) rivalry

    h. The wind blew *incessantly* across the island.

      (1) constantly (2) disagreeably (3) occasionally (4) icily (5) noisily

i. Some girls wrote descriptions of *quaint* customs.
  (1) local (2) odd (3) family (4) feminine (5) neighborly
j. They were surprised by the *solidity* of the ice.
  (1) firmness (2) smoothness (3) unevenness (4) clearness (5) color
k. The soldiers *repelled* the attackers.
  (1) fled from (2) surrendered to (3) joined with (4) caught sight of
  (5) forced back
l. He was *nauseated* by the sight.
  (1) pleased (2) sickened (3) scared (4) embarrassed (5) made lonesome
m. The *solitude* of the sod hut depressed him.
  (1) loneliness (2) coldness (3) crudeness (4) poverty (5) smallness
n. *Fertile* ground is one of our most valuable resources.
  (1) Moist (2) Idle (3) Level (4) Cultivated (5) Productive
o. His assignment was done *piecemeal.*
  (1) satisfactorily (2) a little at a time (3) before dinner (4) unwillingly
  (5) all at once

Part II

Answer all questions.

1. Credit will be given on handwriting (0 to 10 points), based on the average quality of the handwriting on the paper as a whole.   [10]

2. *Directions:* After reading each selection below, read the statements and questions at the right. Then choose the word or expression that most satisfactorily completes *each* in accordance with the *meaning of the selection,* and write its *number* in the parentheses.   [2 credits each.]   [30]

A. Powdered zirconium is more fiery and violent than the magnesium powder which went into war-time incendiary bombs. Under some conditions, it can be ignited with a kitchen match, and it cannot be extinguished with water. Munitions makers once tried to incorporate it into explosives, but turned it down as too dangerous for even them to handle.

But when this strange metal is transformed into a solid bar or sheet or tube, as lustrous as burnished silver, its temper changes. It is so docile that it can be used by surgeons as a safe covering plate for sensitive brain tissues. It is almost as strong as steel, and it can be exposed to hydrochloric acid or nitric acid without corroding.

Zirconium is also safe and stable when it is bound up with other elements to

a. The title below that best expresses the main theme or subject of this selection is:
  1. A vital component
  2. A safe and stable substance
  3. Zirconium's uses in surgery
  4. Forming mineral compounds
  5. Characteristics of zirconium ...( )

b. Zirconium is *not* safe to handle when it is (1) docile (2) lustrous (3) powdered (4) in tubes (5) in bar form ....( )

c. The selection tells us that zirconium (1) is a metal (2) is fireproof (3) dissolves in water (4) is stronger than steel (5) is familiar to fewer than a dozen scientists ....( )

form mineral compounds, which occur in abundant deposits in North and South America, India, and Australia. Although it is classified as a rare metal, it is more abundant in the earth's crust than nickel, copper, tungsten, tin, or lead. Until a few years ago, scarcely a dozen men had ever seen zirconium in pure form, but today it is the wonder metal of a fantastic new industry, a vital component of television, radar, and radio sets, an exciting structural material for chemical equipment and for super rockets and jet engines, and a key metal for atomic piles.

B. Few animals are as descriptively named as the varying hare (Lepus americanus), also commonly known as the snowshoe hare, white rabbit, or snowshoe rabbit. The species derives its various names from its interesting adaptations to the seasonal changes affecting its habitat.

The color changes are effected by means of a molt, and are timed (although the hares have no voluntary control over them) to coincide with the changing appearances of the background. The periods of transition, from white to brown in the spring, and from brown to white in the fall, each require more than two months from start to completion, during which time the hares are a mottled brown and white. In addition to the changes in color, in the fall the soles of the feet develop a very heavy growth of hair which functions as snowshoes.

In New York State, hares are most abundant in and around the Adirondack and Catskill mountains. Thriving populations, with less extensive ranges, are found in Allegany, Cattaraugus, Rensselaer, and Chenango counties. Smaller colonies of limited range are found in scattered islands.

d. The selection makes it clear that (1) zirconium rusts easily (2) chemists are finding uses for zirconium (3) keys are frequently made of zirconium nowadays (4) zirconium is less abundant in the earth's crust than lead (5) makers of explosives are searching for ways to use zirconium ....( )

e. Zirconium is likely to be useful in all of the following fields *except* (1) surgery (2) television (3) atomic research (4) the manufacture of fireworks (5) the manufacture of jet engines ....( )

a. The title that best expresses the main theme or subject of this selection is:
1. Seasonal changes in birds
2. The varying hare
3. An American animal
4. The abundance of hares
5. The effect of color changes ....( )

b. Terms used to name these rabbits are related to their (1) abundance in many parts of New York State (2) sensitiveness to weather conditions throughout the State (3) ability to adapt to the change of seasons (4) thick white coats (5) peculiarly shaped feet ....( )

c. These rabbits have both brown and white markings in (1) summer and winter (2) spring and fall (3) spring and summer (4) fall and winter (5) winter and spring ......( )

d. The parts of New York State where rabbit populations are most plentiful are (1) Allegany, Cattaraugus, Rensselaer, and Chenango counties (2) Adirondack and Catskill mountain regions (3) islands within the state (4) snowy areas in the hills (5) extensive ranges ....( )

e. Which statement about these rabbits is *true* according to the selection? (1) They are becoming fewer in number. (2) They are capable of leaping great distances. (3) They are more plentiful in winter. (4) They prefer rapidly changing backgrounds. (5) They have no control over their changes in color ....( )

C. In August of 1814, when news came that the British were advancing on Washington, three State Department clerks stuffed all records and valuable papers — including the Articles of Confederation, the Declaration of Independence, and the Constitution — into coarse linen sacks and smuggled them in carts to an unoccupied gristmill on the Virginia side of the Potomac. Later, fearing that a cannon factory nearby might attract a raiding party of the enemy, the clerks procured wagons from neighboring farmers, took the papers thirty-five miles away to Leesburg, and locked them in an empty house. It was not until the British fleet had left the waters of the Chesapeake that it was considered safe to return the papers to Washington.

On December 26, 1941, the five pages of the Constitution together with the single leaf of the Declaration of Independence were taken from the Library of Congress, where they had been kept for many years, and were stored in the vaults of the United States Bullion Depository at Fort Knox, Kentucky. Here they "rode out the war" safely.

Since 1952, visitors to Washington may view these historic documents at the Exhibition Hall of the National Archives. Sealed in bronze and glass cases filled with helium, the documents are protected from touch, light, heat, dust, and moisture. At a moment's notice, they can be lowered into a large safe which is bombproof, shockproof, and fireproof.

a. The title that best expresses the main theme or subject of this selection is:
1. Three courageous clerks
2. The Constitution and other documents
3. How to exhibit valuables
4. Preserving America's documents of freedom
5. The importance of government papers ....( )

b. Before the War of 1812, the Constitution and the Declaration of Independence were apparently kept in (1) Independence Hall (2) Fort Knox, Kentucky (3) the office of the State Department (4) a gristmill in Virginia (5) an empty farmhouse( )

c. Nowadays these documents are on view in the (1) Library of Congress (2) United States Bullion Depository (3) United States Capitol Building (4) United States Treasury Building (5) National Archives Exhibition Hall ....( )

d. An important reason for the installation of a device for the quick removal of the documents is the (1) possibility of a sudden disaster (2) increasing number of tourists (3) need for more storage space (4) presence of foreigners in Washington (5) lack of respect for the documents ......( )

e. The documents have been removed from Washington at least twice in order to preserve them from (1) dust, heat, and moisture (2) careless handling (3) possible war damage (4) sale to foreign governments (5) the stares of curious visitors .....( )

3. Answer either *a* or *b*:   [20]

   a. Suppose that during Christmas vacation you received a letter from a former neighbor and classmate who now lives in a different section of the country. Answer the letter, giving news about your neighborhood and school that you think will interest this person.

   b. Suppose that your class is making a study of local industry and that, as class secretary, you have been asked to make arrangements for your class to visit a nearby factory or place of business. Write a letter to the manager, explaining why your class is interested in making such a visit and asking his permission to let your group come on a particular date.

4. Answer either *a* or *b*:   [20]

   a. Choose *one* of the following topics and write a well-planned composition of at least 100 words:

(1) Being a good citizen	(6) If I had my school career to live over
(2) My pet's good sense	(7) The music I like
(3) Bedtime snacks	(8) Homemade sports equipment
(4) How I irritate my parents	(9) Why we need more scientists
(5) Looking forward to spring	(10) When my pride was hurt

   b. Suppose that a civic planning committee has invited the eighth grade of your school to help in preparing a booklet to be called "Our Community." The topics suggested for your particular school are:

   (1) Health services in our community
   (2) Recreational facilities in our community
   (3) Transportation in our community

   Choose *one* of these topics, and in at least 100 words write a discussion of it that might appear in the booklet.

5. Answer either *a* or *b*:   [20]

   a. Books add to our store of information and experience. In a paragraph of about 100 words show how a book you have read *either* has provided you with information that you could not have obtained otherwise *or* has described an experience that you could not have enjoyed first-hand. Give title and author.

   b. Poetry can express humor, sadness, patriotism, pride, joy, love of nature, and love of neighbors. In a paragraph of about 100 words show how a poem you have read expresses *one* of these feelings. Give title and author.

ENGLISH (8TH GRADE)—JUNE 1959 (1)

Part I

Answer all questions.

1. Dictation (to be given by the examiner)   [10]

The examiner should dictate the following paragraph to the pupils, without emphasizing or otherwise indicating the italicized words. The pupils should write the entire paragraph. Only spelling of the italicized words should be considered in rating papers.

Our class is *making* plans for the last party of the *school* year. We hope to hold the *affair* outdoors, but we shall *use* the gymnasium if the *weather* is unpleasant. This *event* will be an excellent opportunity for everyone to *congratulate* the class *officers* who have been *elected* to *serve* next year. The *committee* in charge of *arrangements* will meet on *Friday* to *discuss* the *final* plans. It will, of course, be *necessary* for every *member* of the *eighth* grade to work *toward* the *success* of the class party.

2. Spelling words (to be given by the examiner)   [20]

The following words are to be dictated to the pupils and each should be used in a sentence to make the meaning clear:

1. because	11. knowledge	21. pale	31. education
2. brought	12. principle	22. hoped	32. agreeable
3. address	13. business	23. familiar	33. phrase
4. believe	14. writing	24. hitting	34. possession
5. herd	15. colonial	25. slavery	35. actually
6. beginning	16. companies	26. strict	36. column
7. favorite	17. millions	27. customs	37. individual
8. truly	18. beneath	28. ballot	38. persuade
9. quarter	19. communication	29. interfere	39. curiosity
10. waist	20. precious	30. purchase	40. recognition

3. In the spaces provided, write the *plural* form of the word in parentheses. [No credit for misspelled words.]   [5]

a. Many (factory) have been built in the South recently.
b. Several bushels of (tomato) were given away by the farmer.
c. Two (donkey) were seen grazing along the trail.
d. The children sang several (solo) at the concert.
e. We watched a flock of graceful (goose) in the air.
f. The (wife) of the governors were also invited.
g. A cluster of (bush) surrounded the old house.
h. The party of (fisherman) made a large catch.
i. She added two (spoonful) of sugar to the fruit.
j. There is a sale of (handkerchief) at the department store.

4. In the spaces provided, copy the following, capitalizing and punctuating wherever necessary to make correct sentences: [10]

miss parker our english teacher read the class some of sandburgs poems

will you read us one of your favorites she then asked

yes Id like to a student replied

5. In the spaces provided, give the part of speech of *each* italicized word as it is used in the sentence. [5]

a. Did the team *score* any *runs?*

b. *Every* day Mary *runs* to get the bus.

c. *Must* you finish that work *immediately?*

d. Jack is *not* going with *us.*

e. *For* many weeks the meetings of the *historical* society were held at our house.

6. Print a capital *S* on the line after each of the following that is a complete sentence, a capital *N* after each that is *not* a complete sentence, and a capital *T* after each that consists of more than one sentence. [10]

a. The Gulf Stream, which runs like a friendly blue river across the cold green Atlantic Ocean.

b. This stream is indeed mighty.

c. Comparing the Mississippi and the Amazon to this stream.

d. The stream gives England warmth it makes it warmer than Labrador.

e. The general course of the Gulf Stream has never been known to change.

f. Flowing north from Florida following the curve of the coast, staying well away from the shore.

g. Nearing Europe, the stream divides north and south.

h. The northern drift mixes with the Arctic Ocean, while the southern drift comes into the path of Africa's hot trade winds.

i. Scientists think it takes three years for the stream to make a complete round trip this belief is based on the courses of bottles tossed into the stream to drift.

j. Other oceans have such currents in the North Pacific, the Japanese Current makes the climate of coastal Alaska warm.

7. In column II below there is a list of titles in italics and of authors and subjects in regular print. In column I are listed the guide letters which appear on the front of some of the drawers of a card catalog in a library. In *each* space provided, write the *number* of the drawer in which the title, author, or subject card in column II would appear. [The same number may be used more than once.] [5]

Column I	Column II
(1) Ab-Bru	a. Camping
(2) Bu-Com	b. *Famous Ghost Stories*
(3) Con-De	c. Elias Howe
(4) Di-Fac	d. *Black Beauty*
(5) Fad-Grim	e. Henry Wadsworth Longfellow
(6) Grin-Huf	f. Fishing
(7) Hug-Kn	g. *David Copperfield*
(8) Ko-Mif	h. *A Christmas Carol*
	i. Kites
	j. Albert Einstein

8. Below is a partially completed outline. Using the list of topics and subtopics given, fill in the outline completely.   [5]

Topics and Subtopics

Beverage

Meat Loaf

Clam Chowder

Mashed Potatoes

Apple Pie

String Beans

Dessert

Main Dish

Milk

Cream of Mushroom

Today's Menu

I. Soup

   A. ....

   B. ....

II. ....

   A. ....

   B. Roast Lamb

III. Vegetable

   A. ....

   B. ....

IV. ....

   A. ....

   B. Ice Cream

V. ....

   A. ....

   B. Hot Chocolate

9. Some of the following sentences contain errors. If a sentence contains an error, underline the incorrect expression and write your correction on the line at the right. If a sentence is correct as it stands, write *C* on the line at the right.   [15]

   a. Have you ever went to camp during summer vacation?

   b. My best friend and me have been campers at Hyledge for the past three years.

   c. The director has organized the camp very good.

   d. The camp membership use to be small, but it has grown rapidly under his direction.

   e. Last year there were approximately two hundred boys registered.

   f. Two hundred fifty have already paid there fees for the coming season.

g. Because of the increased registration, the director has chose more junior counselors.

h. He has written to invite me to serve as one of them.

i. My friend has always swam better than any other boy at camp.

j. He began to help the swimming instructor two years ago.

k. Now, as a senior swimming instructor, he don't pay any fees at all for a whole summer at camp.

l. One full month of enjoyable camping activities is to be mine without cost this year.

m. My parents are even more prouder of my appointment than I am.

n. What a memorable vacation we two boys plan to have!

o. I can hardly wait to reach Hyledge and to enjoy them interesting sports and crafts.

10. In each sentence below one word is italicized. Underneath the sentence is a group of five words or expressions. From these select the word or expression that has most nearly the same meaning as the italicized word and write its *number* on the line at the right. [15]

a. The movie appealed chiefly to *adult* audiences.

  (1) small (2) hard-to-please (3) grown-up (4) educated (5) well-behaved

b. The pupil sounded each word *distinctly*.

  (1) promptly (2) pleasingly (3) cautiously (4) carelessly (5) clearly

c. He *declined* our offer of help.

  (1) suspected (2) misunderstood (3) consented to (4) refused (5) was annoyed by

d. When his friends went home, the author *resumed* his writing.

  (1) put aside (2) read over (3) corrected (4) went on with (5) destroyed

e. Do not *loiter* in the halls.

  (1) linger (2) make noise (3) scribble (4) run (5) drop papers

f. The boy *customarily* wore a tie to school.

  (1) recently (2) usually (3) rarely (4) unwillingly (5) finally

g. He tried hard to *avert* the accident.

  (1) describe (2) prevent (3) forget (4) make light of (5) pay for

h. We checked the *accuracy* of the statement.

  (1) background (2) recentness (3) length (4) completeness (5) correctness

i. They discovered that the doctor was *an impostor.*

  (1) a specialist (2) a pretender (3) an inventor (4) a foreigner (5) a magician

j. Many *calamities* can be traced to simple causes.

  (1) disasters (2) joys (3) expenses (4) peaceful moments (5) loud noises

k. The knight came upon his *adversary* in the forest.

  (1) servant (2) sweetheart (3) enemy (4) leader (5) relative

l. We found his attitude *baffling.*

  (1) understandable (2) tiresome (3) embarrassing (4) puzzling (5) discouraging

m. Penn's treatment of the Indians was always *humane.*

  (1) intelligent (2) cautious (3) natural (4) dignified (5) kind

n. The young man *squandered* a fortune.

(1) wasted   (2) invested   (3) saved   (4) hid away   (5) fought for

o. He seemed *casual* as he was called upon to make a speech.

(1) absent-minded   (2) unconcerned   (3) delighted   (4) unprepared   (5) dissatisfied

Part II

Answer all questions.

1. Credit will be given on handwriting (0 to 10 points), based on the average quality of the handwriting on the paper as a whole.   [10]

2. *Directions:* After reading each selection below, read the statements and questions at the right. Then choose the word or expression that most satisfactorily completes *each* in accordance with the *meaning of the selection* and write its *number* in the parentheses.   [2 credits each.]   [30]

A. One reason that so many people fail is that they lack confidence in themselves. If you think of yourself as being unworthy of great achievement, you will never achieve greatness. If, on the other hand, you know yourself and understand what your abilities are, and if then you determine to accomplish everything of which you are capable, you will certainly stand a much better chance of success. How may one become inspired to realize all his possibilities or to gain confidence in himself? One of the surest ways is for him to associate with persons who have really achieved greatness. It is impossible, however, for most people to come frequently into the actual presence of the great. The next best thing, perhaps, is for him to spend part of his time in reading about great achievers. Biography is a powerful stimulant to action. But these processes will not avail unless one rids himself of a sense of inferiority and determines to do the best that he possibly can. One of our great philosophers expressed the idea in a single sentence when he said that each individual should hitch his wagon to a star.

a. The title that best expresses the main theme or subject of this selection is:
1. Ways of becoming successful
2. Worthy use of time
3. Outstanding persons
4. A sense of superiority
5. The value of biography .....( )

b. According to the writer of the selection, a basic cause of failure is lack of
(1) perseverance   (2) pride
(3) thoughtfulness   (4) self-confidence
(5) friendliness ....( )

c. The writer advises that, as a start toward greatness, a person should (1) get a college education (2) think only of himself (3) read biographies (4) consider himself unworthy (5) enter politics ....( )

d. The author of the expression "Hitch your wagon to a star," was most likely advising people to (1) travel widely (2) study astronomy (3) ignore details (4) determine to do big things (5) write great books ....( )

B. Although man has known about asbestos for many hundreds of years, it was not until some eight decades ago that it was mined for the first time on the North American continent. H. W. Johns, proprietor of a New York City supply shop for roofers, was responsible for the opening of that first mine.

Mr. Johns was given a piece of asbestos which had been found in Italy. He experimented with the material and then demonstrated its miraculous powers to his astounded customers. After donning a pair of asbestos gloves, which looked much like ordinary workgloves, he took red-hot coals from the fireplace and juggled them in the air. How amazed the spectators were to discover that he was not burned at all! You can well imagine that he soon had a thriving business in asbestos roofing materials. However, because the transporting of the asbestos from Italy to the United States was very expensive, Mr. Johns sent out a young scientist to seek a source nearer home. This geologist located great veins in the province of Quebec in Canada.

Ever since 1881 Quebec has led the world in the production of this unusual mineral, which is a compound of magnesium, silicon, iron, and oxygen. When it is mined, the asbestos is heavy, just as you would expect a mineral to be. When it is picked apart, a strange thing happens: the rock breaks down into fine, soft, soapy fibers.

Geologists have not yet solved the riddle of this rock that can be separated easily into threads, but they have found thousands of uses for this fireproof material, often called the "cloth of stone."

a. The title below that best expresses the main theme or subject of this selection is:
1. Fireproof substances
2. The contributions of H. W. Johns
3. A "wonder" mineral
4. A new roofing material
5. Asbestos mining in Canada ...( )

b. Johns proved his ability as a salesman by (1) going into the roofing business (2) hiring a trained geologist (3) importing asbestos from Italy (4) demonstrating the use of asbestos gloves (5) proving to be a clever juggler ....( )

c. Johns sought a nearby source of asbestos in order to (1) impress his customers (2) locate better raw material (3) attract new business in Canada (4) make use of scientific help (5) lessen transportation costs ....( )

d. Which property of asbestos does the author emphasize? (1) its unusually great weight (2) its thread-like consistency (3) its composition of elements (4) its soapy taste (5) its tendency to burn easily ....( )

e. The author's chief purpose in writing this passage was to (1) show the need for more geologists (2) improve business relations with Canada (3) present facts about asbestos (4) increase the sales of asbestos (5) compare asbestos with other minerals ( )

C. In the back country of British East Africa is a vast stretch of land untouched by civilization. No foreigners, except occasional big game hunters, penetrate its area. Even natives, with the exception of the Wandorobo tribe,

a. The title below that best expresses the main theme or subject of this selection is:
1. Life in the backwoods of Africa
2. The menace of the tsetse fly
3. The food of the Wandorobo tribe

shun its confines because it harbors the deadly tsetse fly. But the Wandorobo nomads depend on nature for their lives, eating the roots and fruits of the forest and making their homes wherever they find themselves at the end of the day.

One of the great staples of their primitive diet is wild honey, their only sweet. They get it by means of an ancient and unique partnership set up between them and the bird scientifically known as the Indicator. The scientific world finally confirmed the report, which was at first discredited, that this Greater Honey Guide Bird purposely led natives to trees containing wild bees' honeycombs. Other species of honey guides in Africa take advantage of the honey-foraging of some animal in much the same manner as the Indicator uses men.

When this amazing bird wants a meal, it settles in a tree near the encampment of the Wandorobos. It chatters noisily until it is answered by whistled responses from the men. When it senses that it has been spotted, it starts its leading flight. It chatters from tree to tree as the men keep up their low musical answering call. When the bird reaches the tree, its chatter becomes shriller and the men look the tree over carefully. Usually the spot is just below where the bird perches. The men hear the humming of the bees in the tree's hollow trunk. They start a fire to stupefy the bees and scatter them with their smoking torches. As they chop open the hive, the many bees who escape the nullifying effects of the smoke sting the men viciously. Completely undaunted, the men free the nest and gather the honey, leaving a small offering for their bird guide, who, as they leave, drops from his perch and takes his reward.

4. A strange partnership between bird and man
5. How to locate a bee tree .....( )

b. According to the selection, a characteristic of the Wandorobo tribe is that its members (1) have no permanent homes (2) avoid the country of the tsetse fly (3) hunt large game (4) lack physical courage (5) live entirely on a diet of honey ....( )

c. The report that Indicators *purposely* lead men to honey was (1) based on a local superstition (2) spread by members of the Wandorobo tribe (3) greatly exaggerated by big-game hunters (4) not known outside of British East Africa (5) at first not accepted by scientists ....( )

d. The Indicator leads men to the honeycomb because the Indicator (1) has no other friends in the animal world (2) wants its share of the honey (3) is unaffected by the tsetse fly (4) has been trained to act as a guide (5) fears the stings of wild bees ....( )

e. After locating a honey tree, the Wandorobos use fire and smoke in hope of (1) hiding their activities (2) driving away the guide birds (3) softening the honey (4) weakening the trees (5) making the bees harmless ....( )

f. Which statement is true according to the selection? (1) The tsetse fly is kept confined to one area of Africa. (2) No foreigner has visited an encampment of the Wandorobos. (3) The Indicator is also known as the Greater Honey Guide Bird. (4) The Indicator sets up a humming sound when it locates a honey tree. (5) The Wandorobos expect a reward for providing honey for the birds ....( )

3. Answer *a* or *b* or *c:*   [20]

  a. Suppose that you have just acquired a pen pal in Melbourne, Australia. Write to him or her to tell about your plans for the summer vacation. Remember that Australia will be having its winter season while you are enjoying a warm-weather holiday.

  b. Suppose that you have been elected secretary of the newly organized Safety Club. Write a letter to Mr. John Smith, Universal Insurance Company, Hometown, New York, requesting pamphlets or other material that might be useful in your club activities.

  c. Suppose that one of your former classmates, who has moved to another city, has won first place in a statewide public speaking contest. Write a letter to congratulate him or her on this success.

4. Answer either *a* or *b:*   [20]

  a. Choose *one* of the following topics and write a well-planned composition of at least 100 words:

My picture in the paper	There ought to be a law!
My earliest ambition	The United States in 1970
The wrong road	If my desk could talk
The clothesline	An interesting hobby
My mother's (*or* father's) favorite story	I wish I were twenty-one

  b. Recently there have been a number of accidents in your school and on the school grounds. In an article of at least 100 words that might appear in the school newspaper or in a local newspaper, call attention to the number of accidents and suggest ways in which the safety record might be improved.

5. Answer *a* or *b* or *c:*   [20]

  a. There are many stories about animals that seem to have almost human characteristics. In a paragraph of about 100 words show how an animal character in a story you have read is like a human being. Give title and author.

  b. In books we may become acquainted with persons who interest, inspire, entertain, or teach us because of their ideals or accomplishments. From a book you have read select such a person, and in a paragraph of about 100 words show how you feel you have benefited by making this person's acquaintance. Give title and author.

  c. It has been said, "The pen is mightier than the sword." In a paragraph of at least 100 words tell why you think that a story or a poem you have read might influence people toward action of some kind. Give title and author.

INDEX

2

4

AMSCO SCHOOL PUBLICATIONS

SCIENCE

General Science	*Chemistry*	*Health*
Biology	*Physics*	*Earth Science*

MATHEMATICS

Preliminary Mathematics (7th and 8th Years)

Ninth Year Mathematics	*Intermediate Algebra*
Tenth Year Mathematics	*Advanced Algebra*
Eleventh Year Mathematics	*Solid Geometry*
Plane Geometry	*Trigonometry*

FOREIGN LANGUAGES

French	*Spanish*	*Latin*

HISTORY

Social Studies	*World History*	*American History*

BUSINESS EDUCATION

Typewriting	*Business Law*

ENGLISH

English Language Arts—Preliminary
Comprehensive English (Three and Four Years)
Vocabulary for the College-Bound Student
Lessons in Reading Comprehension
Words at Work
Essentials of English
Drill for Skill
Corrective English
Adventures With Words
Journeys Through Wordland
Lessons in Vocabulary and Spelling

14